T0368396

ALIVE AND KICKING

THEN & NOW

TERRY DOBSON

authorHOUSE

AuthorHouse™ UK
1663 Liberty Drive
Bloomington, IN 47403 USA
www.authorhouse.co.uk
Phone: UK TFN: 0800 0148641 (Toll Free inside the UK)
        UK Local: (02) 0369 56322 (+44 20 3695 6322 from outside the UK)

Published by AuthorHouse 01/21/2025

ISBN: 979-8-8230-9174-9 (sc)
ISBN: 979-8-8230-9175-6 (e)

Library of Congress Control Number: 2025900672

Print information available on the last page.

CONTENTS

LOVING MEMORIES OF

Julia Fentiman
26.12.1942 -14.09.2024

R.I.P

For a special lady who granted me the opportunity, not once, but twice, to visit the Holy Land of Israel.

Enthusiastically joining a large group of Christadelphian celebrants on both these occasions.

Bringing together life stories of people and places, in a land I have wanted to visit once again.

Establishing friendships, faith, and many other awe-inspiring accounts contained in this publication.

INTRODUCTION

This book is a work of non-fiction, and based on experiences, recollections, and many unforgettable moments during the lifetime of the author, Terry Dobson.

In some extremely limited cases, the names of people, places, dates, and the sequence of events altered, solely to protect the privacy of those that feature in these stories.

The contents of this book are true; however, because of the timescales involved, and citations revealed by the author, some minor inaccuracies may occur.

Nevertheless, they should not affect the overall honesty and integrity of this work.

The author apologises for any omissions, recollections, opinions, and events covered in these stories that may be remembered differently by others, including narratives already disclosed, and further adapted from my previous works, namely:

- ➢ **And then came Agadoo - Black Lace.**
- ➢ **ABRI - My Oasis.**
- ➢ **Another Day Another Time.**
- ➢ **Afterwards - Dare to Dream.**

The author, immediate family, and close friends have supplied the photographs contained in this work, and in all of the above publications.

John Dales the artist, and former work colleague, has prepared the cartoon drawings in this book, and in all the above previous publications.

An extraordinary imagination, with stunning caricatures that have taken many hours to produce, and as yet, an undiscovered talent.

A DEDICATION

For the fifth time, I feel in debt to my immediate family, friends, and acquaintances.

For their continued patience, understanding and help during the many hours of questions and research while drafting my latest book, "Alive and Kicking –Then and Now."

A book about my many ongoing aspirations, recollections, unfolding issues, never ending bucket list, and a life still very much enjoyed.

The constant queries, prompts and difficulties during my working life, while married and becoming single, my band, my time prior to and during retirement, and our family's past and present endeavors, all remembered with fondness.

To all my friends and colleagues at the Rosse Observatory Pontefract, for putting their trust and electing me, to the position of Chairperson once again.

To my Supporting Music for All colleagues, (SM4LL) who have elected me as their chairperson, and long may our small, nevertheless diligent, and conscientious fund-raising group continue.

Also, and once again, to my stargazing companion, Amanda, for taking time out of her own busy home, work, secretarial duties at the observatory, and inclusive voluntary calendar, in helping with some proofreading, and suggestions of immeasurable punctuation.

To my band mates for listening to these, and many more anecdotes, and other prolific stories during rehearsals and gigs, over our many years together.

And finally, to my mum Jean, who, at 93 years of age and counting, a continued inspiration to me, and all our extended family, with her own recollections of an extremely long, at times sad, frequently happy, fun-filled, and fascinating family life.

Thank you! ♥

FOREWORD

A further compilation of stories, recalling times, events and experiences that have transpired over the years, involving family, friends, associates and the author, Terry Dobson.

I have to say I have thoroughly enjoyed putting this publication together, recalling, and as it happened stories that I hope you will enjoy reading.

At times writing some of these anecdotes have taken their toll, both emotionally and physically, as only recently come to terms with incidents that have taken place over the last five months or so.

A personal emotional rollercoaster for me, and for all my family too.

Common knowledge that my childhood memories are becoming vaguer as I get older, relying on others to remind me of past times, and how they enjoy correcting me if exaggerating, or under or over explaining a particular issue of conversation.

However, I can honestly say these last few months remain vividly imprinted, and because of these repressed emotions of mine, finding my recollections of these events not easily put into words.

I have sincerely enjoyed researching and writing this further account of my life and involvement during these at times, traumatic stories.

Enjoy the read.
Terry Dobson

INSPIRATIONAL WORDS

Simple Minds
From the Album Once upon a Time -1985

You turn me on
You lift me up
Like the sweetest cup I'd share with you
You lift me up, don't you ever stop, I'm here with you
Now it's all or nothing
Cause you say you'll follow through
You follow me, and I will follow you.

What you gonna do when things go wrong.
What you gonna do when it all cracks up.
What you gonna do when the love burns down.
What you gonna do when the flames go up.
Who is gonna come and turn the tide.
What's it gonna take to make a dream survive.
Who's got the touch to calm the storm inside.

ALIVE AND KICKING

Stay until your love is alive and kicking.
Stay until your love is until your love is alive.

Oh, you lift me up to the crucial top, so you can see.
Oh, you lead me on, till the feelings come.
And the lights shine on.
But if that don't mean nothing.
Like if someday it should fall through.

You'll take me home where the magic's from.
And I will be with you.

What you gonna do when things go wrong.
What you gonna do when it all cracks up.
What you gonna do when the love burns down.
What you gonna do when the flames go up.
Who is gonna come and turn the tide.
What's it gonna take to make a dream survive.
Who's got the touch to calm the storm inside.
Don't say goodbye, don't say goodbye.

In the final seconds who's gonna save you.
Oh, ALIVE AND KICKING.
Stay until your love is, love is, alive and kicking.
Oh, ALIVE AND KICKING.
Stay until your love is, love is, alive and kicking.
Oh, ALIVE AND KICKING.
Stay until your love is, love is, alive and kicking.
Stay until your love is, love is, alive and kicking.

Words :- Jim Kerr, Michael Joseph Macneil,
Charles Burchill.

CHAPTER ONE

Alive and Kicking

(Just about)

Finding it increasingly difficult these days in keeping track of just where my conscious hours go, giving me the distinct impression of time completely vanishing into thin air.

From minutes to hours, one day to the next, from weeks to months, and now years, continually rolling along, and now just a little faster than I would expect.

Making no wonder all I appear to do is reminisce of my time, and that of family and friends, either still with us, or have passed away.

Nonetheless, I can say with some confidence, that these past years have given me lots of anecdotes to fondly remember, and bring to "life" past and present events in these memoirs of mine.

Plenty of recollections to look back on, and at times with extreme bias, a certain amount of vanity, and without any doubt, an enormous amount of love, affection, and utmost pride.

Fair to say, that upon reaching my seventy second year, lots of trepidation has taken place, with more action-packed years now way behind me, than super fast-moving quality time left ahead.

Nevertheless, feeling I can hold my own, most certainly, with others of a similar age and disposition.

Making a conscious decision to give myself plenty of things to do in these, my later years, to organise and plan my days far ahead.

To coordinate my time with family and close friends in my retirement, so much so, I have actually found the need to use my mobile phone diary to keep track of up-and-coming events.

Following my departure from full-time employment, on December 18th, 2018, I have never felt more industrious.

Certainly not my intention of becoming a person in the domain of developing, or converting into a superannuated lazy person, or a frequent TV watching channel hopping, couch potato just yet.

The hours that I am up and about, mean so much more to me these days, feeling that I must squeeze in as much as possible, and physically able to do, during my awake hours.

To ensure I have a fulfilling day, although tiring at times, but rewarding, and certainly giving me, and optimistically others in my friendship circle, a little pleasure, some satisfaction, and perhaps experiences too...

At this point, I must confess, my "work" certainly not like in employment, with a monthly salary, a paid job, or given a fee, for an operational day, with hours from eight until five, an hour lunch break, and a boss or manager, giving me instructions to do this or that.

Obviously, an unequivocal, NO to those remarks.

I now aim to do whatever I want to do, and when I want, and, for whom I want to "do it" or that for...

As an explanation needed as to what I mean to "do it," usually means becoming involved in a variety of motivating factors.

From manual work as in my former joinery role, but not house building or time in a joinery workshop.

Now manufacturing and constructing anything from garden decking, flower planters, and nesting boxes.

Also, boarding out loft spaces, or becoming a part-time roadie for young musicians, especially my youngest son, Liam, or engaged in an interesting inspiring hobby, or just a man about the house sort of thing.

Either way, to ensure I'm always active, and constantly enjoy my doing "it" or "that" for someone, whatever "it" or "that" necessitates.

However, because of this "work," my relaxing hours now exceedingly rare, nevertheless, my rare down time, can, and usually does, result in a much-needed nap.

Not over long, fifteen to twenty minutes of peaceful shut eye, an essential catch up needed to replenish all my long-expired energy.

These tranquil periods usually taken in our conservatory, along with

Lottie and Ted, my Lhasa Apso dogs, where they lay tightly at either side of me on the sofa.

A cosy time, that usually results in keeping my outer thighs nice and warm, in fact, at times just a little too snug.

Unfortunately, Lottie snores, and quite loudly, and how Ted sleeps during his time through it, anyone's guess.

Nevertheless, Lottie's doggy snoring interference does function as a sort of alarm, an alert to slowly open my eyes, and usually bringing me to my senses.

Stimulating my brain, the grey matter supposed to belong in my head, into some sort of attentive action.

Now, this may prove dangerous, and for a variety of reasons.

My resting periods during the day, or evening, consists of more than just having a nap, it could include an abundance of diurnal one-hour sessions, sat in ever so comfortable surroundings, immersed in my Lazy Spa hot tub.

A watery delight, aptly named Hector, and made for six adults, although 99% of the time just me, marinating in forty degrees of bubbling steamy hot water.

An ideal situation, where I can serenely listen to music of my choice, Alexa supplying these tunes, yet another wonder of our fast-evolving electronic communication age, located in our rear garden summer house, next to Hector.

Usually a peaceful period, lending itself to becoming a perfect point in time for prolonged contemplation, to gather my many thoughts and considerations, and expand them on future possibilities.

This the precarious bit…

At times I am impulsive, where my thoughts, because of their spontaneity, can, and usually do, cause mayhem, and not necessarily just for me, but for family members and others around me, and where I can continually find myself oblivious to the consequences, that my many ponderings could amount to.

These deliberations of mine thankfully a lot less embroiled from a physical, mental, and financial point of view, however, some of my initial thoughts and actions, have over time evolved, and just a bit bizarre, considering my age.

Again, an explanation required what I mean using the word bizarre, on at least one of these particular thoughts...

Well...

I do have a fascination with astronomy, and have done so for several years, and unbelievably, because of my regular attendance at an observatory located in Pontefract, West Yorkshire, and now elected as the chairperson of West Yorkshire Astronomical Society.

Although, I have to say it, my knowledge of astronomy as a whole, somewhat lacking, more so, when listening to, or overhearing conversations about the cosmos between members, that at times all way over my head.

Also, looking in profound amazement at images of distant objects, thousands of lightyears away, perhaps beyond our solar system, our observatory's members photographing lots, that to me, equally as good, as others photographed using NASA/ESA Hubble, or NASA/ESA/CSA JWS telescopes.

Opening our doors two nights every week, Tuesday, and Friday, with other accessible nights, especially during the winter months, where the team become involved in lots of outreach activities, regardless of our inclement weather.

These outreach nights, typically welcome young children to our observatory, attending as Cubs, Scouts, Beavers, Girl Guides and school visits, and other planned events in and around our building.

Alternatively, other nights also includes our ever-popular Young Astronomers Evenings, held on the last Friday of each month, except August and December.

These nights regularly attracting up to forty children, along with parents for a fun filled educational two hours, where online booking becoming essential to guarantee places.

As part of the merriment, our volunteers take lots of time to carefully prepare a number of art and craft items, to make, and enhance, whatever our agreed monthly astronomical subject matter may involve.

These objects of astral interest, have to remain suitable for children from the ages of four to twelve, with the occasional fourteen-year-old joining in too.

Frequently, paper or cardboard used, in all colours, shapes and sizes, and held together using Sellotape, Pritt stick, staples, elastic bands, string, and drawing pins.

Balloons of all colours, shapes and sizes, crayons, felt tip pens, pencils, glitter, paper clips, baby oil, shaving foam, food colourings, and of course our tools, scissors, and hole punches.

You name an arts and craft product, and sure our team will have undoubtedly acquired and used it, or them, at some point or other during preparations for these sessions.

Amanda, my nonpareil accomplice, and chief organiser of the arts and crafts segment of these evenings.

Also, Amanda, the elected secretary of the observatory's committee, and the reason I am involved with taking part in this particular hobby, and time-consuming enjoyable pastime, in the first place.

The items used on these evenings easily obtained from an exceptionally large popular online company, or, more often than not, from a local garden centre pound shop, as possible to thoroughly inspect, and feel the goods prior to a decision to purchase...

Inevitably this means a fleeting drive to investigate availability around the whole centre, looking at, or purchasing, plants, wool, or coffee and cake, or lunch.

Also to purchase much needed items located in the "pound shop," and anything and everything else, and most definitely the intended reason to drive there in the first place.

At my time of life, I never thought in a million years that I would find myself occupied with what has now become a kind of enjoyable pastime.

However, I must confess, I do love every minute of the camaraderie, shopping, expressly eating, drinking of tea or coffee, and of course our experimentations.

The testing assessments, and experimenting sessions frequently conducted at the home of Amanda, and usually full of conversation, encompassing a variety of topics that typically extends to copious amounts of giggling and laughter.

Not quite the same without a few essential cups of tea, and umpteen pieces of delicious homemade cake or biscuits, that certainly help with managing these once monthly, afternoon creational considerations.

Then to realise whatever items now made, and without doubt, it, or they, actually work, and easily produced with children in mind, along with assistance from their parents, and with a bit of a synopsis from observatory volunteers, at these young astronomers' events.

As a former carpentry and joinery tradesman, albeit many years ago now, I am able to confidently use a variety of hand and electrical tools, and I can measure, mark out, and make and construct most things to a notable standard.

In my previous profession of using "sticks" to play drums, while performing with pop and rock bands all over the UK and Europe, also confidently using chopsticks at Wagamama's, giving the insinuation that I can successfully use a pair of sharp scissors.

Although, when I say, "to play drums," a term I use very loosely, considering my meagre efforts, when looking, and listening to the amazing talents of my youngest son, Liam, and Rosie, my stargazing partner Amanda's daughter, both extremely talented, excellent musicians.

Said by many, that I too have an effective good strong pair of large hands... with an exceptionally solid and formidable right-hand grip, common knowledge amongst all my associates, and exclusively for those who have had the unfortunate pleasure of receiving a firm handshake, will tell you.

Fortunately for some, I can also gently squeeze, with little or no pressure, ensuring that the person I am welcoming survives the ordeal.

However, recently hearing a little light hearted story making me smile, when offering out my hand in greeting.

Imagine the scene, an NHS blood donation session, the nurse already inserted the needle into his left arm vein to collect a near pint, or four hundred and seventy mils of blood, when a comment from the nurse instantly raising the donors blood pressure no end.

The nurse reaching across the donor to retrieve a utensil from her tray, inadvertently placing her left boob gracefully in the donors left open palm, at the same moment saying, "you can begin to squeeze now."

A moment of absolute sheer pleasure, extreme panic, or verbal abuse prevented, when the nurse immediately regained her upright posture.

Perhaps this just under a pint of appreciated blood retrieved in double quick time, with the blood bag almost full to overflowing in a matter of minutes.

Squeezing his hand in double quick time, just one pint, of three blood donations required every minute to handle critical treatments.

If I mention squeeze once again during my many stories, please do not bring this episode to mind.

I do digress.

Nonetheless, for me using scissors, card, and colouring pencils to make items of celestial relevance, in a sort of "Blue Peter" setting, held at Amanda's home, or at the observatory for our young astronomers' evenings.

Certainly, and without question, not in any of my aforementioned wildest dreams, and never ever a contemplation at my time of life did I think I would undertake a hobby of stargazing, and where the bizarre nature of my particular monthly afternoon sessions originate.

This year our observatory celebrates forty years in existence, with West Yorkshire Astronomical Society (WYAS) celebrating fifty years, this in its self an amazing milestone to achieve.

Our committee putting a few things in place to applaud the founder members and all the previous committees and past observatory members, to recognise their time and constant hard work in keeping our facility open for all to visit.

To think none other than Sir Patrick Moore actually attended, along with Sir Bernard Lovell to the opening ceremony way back in September 1983.

Including many hundreds in the audience to hear Patricks speech, and all recorded in many photographs for prosperity via Paul Dobson(no relation) for regular talks at the observatory.

Writing letters to various people, some quite famous, two of which submitted in this manuscript, to ask for a signed photograph in recognition of our societies fiftieth year.

One reply I am certainly proud of, a signed photograph from Sir Brian May, lead guitarist from the band Queen, a band admired since the early seventies, and music I have enjoyed emulating during our Black Lace days in clubland.

Where was I…

Oh yes…

My deliberations…

While sat in Hector, my hot tub.

My obvious water filled delight one of my best purchased items, over five years ago now, and becoming an absolute essential requirement during those lock down distressing covid times of the early 2020s.

Where, exploiting the continual use of Hector now turning out the norm, either during the daytime or evenings, especially on a cloud free, clear night sky, where depending on the time of year, stars, planets, and constellations now in full view.

All helping to successfully erase those continual TV and radio bulletins of traumatic times away, enabling me to thoroughly, although, I say shamelessly, enjoy these idyllic moments.

And, unfortunately for some, allow me to contemplate and reminisce...

One of these contemplations giving me the idea of walking the two miles each morning to mum's, more so, when our local meteorological conditions indicate a sunny and fine day.

Although, I do not mind a quick pace in the wind or rain, as long as not overly stormy.

I feel that walking at a quick pace, will help with my struggling fitness, and assist in reducing my tummy and "love handles," Sadly, my regular perambulating does not appear to accomplish either of those, so far...

However, what it does do, can and does effectively save me fuel in driving to mum's.

Where, taking the car to drive the two-mile distance either way, can take up to 30 minutes at the time I set off.

This due to an extended rush hour, where commuters not only driving to work, and in addition, dropping off their children at our local schools too.

Our Girl's High, Queen Elizabeth, and St John's schools, Wakefield College, also Silcoates School, and three neighbouring junior and infants' schools, inevitably brings our village of Wrenthorpe, to become almost gridlocked with traffic heading out towards the north of Wakefield.

Adding to my dilemma, major road improvement works at Newton Bar, ongoing for almost eighteen months now, that does not offer any respite either, whilst what accomplished so far, beginning to look promising.

On the other hand, I have noticed that this new meticulously planned road layout, involves the installation of new traffic lights, and lots more than previous.

I would think, put there to manage more vehicle and pedestrian crossings, throughout vast amounts of white dotted lines painted on immense amounts of additional tarmac, through the middle of a roundabout, which includes extending the length of an existing bus lane too.

At this time, I am not entirely convinced, that all this work when finally completed, will provide a uniformed continual flow of transportation, and reduce lengthy queues of traffic that develop when coming from our direction towards our town centre, during busy rush-hour times.

Oh well.

Yet another "becoming fitter" attempt of mine, to attend a local gym, however, faded into a sort of insignificance quite some time ago now.

Not that during my twice weekly visits, I did not enjoy spending around thirty minutes cycling, or an equivalent amount of time on one of three rowing machines.

Also, a variety of floor, and various apparatus exercises on each morning, I did enjoy all of these, sort of.

A much better motivation to transmute my choice of exercises occurred, that I would positively enjoy doing such a lot more.

Swimming...

As I said earlier, I do feel like I need to keep up with a method of exercise, an application of some sort to maintain, or at the very least, make me feel as though I am reasonably fit.

However, keeping up, is just what I try to do on each occasion, when I enter the pool.

Always healthier when you work amongst, or become part of a team, a selection of people around you, that can motivate, encourage, inspire, and support you during these demanding, somewhat punishing times.

During my many years as a Survey Manager, teamwork has always proved to work agreeably, and where everyone unanimously getting "stuck in," to achieve the absolute possible best results.

Also, my groups and bands over these last fifty-five years, consisting of four or five musicians, who harmoniously and seamlessly gel together.

Making great melodic music and turning out amazing performances, irrespective of our individual skills and attributes.

My just two swimming team, now a successful partnership, that initially came about to "kill" a few hours while waiting for a brass band rehearsal to finish.

I will explain.

My youngest son, Liam, and Rosie, the daughter of Amanda, attended Manygates Music hub to learn their craft, and where the friendship between me and Amanda commenced, not only in music, but astronomy too, both becoming a mutually shared interest.

Rosie, now a student at Nottingham University, and while on leave, asked to "stand in" for The Carleton Main Frickley Colliery Brass Band, a band that both Liam and Rosie former members of.

Rehearsals take place twice a week, during the evening in a band room, located in South Kirkby, a small village south of Wakefield, fourteen miles away, and depending on traffic, takes approximately forty-five minutes to drive there.

A quick deduction of distance and time, meant to drive, drop off and return home, then to repeat to pick up and return home once again, amounted to just traveling, with no quality time left to do anything at all in-between.

An alternative, to drive there, drop off, and do something during the time Rosie would attend rehearsals.

It just so happens, Minsthorpe Leisure centre less than a mile away, incorporating a full-size swimming pool.

The problem of "killing time," now solved, it's more like killing me, that's now the problem.

A joint initiative, to best use our down time while Rosie attends rehearsals.

The both of us would swim lengths in the twenty-five-metre pool, just a few at first, I think twenty-four in the hour or so before the centres nightly closure, became achievable, even with an amount of chatting.

When Rosie returned to University in Nottingham, our resolute swimming escapade, continued in the new Wakefield Sun Lane leisure centre, regularly in attendance, at least once a week, or when convenient, and when the centre's timetables for lane swimming allow.

A pool where the both of us have surpassed our original expectations, and on one occasion, swimming sixty-four lengths in the twenty-five-metre-long pool, one full mile, although our regular average around fifty lengths during the permissible time allowed.

Albeit not aiming at becoming an endurance race at all, simply good exercise, and just as well, as I mentioned earlier, I have all on in keeping up, when considering Amanda's breaststroke swimming abilities.

Also, time for a brief chat, every two, or four lengths, or until either one of us says, "come on," our much-needed recuperation now over until the next break, certainly a requirement for me.

Our active leisure centre watch, and phone app, in association with poolside displays, gives us the number of lengths completed.

Making it much easier seeing the numbers, as recalling how many lengths completed becoming increasingly difficult, especially when chatting every few lengths.

When our swimming completed, showered, and changed, this amazing app, sends an email displaying our actual swim time, rest time, length of stroke, average pace, and calories used.

Always becoming a light-hearted topic of conversation, over a coffee and chocolate bar snack, in the café area.

So, I remain very much alive and kicking … just…

Although, another chapter of mine, may give you a unique, and perhaps amusing explanation on that perspective.

CHAPTER TWO

It's a Cruel World

How many times have I listened to family and friends remarks about their particular future plans and ideas, only for them to come cascading down in an instant.

Preparations taking long weeks, months, sometimes years in the making, no doubt causing lots of undue stress and upset, and possibly with some considerable financial outlay too.

An episode continually and respectfully brought to "life," when considering the events of September 11th, 2001, commonly known as 9/11.

When twenty-three years ago, terror attacks carried out by Al-Qaeda, would bring an abrupt end for a number of people who made meticulous personal plans, unaware of what would unfold in the coming few hours.

Two-hundred and forty-six people went excitedly to sleep in preparation for their morning journey to the airport and subsequent flights.

Two-thousand six-hundred and six people went to sleep to prepare for a full day at work.

Three-hundred and forty-three firefighters went to sleep, unaware of what their morning shift would demand.

Sixty Police officers went to sleep ahead of their morning patrol.

Eight paramedics turned in for the night in preparation for their morning shift.

From the time of 08.46 on a bright cloud free Tuesday morning, all of the above would perish before10.15 in the north and south towers of the World Trade Centre, the Pentagon, Summerset County, and four hijacked aircraft.

Just one-hour-twenty-nine minutes of absolute mayhem, inflicting untold pain, injuries, and suffering, killing thousands upon thousands.

Catastrophic does not tell of the grief experienced of their families and friends, and witnessed alongside the population of the whole world.

An incident that will bring back those memories for all onlookers who can recall what they had planned, and doing on that fateful day, year after year.

One fateful single moment in time, and all the more reason why everyone should enjoy the breath you take today.

Tonight, before you go to sleep, kiss the ones you love, snuggle up just that little bit tighter, and never take one second of your unique life on our remarkable planet for granted.

I can count a few of my own plans and those of my ex-wives and former partners that have similarly met their demise, and although upsetting and life changing for those family and friends around me, certainly not in any way like what happened on that fateful day.

Notably, one such idea that materialised into a formidable plan way back in 2006, with my partner Tricia, mum of my youngest son, Liam.

The both of us buying into this proposal in a big way, that undoubtedly would affect our futures together as a couple, as parents, and in a little while, our modified working lives.

Our plan, on the face of it, sounding simple by comparison to other endeavours I have found myself involved in.

Easy to say, some ideas falling into place quickly, with little or no brainstorming, no hard work to call of, or financial input required.

While other ventures take a while longer to fathom out how things will work, a joint agreement involving compromise, both in financial terms and time, coordinating the various pieces of the intended complex conundrum.

Tricia's idea would inevitably change our future together, coming about as a result of her switching jobs within the same organisation, and not necessarily to the liking of what Tricia would have liked or wanted to do.

That aside, Tricia's initial plan to own and run a sandwich shop now developing into a joint venture, both in finance to purchase or lease premises, then carry out any work required to bring the project to life.

Not taking too long to find the ideal premises, although, a few false starts in the procurement process, businesses that appear to function correctly with a good gross turn over, proved otherwise, however, all falling quickly into place with our latest viewing.

These premises came complete with an existing long-standing established proven profitable business to purchase, and included in the acquisition, a two-bedroom first floor flat directly above the shop.

Raising the full purchase price including a contingency sum, released from capital equity contained in our respective homes, a recommended financial advisor helping us, giving expert advice along the way.

Meeting the business vendor quite a few times during the progression of sale, with agreements made over the purchasing of various items contained in the premises, essential in continuing to make our venture a profitable one, and introducing other ideas into the pot.

The both of us really happy, especially Tricia, as she had already made enquiries with her HR department to take a three year with-out pay sabbatical from her day job, with her remaining expiry date for working in the civil service, now just a few weeks away.

The date now a fact, and set in stone, as the solicitor acting on our behalf giving a date and time when the exchange of the agreed contracts will take place.

I will continue in my day job as a Survey Manager, nevertheless, my role as a parent outside my day job, and our business arrangement, to also get more involved with our son Liam.

Taking him to a local pre-school club, and picking up from the after-school club each day, and then after working a full week in my own job, taking the lead at the sandwich shop on a Saturday morning, and at night, performing with my band, Mister Twister.

This arrangement will allow Tricia to have a lay in from her planned 06.00hr Monday to Friday start, and anything else needed to ensure our business partnership, including our own relationship, my day job, our son Liam, my band, including any family social activities, will remain on track for the foreseeable future.

A tall order, but thoroughly thought through, as the pieces of our complicated, yet evidently straightforward jigsaw puzzle, beginning to steadily fall into position.

The edges all fully in place, and now most of the middle, our complete picture coming clearly into view as the last remaining pieces of our jigsaw put carefully into place.

Nonetheless, confident that things will not go exactly as planned once our working partnership in place, but absolutely sure the both of us, including existing staff from our business seller, will give it our best shot.

Who would have thought that just four years ago the both of us would meet, conceive, and our son Liam born.

A birth not exactly planned, but after weighing up all the odds, considering our ages, moving forward in earnest, to the next chapter of our lives, and future together.

The single-story brick and tile extension along the house side, now almost completed, ten months of building work carried out almost every weekday evening, and weekends too.

Taking its toll on my physical appearance, weight dropping from me, but making a huge difference to the adjoining dining room and kitchen, also bringing about the introduction of a toilet, created with-in the now enlarged front entrance hall.

Just a few snagging jobs to carry out, decorate, then enjoy the added space and additional facilities.

Tricia passing all the necessary food hygiene courses, health, and safety awareness course, purchasing clothes, appropriate shoes, tea towels and anything else required for her time engaged behind the sandwich shop counter.

All the staff now in place, home addresses and telephone numbers, details of national insurance numbers, and of course income tax details.

A tenant in place for the first floor flat, an added bonus, as just decoration and a few maintenance items to complete, with a totally separate access from the rear of the shop premises.

Our business venture had taken lots of preparation time, although not seeming to make much difference to our daily working lives, no fallouts or stress related incidents, simply good old common sense bringing about amicable and doable solutions.

Now just a few days away from the start of our imagined working future.

The many months of preparation and imminent signing of purchase agreements would come crashing down in the blink of an eye, a tearful and life changing one at that.

Not financial, exchange of contracts or anything associated with our business venture, but the ever so sad and untimely sudden death of Tricia, my partner of almost five years, and mum of Liam.

Finding the words to describe this dreadful situation beyond me, as this lovely lady had put her heart and soul into our relationship, and even more so since the birth of our son, a joining of hearts and minds.

At forty-seven years of age, with so much planned in front of her, and for the three of us as a family, a sudden and devastating dissolution.

Much too young, the date of July 17th, 2006, will stay with Liam, me, Tricia's family, and friends for the remainder of ours and their lives.

Everyone aware of the term, "life goes on," but until you have experienced such an unexpected loss, as too those persons who came so close to living the dream have done, much harder to do than those few words would have you believe.

Nevertheless, life does go on, and has to take place for the sake of those around you, to "move on," but never forget what you had almost accomplished or had in your grasp, if only for a fleeting time.

That said, brings me back to yet another deeply rooted date, and there for almost thirty years and counting.

Remembering that distressing telephone call as though yesterday, received from my former band mate and friend Ian Howarth's wife, Lynne.

In the early hours of this morning, an accident occurred in Germany involving Bradford 70's band Smokie, and some of the band in a critical condition, including Alan Barton, my band mate and friend from our Black Lace days.

Of course, the message shocking, even more so when just a few days later, receiving further terrible news that Alan had died as a result of his injuries.

How do you reconcile that news, a chap, friend, and band mate since early1969, who had accomplished so much in his forty-one years, no longer around.

On reflection, our first meeting at Wakefield Music Centre a memorable one.

Myself, Ian Howarth, met Alan and Neil Hardcastle while looking at drums, guitars, and other necessary equipment required to form a band.

Ian, already fresh from a recently disbanded group, eager to get involved in playing music with fellow interested musicians, and what better place back in those days to meet these people, but in a Music Centre.

Neil, a drummer had recently returned from Hong Kong, playing drums in a band, and received an element of stardom, and now keen to play in a UK band.

Alan, on the other hand, already a song writer and self-taught guitar player, had not yet had the experience of performing in a band, however with-in half an hour, the four of us on our way to Alans house in Horbury to discuss just that, forming a band.

The bus journey full of anticipation, Ian mentioning his former band lead singer who I had met months before, Steve Scholey, also looking to join a band once again.

Alan saying his school friend Nigel Scott could play bass guitar, and there you have it, our five-piece band in place.

A band that would eventually turn professional in early1976 to carry out summer season work in Skegness, but now as a four-piece band, including a new member Colin Gibb, and excluding Nigel and Ian, who remain close friends to this very day.

Our four-piece band, Black Lace becoming a household name when representing the UK in1979, competing in the twenty-fourth Eurovision Song Contest, held in Jerusalem, Israel, with our song "Mary Ann," and also appeared in the Golden Orpheus Festival held in Poland during the same year.

Following a busy two years, Black Lace the four-piece band, now a duo, Alan, and Colin.

I joined the Castleford band Stormer, (formally Method) and Steve "retired" from singing, as you will read in forthcoming chapters.

Alan and Colin had further hit records with Superman, Agadoo, Do the Conga, Music Man and Party-Party Albums to their credit.

A memory I recall following a tragedy beyond belief.

After the Bradford City stadium fire disaster on May 11th, 1985, where fifty-four Bradford supporters and two Lincoln supporters perished, smoke and fire consuming them.

Lots of pop artists amalgamated to bring out a charity record in support of all the grieving families of those that perished.

Black Lace added to a long list of superstars recording the anthem "You will never walk Alone."

Rubbing shoulders with the likes of many popstars of the day for a photo shoot, to give the record as much publicity as possible.

Including Gerry Marsden, Tony Christie, Rick Wakeman, John Entwistle, Paul MacCartney, Phil Lynott, Zac Starkey, Motorhead, Kiki Dee, Keith Chegwin, Graham Gouldman, and The Nolans, to name but a few of those taking part.

Also included, Chris Norman, and Smokie, this meeting becoming the catalyst for Alan to explore new horizons.

Changes to the Black Lace line up taking place when Alan had a further opportunity that only he could dream of, re-establishing the band Smokie, and becoming their lead singer.

An unbelievable nine years, from singing our Eurovision Song in the contest, to further success as a duo releasing songs regularly played to this day.

Alan then taking on the role of lead singer in a band he had always admired, to achieve even further esteemed goals in his musical career, that a story in itself.

Success after success for Smokie followed during the years 1988 until March 23rd, 1995, when I received the call that Alan had died.

Smokie still performing and playing music, with further line-up changes, although no original members now, following the recent sad death of Terry Utterly, bass player from conception in the mid-sixties.

All that aside, Smokie always the band Alan looked up to from our own bands conception, and who knows what they could have achieved with Alan remaining at the helm.

Alans enthusiasm agreeably known amongst all his close friends, always ahead of the game, and no doubt continuously planning ahead, now sadly snatched away in an instant.

Following Alans death, Colin continued to perform under the name of Black Lace with a few different resolute "partner," the longest, Rob Hopcraft, from 1991 until 2000, Rob passing away in May 2020, as a result of a fall.

Colin leaving the UK for the sunnier climate of Tenerife in 2002 to carry on his Black Lace musical activities until the announcement on Facebook of his forthcoming retirement on May 13th, and last ever gig on May 16th, 2024.

Lots of plans in place, and one in particular, moving from Tenerife to mainland Spain.

Ian Howarth, partner Carol, Stuart Duffy, and his wife, fresh from a recent Bradford charity gig at St Georges Hall, all meeting up with Colin and wife Sue for a get together near Colins home in Tenerife.

A meal and drinks, with fun and laughter, and no doubt all of these future retirement plans of Colin and his wife, high on the discussion agenda.

Colin, the last but one of our former band to hang up his guitar, and conclude a long and illustrious career in music.

Involved for almost fifty years as a band member in Black Lace, also, performing throughout the UK, Europe, Canada, USA, and Australia in a duo of the same name, and finally at the age of seventy, bringing an end to his vocation as a single entertainer

"Colin Gibb Black Lace" Facebook page, awash with congratulations from past band mates, musician and entertainment friends, close family, and well-wishers about Colins imminent retirement.

Colin and wife Sue to finally settle down and enjoy a retreat in their new home on mainland Spain.

That in itself no mean task, having to load up two cars of belongings, take the overnight ferry from Tenerife to mainland Spain, and drive to their new residence, not once, but a round trip carried out three times.

A date already in the diary when they leave their home in Tenerife, Thursday June 6th, 2024, but not before all their valued possessions safely transported.

Their last journey to Tenerife prior to the agreed departure date, a together overnight voyage taking place with just one car, the other left at their new home on mainland Spain, awaiting their imminent return.

Just a few days remaining to say their goodbyes to friends they had both come to know during their twenty-two years while residing on this home for some, and holiday island for others, before loading those few remaining items into their car.

Everything now in place…

Sunday 2nd June 2024, I had just returned home from a Bible study meeting held in Batley, and changed into shorts and t-shirt.

Now outside at the front of our house, clipping merrily away at our overgrown and out of shape privet hedge.

Amazed at how quickly it had grown, long shoots with newly grown leaves appearing, and at some length, everywhere, and only a few weeks since its last rigorous prune.

This supposedly summer weather of rain, sun, and even more rain helping my hedge growth no end.

My shears making short work of approximately twenty-two feet long, and five feet high hedge, two sides and top, as cut after cut, leaves began to fall in heaps onto a plastic sheet.

An expanse of plastic placed on the front pavement making clearing up hedge cuttings much easier, and funnily enough, I do enjoy manually fashioning the hedge with my sharp shears, rather than using an electric powered or battery-operated hedge cutters.

Only ten minutes into what is becoming rather hot sweaty work, I could feel my phone vibrating in my side pocket, making me think, who could want me, and on a Sunday afternoon, don't they know I'm extremely busy.

I had hoped to get my cutting and clearing job done quickly, and then on to mums, woe betide if I am late, as she keeps an eye on the clock, and also the TV.

Wiping sweat from my brow, and both hands with my developing damp t-shirt, before pulling out my vibrating phone.

Finding it a little difficult to see the screen in blinding sunlight, just a reflection of my sweaty red face visible.

After answering my device many times, and finding it's a scam call, I now have a different philosophy.

If a contact name not visible on my screen, I seldom respond, thinking if they need me, and urgent, whoever wants me, they will at least try once more, or send a text message.

With all these billions of mobile phones in circulation, and our plethora of technically minded inventors around, you would think it not an impossibility to make an anti-glare screen.

Perhaps a white screen, similar to an Amazon Kindle, or anything far better than this reflective display.

Finally making out a name, and answering, hello, hello Terry, its Ian, oh, hi Ian…

I have spoken to Ian on the phone such a lot over this last year or so, mainly due to the organisation of last year's Bradford charity gig rehearsals, and the show itself.

A heavenly seventieth birthday fund raising event in Alan Bartons name, and also calls in relation to planning to see Ian performing in local clubs or pubs.

However, instantly picking up the tone of his voice, certainly not one of those calls, asking Ian what's the matter.

I didn't hear his response, as a car driven past, then another one, unusually busy, a car travelling up our street, and at close quarters, bad timing or what.

Just a minute Ian, I cannot hear you, now going inside.

Slipping off my shoes, the phone to my ear, sitting down on the living room two-seater sofa, and for what I am about to hear, a good job I did too.

Terry, I have some terrible news, Colin from Tenerife has died…

WHAT!!!

Ian, a funeral director for over forty years, and born into a family who's occupation also in funerals, more than suitably trained in dealing with, and delivering such sad news.

Nonetheless, I could tell that Ian clearly upset at receiving this devastating news about our long-time friend, Colin.

Initially finding this terrible news extremely hard to take in, then asking how, and what had happened, where, and when, just blurting out anything, question after question.

Ian reiterating that Colin and Sue had just returned from mainland Spain, Colin collapsing outside their home, complaining of severe chest pains, and after several attempts to revive him, passed away right there on the pavement.

Such sad news, and only a few hours after listening to the news on TV that the former rugby player, Rob Burrows aged just 41, had also passed away.

Rob Burrows, diagnosed with Motor Neuron Disease (MND) in 2019 at the age of 37, had courageously fought his personal battle for over four years.

I dropped in to see Kevin Sinfield during one of his fundraising runs, when after running almost twenty hours of a twenty-four-hour non-stop running challenge.

Kevin passing through Stanley, Wakefield, at 05.00hr, running to the finish line at Leeds Rhinos stadium.

Having watched lots of footage on TV of Kevins fund raising activities, and seeing Robs wife Lyndsay and children, and how they all coped day after day, I can only imagine the grief that all are going through at this time, ever so sad.

Gordon, Colins former stage partner had telephoned Ian to tell him about the news of Colins untimely death, just after Sue had let him know.

News traveling fast by telephone before anything published on the many media outlet platforms.

Unbelievable… how could this have happened.

Listening intently to Ian describing the third, and forth hand details, and the possibility of Ian, myself, and Steve travelling to Tenerife for Colins funeral as early as tomorrow afternoon.

What, so soon, Colins death only confirmed half an hour ago, however, I am told a normal period in Spain.

The funeral arrangements made, and taking place within two-or three-days following a death, unlike here in the UK, where it can take up to four or more weeks for interment to take place.

Ian taking on the role of organiser, nipping in to his local travel agents in Ossett to search for appropriate flights and accommodation, for three aging single travellers.

Just over four years since my last visit to this sun-soaked tourist resort, meeting with Colin at two of his regular venues, one in particular Princess Di's, where I met Gordon and his wife.

Colins on stage enthusiasm like that of a man possessed, still jumping up and down, arms waving as he sang and played guitar for Agadoo, like a young fit twenty something.

The rest of his show consisted of other memorable Black Lace hit tunes, along with similar danceable sing along ditties.

Where he gets the energy from anyone's guess, but giving 100% at both of these packed-out venues, and sure nothing less at all his other gigs.

Ian ringing to say he had sorted flights and accommodation for a Monday departure of 17.15 arrival at Tenerife 21.50, a four-hour thirty-five-minute flight, and three single rooms with a breakfast.

Just the one overnight stay, which if Colins funeral takes place during Tuesday, preferably early in the day, as our return flight on Tuesday evening at 20.45, arrival in Leeds on Wednesday 01.25.

However, no confirmation of a day or time at this early stage received from Colins wife, Ian thankfully did not confirm our prior arrangement, so all waiting for a further announcement.

Sue speaking to Ian late Wednesday saying that the coroner had finally released Colins body, and the funeral taking place on Thursday June 6th at 10.00hr.

Sadly, now far too late to make any further arrangements for the three of us to travel to Tenerife to pay our respects.

Nevertheless, to help those living in the UK that cannot attend, and other family or fans living in further afield locations, the service available to watch on YouTube from the Memora Funeral Home in Elena Cho.

These last few days full of memories, far too many to jot down, nevertheless, most bringing an immediate smile to my face, some as a direct result of drink, far too much alcohol, and not me, but the aftermath of others, namely Colin.

Always keen to get his point of view over, disappointedly argumentative, and even more so after a drink, or two.

Living together in digs and hotels for over five years you do get to know each other extremely well.

Colin usually paired up with Steve, sharing a room together, while me with Alan also sharing, and as our bedtime much earlier than Colin and Steve, always the first up for breakfast.

The two of them, loveable rogues, who time after time got into all sorts of mischief, some of which I would rather not say, but certainly not criminal in any way.

Memories shared on many platforms too, and thinking of Colins cousin, Debbie, living in Wetherby, who had planned to visit Tenerife to see him after almost forty years, only cancelled because of the covid epidemic.

Visiting my ninety-two-year-old mum on the Thursday morning, enjoying the almost two-mile walk, clearing my head, and enjoying the fresh after rain smell while on the meadows, wildlife in abundance.

Squirrels, hedgehogs, crows, magpies, blackbirds, and a variety of others either flying, running, or climbing.

Plenty of dog walkers too, most on a leash, that's the dogs, others allowed to roam freely.

Lots of life, busy for 08.30hr as my pace picking up a little, walking quite quickly now, making mums in around eighteen minutes.

Much sooner than driving around the same 08.30hr time, with two possible routes from my home, and out of the village of Wrenthorpe, both having to pass schools, and one direction in particular, three schools and a college.

The plus side for me, I can make up lots of steps, and exercise at the same time, although not exactly cartwheeling, but keeping up a quick, almost running pace.

Explaining to mum what will transpire in just over an hour, almost having to shout over the TV volume, before realising a remote control on her lap that can reduce the sound.

Mum saying its marvellous what everyone can do today, watching a live transmission from almost anywhere in the World, either on your phone, iPad, or smart TV.

My duties carried out, including having a cuppa and slice of toast for my breakfast, a little perk when making mums, before heading back home to watch Colins funeral service.

On reflection the service carried out to perfection, Bill, the spokesperson spoke highly of Colin, even remembering that he had watched and danced to Black Lace at Butlins Minehead.

I particularly enjoyed Bills rendition of Ecclesiastes 3 from the Holy Bible and how he envisaged "everything has its time," relating to Colin, his success, and achievements.

Also, something he brought to everyone's attention, and all aware of, and viewed often without comment.

Colin Gibb, Born December 8th, 1953 – Died June 2nd, 2024.

Nothing you would think erroneous with that, nonetheless, the ever so unrecognisable dash or hyphen between the born and died date, actually represents a whole life, in Colins case, almost seventy-one memorable years.

Years and years full of everything you can bring to mind, and more so in Colins eventful career.

Colins long-time friend on Tenerife, Feddie, the former singer, and front man from the UK band Freddies Beano, giving a brilliant account of his time and friendship with Colin.

Ian arranged to send thoughts from the three of us in an email to Sue, for Bill to read out during the service.

Ian and me focusing on our many years as friends and musicians, performing and playing music together, representing the UK in the Eurovision Song Contest, all formal under the circumstances.

However, Steve had put together a masterpiece, in particular pointing out an instance when Colin gave our then manager, Keith Mills a punch in the face, when he commented to Colin and Steve, "isn't it time you two went to bed."

Colin not a threat to Keith at all, Colin only five-foot five, while Keith over six-foot, and at least sixteen stone.

Nevertheless, it's not the size of the dog in the fight, but the fight within the dog, comes to mind.

Steve also mentioning that Paul Young and his band Q tips, staying in the same hotel, and on the same show as Black Lace, thought the incident very funny too, raising lots of hearty laughs in the service.

Alan and I going up to bed over an hour before this incident, but mentioning in my email to Bill, via Ian, that they regularly got up to lots of mischief.

Others in the UK now making up the famous Black Lace name, a duo singing all the hit tunes that survive to this day in clubs, children's discos, summer festivals and schools, even after forty-years, and counting.

A saying comes to mind that brings my personal thoughts about this particular chapter:-

"The heart of man plans his way, but the Lord establishes his steps"
Proverbs 16:9.

As human beings, we will never stop making plans for the next hour, the following day, or our futures, but a cautious lesson for us all is to hold our plans lightly.

CHAPTER THREE

A likely Story

When you think of all the electronic emails that continually reach my mobile phone or PC, and, if left for just a few days, it can take some time to read through them all.

In my case usually advertisements, from companies or businesses, where I have browsed, or purchased on-line goods, or reluctantly elected to receive an automated receipt, when acquiring goods from an on-line store or shop in town.

In my case, I grudgingly get all of these, and more, including additional valid emails, from two establishments, that I spend most of my time involved with.

The observatory members and committee, and the committee of Supporting Music for All, (SM4LL), where this year, I am chairperson of both.

Sm4ll is a music innovation group, which raises funds to help support young musicians in Wakefield and the five towns area.

Occasionally, I also receive reminders from my prescription delivery establishment, prompting me to reorder using my NHS app, and also a variety of others from my favourite on-line company, either confirming orders or delivery dates.

Including legitimate reminders for my TV licence, car tax and insurance, and a few others, however further ones received obviously sent in an attempt to defraud.

These so-called spam emails becoming more frequent, and on all platforms involving personal contact details, most of which invite people to part with savings or pension funds for all sorts of ridiculous reasons.

So far, the ones I consider spurious, I delete without even opening, and definitely all those that appear in my spam folder, subsequently, and in my case, these attempts to defraud, have failed miserably.

However, on two such occasions, I did open emails in my spam folder, that from one line of information I could read, looked like they originated from authentic organisations.

Discovering that the first one, an offer of a film adaptation of my second book, named, "Abri, My Oasis."

The other email outlined the possibility of making a documentary about the contents contained in my first biographical book, "And then came Agadoo."

Just a little apprehensive, I did hesitate, however, my enquiring and inquisitive nature succeeded.

I eventually decided to reply to the documentary offer, to my surprise, and disbelief, it proved the genuine article.

The gentleman I spoke with after sending a confirmation email, definitely up for a meeting with me, and as he lived in a village near Huddersfield, just a few miles away, I jumped at the chance.

Arranging to meet at a popular local garden centre, about halfway from both our homes, where, over a bacon sandwich and cuppa, chatted about his documentary proposal.

Not too much intensity at this early stage, nonetheless, soon becoming clear that he had certainly done his homework, and in some detail, knowing a great deal about me, and the other members of our Black Lace band.

He had purchased, and clearly read, all fifty-seven chapters of my book, "And then came Agadoo," which he referred to at every opportunity, when discussing proposals of episodes and characters.

He had also taken the time to read all about our band Black Lace, on all of the on-line search engines too, in particular, YouTube and Wikipedia.

I also took along my now aging scrap books, for an instant and visible look at articles of our band years of yesteryear, which raising a few hearty laughs from the two of us, in a now busy café area.

To date, only short notes and possible locations discussed, as immediately after our meeting, told that a former member of the Black Lace duo, had already met a producer, and made considerable progress in creating a documentary about his time performing in the band, and its former participants already.

So, our forthcoming Black Lace documentary now put on the so called, proverbial shelf, deferred until a later date.

Hopefully not too late, as age definitely a factor, and one that waits for no one, and with two surviving members left of the original four, the sooner the better.

Although, I do recall that I am a founding member of Black Lace, along with long-time friend, Ian Howarth.

At this time, neither asked to contribute anything to this other forthcoming documentary, from a much later incoming, and now former long gone former band member.

Oh well…

However, I also made the decision to reply to the request of a film adaptation of my second book "Abri, My Oasis" too, via a return email.

I received an almost immediate reply to my correspondence, saying they would like to meet me in person, or at least, contact me via telephone to discuss finance and future possibilities.

One problem of many, this film establishment resides in California, on the west coast of America, a distance of five thousand miles, so absolutely not a chance of me visiting.

Unless of course, all my overheads paid for, including flights and accommodation, arranged beforehand, and all at the company's expense.

Strange that an on-line zoom meeting not deliberated or included in the return email, considering the vast distance between us.

At the very least, to connect us, a face-to-face zoom chat could have taken place.

Instead, I opted to receive a telephone call on a specific day and time of my choice, from this renowned and celebrated film producer.

I only confirmed his call once I had thoroughly checked him, and his associates out, and established that the film titles he had allegedly produced, actually existed.

Unfortunately, I missed his call, however, the voicemail message did infer that the original email, and proposition, including film producer, appeared in fact from a legitimate source.

On the other hand, just a subordinate who replied, leaving his name and voice message, giving me, amongst other things, instructions to return his call on a telephone number provided.

Slowly tapping out the many digits on my mobile, and when connected, instantly giving me a warning, that this particular telephone number, confirmed as suspected spam.

Immediately ending my call...

Feeling so disappointed, and let down, although, I should have known better, as I am sure had a film producer, or company who wanted to exchange details with me, he, she, or they, in the first instance, would have contacted my publishing company.

So, a possibility that I could have squandered an opportunity of a plausible film adaptation of my book, "Abri, My Oasis."

Or had I continued with the telephone call using my landline, unaware of a warning message, would it have just turned out to become an audacious elaborate rip-off, a clever deception to obtain bank details and money from me, after all.

Funnily enough, I have not heard anything from this possible spam company, or individual since, now a few months ago.

Oh well.

Which brings me to emails I should not readily refuse to acknowledge, and one in particular, notification of my forthcoming dental appointment.

Visiting dental practices not at the top of my preferences to attend, and hospitals too, however, at times, I have had no choice when relatives, or close friends admitted, and prompts the choosing and taking of drinks and snacks, usually all devoured during the visiting time.

I have attended this particular NHS dental practice for almost fifteen years, located in Ossett, around five miles away, a short cut, I use regularly when visiting my son, Warren, along Low Laithes and past a popular golf course, and one hobby that I am pleased does not appeal to me.

My short, fifteen minutes of agony car drive, giving me ample time to prepare for what awaits me on my arrival, when the dentist begins to assault my mouth and teeth.

Over the years, I have conducted some unique DIY dentistry, only because of my reluctance to go to a practice, which almost resulted in a few near disasters.

I should have known better, as attempting to pull teeth with a pair of plyers from my toolbox never going to turn out satisfactory, regardless of how careful I am.

However, and on a few occasions, my attempt at pulling out the said teeth, did work, and with little, or no blood, and essentially no pain.

Removing the troublesome incisors, a couple from the rear top of my mouth, and on both sides, immediately relieved me of a troublesome, annoying, throbbing ache, which I had put up with for what I believe months on end.

Not to mention the removal of two wisdom teeth in my early teens, an experience that I feel, this particular visit put me off attending these dental practices for life.

If hereditary ailments anything to go by, my mum had all her adult teeth removed at an early age, just forty years old, due to an infection, and acknowledged receding gums.

Though, now at the age of ninety-three, mum often repeats during conversation, she would never turn the clocks back, or have a new set of dentures made, and completely satisfied using the very same dentures for over fifty years.

Now, that is what I call a bargain, with no further charges incurred for dental work, and over many years, as at the time of the NHS launch, dentistry free, and no financial contribution required from the patient.

This dramatically changed access to receive good oral healthcare, and brought about obvious grand expectations and appreciation of patients, nonetheless, in 1951, a charge of one pound introduced for dental treatment.

However, these days, when using NHS dental care practice, now at an astronomical expense, especially for a clean and polish, tooth removal, fillings, or the making and fitting of small dentures.

Also, if using a private dental practice, the cost to acquire a full mouth implant, now tens of thousands of pounds, or, if a replacement single adult tooth required, these too can cost over a thousand pounds, for each tooth!!!

My own teeth, well, those that now remain, cleaned consistently, at least twice a day, including a regular mouth wash, and in good condition, but sadly, some now becoming a tad loose, because of the deteriorating condition of my gums.

The dental hygienist at my practice, usually books me in twice a year, as a minimum, to take measurements and thoroughly give my teeth a good clean and polish, which does give some satisfaction, regardless of cost, well looked after.

Listening to the hygienist calling out various numbers, three, four, two, and five, seemed the most frequent ones, while she continued with the examination of my mouth.

The assistant busily working away at the computer, overhearing six and seven also mentioned a few times, now finding the taking of my measurements interesting.

Being somewhat an inquisitive person, I felt I should ask why these are taken, and how and why used once all my cleansing work completed.

As an explanation, the dental hygienist said that these numbers are measurements of gaps between my individual teeth and gums.

The smaller the numbers, the healthier the gums, which on my last visit, gave an indication that my gums now healthier and much improved.

However, I do have two dentures, one to my right top, and a middle bottom one, just a single tooth fitted to each acrylic plate, and both fit perfectly, but they do require adhesive to hold them in place, and in particular, when consuming hot foods, and drinking tea or coffee.

Before the hygienist starts my check up, I always remove my dentures, and place them on a tray to the side of my chair, so she can get to work with my sterile clean and shine.

Some one-sided conversation taking place during this time, usually about my teeth and mouth, but with an active noisy drill, water jet, and suction pipe roaming around my mouth, I do not think she expected to receive a reply, even if I could.

I also asked about the possibility of extracting all of my bottom teeth, and fitting a complete full lower denture, but I could tell from her facial expression, not a favourable idea to suggest at this particular time.

Oh Well…

I had the rest of my evening all planned once home from the dental practice, making tea, go to mum's, and then, regrettably, unload our groups van, for the very last time.

Making my tea would not take too long, a salmon steak wrapped in foil, soon placed in a hot oven, new potatoes now boiling in a pan, and just mixed vegetables to steam in the microwave, not a problem.

This evenings look in on mum, now a quicker than normal visit, just a few minor chores to conduct, and then onwards to Jim's home, to unload the van.

At a previous rehearsal, Jim and I had discussed dissolving the partnership, and bringing an immediate closure, and the end of our band, Mister Twister.

Performances up and down the country had taken place in working men's, and private clubs for over twenty-five years, not bad, when the original idea came about to form our band, to play for just a couple of years, way back in 1997.

A good run considering, and an enjoyable prolonged musical experience.

Those years added to other bands I have played in, amounts to over fifty-four years, and as said by most of my musician friends, the absolute best times had by all in clubland.

On the other hand, my tea now cooked and looking professionally presented in a white ceramic dish, and feeling hungry, I began to enthusiastically eat my concoction.

If I say so myself, a tasty meal, a definite gastronomical delight suiting my taste buds perfectly, and one I have made a few times now, the salmon cooked to perfection, as too the potatoes and vegetables.

Tucking in, and savouring the many flavours, and all while watching Pointless on BBC TV, even though, my mind elsewhere, when suddenly, and shockingly, even more delicious food going effortlessly down my throat…

AND

My top denture too…

Talk about panic…

A fear I have never experienced, came over me, and a million different thoughts, now rushing through my head…

Why I did not remove my denture before tucking into my tea, as I usually do when eating on my own.

Better still, why, when I arrived home from the dentist, did I not use my denture fixative to ensure it is secure, before starting to eat…

Too late for all that now, and more importantly, and with some urgency, I need to dislodge this odd, single tooth, unusually shaped denture, from my throat.

I began hitting my chest with a clenched fist, and also attempting to force a cough, to try and release it from midway down my oesophagus.

No luck, again beginning to panic, while attempting to think things through at the same time.

A drink of water, or more food required, a shame to waste the last tasty bit in my dish, and with any luck, eating will not make things much worse, and may also help to displace, and potentially help to carefully ease the denture from my throat, into my stomach...

What a dilemma to find myself in, and nobody here to give my back a good thumping, or perform the Heimlich manoeuvre, if they could get their arms around me, to give the required abdominal thrust.

Talking of the Heimlich manoeuvre, I actually carried out this on my former partner, when she inadvertently swallowed one half of a tinned pear.

Talk about panic, not me, my partner, tapping me on the shoulder as I cleaned the living room window, gasping for air, and looking a tad blue in the face, pointing to her mouth.

Instantly turning her around, and putting my arms around her, (a first for quite a few months) and gave a huge tug towards me.

Out popped the pear, to a near collapsing partner, now relieved she could breathe once again.

Where am I...

So much for my astutely planned evening, all pretty much down the drain, or in my immediate and now pressing case, stuck in my throat.

Success, a glass of water, and eating more of my food, actually did work, persuading my denture to continue slowly down my throat, and into my stomach, which possibly averted my own near-death event.

But what to do now...

Immediately sending out a few WhatsApp messages, to inform close family and friends of my dilemma, would give me some assurances that others now knew if any further problems should occur, during what remains of the evening.

I do have a key safe fitted to the outside wall, next to the front door, with a pass code to open, for those that do not have a house key.

My son Warren's initiative, so again, relieved that access to my home, in such an emergency can take place, although possibly a bit late, had I choked.

I contacted Warren, and his partner Sommer, both qualified

paramedics, for some professional advice as to what to do next, and by chance, they also had two further paramedics over to their home for tea.

The conversation that followed laughable, but also with a serious connotation too, nevertheless, everyone said that I should attend the A&E department at Pinderfields hospital, and as soon as possible.

Oh Well.

Characteristically, now thinking of the evening's earlier arrangements, a short drive to mum's and then on to Jim's to unload the van.

I did not feel uncomfortable, and certainly not in any pain, my denture now out of harm's way, for now.

Optimistically sat there in my stomach with the rest of my tasty food, so nothing anyone can do at this point, so I might as well just continue as originally planned.

Scraping the remaining few leftovers of my now cold tea in the bin, and putting my dish and cutlery in the dishwasher, wiping down the worktops, and quickly giving everywhere in the kitchen area a quick tidy up, and not forgetting to leave one of two patio doors slightly ajar, for Lottie and Ted.

Then, quickly on my way to mum's.

The short, two-mile drive as you can imagine, thoughtful, with my mind full of possibilities and "what if's"...

What if, the denture stays in my stomach.

What if, it gets stuck in my intestines.

What if, I require an operation to remove it.

What if, when I go to A&E, they keep me in.

No matter, I will now have to wait and see, and definitely not saying anything to mum at this time, so as not to worry her, as I took her stainless-steel water bottle, and a clean drinking glass into the bedroom, closed the vertical blind, partly closed the curtains, and pulled back the quilt.

Deciding not to stay too long, and even declining a cuppa, and KitKat, saying to mum, I do need to go to Jim's home to unload our van as soon as possible, and in my thoughts, a very quick drive to A&E.

Giving mum a kiss on her cheek, and then I am off, saying, see you in the morning mum, and locking the door on my way out.

I do hope around to see mum in the morning, and not admitted to a ward on an upper floor in Pinderfields hospital, awaiting an emergency operation...

Unloading our van an almost silent affair, apart from me explaining what had happened less than an hour before.

Raising a few laughs and insinuations, making our toil of carrying and wheeling all of our equipment down Jim's drive to his garage, a high-spirited visit, instead of a sad event.

I had already asked if my drumkit could remain in Jim's garage until I sorted out my shed before picking it up, now agreed.

The many times unloading our equipment in the past, at every gig, taking it all in, and then after our shows, everything back out of clubs and back into our van.

Also, unloading our equipment for the van to have its yearly MOT test, but this time around, so different, hugely different, as our equipment not put back in our van, ever...

Taking about twenty-minutes, Jim saying to get myself off to A&E, and he and his son, Chris, would put all the unloaded equipment in his garage, where it would remain securely locked, and alarmed until whatever decided in the not-too-distant future.

A unanimous decision agreed some time ago, to finally part with our van, selling it on, when the appropriate time finally arrives.

However, it would require a valid MOT, to obtain a competitive price, as overall, generally in good condition, for a twenty something year-old vehicle.

Our equipment had "lived" in our van all of the time of our playing days, so not only a vehicle to get our band Mister Twister, to and from clubs up and down the country, but also a protected equipment storage unit too.

Additionally, and mandatory in this case, a massive thank you to our long-established friend, Mick, a former band mate, for allowing us to park our van for all of these years securely in his more than ample, huge rear garden, located a few miles away, in Warmfield...

Furthermore, and to make matters even worse, my misfortune happened on the seventeenth anniversary of my son Liam's mum Tricia, my partners sudden death, and on the very same date, one year ago since Liam's grandad passed away too.

Memories of this day and date, firmly etched in my mind, nonetheless, I must get my own serious matter sorted, and quickly too, so as not to add another name to this date...

Now becoming a little worried, the main hospital carpark looked extremely busy, no visible empty spaces.

Luckily, a car pulling out just as I approached, and close to the pedestrian exit too.

The A&E carpark not accessible, due to major extension work conducted to the hospital, now just a drop off facility, so a much further walk from the main carpark, and one feeling a little apprehensive about taking.

The waiting area manic, remarkably busy indeed, hardly any available chairs, and so late too, as I quickly passed through to reception.

Glancing at the informative TV screen, I noticed seventy-five patients either waiting or currently checked in A&E at this time, which got me thinking, It could take hours, and maybe here for quite a while.

Luckily once checked in, only waiting thirty minutes before a nurse called me into a private room, along with two further nurses looking on.

I explained what had happened, which, once again, did raise a giggle or two, however, NHS professionalism did then take effect.

Given lots of sound advice from the nurse, and what would take place next.

In the interim, to wait until a doctor called me for a checkup, then an Xray, and depending on the results, either wait for my denture to cautiously pass through over five feet of large intestine, and appear with poo, which could take a few days.

Or, if it did remain in my stomach, or get stuck while making its way out, the alternative, an enema, and possible minor operation to remove, a thought I would emphatically put to the back of my mind.

Finally getting home around 03.00hr, almost eight hours, spending the majority of my time sat in the waiting room, watching patients of all ages, coming, and going, and looking at hospital statistics on TV, showing continual movement of patients, to who knows where.

The doctor giving me a thorough examination, listening to my chest and back with a stethoscope, and having seen the Xray, gave me an almost all clear, to go home, and to wait patiently for my bowels to take their course.

Also told to carry on and continue as normal, with an indication to eat plenty of food, especially those that have natural lubricants, and to drink plenty.

Perhaps lots more than usual, and anything else that involves an amount of exercise, which will all help with my denture taking its long and hazardous journey.

This relatively good news had given me a clear indication, to arrange an afternoon swimming session.

Now, and more than ever, definitely, a much-needed exercise.

Amanda picking me up at the usual time, for a fun filled couple of hours, and maybe, just maybe, reaching a further milestone with our swimming, for the both of us.

Also, following a text to ask if this inconvenience a possibility, thanking Amanda for calling at my home the previous night.

Visiting to lock up my rear patio doors, and feed Lottie and Ted their tasty cheesy cheddar snacks, while I sat in the hospital waiting room, twiddling my thumbs, and uncertain of what would take place.

I am pleased to say, all did eventually turn out well, thankfully, as my denture did not get stuck in my stomach, and after almost sixty hours of sightseeing in my large intestine, finally, and with little fuss, it emerged during my regular morning ablutions.

Although, it did not come without some earlier discomfort, waking me at 04.30hr in the morning, a sort of lower abdominal pain giving me an indication of its approaching appearance.

I did roll over, and fall back to sleep, until my bedroom TV alarm came on at 07.15, then up and about, and immediately down to business, so to speak.

Everything taking place as told it would happen, although, thankfully, an expectation of experiencing some acute pain, did not materialise.

After its long, slow, perilous journey, a thorough soapy wash, and a full day and overnight soak in steriliser, my denture now looks ok, and I am able to wear it once again...

However,...

I will, ensure that from now on, I do remove my denture before eating, or make absolutely sure secured in place with denture adhesive...

CHAPTER FOUR

A Sightseeing Holiday

(With a Difference)

Over many years, I have travelled on countless overseas holidays, to lots of European countries, Sri Lanka, the Maldives possibly the furthest, and visited many comparable destinations while playing drums, professionally in my band.

Nonetheless, some destinations did not turn out that good, and certainly not as the holiday brochure booklets, photos, or, as our bands manager and booking agents described them.

On-line reservations made with travel agents, not that much different either, all offering three, four and five-star accommodation, and upon arrival, did not actually meet expectations.

Nevertheless, some holidays took place that felt exactly right, and some much better than anticipated, turning out exceptional, and becoming a destination where I would like to repeatedly return.

One of which, a location on mainland Spain, situated on the Costa del Sol, known for its beaches, the Puerto Marina, Theme Park, Sea Life centre and a castle style monument, dedicated to Christopher Columbus following his discovery of America.

The coastal city of Benalmadena...

Staying at three family style hotels, over six visits, and each displaying an array of different, distinctive qualities, which captured my imagination over and over again, with so much to see and do, including enjoying long walks, at a practical time of year, and while in tolerable temperatures.

The destination of Benalmadena remarkably close to the town of Coin, and the villa residence of Baz, my ex-father-in-law, where all the family enjoyed quite a few daily visits over these years, to relish in his home surroundings, and superb hospitality.

On a few occasions, my sons, Ashley and Warren, and their mum and husband Martin there at the same time, bringing our somewhat segregated family unit together.

That included my partner, and youngest son Liam, where collectively all enjoyed our prearranged time, in amazing idyllic, picturesque surroundings.

A destination that I visited, over an eight-day period, way back in 1979, similarly, one of those that I have always had the desire and determination to return to one day, and following just the one short eight-day visit.

To the state of Israel.

During the first few days, totally transfixed with all the locations that I actually visited in this remarkable country, and the potential of those that at the time did not permit our party to visit.

So disappointed that our stay in Jerusalem, turned out nowhere near long enough, to take in everything the country of Israel had to offer...

Not that I would want to return there on a package type of holiday, where I would stay in the same hotel for the whole of my visit, traveling to various places, arranged through holiday representatives, and returning each day for some leisure time, my meals, and to sleep.

My personal preference to organise and plan a unique sightseeing holiday, where I could travel all around the country, staying at various city hotels, or maybe at a kibbutz, and able to visit numerous historical and biblical locations enroute.

Some of which, I did get the opportunity to visit and explore, during my time there in 1979.

I will explain...

Our four-piece band, Black Lace, becoming the British entrant to represent the United Kingdom, in the twenty-fourth Eurovision Song Contest, to take place in the city of Jerusalem, Israel, and televised across the whole of Europe and nearby countries, on March 31st, 1979.

While on location, Black Lace had to wait until mid-afternoon each day for our proposed seventeenth position rehearsal time, a welcome on-stage slot that gave us plenty of free time, and a perfect opportunity to see parts of this amazing country.

A coordinated, after breakfast outing began to take shape, and tailored to fit with-in a limited radius of Jerusalem.

The British Broadcasting Company (BBC) and local Israeli tour guides arranged our daily visits, along with CBS music (now named Columbia Records after Sony acquired the Columbia name and trademarks from EMI), who took us to various locations.

However, because our UK entourage so large in numbers, it became necessary to divide into two smaller more manageable groups.

Some traveling in a fifteen-seater mini-bus with prominent personnel from the BBC, and others in similar transport with representatives from CBS.

After an early breakfast buffet each day, Alan, and I, merged with associates from the BBC, while Steve and Colin joined with the CBS record company representatives, visiting as many historical and biblical places as possible, during the limited time available.

Our trips took us to see the partly excavated ruins of Jericho, and a region where the famous Dead Sea Scrolls existed before discovered, an on-going archaeological digging site at the time.

Our small group visited the infamous Dead Sea, where an attempt to do a bit of swimming took place, or should I say floating, such a strange experience.

A stopover to Yad Vashem, (memorial of the WW2 holocaust) and the museum of the Dead Sea Scrolls, as well as local stuff, like the Jerusalem markets, the mount of Olives and Wailing wall also taking place.

Steve and Colin did not follow our precise route, as they had a different itinerary, nevertheless, after daily discussions following our trips out, both parties had attended sites with similar historical and biblical significance.

For almost forty years now, my averred return visit to Israel has eluded me, as sadly, I have not had the same determination and gusto, I spoke of earlier, which over these years had somewhat faded.

Nevertheless, and for several reasons, I continually booked overseas poolside holidays, where I would remain stuck in the same location most of the time, eating, drinking, swimming, and sunbathing, with just an occasional trip out, or walks around the town or city where our hotel located.

An opportunity came my way in 1994 to take the three hundred mile, south bound trip across the Mediterranean sea while on holiday in Cyprus.

However, our island holiday only lasted seven days, and the Israel excursion would assume four of those days, and so expensive to travel and stay there too, so my temptation scuppered, and that trip did not materialise.

Although, just recently, and because of changing circumstances, I have an opportunity to visit Egypt, where I will certainly see ancient historical monuments, and as much of the country as possible, during my proposed stay.

My trip only coming about because of a rekindled friendship with a former local lady, whom I knew years ago while at senior school, and after all these years, becoming friends once again, on a large social network platform.

I mentioned during one of our text conversations, that I would like to visit Egypt, to ride on a camel, and view the pyramids, and if time permits, visit museums, and also travel on the river Nile, anything, and everything instead of just watching documentaries about them all on TV at home.

Some twenty years ago, Caroline met a local resident from Egypt while sailing on a Nile Cruise, called Tommy (for short), and permanently moved there, became engaged, and got married.

Tommy and Caroline own and manage a travel company called T&C Tours, and because of our on-line friendship, they would arrange this sightseeing holiday, with a little assistance and constructive suggestions from me.

Perhaps, if I knew a local resident or someone who owned an Israel travel company, and fully aware of all the Historical and Biblical locations, that would also make an Israel holiday perfect too.

Or perhaps a person who regularly visits Israel, and similarly knows of these places and could conceivably arrange an equivalent touring holiday, similar to my time in Egypt, for me to visit this amazing country and various exciting locations...

Would you believe it, and unbeknown to me at the time, it just so happens that a friend of mine, actually has a long-established acquaintance, who could perhaps help with arranging just this type of sightseeing holiday in Israel.

Once again, I will explain.

The secretary of our observatory and my stargazing companion,

Amanda, has known a lady for over twenty years as part of a congregation attending worship.

Frequently meeting at Bible study classes in Heckmondwike, a village just a few miles away.

During conversation, and quite a while ahead of Amanda and I becoming members at the observatory, sat in the café, at Manygates Music Hub.

All waiting patiently for our youngest children while having a coffee and scone, both children either having percussion lessons, or in orchestral rehearsals, when my inquisitive nature got the better of me, and amongst talking of other enjoyable and interesting subjects, religion also became an appealing topic.

Amanda said that she and her immediate family are of the Christadelphian faith since childhood, as too her parents and grandparents.

I am aware of some religions, at three years old, along with my new younger brother, Brian, both christened in the church of England faith, my stepdad christened as Catholic, while mum is church of England.

I have friends and people I know of who practice the Jehovah's Witness faith, and a chap in college in the Mormon faith, and also Muslim students, but in my naivety, I had not heard of the Christadelphian faith.

I did attend church while at junior school, singing in the choir at Alverthorpe church, but thereafter, I only found the necessity to visit church while in attendance with family and friends at christenings, weddings and sadly, funerals.

Saying to Amanda, during our many tête-à-têtes, I would like to return to Israel, someday, following our bands visit there in 1979.

When, unexpectedly, Amanda announced a lady friend called Julia often takes a party of believers of the Christadelphian faith to Israel from their places of worship.

What amazing news, and certainly music to my ears, and I wanted to hear more.

Questions and more questions followed, about all the if's and buts, and what it all entailed, and if at all possible, could I actually join this party, and travel to Israel too…

My excitement at the opportunity of once again visiting Israel, now topmost in my thoughts, certainly rekindling those long-standing memories and my desire of yesteryear.

Amanda, said that I had actually met her friend Julia, at a few summer and Christmas school concerts, where Julia had attended to watch Amanda's two daughters, Holly and Rosie performing, playing various instruments in the school orchestra, although, at this time, I could not recall, seeing or speaking to her.

My youngest son Liam played percussion in the orchestra too, and I travelled there to watch and listen, however, I also liked to help out in the café area.

Serving tea and coffees, selling raffle tickets, and offering delicious looking buns and cakes, lovingly made by Amanda, and mum-in-law Jennifer, where I probably met and spoke with Julia.

Julia has attended studies of the scriptures at the same Heckmondwike meeting room since her early childhood, and started arranging these visits to Israel over twenty-five years ago, each visit taking place at eighteen-month intervals.

Amanda said she would ask Julia at their next meeting, if any available places remain for the forthcoming planned trip, and as I am not in the Christadelphian faith, acceptable for me to join the party.

Sadly, the next two trips already fully booked to capacity, and quickly doing my sums, realised a minimum of four and a half years, before I could go.

Julia gave Amanda an indication that if a place did become available for a later trip, a place reserved for me to join the party.

A sort of delayed disappointing reaction ensued, four and a half years to wait, that is such a long time, and one thing that I have learnt during my retirement, to take preoccupations a little slower, and also to have lots and lots of patience.

One thing is for sure, I will remain in regular contact with Amanda, and so, if for any reason individual cancellations did take place, and passed to Julia, a slender chance may arise much sooner rather than later, when I would finally fulfil my wish, and, after over forty long years, return once again to Israel.

Where was I …

Oh yes…

My Egypt holiday now all planned with Tommy and Carolyn, but only after a few deliberations about the itinerary and length of my holiday.

A couple of points in our discussion took a while to resolve, should I stay for ten, fourteen days, or four days cruising the River Nile, or maybe a four-day poolside break in Sharm El-Sheikh, choosing becoming a little more challenging.

Having had lots of poolside holidays, perhaps sailing on the Nile may turn out the more appealing.

Finally, agreeing a duration of ten-days, including a Nile cruise, a perfect length of stay suiting me better on this occasion.

However, I did say if all goes satisfactory, and I like the country and its culture, perhaps then, I will propose a fourteen-day trip the next time.

If agreed, beginning my sightseeing holiday at the start of March 2020, which would include my birthday.

Surprisingly, I received confirmation, via Amanda, that Julia, has added my name to the list for a forthcoming Israel trip, taking place in November 2020.

2020, an amazing year for my touring and visiting all of these incredible Biblical and Historical attractions, and hopefully, some others away from the beaten track.

As I do like watching lots of documentaries on TV about biblical events and the cultures of Egypt and Israel, and historical artifacts contained in these ancient countries.

Who would have thought, sending just a few text messages, and in conjunction with close friends, and word of mouth, both of these amazing sightseeing holidays have now become a reality.

Excited, I am beyond that, in fact, deliriously happy, a feeling I have not experienced for years.

However, and what has now become world history, an epidemic of enormous proportions, resulting in worldwide chaos and death, would soon hang over all of us, and bring the world economy to its knees.

Including serious doubts about my planned November trip to Israel.

Just a few weeks prior to me leaving home for my tour of Egypt, news of a brewing pandemic hit all the news channels, allegedly emanating from China.

These flu-like symptoms began to bring down people from all levels of society, a serious illness, and for some, eventual death.

That aside I contacted Caroline and Tommy, excepting their offer with my tour and confirmed itinerary of Egypt.

Such an amazing schedule, visiting the Pyramids, Saqqara necropolis, including a river cruise lasting four days sailing on the Nile, and all while taking short visits seeing other amazing wonders.

On the other hand, and more importantly, hearing horrific hourly news bulletin updates informing everyone that this ongoing pandemic, certainly getting much worse.

I suppose listening to the daily news, thinking my stay here in Egypt could falter, yet, and as luck would have it, I did complete my amazing ten-day stay, but only just.

As when I returned home, Governments from around our planet decided in an attempt to protect the world's population, carry out something never ever experienced, an unreserved "lock down."

No attending work, school, or play, except for key workers, as children and the elderly, considered most vulnerable.

Months and months of listening to appalling news bulletins informing the public of the continuing world-wide coronavirus pandemic situation.

The United Kingdom Conservative Government putting all sorts of measures in place in an attempt to stop the virus spreading, passing from one person to another.

A minimum, two-metre distance between people now put in place, hand sanitiser dispensers fitted everywhere, and in particular the use of facemasks.

These now worn at all times when travelling or visiting shops and supermarkets for food essentials.

Financial implications a huge threat to businesses and members of the public, and if found guilty of not observing strict new rules and regulations, huge fines, and possible prison sentences imposed.

Police officers involved with issuing these fines for non-compliance, solicitors and court hearings on hold and not sitting, all bringing about huge backlogs of impending punishments or possible imprisonment.

Sounding almost like an impatient, overburdened Government had imposed martial law, eager to bring things under control, and fast.

My long-awaited sightseeing holiday to Israel now postponed, indefinitely, or until such a time as the UK and the rest of the world return to something like normality, and how long that would take, is anyone's guess.

Our band, Mister Twister, had more than a few gigs cancelled from our diary, and businesses going bankrupt, or facing ruin left, right and centre.

Most of us now housebound and fearful of contracting covid-19, what an unbelievable and aberrant situation, and during our supposedly modern and technically excellent, twenty first century.

My mum and partner, Peter, both spent time in hospital after contracting covid, thankfully recovering, that sadly, not the case for many others.

A few of my friends suffered severe debilitating symptoms, including Amanda, and all over the Christmas and New Year period.

Liam returning from a Manchester party with college friends brought the dreaded covid indicators back home too.

Both of us testing positive on Christmas day morning, although, in my case, not feeling particularly ill, just having flu-like symptoms and a thick head, and at this point I had not touched one drop of alcohol.

Nonetheless, under government guidelines, confined to our home for ten days, or until testing negative.

Anything and everything put on an immediate hold, until who knows when.

With minimum delay the UK becoming the first to develop an effective vaccine, and within a brief time of creation and development, certainly some resolve from the pharmaceutical engineers, and administered it to pop-up centres around the UK…

The Government quickly ratified a sliding scale of importance for everyone to receive their inoculations, with the elderly, infirm and pensioners, receiving the highest priority, and eventually everyone else over twelve years of age.

In the interim, this course of action began to give everyone a little reprieve, now allowing some reasonably close contact, and a full return to work, children back into schools and colleges, and the entertainment industries allowed to open up once again too.

After a number of deceptive starts and stops, and a second injection of this notable vaccine, things eventually began to improve in the UK and around the world once again.

Finally, and appreciatively, I received confirmation that my long-awaited Israel trip, now scheduled to take place in May 2022, almost eighteen months from its postponement.

Emailing my holiday request to our band members, informing them of my departure time, and at last a date now firmly set in stone, nonetheless, sent with some apprehension and trepidation.

Feeling a little guilty, as our band had not played music around clubs for almost eighteen months.

Not a single penny earned to take care of our van's upkeep, all the while standing charges to our bank still taken, and all of the above because of the coronavirus pandemic.

An interesting conversation urgently needed at our next rehearsal, when face to face with each of our band members.

Feeling sure my band mates would understand, as we have all had a period of prolonged incarceration in our homes during this time, and they may also want to instigate reserving holiday places for their families.

No doubt about it, certainly a testing time for everyone, and still early days for everything to get back to a pre-pandemic routine, lifestyle, and operational levels.

Including, all public transport, such as airports, ferries, trains, buses, and coaches, all necessary for our economy in the UK, and worldwide population to travel, and deliver goods, and enable my long-awaited sight-seeing holidays to take place.

CHAPTER FIVE

Israel – 2022

(Itinerary One)

Following a disastrous couple of years, our lives now beginning to get back to some sort of organised mandate.

Most surrendering to their initial fears, and having the fortitude to try and venture out and about once again, visiting pubs, clubs, and other former prohibited premises.

Our ever-increasing communication platforms favourably thrust down the list of priorities, possibly with the exception of zoom, or other face-to-face IT systems, which came into their own, along with other similar packages, during lockdown.

Our local pubs, clubs, restaurants, music, and entertainment venues, anything, and everything else which survived during two restrained periods becoming those places to go.

However, lots of office spaces and buildings remaining empty, or skeleton staff operating in them, as working from home continued, furthermore confident this action will take precedent over commuting to work, for some time to come.

Our own city centre, and quite sure others, becoming ghost cities, along with many towns and villages, street style café areas empty, all missing customers wanting a break from visiting shops, or thirsty staff from these now empty office structures.

Now, following our holidays postponement, and after such a long wait, prior to, and over the covid period, eighteen long months, nevertheless, my National Express bus journey to Luton now confirmed, as too the overnight IBIS hotel, prior to our ELAL early morning flight to Tel Aviv, Israel.

Undeniably real, and in only a few short weeks, I cannot wait, as at last my forty-three-year holiday desire definitely about to take place.

Our sight-seeing party will consist of twenty-seven travellers, of all ages and abilities, and all of Christadelphian faith, except me.

What should I expect, would they all welcome me, like Julia, the only person I have come to know so far on our planned trip.

All this made possible, following an invitation to Amandas home for tea.

The evening becoming a lovely get-together, with a tasty meal, including a delicious pudding, and wine, and my first introduction to a blessing, and a short reading of the scriptures prior to eating our meal.

I had said a blessing before a meal a few times, long ago, just the usual one liner, although at the time I did not think of it as a religious appreciation, even though mentioning "Lord."

"For what we are about to receive, may the lord make us truly thankful, Amen."

Then quickly tucking into our food.

On this special occasion, the blessing spoken via Amanda's husband, Dave, appearing so much lengthier and worldly poignant, than my one-liner.

I had not heard of Christian Bible readings held in a house either, as these regularly taking place, or so I thought, always occurring in church.

I have held many a Bible, especially when collecting and stacking them in Alverthorpe church during my choir member days, but never owned one, or ever had one in my home, on a bookshelf or tucked away in a drawer.

Of late, only browsing through an on-line Bible to use as a confirmation of story lines, when reading Chariots of the Gods, the Swiss author, Erich Von Daniken, writing this, and published in 1968, also Return to the Stars, published in 1970, but especially Chariots of the Gods.

The books of Ezekiel, and Revelations in particular referred to, narratives written in the scriptures to corroborate what Erich had written about in his many publications.

Erich uses modern technology objects to explain Biblical terms of reference, inferring extraterrestrials in the form of ancient astronauts, which allegedly visited Earth pre-Biblical periods.

Leaving behind lots of artifacts which exist to this day, continuing to defy accurate clarification and explanation.

However, because of my forthcoming Israel trip, Amanda has given me a King James Version Bible, and loaned me a Christadelphian Hymn book, as daily meetings already prearranged, will take place in the hotels our group stay in, which includes Bible readings and singing hymns after our evening meal.

Julia had already informed me, that as part of our trip, these meetings will take place each and every evening, although, given a choice to join in, or not, as enrolling, would mean actually taking part with readings and singing hymns.

You would think my role as a former team manager, and with over fifty years' experience performing, playing my drums, singing in bands, and my brief though enjoyable time singing in a church choir, not a problem for me talking, or using these thoroughly used tuneless vocal chords for just a couple of hymns each night.

I have to admit, certainly not the case, as I had given this matter lots of thought, and having listened to my dulcet tones and meagre attempts at just singing anything these last few years, I quickly realised my vocal chords did not amount to a good sounding melodic tone, or vocal range at all.

Reaching every musical note within a passage, except the notes I should achieve, or perhaps the saying, "singing all the right notes, but not necessarily in the right order" comes to mind.

Possibly tone deaf also comes to mind, a much better description of my meagre choral abilities.

However, my determined positive temperament, will always give everything and anything a go, at least once, so looking forward to meeting the twenty-seven other sightseers at the Luton IBIS, and take it from there.

Becoming aware early on in the booking process, that I would share a bedroom containing two single beds, with a gentleman from Sheffield, not only at the Luton IBIS, but throughout my stay in Israel too.

Same gender room sharing, has become the norm for other single travellers on these trips, as the charge of a single room supplement, can cost almost half as much again, as the full holiday, consequently, a massive financial saving all around, when agreeing to share.

Although again all of this a bit daunting, as I have not met Trevor my roommate before, feeling more like a dating agency, and immediately sharing a bedroom.

Thinking back to our band days, and staying in pro-digs all over the country, where the four of us, in most cases shared a room, and sometimes even a double bed.

If given a choice, undoubtedly, Alan and I share a double bed, while Colin and Steve take the two singles, as staying in digs for entertainers, most classed as family rooms, and configured in this way.

Sometimes, when making a reservation, when working in clubs away from home, availability would consist of three single beds in a bedroom, so I always opted to take a single room, which gave me lots of quiet time to read my many books.

Musician friends, sharing anything and everything, full co-operation with each other, to ensure our band could last out the long weeks away from our homes and families, and these many occasions a vivid memory of just how each of us coped.

Other artists I frequently met in pro-digs, did not survive in the music business to tell the tail, with lots of arguments and continual fallouts, bringing about many lineup changes, or a full disbandment.

Meeting Julia at 06.55 in Dewsbury bus station, to board our National Coach to Luton, on a damp day, gave me much delight when waving off my taxi driver brother.

Removing my coat, and pushing it tightly to the bottom of my holdall, knowing that our weather conditions in Israel will remain much warmer.

Certainly, no mentioned of rain or damp conditions at all in the Israel forecast during our ten-day stay.

Arriving at Luton airport mid-afternoon, and actually passing our IBIS hotel enroute, just a short walk back down the road, taking approximately fifteen minutes, said Julia.

Taking the largest of Julia's two cases, I set off, with my suitcase in the other hand, pulling them along a tarmac path that at times becoming a bit narrow, for both cases and me, just about fitting on this busy airport access road footpath.

Downhill most of the way to the Ibis hotel, although thinking in just a few hours, doing the very same, but this time, an uphill walk, pulling two large cases from the hotel, to check in to departures at the Airport terminal tomorrow.

I did say to Julia that I could take care of her larger than average case, a sort of chaperone, because her case did appear full to capacity, certainly up to an allowed weight limit, and difficult to manoeuvre, even for me.

Thankful the forecast here in Luton remained dry, and confident it would continue for our walk back to the terminal in the morning.

Meeting most of our party at the IBIS hotel during the afternoon becoming an absolute pleasure, and finally connecting with my roommate Trevor, who had a similar handshake to me.

Trevor arrived a little later, because of the earlier flight change that did cause a few transport issues, as what transpired not necessarily a common practise, when booking holidays.

Our original flight from, and it's return to Heathrow, for some reason changed at short notice, causing issues where best to park cars for those driving to the airport, as our outbound journey will now take place from Luton Airport, with an arrival at Heathrow.

Trevor living in Sheffield, and chose to park his car at Heathrow, driving a further thirty-five miles south from Luton, and taking in the busy M25 motorway, and then a taxi arranged for his journey to Luton and the IBIS hotel, close to the airport.

Trevor's brother, Robert, deciding to join our trip at the last minute, travelling to Heathrow from the south coast in his car, and joining Trevor in the taxi to our Luton hotel.

Robert opted for a single room, making his holiday more expensive than those of us sharing, although, amid the three of us, I did suggest perhaps Trevor and Robert should share, and I would pay the room price difference.

However, my proposal immediately declined, as soon becoming clear all the paperwork and everything else would have to change.

No matter, Trevor certainly did not mind, or me, as everyone in our party getting along extremely good.

How long I had known Julia, and becoming friends, soon developing into the main topic of conversation, and with me the only none-Christadelphian in our party of twenty-seven, I suppose it did require some clarification.

Starting my explanation in every case, as I did get asked such a lot, saying that my friendship began with Amanda and youngest daughter Rosie, as others in our party knew of their family extremely well.

Rosie, along with my youngest son Liam, both musicians attending a music hub in Wakefield, learning their craft, and became the preliminary place of contact, between both families.

Amanda and I sat in the café, at the music hub, along with other parents, all chatting, while waiting for our children to appear from lessons or rehearsals.

Our discussions covered a variety of subjects, and one in particular, about my visit to Israel, way back in 1979.

Mentioning my previous 1979 visit to Israel, to Christadelphians in the IBIS hotel, and while in Israel, led to many more conversations, I will come to those later.

Continuing with how I met and got to know Julia.

Rosie and Liam attended Outwood school, and held a few music concerts in the main hall, Julia attending a few of these, and where told I possibly first met her.

These few words, in the interim, achieving the necessary results, however, others in our party, having an inquisitive, enquiring nature, just like me, brought about many other innovative questions, and all heading in my direction.

I did enjoy the attention, feeling rather special for just a fleeting few hours, in a funny sort of way, and my numerous replies, albeit a little vague at times, now flowing freely over the length of our holiday.

While not sure how much of my "life" now common knowledge during the provision of all my particulars Julia, and tour company required, to enable important levels of security, a prerequisite via the Israeli authorities to take place.

Nevertheless, I did give a truthful accurate account of my multifaceted past, openly presenting as much information as possible, although, at this incredibly early stage of our sightseeing get-together, I certainly did not want to upset anyone, or give out a wrong impression of myself.

Finding it difficult to describe the emotions I felt when our ELAL aircraft touched down on tarmac of the Tel Aviv airport, but I can assure you that I had all on to hold back a tear or two.

Arriving in Israel once again, after a period of forty-three years and two months, just a drop in the ocean, as those somewhat bewildering years, with some individual times more memorable than others, have certainly flown incredibly quickly.

After visiting those sites way back in March 1979, and now some of them mentioned in our itinerary, how would I feel when seeing them for a second time, anyone's guess, but could not wait to get started.

Reading up the history of this amazingly small area of land prior to my visit, just eight-thousand square miles, with a current population of around ten million, just 3% of the world's population, and an area of just 0.2% of all Arabic lands.

A state since its formation on May 14th, 1948, Israel bordered with Lebanon, Syria, Jordan, the Gasa Strip, Egypt, the Mediterranean Sea, and gulf of Eilat.

However, in 1979 when I stood at the open door of our aircraft, waiting to descend steps on to the tarmac, taking in a huge breath of the aroma of Israel, an unmistakable fragrance, that sadly did not materialise on this occasion.

My initial thoughts that our aircraft and airport now as one.

An attached linking tunnel, taking us directly from the aircraft, into the main building, through to security and passport control, and our suitcase retrieval area.

Aircraft linking tunnels or jet walks, positively a brilliant innovation, especially when windy or raining, and from what I remember of airports, these possibly not around, or used at some airports in1979.

Although, travelling via aircraft, definitely not a regular mode of transport for us individuals, or our band in those early days.

These passageways, airbridges or passenger boarding bridges, whatever name used, certainly not available for our arriving aircraft to Israel in 1979.

As all passengers left our aircraft, front and rear, using traditional steps descending to the tarmac, some distance from terminal buildings, and from memory, requiring a bus to get us to there.

Oh well.

A meet and greet with Da'vid, our guide for the next ten-days, now showing us a way out, Julia walking and chatting with Da'vid, no doubt lots of catching up since their last meeting.

Leaving the airport terminal full of enthusiasm, our coach ready and waiting, engine running, ensuring air-conditioning units worked to capacity, a definite much-needed appliance, as it did appear quite hot, even at this late hour.

Identifying our own suitcases, allowing our driver and helpers to load them underneath the buses seating area, and then without delay, on our way to Netanya.

Our first night stop over, The King Solomon Hotel, just thirty minutes north of Tel Aviv, sitting directly on the amazing coast of the Mediterranean Sea.

Our hotel centrally located on a coastal expanse of the Holy Land, and although dusk, and quickly getting dark.

The beach promenade appears to offer amazing views over the Mediterranean Sea just now, and sure much improved when waking up at sunrise, or whatever time in the morning.

How wrong, totally the opposite.

Both Trevor and me, disrespectfully woken up during the pre-daybreak hours, to thunderous thrashing of wind and rain, beating against our eighth-floor balcony door and window.

Certainly not what I had in mind for a start to my sightseeing trip, and thinking less than thirty hours ago when leaving home, saying, it can hit a rather hot thirty degrees, or even higher in Israel during this time of year.

Unquestionably, an escalation to anywhere near these elevated temperatures did not seem possible today.

Nevertheless, after a tasty and filling buffet breakfast, the weather had already begun to brighten up no end.

As looking through large hotel windows over towards the Mediterranean Sea, evidently not a sign of earlier stormy conditions, no rain, wind, or clouds, just perfectly still palm trees and a clear blue sky.

Perhaps normal weather for an early May start of day in this seaside location, who knows, but sure I would soon find out, as our one-night stay at the hotel had ended, and all our suitcases, once again, loaded into the enormous lower boot section of our waiting coach.

Next stop, Caesarea, around thirty minutes away, and seventy miles northwest of Jerusalem, and again, located on the coast of the Mediterranean Sea.

Originally a Jewish city, until the Romans conquered it in 63BC.

Lots of amazing ruins, most still visible, and following some excavation and restoration, an amphitheatre standing out, now in use to this day, as an entertainment open air venue, with seating for twenty thousand spectators.

Also, positioned almost at the seas edge, remains of a huge oval shaped stadium, unmistakably, once used for chariot racing, that in its day could seat up to a hundred thousand spectators, with spectacular views overlooking the Mediterranean Sea.

Bringing to mind one of my favourite actors and films, Charlton Heston, as Ben Hur, and in particular, its more than impressive chariot race, and when looking from our inspiring, elevated location, you can almost imagine the very same excitement.

Following lunchtime, our coach began to make its way to Mount Carmel, fifteen miles inland, and once again, more spectacular views awaited our party, looking across the Valley of Jezreel.

Our guide Da'vid, giving a brilliant verbal account of this historical location, and its Biblical significance, and made all the better when using a "whisper."

A battery operated in-ear headset, everyone wearing one, bringing Da'vids voice, clearly to all of us, wherever our location or situation, with-in signal distance.

Onward to our next visit, just a few miles away, Mount Carmel, and then on to view the Baha'i Gardens, then making our way to Tel Megiddo, an ancient stronghold, ranging from 4000 BC.

These structural remains, situated on a great "highway," linking Egypt with Mesopotamia, and from 1468 BC to AD 1918, a location where many battles and enemy attacks have taken place, the British Government also involved, with the Belfour declaration, a public statement issued in 1917, and valid until May 1948.

During these long sightseeing walks on our first day, I began to think, having a large brolly maybe useful, and not to offer protection against rain, but a mobile functional shade, from the intense heat of a glaring sun.

Yes, it had now reached its maximum day time temperature, and so pleased I had put on my factor 30, even though it had rained while in Netanya.

Now much further inland, and thankful for my free white baseball cap, the tour company supplied as a "freebie" a definite welcome package, including a shoulder bag, and detailed map of Israel.

Heading down to the sea of Galilee and our next stop over at The Restal Hotel, and the fourth most holy city in the land of Israel, after Jerusalem, the city of Tiberias.

Tiberias, named after a roman general, Tiberias Caesar, originally Herod Antipas founded this city, positioned on the banks of the Sea of Galilee since AD18.

A lovely hotel awaited our party, and after a recent refurbishment, looked amazing from outside, with huge palm trees all along the main frontage of this building.

Lots of useful amenities, including a gym, although, with all our everyday walking, some uphill treks, and oh so many steps, I do not think spending any time in there would offer additional benefits during my three-night stay.

Our room has all mod-cons, twin beds for starters, flat screen TV, Wi-Fi, sea views, and of course an up-to-date modern bathroom.

A large pool and sunbathing area situated directly to the rear, a welcome sight, and if our busy itinerary allows enough time, almost sure I am able to fit in a swim during our stay, in an excellent choice of hotel for our party.

Trevor claiming a bed next to the window, closest to a double plug socket, essential for charging his laptop, mobile phone, and my phone too, as a plug adapter I had bought did not fit, so sharing charging time using Trevor's adapter.

After just one night, already settling into a routine, Trevor using our bathroom first, while I turned on our room TV to catch up with news from home and around the world, tonight no different.

A very tasty looking buffet tea once again on offer, and I could not wait to get stuck in, a little hungry, no, starving, but I would not make the same mistake, when sitting down during our previous days evening meal.

Last night's feast, a huge buffet, arranged purposely on platters to get those taste buds anxious to eat.

I sat on an empty table with my overflowing plate, consisting of a mixture of potatoes, vegetables, and roast chicken, you name everything on display I had it on my dinner plate.

However, already munching and enjoying my second forkful, when Trevor and Robert, along with others from our party, joined me on our now fully occupied, large circular table.

I began to say, this food tastes exceptionally good, when instantly realising, everyone had their head bowed, and clearly in thought, saying their own private blessings before starting to eat.

Feeling a little embarrassed, I did apologise profusely, but told not to worry, and enjoy my food.

Tonight, I would definitely refrain from talking, until absolutely sure everyone on our table had said a personal blessing, and began to eat.

Once again, our buffet meal did not disappoint, very tasty indeed, all three courses, starting with soup, main meal, and pudding, delicious.

A side room once again sorted for our Bible readings and hymns, just one floor down from the restaurant, situated at the very end of our hotel building.

A bit compact for twenty-seven of us, nevertheless, our chairs still organised in a circular formation, so all sat facing each other, similar to our previous first night's room setting.

My original fears unfounded, as I voluntarily joined in, and fully taking part in last night's meeting.

Singing hymns, I had not sung before, from a hymn book loaned to me, and speaking five verses from my loaned Bible, although, that did begin to terrify me, as each of our party read their allotted verses, and soon my turn.

I counted those in our party to the left of me, yet to talk, and quickly determined which five verses I would read, when it became my turn.

Having a little time to have a few practice attempts, mainly to familiarise pronunciation of some of these alien names and words, and I think I did speak my verses with some confidence.

After our meeting, a few of our party said well done, pleased I had joined in, and giving a good articulation of untried names and words.

When Amanda had given me the King James Bible, it came with recently purchased printed cards, three separate bookmarkers with a difference.

These three cards, or scripture Reading Companions, first, second and third portions, each having all 365 days printed on both sides, including months, and which of 66 individual Bible books, and verses of the Bible to read on each day.

Quickly deducing, that I would read all of the old testament once, and the new testament twice, in a full year if keeping up to date with my studying.

Now in the month of May, while here in Israel, and where this three-card system of reading the Bible would continue, and consistently followed throughout our stay.

I did have a few weeks to practice each day with Bible readings, using my card system, prior to my holiday departure, so becoming reasonably familiar with some words and pronunciation, and how things would take place during our meetings.

I also asked questions and picked up other information from Amanda, about Christadelphian beliefs while driving many times to the observatory.

Nonetheless, remembering names has always remained a problem for me, as I usually end up calling everyone "love."

Ok "love," you ok too, no problem "love," yes "love," to name a few, so you can imagine what problems I had when trying to remember twenty-seven first names.

However, each person in our Christadelphian party, referred to as brothers and sisters, so when describing one or the other, it became a little more relaxed, at least getting the male or female bit right.

Sister Helen for example, or brother Trevor or brother Robert, did come much easier to me, and I do not think I used my "love" term once, during my stay.

Each night a different brother, or Brethren, would take charge of our meeting or Ecclesia, opening with a hymn, then a prayer, before starting the reading journey, either clockwise, or anticlockwise from the Brethren.

Taking turns to read Bible verse, all around our circle, until the days reading fully completed, another hymn, then a final prayer, following on with a final short piece of piano music, bringing our one-hour evening gathering to an end.

Tonight's meeting just the same, chairs already set in a circle, in a much larger room, but unsure who would become Brethren for tonight's meeting.

Trevor did say, he would take charge of tomorrow's meeting while sat at the table eating our tea, as he remarked at having some preparation to do after tonight's assembly.

A sister would accompany singing hymns on an electric piano already set up in our hotel meeting room, playing a brief musical introduction or voluntary, to our meeting, before tonight's opening proceedings.

I did feel considerably more confident, and looking forward to tonight's meeting, as I had not spoken a single word over tea, certainly not before everyone had said a personal blessing.

My previous night's singing, and reading had taken place with little, or no nerves at all, considering I only really got to know Julia just prior to leaving the UK, and now beginning to get to know the remainder of our party.

Perhaps easily falling into place due to all of my years performing and playing drums in bands, always an audience watching and listening to our music, but I did feel, and made to feel extremely comfortable with everyone in our party.

Incredibly pleased with our meeting, and to me, everything appeared to proceed efficiently, and to a meticulously organised plan.

Two nights in a row, I have spoken verses assigned to me, in clockwise order from brother Trevor sat to my right, and feeling more confident singing, my voice in unison with Trevor's, on the one side and a brother on my righthand side, and with their assistance, I actually "hit" each note, there or there abouts.

Turning on the air-conditioning unit to full, prior to eating tea and our meeting, would ensure a good night's sleep, although, I still needed to get used to sleeping in pyjamas.

I had always slept in the nude, or my boxers, so another first, and obviously essential attire when sharing a room with a stranger, granted, after just two days and nights, now friends.

Two amazing days now completed, and a further eight days to go, with lots more to see and do, and in particular, visits in our itinerary to destinations where I visited in 1979.

CHAPTER SIX

Israel - 2022

(Itinerary two)

Settling into my holiday, and making new friends daily from within our group, however, even with expanding my knowledge, about the understanding and beliefs of my Christadelphian friends, obviously I have so much more yet to learn.

After almost three days, two of which, spent here in the warm climate of Israel, I can honestly say, thoroughly enjoying every minute of my sightseeing holiday.

Our numbered roll-call procedure now firmly in place, and used when everyone is seated on the coach, either when leaving the hotel, or, before departure from each and every one of the many daily destinations, and in hindsight, an obvious necessity to ensure no one left behind.

My allocated number is eleven, with Trevor and Robert sat across the aisle from me, twelve and thirteen respectively, and Julia, as leader of our group, given number one, as she commands the front seat, and usually, along with Da'vid, last to board the coach.

Da'vid making this arrangement, as he had successfully used a similar numbered roll-call system, when signed up as an army recruit during the seventies.

A system now proving extremely useful for each and every one of our party, especially if having to walk a long distance when heading back to the locations coach parking vicinity.

While on a rocky, uneven walkway, one of the elderly brothers took a fall, and although not serious, bruising and swelling had already begun to show, causing some distress when walking, a stick, and his wife, becoming useful.

Also, prior to setting off on our daily visits, getting used to, and enjoying hearing a blessing pronouncement from brothers over the coach microphone, and again, upon the safe return to our hotel.

All in all, feeling extremely happy, that, in the first instance, I received consent to join the party, and not made to feel like an impostor or pretender, and certainly on our trip, accepted as a friend, from each and every one in our group.

More questions continued about my past, and how I had come to know Julia, whenever in a smaller group, and found to repeat myself on a number of occasions, however, these conversations always light-hearted, amusing, and jovial.

I wanted to know more about Christadelphian faith, so a bit more of a tête-à-tête, relaxed, and undoubtedly enjoyable conversations taking place, whenever Da'vid resting from giving his extremely knowledgeable location oration, via our whisper headsets.

My alarm set for 07.00hr, as today's visits commence at 08.15, Trevor saying he had had a good night's sleep, so much for earplugs that Julia gave me, because information received from others, suggested that Trevor snores such a lot, and ever so loud.

I had forgotten that I had them, so not used them, but not heard a sound during the last three nights, apart from the storm in Netanya.

Saturday in Israel called shabbat, (he rested), however, beginning at sunset on Friday, and ending at sunset on Saturday.

A day of rest, like Sundays at home, but with few hotel staff working (melachah) today, even one, of two lifts pre-set to stop at each floor, up or down, with no need to press a button once in the elevator.

My no frills, but tasty breakfast eaten, and rucksack packed with all of my usual items, mobile phone, bottles of water, suncream, sunglasses, baseball cap, hand towel and map.

I have today's itinerary on my phone, and now looking forward to whatever and wherever our exploring and viewing will take us.

A busy day, visiting Beit She'an, Harod Valley, Ein Harod, Mount Gilboa, Mount Arbel, plain of Gennesaret, and fitting in an enroute much needed lunch break at some point.

A mid-day lunch not provided as part of our holiday package, however,

Da'vid knows of some great eateries, and all selling prepared hot food, usually Falafel, or Schnitzel.

I like both, and with a portion of chips and a drink of choice, costs the equivalent of around ten English pounds.

Lots of other available foods on display, tasty looking Salads, Shawarma and Laffa, the majority of our party sat in my proximity, opting for Falafel or Schnitzel.

These cafes also good times for a catch up on the morning's events, with brothers and sisters taking time to enlighten me of the biblical and historical significance, of places visited so far, and those ahead.

The passing on of a little more biblical knowledge than our excellent informative guide, Da'vid, and all in accordance with Christadelphian beliefs, helping me lots.

Another full nine-hour day of sightseeing ticked off from our itinerary, arriving back at the hotel at around 17.00hr, a final blessing talking about today's experiences, another brother delivering this, prior to leaving the comfortable seats of our coach.

Tea, delicious, and another meeting over, enjoying listening to tonight's brethren Trevor, my roommate.

When leaving the meeting room, Julia asked if I would like to conduct a reading while at one of the locations our party have yet to visit.

A little hesitant at first, then enthusiastically agreeing, and asking if I could see the reading up front, so that I could have a little practice.

I had listened to a few of these already, brothers verbally delivering these verses at various poignant locations.

Gathering around, closely together, as each brother would read these chosen Bible verses while stood directly next to Da'vid, the short lead, just about long enough for the whisper microphone, so that everyone in our group could hear these emotive words.

I would have to do the same at a proposed location, Julia, and brothers yet to decide where.

Me, Trevor, and Robert getting along famously, sitting together at breakfast, lunch, and tea, and sitting across from each other on the coach, and when possible, during the evening meetings too.

Many conversations taking place, and during one of these, Trevor mentioned he worked for a number of years at the main Royal Mail delivery office, on Denby Dale Road Wakefield, commuting each day from Sheffield.

Just a few miles from my residence in Wrenthorpe, and calling at this building many times to collect missed parcel deliveries, and frequently driving past it.

Yet another snore free night, Trevor already in the bathroom, I had not heard a thing, I do hope I do not snore, although, no one as yet, has made me aware that I do.

After breakfast, first stop, a short bus ride to a jetty, and sailing on the sea of Galilee, after about an hour, our boat, docking much further north, embarking, and a short walk to visit Capernaum, and then boarding our coach once again to call at Nof Ginosar, and Chorazin.

Lots and lots of New Testament biblical significance with these locations, and heaps of historic issues, especially, alarming problems over a number of years, with fluctuating water levels on the fresh-water Sea of Galilee.

According to Trevor, other brothers, and sisters, Da'vid giving an amazingly accurate account of all of them.

Confirmation, corroborated of this, when consulting our itinerary and information booklet, pre-prepared each year via Julia when the holiday information and itinerary finally confirmed.

Although subject to change at short notice through our tour company, but a great brochure to use as our own daily guide.

Our days extremely long from the sound of our alarm to finally turning in for bed.

Plenty of travelling between locations, and lots of walking, not always on flat even surfaces, some on uneven ground from our coach to elevated sites, lots having many steps or steep footways.

Today no different to others, almost collapsing into bed, after eating a delicious tea and attending yet another excellent informative meeting.

Day Four, and a long drive to the furthest point north of Israel, almost on the boarder of Lebanon, to visit Tel Hazor, Tel Dan, Dan Nature Reserve, Banias (Caesarea Philippi),Golan Heights, and Mount Bental, where I will read my assigned Bible verse.

The verse mentions Mount Herman, overlooking the mountain across the valley from today's location, Mount Bental, where my Bible reading will take place.

I had practised my brief three verse reading a few times now, but only under my breath, my first time reading out aloud, and in a public place at that, using Da'vids whisper microphone.

My verse.

Psalm 133 1-3

1 Behold, how good and how pleasant it is for brethren to dwell together in unity!

2 It is like the precious ointment upon the head, that ran down upon the beard, even Aaron's beard that went down to the skirts of his garments.

3 As the dew of Hermon, and as the dew that descended upon the mountains of Zion: for there the LORD commanded the blessing, even life for ever more.

Following my reading of this verse, giving back the use of microphone to Da'vid, opening my Christadelphian hymn book, and singing hymn 65, "behold, how good a thing it is."

Confident I managed my talk satisfactorily, a little advanced practice helping no end, considering I have never ever done anything like this, in all of my sixty-nine years.

Taking everything into consideration, I have really enjoyed today, and pleased I decided to read those Bible passages, although no pressure to do so.

Another tiring day, even for me, as I had considered myself as reasonably fit until now.

However, other brothers and sisters found our walks today a little more intimidating than at previous locations, but still managed to visit everything on our itinerary, regardless of the prolonged heat and walking distances.

Browsing through my travel plan, and so looking forward to tomorrows visits, spotting three of the sites I visited in 1979, The Dead Sea, Qumran, and Jericho.

Remembering the 1979 experience as though yesterday, although, the minibus ride from Jerusalem, became an occurrence I would not forget either.

While descending to the lowest point on earth, our small bus immediately halted, a zig-zag roadblock in the way, and with the Dead Sea in view just a few miles away.

Armed military personnel boarded our bus, and talked at length with our guide, while other guards looked intensely around our vehicle.

An unnerving fifteen minutes of discussion taking place, and not daring to look at anyone for fear of accusation, or whatever, before finally allowed to continue.

This altercation the first instance of intense armed security we had come across while in Israel, other than as expected, around the hotel where all the contestants reside, and so close, the venue for the forthcoming 1979 Eurovision Song Contest.

I do digress…

After breakfast, leaving our hotel in Tiberius, and heading south.

Today's travel plan includes the Jordan Valley, Damiya (Biblical Adam) Beth Arabah, Mount of Temptation, Wadi Kelt, and Red Ascent.

Astounded at the changes to the whole region surrounding the Dead Sea, yes, over forty-three years since I stood on this actual shoreline, and how things have changed.

The Dead Sea now way in the distance from my previously remembered shoreline, at least a hundred metres walk, heading down steps, and footpaths, in advance of reaching the current waterline, and an estimated, forty metres lower in depth than in 1979.

Apparently, loosing over a meter a year since my last visit here, all due to evaporation, and a poor water supply from the river Jorden, as water now drawn from the river for irrigation of agricultural crops way up north, prior to reaching the Dead Sea.

Also, lots of newly built infrastructure, toilet blocks, changing rooms, shops, a bar, and hundreds of people, evidently not just tourists, lots of locals too.

An enormous difference from my memories back then, with just our minibus, a small toilet block, with a single shower head protruding from the wall, and walking straight into the water from a level shoreline.

However, still enjoying my time, more so than in March 1979, as in no immediate rush to leave for our band rehearsals.

Experiencing floating, and bobbing up and down, ensuring that I did not submerge above my shoulders for fear of this rather buoyant salty water.

The water of the Dead Sea contains extremely high levels of salt, and if getting it in eyes, nostrils, and mouth, definitely a visit to the hospital required, one location I did not want to attend...

This body of water is nine time saltier than any other sea or ocean and approximately eighty kilometres long (49.7miles), and varies between seven to twenty kilometres (4 – 12 miles) wide.

Due to the these extremely high levels of salt, no living creature can live there, hence the name Dead Sea, so no worries about receiving a bite from something, and absolutely no fear of drowning as sinking practically impossible.

Nonetheless, this high level of buoyancy making it extremely difficult to scoop handfuls of mud from the seabed, but finding a way.

All our party staying close to the shoreline, as I began smearing it thickly over my whole body, assured this grey gooey sludge has good skin reviving mineral properties.

Letting it fully dry, before taking a much-needed shower, in one of several open-air shower blocks.

In this hot climate, the ice-cold water feeling rather refreshing, and not even bothering to dry off, confident my skin, and swim shorts bone dry within minutes, aided with a rather lengthy uphill walk ahead to reach the changing rooms.

Moving on to Qumran, bringing back lots of memories of my time while here in March 1979, a location where the Dead Sea Scrolls existed for thousands of years, until found in various elevated caves, between the years of 1947 to 1956.

This site, a virtually desolate digging area during my previous visit in 1979, famous for what existed here, and now, so much more to visualise and theorise about those ancient times.

Boasting, additional extensive excavations, including a newly built modern visitors' centre, a new toilet block, and lots of tourists making their way around a newly constructed safe wooden walkway, looking at all of this remarkable, noteworthy site.

A massive improvement, and clearly attracting lots of tourists, viewing excavated cisterns for holding water, and buildings, where in ancient times, these scrolls existed and possibly written, and eager to view those caves from across a narrow valley, where the discovery of the scrolls took place.

Accidently found when a young shepherd boy, looking for lost sheep, threw stones into an elevated cavern, and his stones hitting something like the sound of breaking pottery.

Informing his parents, who went to investigate, finding earthen wear jars, containing what is now known as the Dead Sea Scrolls.

Words that when translated provided a window to the past, and a wider spectrum of ancient Jewish beliefs and practices, still investigated to this day.

Sadly, not visiting Jericho, due to some previous troubles in the vicinity, however, now making our way to our next stop over, a little earlier than planned, and before tea, finding time to take a swim in a huge rectangular pool.

The Kibbutz Kayla, only a short distance from the Dead Sea, where our group will spend two nights.

Da'vid handing out keys to our respective room, number 75, (also my flat and mums house numbers) and an opportunity to have a laugh at Trevor's expense, as when I opened the door, and just about visible in the dim light, bunk beds.

Saying to Trevor, on no account could I sleep in the top bunk, it is your bed for the next two nights.

Trevor instantly replying, not a chance, I could not get up there, so for sure not my bed.

However, noticing a bedroom directly to my left, having a double bed, saying Trevor could have that, and I would still have the bottom bunk.

Both laughing, a problem, or not, now solved…

Tonight's tea cooked to perfection, in the dining hall, quite some distance away from our room, and for others in our party too, as if we had not done enough walking during the day, even more now, just to eat.

All taken in good spirits, as it would certainly offer additional help working up an appetite.

Our after-tea meeting, held in a large room below the dining room, and fully air-conditioned, thankfully, as still so hot, even at this early evening hour.

Checking tomorrow's itinerary, and confirming my alarm pre-set before bedtime, a few more places to look forward to visiting, in particular, Masada.

Located in the Judean wilderness, and two and a half miles from the Dead Sea, another location steeped in history.

Although only 161 feet above sea level, the mountain of Masada, is actually 1475 feet above Dead Sea level, and fortified in BC167.

The Judean Wilderness and Ein Gedi both Biblical and historical places on our list for tomorrows visits.

My bunkbed amazingly comfortable, falling asleep almost instantly, waking up to the sound of my alarm.

I must have slept very well, as Trevor already in the shower, and I did not hear a thing.

Trying a few channels on the TV, finally finding one I could understand, CNN, just as Trevor exited the bathroom, now my turn, not taking over long, my roommate already dressed, and waiting for me to take our walk up to the dining room for breakfast.

Lots of food on offer, deciding on a cereal, and scrambled eggs on toast, accompanied with a glass of fresh orange, and a cup of tea.

The coach ready and waiting, parked just a few meters from our room, really hot and sweating when walking back from the dining room, eager to get to my second from the front window seat, and appraise the extra cold air-conditioning.

My bag packed the previous night, and plenty of water available on the coach for just a few Shekels, now making our way out from the Kala Kibbutz.

Along with Alan, and representatives from the BBC, I visited a Kibbutz local to the Dead Sea in 1979, although fairly confident not this particular Kibbutz.

However, lots of improvements and alterations conducted all around this region during the past forty years, so perhaps possible the same one.

First stop, The Judean wilderness and Ein Gedi.

Once again, lots of biblical significance in this location, and an exceptionally long elevated hazardous walk, on rocky terrain, including steps, with little or no safety barriers ahead of us.

Our parties no rush saunter, taking a path that steadily gained in height, and rather steeply at times, the further up we walked; Da'vid ahead of us giving a commentary on the views and what to expect.

Following a fast-flowing freshwater stream, all the way up the mountain to a fairly large shallow pool area, finally coming across David's waterfall.

The end result, spectacular, with water falling from over fifty feet above, an amazing sight and sound.

Ein Gedi renowned for its wildlife, sweet-smelling herbs, and spices.

The long walk back becoming much easier, a decent still every bit as hazardous, treading very carefully all the way down.

However, the downward journey made all the more enjoyable, as now able to gaze at stunning views between the hills, and mountains over towards the Dead Sea and Jordan.

CHAPTER SEVEN

Israel - 2022

(Itinerary Three)

Next stop, the ancient Roman plateau fortress of Masada.

Instantly spotting the flat-topped mountain from our coach, and still quite a way off, looking ominous in the distance, with clear blue skies and mid-day sweltering heat, waiting for us.

The visitor's centre and cable car informed as the only shade available, everything else when on top of the mesa, open to the elements.

Clips of the mountain top and its ancient past shown on a large TV screen prior to our ascent, giving an historic account of what transpired around on top of this location in AD 73, when the 10th Roman Legion laid a sustained three-year siege of this mountain top fortress.

The Romans tried unsuccessfully to starve the inhabitants of Masada, finally building a huge stone and rubble ramp in order to reach the walls and gates at the top, then setting fire to them.

However, 967 Jewish zealots under the command of Eliezer Ben Yair, committed suicide, rather than face their lives in Roman slavery.

A six-part, mini-TV series, made of this historical event in 1981, featuring Peter O'Toole, Peter Struss, and Anthony Quayle, a DVD disc set, and if still available, I will definitely order on my return home.

Two huge cable cars, taking 80 passengers in each, both up and down, ours full to breaking point, on the three-minute ride up.

Incredible views across the Judean Wilderness and Dead Sea, and a visible wiggly path all the way to the top, and people of a more resilient nature, still prefer to use this irregular and dangerous looking track to the top, even in overpowering heat.

Da'vid giving a notable running commentary all the way around the top of the mountain fortress, fascinating that the remains of eight Roman forts exist, and clearly visible from here while looking way down onto the plains below.

A perimeter wall surrounding Masada at ground level, and amazingly including a ramp, rising to just below the base of the wall, ancient, recorded history for all to see.

I can understand why Masada attracts over 750 thousand visitors each year, with so much to see, and after all, thankfully much needed purpose-built shaded areas on the top.

No queues at the cable car, our descending journey, and walk to the bus, bringing an almost two-hour amazing experience to an end.

Our now familiar rollcall taking place, number 7, sounding just like Len Goodman, Severn, on Strictly Come Dancing, and achieving number 27 without stopping, all present and correct, making our way to our next stopover location.

The Caesar Hotel, Jerusalem.

Taking roughly two hours to cover the sixty-five-mile journey, stopping on the Mount of Olives to gaze over an extraordinary ancient city, again steeped in biblical importance, and numerous historical events taken place over many centuries.

This locale packed with coaches, with a constant stream of disembarking tourists, all eager to take photos of an extraordinary view of Jerusalem, looking from an elevated position, across the Kidron Valley.

Lots and lots of street vendors milling around, constantly wanting you to purchase camel type teddies, maps, and panoramic prints of this very same Jerusalem view.

Making our way to yet another busy district, and lots of coaches parked up anywhere and everywhere possible, however, our "slot" to visit the gardens of Gethsemane, almost upon us, so not an over long wait.

Our driver pulling up on a busy main road, awash with tourists, quickly dropping our party off, as no available parking spots close enough.

The gardens coming to mind from my limited knowledge of the Christian faith, where Judas Iscariot betrayed Jesus.

A reading taking place on an elevated, tiered, semi-circle seating space, including an opportunity for group photographs, and singing of a number of hymns.

Especially hymn number 61, "Pray for the peace of Jerusalem," sang from the Christadelphian hymn book, and when listening to the words and hearing vocal harmonies as good as this, all becoming a bit emotional, even for a big softy like me.

Prior to my trip to Israel, I had never considered myself as a religious sort of person, however, listening to this tune, sang so beautifully, and in this location, I doubt anyone, no matter how "hard" they appear, could not feel emotionally moved.

Our hotel located quite central, and not far from here, but now coming across lots of commuter rush hour traffic, before finally arriving at the Ceasar Hotel.

How all of these coach drivers do their amazing job, beyond belief, narrow roads, right and left angled elevated and descending bends, steep hills, and of course, dodging lots of horrendous moving and parked traffic, astounding me.

Over our many days of travelling the length and breadth of Israel, I had experienced more than a few "We're all going to Die" moments, while covering hundreds of miles during the first week here in Israel.

However, our driver, succeeding in doing an excellent job in avoidance procedures, and in the toughest of circumstances.

The Ceasar Hotel, situated in a sort of off-street cul-de-sac carpark, again, a complicated manoeuvre required.

Our more than capable driver, making it look easy, getting our coach tucked in there, and from a busy main road too.

Our seventh-floor room, overlooking our bus and carpark, unfortunately, little else of a view, as several buildings surrounding our hotel, all so many floors higher.

Nevertheless, our room rather large, with ample space for two comfortable looking single beds, two suitcase holders, an easy chair, a desk with chair, a large customary wall mounted flat screen colour TV, and of course, an expected air-conditioning unit.

Taking the bed nearest the bathroom, while Trevor acquired the remaining bed, and again, next to the window, no compromise required, as clearly both happy with our sleeping arrangements throughout our holiday, and this no different, spending four nights in the last hotel of our stay.

Taking another look at today's itinerary, as during these next three and a bit days, all of our visits in and around a close radius of Jerusalem.

Absolutely lots and lots to see and do, and yet another outdoor reading for me.

At least one reading had taken place at all of our previous locations during our stay, and all pre-prepared in a black coloured A4 lever arch file, passed around from Brother to Brother following each reading.

Taking a phone photo of my suggested reading in advance, to prepare myself once again, and in particular, taking the pronunciation of names and places, expressly serious.

During our nightly meetings, I had read my customary five verses while here in Israel, and all as the three-card system indicated, and more than happy with my first-time results, as now getting used to each of our assembly's format.

Again, keeping an eye on the last three or two brothers or sisters speaking prior to me, so I could count five verses ahead, and pre-read what I would say.

Unfortunately, because of this unorthodox practise, I missed hearing many verses, apart from the last one of five verses spoken from the person sat next to me.

However, my perseverance in the few weeks leading up to my holiday, and while here in Israel, I will definitely continue with daily readings of the Holy Bible when arriving home.

It has, without any doubt, while here in Israel, enthused my emotions, especially when reading about biblical individuals, places where they lived, and actually visiting these locations, genuinely amazing.

Breakfast eaten with some urgency, yes I did feel a little hungry, now totally satisfied with everything on offer, as I made my way to the coach.

Our hotel remarkably busy indeed, with a number of vehicles and three coaches in the carpark, but ours not in sight.

Apparently, waiting for a different coach and driver to arrive, taking our party around this locality for the remainder of our stay.

Rumours circulating around the restaurant during the previous night's meal, saying our party would board a bullet proof coach to visit Shilo in the morning.

Nonetheless, and thankfully, this did not materialise, Da'vid saying it's not mandatory, or an essential requirement, on this occasion.

Starting our day with a visit to Samaria, and Shiloh, Mount Ebal, Mount Gerizim and the tomb of the prophet Samual.

Not a taxing day, more and more walking though, and lots and lots uphill and downhill, only guessing, but when mountain locations mentioned or featured in our itinerary guidebook, I cannot see a bus making the journey up them, leaving us climbing the remainder of the way.

Not actually climbing, as in mountaineering, nevertheless a steep walk, using up lots of energy, and requiring sufficient amounts of refreshing water to keep hydrated.

All that aside, twenty-seven of us, have continually commented on the many locations visited and enjoyed, so far, with little mentioned of the at times long hilly walks.

Although not of the Christadelphian faith, I feel wholly entwined, and totally part of our friendly, sociable, and approachable group.

Once out of the city, a drive north to Shiloh (Tel Shiloh) not taking exceptionally long, to cover about twenty miles, to view yet more excavated ruins, or in Julia's words, lots of stones.

A circular visitors' centre elevated on legs, with a slowly rising ramp following the contours to its entrance awaited us, almost looking like a UFO from a distance.

When indoors, a stepped seating quarter fully wrapped around half of the centre, while a huge sectional screen fitted to the other half, providing images, once the engineers had got the IT system working, showing a roleplay storyline about this ancient site,

Over the next three days, our group would visit lots of amazing historical and biblical sights, and a couple in particular that took my breath away.

Yad Vashem, and Hezekiah's Conduit, without doubt amazing places to visit, from modern structures to an almost impossible ancient accomplishment.

Visiting Yad Vashem brough back more memories from 1979, and one I would always repeat when asked about our bands time there over forty years ago.

Sights, photographs, vivid black and white images of the WW2

Holocaust, listening to a commentary in disbelief of the atrocities conducted, and now here once again.

Not recognising anything on this visit, everything appeared new, nothing as I remembered it.

However, not deterring my experience, as our party walked and talked around most of the site, Da'vid giving a thought-provoking description of the location along the way.

A new "attraction," or enticement, if that is the correct term, did stand out, a memorial to all the children who perished in the WW2 concentration camps.

A dark, purposely made cave, electric looking candles dimly lighting up the whole building, shining on hundreds of floor to ceiling mirrors, where the journey takes you on a winding, twisting level walkway.

Listening to all the children's names broadcasted in an almost whisper, spoken with conviction, over the public address system, eerie, and significantly poignant.

My visit to Hezekiah's conduit becoming an amazing experience.

Located just outside the walls of Jerusalem, in the City of David, where following a long journey down lots and lots of steps, twisting winding and finally coming to the conduit, or tunnel entrance.

Reading about what to expect on our downward journey the previous night, down and down via Warrens Shaft, and taking over thirty minutes to get to the tunnel entrance.

Now finally here, so looking forward to my trek through the hand-crafted conduit.

As agreed, a torch and waterproof footwear required, bringing both of these, and now getting myself sorted, although, I am quite tall, about 6ft 2", and wide at the shoulders, did not help at all...

The trek to connect the Gihon spring to the pool of Silam, and while slowly walking in fast flowing water, almost to my knees, thankfully surging in my direction of travel, and all-in pitch-black claustrophobic conditions, taking over forty minutes to complete.

Regardless of this extraordinary feeling, so much fun, with singing and chatting, and as far as I am concerned, all while hunched over, for much of the way.

A curving meandering tunnel around 533 metres long, with a fall of just 300mm over the entire length, and all constructed by hand, using primitive tools of the time, amazing.

Even more astonishing, starting from each end, and eventually meeting somewhere in the middle during the late 8th and early 7th century BC, perhaps using a method of sound to know where each team of rock breakers working.

For others, less able, another tunnel available, slightly higher, and a little wider, electrically lit, and bone dry, ending up in the same location, and close to our awaiting coach.

Other planned visits during these next three days, all becoming a similar amazement to me, The Western wall, The burnt house, The Cardo, The Dung Gate, Gihon Spring, Hezekiah's broad wall, King Solomons Quarries, and the Hadassah medical centre and Chagall Windows, to name a few.

However, I did have a further verse to read, outdoors, at The Zion Gate, directly in front of the entrance to Jerusalem.

My verse:-
Jerusalem old city – Hezekiah's Broad Wall.
2 Chronicles 32:1-2 & 5-8

1   Sennacherib king of Assyria came, and entered into Judah, and encamped against the fenced cities, and thought to win them for himself.

2   And when Hezekiah saw that Sennacherib was come, and that he was purposed to fight against Jerusalem.

3   He strengthened himself, and built up all the wall that was broken.

4   (Isaiah 22:10) And broke down the houses to fortify the wall, and raised up to the towers.

5   And he set captains of war over the people, and gathered them together to him in the street of the gate of the city, and spake comfortably to them, saying,

6   "Be strong and courageous, be not afraid of the King of Assyria, nor for all the multitude that is with him: for there be more with us that with him.

7   With him is an arm of flesh, but with us is the LORD our God to
     help us, and to fight our battles" And the people rested themselves
     upon the words of Hezekiah king of Judah.

Definitely a bit of a mouthful, and all spoken to our party, using
Da'vids microphone and whisper, with tourists eager to listen nearby, and
hundreds of armed army personnel also located in this vicinity.

Our last night at Caesars Hotel, made all the more special, especially
when in a conversation with Da'vid.

Da'vid saying to me that Julia had told him of my previous visit in
1979, and asked what I thought of my holiday this time around.

I commented on how much I had enjoyed my sightseeing holiday,
and all of the excellent informative talks Da'vid had given throughout our
stay, and if I had the opportunity, I would like to return on Julias next
organised trip.

Mentioning my 79' visit and what transpired at that time, when he
said that the hotel and concert hall our band performed in, just around
the corner from our hotel location, giving me directions to go to see them.

I could not believe my eyes, here for three days and so close, and yet, I
had not seen it, but now hot footing my way down the street to have a look.

Lots of roadworks taking place, but not much traffic as still in the
hours of Shabbat.

Slowly walking up the ramp to the concert hall, and instantly
recognising the former Hilton Hotel, now called The Vert Hotel, and the
concert hall.

I walked along the exact footpath from the hotel to the stage door, and
then to the main entrance.

Noticing two people, possibly security personnel behind the reception
counter, knocking on the glass door and waving, but not hard or exuberant,
trying to attract their attention.

Now thinking I had made a big mistake, as one of the chaps started
to walk towards me, a serious look on his face, with his right hand firmly
positioned on what I believe a holstered handgun, placed firmly on his
thigh.

Speaking through a gap between the glass doors, and asking if he spoke English, "Of course," came an instant reply, but noticing his gaze had not altered, or hand moved from his thigh.

I gestured to him that I performed here in 1979, showing him images from my phone through the glass door of those days long ago, the stage setting, hotel, and some TV images of the Eurovision Song Contest.

Now smiling, he started to unlock one of the huge solid glass doors, and cheerfully invited me into the vast foyer area.

Thanking him, explaining further what had transpired, all the time showing the both of them more images from my phone, and thinking, all of what I am explaining, probably took place long before both born.

Small chat, and some in Hebrew, with lots of laughing taking place between the young chap who let me in, and the other security guard.

Noticing that he likewise had a firearm, when he stood up from behind the reception desk, and making his way a short distance to a pair of solid wood doors opposite the reception desk, beckoning me to follow.

Imagine my delight, when looking into the concert hall, very dark, but now coming into view, as row upon row, he began to turn on all the concert room house lights.

Asking me to follow him into the actual auditorium that our band had performed in many years ago.

A graphic memory of those times instantly coming back to me, seeing the stage and inclined red seating section, and now able to take in the enormous size of my surroundings.

In our band days, visiting lots of working men's clubs, up and down the UK, time and time again, showing little, or no emotion, just playing our music at a club, a venue to perform and earn our wages, sometimes delighted to return, while others, not so pleased.

However, this venue extra special, and stood right in front of the stage, looking toward the rear of the auditorium, certainly giving me the largest of goosebumps.

Forty-three years and two months ago, repeating several times in my head, feeling very nostalgic and emotional, and sure both security guards could tell this moment in time, meaning so much to me.

Both beckoning me to take as many photos as I wanted, although now thinking more about the cost to turn on all the house lights, just for me to have a quick glance in the hall.

I did take lots of images, including a few of the guards posing behind the reception desk, and a selfie or two with both chaps.

Always finding taking a selfie a little difficult to do, balancing my phone at the correct angle, and getting everything in, while others appear to do this easily, taking lots of selfies with little effort.

Saying my goodbyes, and giving each a "special" handshake, heading back to my hotel, just a few hundred yards away, and essential tea, starving once again.

Feeling hungry once again, and not just for food, but to see yet more of this incredible country and diverse cultures, at least one more time.

Looking through the many phone photographs I have taken over these last eleven days, recalling those amazing visual memories I captured.

Each and every one of the seven hundred images tells a story, and the same said of my pre-covid trip to Egypt, where once again I returned home with just as many photographs.

Bringing to mind the old saying, "Every photograph/picture worth a thousand words."

However, my personal feeling on this subject raises so much more.

As sometimes, "Each and every photograph will raise a thousand QUESTIONS."

CHAPTER EIGHT

My Birthday Bash

(Seventieth)

Of all my birthdays to celebrate, this one, and for some reason finding it difficult to explain, definitely not the one I am looking forward to at all.

Remembering my eighteenth, twenty-first, thirtieth, forty, fifty, sixty, and sixty-fifth birthdays with fondness, my next one definitely appears to point to me progressing rather quickly into an OLD person.

SEVENTY, 70, LXX, no matter how this number is written down, those two numerals, or few letters look such a VAST number for me to reach, and thankfully to get there in a reasonably fit and healthy condition.

Recalling my fortieth birthday at the Lupset hotel, and sixtieth held at our home, both indeed surprises, and not a clue what was going on.

As too, my sixty-fifth birthday held in our office at work, with a further meal actually on the day with immediate family and close friends.

Nonetheless, my band mates, and former working colleagues, would constantly remind me that others much younger than me, have not had that privilege or pleasure of reaching their respective three-score and ten years, in good health and working order.

Pondering the subject of having a party, do I really want to celebrate my birthday, yes or no, at least an opportunity to chat, have a drink and eat tasty food with invited guests, rather than doing all the above at a funeral wake, as it seems others around my age appear to do these days.

This time I want to take matters into my own hands and organise a "bit of a do," and at a local location that should not cause much trouble for those invited who have to travel.

My imaginary invitation list not an exhaustive one, at least aware of those that can, or cannot join me beforehand, with no surprises, although,

81

not really bothered either way if an uninvited guest or guests should turn up, as sure a pleasant experience of enough tasty food and music, to please all anticipated.

For a brief moment, I considered hiring a suitable venue for me and our band Mister Twister to perform at, one way to celebrate my birthday with a bit of panache.

Perhaps at Alverthorpe Working Men's Club, or Balne Lane WMC, both venues our band have performed many times, and ample stage space for our band's PA, lighting and back line equipment, and considerable size concert rooms for my prolific guests.

Perhaps employ a caterer to supply an assortment of tasty hot and cold food, seems a good idea in principle, and the option of me paying someone to perform for my party guests too.

That's it then, sticking to my preferred option to employ a catering company, and coincidentally, my son Warren and partner Sommer, have used one particular couple from Bradford quite a few times, with amazing, tasty results, and at an affordable price per person.

Not hesitating, and asking them for a telephone number to arrange.

I now require a venue, and a performer urgently if I am to book in time, my youngest brother John helping out with one of those, his favoured watering hole, the Conservative club.

Located in our local village of Alverthorpe, and in close proximity to me, and reasonably near to lots of guests already on my mind to invite.

This particular private club still going strong, with a good regular membership, as other renowned watering holes that remain open in the village.

Sadly, The Blue Light, and The Crown, both now developed into private housing, and possibly the only ones I did visit regularly, though, such a long time ago.

Also, the defunct Cock and Crown, that endured major alterations, now a veterinarian practice, at least the building façade remaining, and not looking much different from outside.

Unfortunately, my youngest son Liam involved with training to become a soldier first, and then an army musician, so cannot get time off, either on my birthday, or those weekends before or immediately afterwards.

Had Liam joined me from his base in Portsmouth, he could have performed some table magic, going around each of my guest's seating areas, as he did for my former employees "Love where you live" awards, an interest and hobby becoming really good at, albeit few years ago now.

Nevertheless, Liam's many packs of playing cards, various tricks, and illusions, safely tucked away gathering dust in storage space beneath his double-bed, just in case the urge to rekindle performing his magic returns.

I am thinking live music for the evening, a self-contained act of sorts, and certainly not a disco of any description, as my preference, when possible, letting my guests chat without having to shout, and able to walk around, meeting and greeting each other, rather than a middle-of-the-road DJ taking over the evening.

As in no doubt everyone would complain about deafening loud thumping music, and tunes they do not know, or have not heard of, lots of relentless flashing multicoloured lights, and so-called inaudible comical chat lines after every tune.

Imagine a number, and double it, as preparing my list with names, other than family I wish to invite, becoming longer each hour, and now having reservations that the "con club" not a size large enough to accommodate everyone.

My brother John reassuring me, that he has attended many a party at this club, with amounts of invitees exceeding one-hundred, and as I had not intended to invite so many, the venue now booked, and confirmed for a Saturday night closest to my March 2022 birthday.

Considering the average age of my guests, some in their late eighties, and Mum at Ninety, a little more thought required about what genre of music needed on the night, and what kind of attraction I would like to see and hear for my party invitees.

I began to consider a duo, not that I knew of anyone, perhaps I should contact an agent, and see who or what acts they have available, and at what cost for a night's entertainment.

Pondering, for quite a while, until one of my longest friends, and co-founder of our band Black Lace coming to mind, Ian Howarth.

Ian continues to perform in clubs and pubs, and of late enjoyed good evenings watching and listening to his self-contained show, more than a few times now.

In particular, just recently a performance at an open-air charity concert in Ossett town precinct, and a few local pubs, deciding to raise the question with him, although he and his partner Carol, already on my invite list anyway, but would he mind performing, a question worth asking.

Sending Ian, a text, and waiting patiently for a reply, but then pondering about his health, as not that long ago he spent time in hospital with a heart problem, and required stents to help with blood flow issues.

A positive response from Ian, on both counts, he, and Carol able to join me, the first of my friends to acknowledge their attendance on my birthday celebration night, expressing his enthusiasm to perform two forty-minute sets, and giving his services totally free of charge.

An unexpected surprise, a pleasant one at that, and I can understand his reasoning, saying that if he took the Saturday night off from a gig to attend my birthday bash, he would lose a gig fee anyway, so he might as well come along to my birthday, and play a few tunes at the same time.

Ian had performed at the "Con club" on a few occasions already, so familiar territory for him, and a local gig.

My inventory now totalling an impressive seventy-two people, so much for not compiling an exhaustive list, if all the ones on my directory have no other plans, and can join me.

Not deterred at all, busily getting my fingers sorted in sending out text messages, to those friends and acquaintances not seen that often, but still have regular contact using other means, and verbally informing others, and told to pass on my invitation to further friends in their respective circles.

No posh designer printed invites for my somewhat run of the mill birthday occurrence, an unnecessary extravagance, when emails, texts, social media, and word of mouth can do the trick, and receive a reply in double quick time, as reasonably accurate numbers needed to place my order with the caterers for sufficient food.

Warren and Sommer making all the arrangements with the Bradford caterers, and John lending a hand too, placing orders from a well-known butchers' shop for porkpies and catering size large meat pies, as an additional savoury meaty treat.

Confirmations of attendance now coming in thick and fast, lots of positive marks rather than crosses on my list so far, and furthermore, a couple of surprises in the making.

Our former bandmate from my Black Lace days, Steve Scholey,

confirming he will join us, a celebration on its own, as almost forty years since last meeting up, although, for reasons I am not aware of, declined a few previous offers of joining us on stage once again.

The first of which at an anniversary get together of Black Lace, our band Mister Twister, and Black Lace duo, held on a chilly Wednesday night, March 31st, 1999, at Balne Lane working men's club, exactly twenty years previous of our 1979 Eurovision Song Contest appearance in Jerusalem Israel.

A Black Lace reunion also held at St Georges Hall Bradford, March15th 2015, a twenty-year celebration of the short and esteemed life of our band mate Alan Barton.

Alan passed away on March 23rd, 1995, as a result of a tragic accident in Germany, while touring as lead singer/guitarist with Bradford chart topping group, Smokie.

So, looking forward to having a catch up with Steve, nonetheless, tinged with sadness as he has recently lost his wife following a prolonged distressing illness.

Confirmation received from eight of my former work colleagues, some not seen since my retirement three years ago, and a few more may turn up once word gets out of my celebration "bit of a do."

Liams drum and percussion teacher Rhod and wife Eleanor, Amanda and husband Dave coming along too.

Amanda confirming their attendance when on our way back from yet another non-viewing event at the observatory, with lots of cloud, and light rain, and only a few members turning up, and after double checking the local BBC weather forecast.

A shame Yorkshire TV's amateur weather forecaster, Bill Froggitt not still with us, as his use of using moles, flies, and seaweed, combined with natural folk lore, and an exceptional file of family records dating back to 1771, perhaps he could have given us a more accurate forecast.

However, making for an earlier night home than a usual Friday, although, prior to leaving, I did watch a YouTube documentary video on the observatories big screen about the James Webb Space Telescope.

What an amazing example of technological equipment, costing umpteen billions of dollars to produce, and taking far longer than anticipated prior to a launch taking place from Guiana Space Centre on December 25th, 2021.

The James Webb Space Telescope (JWST) arrived at the second Sun-Earth Lagrange point, or L2, almost one million miles from Earth, on January 24th, 2022, and looking at over thirty years of the amazing Hubble telescope images, I am sure that once fully commissioned, the JWST will provide much better outstanding images, and most available to purchase.

Just a few weeks now to my March birthday bash, however, and shockingly, on February 24th, 2022, Russia invaded Ukraine.

Described as the biggest attack on a European country since the 1939-1945 second world war, although many miles away from home, and so sad that a diplomatic solution could not have resolved issues, prior to the invasion of a sovereign state since 1991, with fighting and immense loss of life taking place.

Not a good start to an encouraging new year, especially after a prolonged period of lockdown, and in no doubt, this apparent unprovoked repugnant conflict will take more lives of soldiers and civilians than the world covid epidemic.

I do digress, where was I.

Receiving notification of my first party no show, Nigel and Sue taking a Mediterranean holiday on a super massive luxury cruise ship for a few weeks directly over my party date.

Nigel, an original member, and bass player of Black Lace from our creation until 1974, leaving to concentrate on his business development.

In the late seventies and early eighties, Nigel's wife Sue, worked for Magnet and Southern, a joinery supplier of superior quality materials, frequently giving me discount on external doors purchased for the odd job I completed during my professional band days.

Everything seems in place for my celebratory seventieth birthday night, the club booked, food ordered, entertainment, Ian ready to go, saying that he will also present an appropriate choice of cultured background music between his sets.

Live music played at the start of the night, and in between Ian's forty-minute spots, and afterwards too, until closing, all an added bonus.

Furthermore, a desirable selection of high-quality food ordered, that will hopefully please all age groups.

What could go wrong…

Ian sent me a text to say he had taken his equipment along to the "con club" in the afternoon, and all set up in readiness in the best room for when my invited guests arrive.

Good thinking, as not the first time I have carried our bands equipment through the front doors of a club, along with audience early arrivals, not a good mix at all.

At least not raining, good for those who choose to walk or take a taxi to my party, unfortunately, I am taking my car, and driving to the club.

WHAT !!!, and on my birthday.

I have agreed to pick up mum at the arranged time of around 18.30hr, (mum no doubt ready and waiting from 18.00hr), an early start, as I must think of the older ones amongst us, as usually tucked up in bed before 22.00hr, at times mum in bed at 19.00hr.

On my arrival, and not the first there, as others, already sat with a selection of drinks, and catching sight of my younger brother John, placing trays of tasty looking pies onto tables already set out waiting for my food order to arrive.

Warren and Sommer appearing in the bar/games room area just after me, in readiness to prepare the food order for a 20.15 serving.

Ian and Carol arriving prior to a planned first set start of 19.30hr, much earlier than working men's club gigs, and on this occasion, Ian will open his show to a full house, as many of my guests starting to arrive thick and fast.

Steve in particular, also driving tonight, arriving from his hometown of Selby around 19.00hr, giving me time to meet and greet, and catch up just a little on over forty missed years.

Both of us gazing at Ian's meagre but impressive stage equipment.

The super massive PA speaker system and amplifiers that our band Mister Twister carry around, definitely not fitting comfortably in this location, with enough space remaining for my drum kit, backline equipment, a keyboard, mike stands, and four players, impossible.

Instead, looking at two five-foot tall, thin flat looking speakers, with a shoebox size bass cabinet at the bottom of each, a mike stand, a couple of guitars, and an iPad.

Oh, the joy of setting up in five minutes rather than our bands hour or so, heaven, and no broken bones or squashed fingers either.

Also, introduced to Richard and his wife, all the way from South Africa, although, not actually making this super extended journey just for my birthday celebrations tonight.

Richard, originally from Ossett moved over to South Africa lots of years ago, becoming a popstar in the mid to late seventies, even having a number one record in the charts, and no stranger to TV either, moving back to the UK just a few years ago.

Now a fully-fledged musician here in Wakefield, playing guitar and singing in a trio called "Cover Story" in local clubs and pubs along with our bands first roady, and driver Mick Lynskey, who formally introduced us.

Elaine, and Diane, sisters I have known from early childhood, keen to embrace, and eager to point out my ever-increasing age, as too their own.

Reminding me of when in my early teens, I used to babysit the both of them, and perhaps in our old age, I could do the same once again.

Perhaps not, and possibly me that will require an all-grown-up compassionate sitter, or sitters long before they do...

A previous bout of utter panic now sorted, as the main food order arrived, nevertheless now extremely late, but everything falling into place thanks to Warren and Sommer for our planned serving time.

Only catching one song from Ian's first set in the concert room, but what an impressive full, and totally mixed sound he creates, and all from his small as a comparison to our bands equipment, and certainly not loud either.

Blown away...

I could hear other tunes and the appreciative wonderful applause he received, as I became embroiled in conversations with whomever pulled me to one side in the bar/games room, an ideal location to chat, and where the tasty looking food tables located.

One of the conversations, and not the first time said, "where's the drummer on stage," it's cheating, came another rather loud interrupting voice, even before I could answer the first question.

Technology moves on, Ian has prepared most of his own backing tracks, and all excellent quality, both in musicianship, and an impeccable sound, the mix first-rate to my ears, and the sound of the applause, the audience ears too.

Self-contained acts using some form of pre-recorded sound, now the most popular form of musical entertainment in pubs and clubs.

Artists can set up in minutes, perform their music, pack up, and away quickly at the end of the night, allowing the club or pub steward to lock up, and staff on their way home, before midnight.

For those that prefer an "all live sound," may become disappointed, especially if paying lots of hard-earned cash for tickets to see their much-loved band or favourite artist, if they did not come up to scratch, hence the use of pre-recorded tracks to support, and compliment the overall live sound.

Even our semi-professional playing gigs once a week band, use a form of orchestration to help with our overall sound, not a problem at all.

I recently watched a recent showing of a recording from Cardiff, The Shadows final greatest hits tour in 2004, on Sky Arts TV channel, an amazing all "live "sound.

The abundance of classic songs spanning over four decades, all played precisely, Bruce Welsh, Hank Marvin, and of course, amazing drums, including drum solo via Brian Bennett, at the time, an awe-inspiring live show, Shadow fans remembering for all the right reasons.

Watching this TV show in total admiration, their amazing musicianship clearly apparent, my surround-sound system working overtime, bringing back so many memories of my teenage friendship with Freddy Pearson, who fair to say, more than over-enthusiastic with the band's timeless music.

Moreover, reminding me of The Shadows 1975 UK Eurovision Song entry, "Let me be the One," finishing second to first place Ding-a-Dong, a band called Teach-in singing this catchy tune from the Netherlands.

Spotting a private secure corner close to where Ian's equipment set up, to safely put all my fully appreciated presents, until home time.

At this rate I will need to look elsewhere, as overwhelmed with the number of cards, and numerous multi-coloured bottle packages, containing my preferred favourite tipple, single malt whisky.

Arriving at just the right time, as only a few weeks ago I had the last drop from a similar number of bottles given as leaving presents at the time of my retirement.

I am pleased to say once again enjoyed in moderation, no need to purchase anymore bottles of this delightful, matured liquid until my next memorable birthday.

Admiring one of a number of thoughtful presents with a difference from Amanda, Dave, and family, in particular, what appears something in a frame, perhaps a photograph or picture, and cannot wait to open it.

All in all, I am so pleased how the night has progressed, lots of delicious food, and from the comments received, everyone had eaten and enjoyed plenty, including a complimentary review of the pork, and meat pies, which I am sure the butchers' shop pleased to hear that good news.

As too the food supplied from friends of Warren and Sommer located in Bradford, not much left to take home for my supper, or following days meals.

Ian had given a great account of his entertaining abilities, played great guitar licks, and sang some great tunes to please all age groups, also playing background music during the interval while the eating of delicious food taking place.

I managed to get around most tables for a chat and to thank my family and friends for all the fantastic presents, some of which I couldn't wait to open wrappers of parcels, bottles, or to see, and maybe a taste of some when home.

Everything cleared away, including Ian's equipment, and way before midnight.

My taxi driving skills taking John, Gill, and mum home, ensuring mum safely in her apartment, a gentle hug and kiss goodnight, locking up and speedily returning home.

I did feel a little guilty saying goodnight to Elaine and Diane, leaving them outside the club, their taxi running late to take them home.

It had taken four of us to put all my delightful presents safely in the car boot, after everyone had left, ensuring all the bottles would remain upright, using throws and other items to pack them in tight, and now alone to remove everything into our home.

My hallway full of multi-coloured wrapping paper, and gift bags at either side, leaving just enough space to get to the front room, and staircase to the first floor.

Picking out Amanda's large colourful gift bag, and now wondering what pleasures packed inside.

Looking stuffed with delights, including a huge bar of my favourite chocolate, Cadburys Whole Nut, the wrapping paper quickly discarded.

Carefully opening the packaging of what I had thought, a framed photo, and not just any photograph.

So delighted to look upon a black and white image of a waxing gibbous moon, with my name, and words pointing out the moon as it would have looked on my birthday in March 1952.

Looking at the rear wall of my living room, and identifying the exact spot to hang it, perfect.

Not one drop of whisky in the house prior to my birthday celebrations, but lots of bottles now, and as only sipped a few tipples during the evening that Stuart supplied, now tempted to have a nightcap.

Opening a bottle of Glenfiddich, a present from Steve, and pouring out just a little to taste, and then turning in for the night.

A lovely day coming to a perfect end, I will look at all the cards, and read all the labels in the morning, and thank everyone for making my day special, although not actually the day of my birthday, but close enough.

Not wanting to wish my time away, nevertheless after a day like today, meeting, greeting, and seeing family and close friends, some at a distance for some time.

A good idea to do it all again.

Roll on my next BIG birthday.

CHAPTER NINE

Egypt – October - 2022

(Second Visit)

I am happy at the thought of my next up and coming holiday, and my second visit to this amazing country of Egypt.

My itinerary now almost sorted, just a few niggly bits to organise with Carolyn, mainly travel arrangements from the UK, flight times, transport to the airport, and arrangements from the airport to home.

Using rail to travel from Dewsbury to Manchester Airport, a first for me in March 2020, ahead of covid hitting everywhere, and confident the start of my holiday journey the same this time, minus the covid epidemic.

About an hour of trouble-free traveling, a ten-minute walk to terminal 3 from the station, and an uncomplicated check-in, certainly much better than driving my car on the notorious M62 westbound motorway.

My preferred method of travel also takes out the need for finding secure carparking, and waiting in long queues for a bus transfer to the terminal, a nightmare if in harsh weather.

On the upside, at least when returning from a wonderful holiday, it can take just a few minutes to join the motorway network, and depending on traffic, about an hour from home.

Taking all of this into consideration, I still prefer the no hassle train journey, a short walk to the terminal, and an arranged lift just a few miles to and from Dewsbury train station, to home.

Sadly, my confidence shattered, now driving to the airport on the M62 after all, as unusually, our flight arrangements with British Airways changed at short notice, and the train timetable indicates, trains not available for a 02.30hr arrival at the airport.

The internet awash with so called secure local carparks servicing customers who use Manchester Airport, although now a little wary of any, if trusted what a newspaper article pointed out.

Apparently, a carpark customer had used an on-line website to book his high-performance car into a secure carpark for two-weeks while on holiday.

However, upon the customers return, he received a speeding fine offence on a day and date while away.

Alleged that his car used as a "run-a-round," carpark staff using his car while the customer enjoyed a much-needed summer break, certainly not the news you want to receive upon your return.

Also, his car possibly utilized for anything and everything over the two weeks, and not only joy riding.

I suppose owning a car of my make and model, I should not need to worry or think it will happen to me, but you never know.

My car now booked into a carpark boasting a five-star rating, lots of complimentary reviews, and including regular buses to each Manchester Airport terminal, however, I will make a note of my mileage and where parked on the day I leave it, so a little bit of insurance.

A few hours ahead of driving the short distance to pick up Carolyn from her parent's house, I decided to make a hot drink, and have a few squares of my favourite wholenut chocolate.

I know, not the usual one-hour before midnight treat, but with a drive of almost an hour ahead of me, helping to keep me wide awake.

A huge mistake, biting down on my fridge kept delicious looking chocolate squares, I instantly realised a nut had lodged firmly between two of my top teeth, pushing one outwards towards my lip.

The immediate sharp pain, or sight of blood, does not normally bother me, but at almost midnight, and about to set off in an hours' time on a two-week trekking style holiday, not a fun time at all.

Grabbing a few pieces of kitchen roll, spitting out the uneaten chocolate, now coated in blood, wiping my mouth and chin, and now looking into the long kitchen mirror to assess the damage.

My tooth, very loose indeed, waggling it just to make sure it would not drop out, and asking myself, why-oh-why, had I decided to eat nut filled chocolate straight from my fridge at the eleventh-hour, in the first place.

A slice of toast with a hot cuppa more appropriate, more fulfilling, far less calories and obviously no hassle.

Too late now, but what to do, I do not know, as the time to pick up Carolyn fast approaching, some sort of quick fix needed, but what.

I had already packed two tubes of fixative gel for my bottom central single tooth denture, perhaps helping to "stick" my latest avoidable tooth calamity in place, at least until returning home to make a dental appointment.

Putting just enough cream in and around my tooth, gently pushing it into position, holding it tightly in place with my thumb and index finger for a few minutes, until confident my tooth feels firm.

Double checking all my travel documents, and once again weighing my case, just to see if it had increased in bulk since teatime, then taking it to my car.

Carolyn staying at her parents' bungalow, after visiting from her family home in Cairo, Egypt, spending four weeks back in our village of Wrenthorpe and hometown of Wakefield.

On my last holiday visit to Egypt, Carolyn travelled from her parents' house to her home with me, husband Tommy, meeting us at Cairo airport, and taking me to my hotel, prior to returning to their home, the same arrangement taking place once again.

However, this time, because of our outward-bound flight amendments, I will get to spend quite a few more daylight hours before starting my first day, rather than arriving in the dark early hours.

Our British Airways flight from Manchester to London Heathrow on time, with no delays on the tarmac, at either end, or our transfer to Terminal 5 at Heathrow without any problems.

The five-hour flight appearing not as long, as our discussions covered many interesting subjects, including what to expect with my itinerary once in Egypt.

Tommy at the airport as planned, and just a short walk to a pre-arranged waiting taxi, for what I remember as a relentless hazardous "we're ALL going to die" drive, into central Cairo.

Our driver did not disappoint, the car horn becoming the usual tool to use instead of verbal abuse, albeit I am sure that does happen, and fairly regularly on our forty-minute drive to my hotel.

Carolyn sending me a text a few months ago, informing me that Mr H, my regular driver during my previous visit, had sadly passed away, after contracting the covid virus during the first few months of the epidemic.

Getting on extremely good with Mr H, right from the start of my ten-day stay, and had lots of conversations during our many hours spent together, the longest being a single journey from Cairo to the coastal city of Alexandria.

One of a few incredibly early starts, and absolutely necessary, as a three-hour, one-hundred-and-forty-mile drive ahead of us.

An early arrival in Alexandria gave me a full day to visit lots of historic sites, including the new library overlooking an exceptionally inviting, deep blue looking, Mediterranean sea.

Eating plenty of tasty food at restaurants, street style eateries, and cafés Mr H stopped at, while enroute.

I am sure everyone who knew Mr H, missing him tremendously, especially Tommy and Caroline, as he had worked for them, and their family members, over many years.

My new driver, appearing relaxed and super confident, and no doubt managing himself, and our car, extremely well in an equivalent hectic rush hour in England.

Nonetheless, just a normal, constant, typical hussle-bustle 24-7 here in what appears a chaotic, horrendously busy Cairo.

Tommy joining me to my hotel, just a few meters away from the Antakh café and bar, where I will have most of my meals while here in Cairo.

Booking in, and taking the lift to my third-floor room, the very same room as I had two years ago.

Thumbing through my itinerary with excitement, eager to get going on my fifteen-day trek around this amazing extraordinary ancient country once again.

My day-to-day journeys throughout Egypt, will take place utilizing, aircraft, cars, buses, boats, and of course walking, on what I am sure yet another precisely organised, and innocuous adventure of a lifetime.

With some time in hand, another visit to see the Pyramids on offer, not part of my itinerary on this occasion, but certainly a trip I could not refuse.

My readily available driver, taking me from my hotel to Giza, and a local world-renowned ancient landmark, where once again I would enjoy a long, and at times, uneasy ride on a camel.

A guide, mounted on horseback, and a teenage camel puller, taking me around the site, Khufu, Khafra, and Menkaure, three principle and largest pyramids on the Giza plateau, although around one hundred and eighteen identified pyramids in Egypt.

Taking in amazing views of the Sphinx, constructed around 2600BC, and cut from the limestone bedrock of the Giza necropolis.

Walking around the top of the excavated perimeter, looking down into the pit, while remembering a riddle supposedly posed by the sphinx in ancient times.

My guide telling me about this riddle on my previous visit to see the sphinx.

"What has one voice, goes on four feet in the morning, two feet in midday, and three feet in the evening"

Answer …

A human being, who crawls as a baby, stands on two legs as an adult, and walks with a stick in old age.

Once both of my feet firmly back on terra-firma, and admiring the many images recorded on my phone.

Now taking a long look around a novelty shop, and finally a much-needed tea break, in the shape of tasty food, served in a local restaurant.

Over three-hours of cloud free blue skies and in just about bearable heat, but not without some help, I must have drunk a gallon of water to keep dehydration and its distressing consequences away.

My bed and sleep would not come fast enough after an unplanned, even though, a thoroughly enjoyable afternoon.

A cheesy omelette, mixture of tomatoes, cucumber, and bread, including two cups of tea, for breakfast, remembering to bring along my prepacked rucksack to the hotel's restaurant, for a quick get-a-way once my driver arrives.

The National Museum of Egyptian Civilisation my first port of call, Carolyn joining me as my impromptu guide for the entire day.

Carolyn had wanted to visit this museum, as it now incorporates twenty royal mummies, (eighteen kings and two queens) from the 17th until the 20th dynasty, relocated there in April 2021, receiving worldwide TV coverage of the event.

The most famous of these mummies, Hatshepsut (Maatkare), Thutmose III (Menkheperre), and Seqenenre Taa II.

These preserved mummies discovered in sealed tombs in the Valley of the Kings, on the west bank of the river Nile, a destination I will once again visit during my stay.

The museum boasts over fifty thousand artifacts, representing the Egyptian civilisation from prehistoric times to present day.

Recalling watching a documentary, where Zahi Hawass, Egyptian archaeologist, Egyptologist, and former Minister of Antiquities Affairs, gave a good perceived explanation about all these, and many more ancient discoveries.

Another day that did not disappoint…

I am so looking forward to visiting the Western Desert areas of the Bahariyn Oasis, Farafra Oasis, the White and Black Deserts and Valley of the Whales, and maybe fit in a swim or two, however, this region such a long way from Cairo.

The transport for my journey, a 4x4 land cruiser, a driver and guide, and a tent, my sleeping accommodation for two nights.

Leaving my hotel at 06.00hr, and introduced to my guide the previous evening, now waiting for me with a driver outside the Antakh café and bar.

The journey to reach Wadi Al-Hatan, and Valley of the Whales, taking over two hours driving southwest, but almost as long just to reach the outskirts of Cairo, covering a total distance of around eighty miles.

I am certainly feeling a lot safer travelling in a 4x4 vehicle, the chassis, and back seats far higher than a traditional car, with a good all-around view.

Sadly, no amazing landscapes in sight just yet, only desert, with a few oasis type garages, and shanty shops, sporadically coming into view for a few seconds, then gone in a flash, when driving past at speed.

Looking forward to arriving at one of the most arid parts of the world, The Western Desert, covering over two-hundred and seventy square miles, and feel I have seen most of it on my journey to our first stop, the Wadi El Rayan waterfall and magic lake.

Arriving at one of Egypt's most famous nature reserves a few hours ahead of all the tourist buses, having the whole expanse to ourselves, taking in the amazing oasis feel, with just desert sands all around us, as far as the eye could see in all directions.

The high and low lakes, with the only waterfall in Egypt, in an area forty-five meters below sea level, and the clear blue water looking spectacular, making it all the more amazing in this secluded barren expanse.

Our departure from this astounding region, timed to perfection, as passing the first coach full of tourists about to enter the site on our way out.

The Valley of the Whales at Wadi Al-Hitan, and petrified forest of Fayoum did not disappoint either, absolutely amazing, that these now horizontal forty-meter-high trees have survived in ossified form for thousands of years, also bones and skeletal forms of fish, sea cows, crocodiles, and whales.

The open air, and fossil museums testament to this well-preserved area, as our driver made easy work of the long uphill journey to our camping zone for the night.

Perched at the edge of a huge inland lake that formally existed here, now just sand, but with a perfect view of the setting sun, and only 18.00hr, a long night ahead until a 05.30hr sunrise.

The wind had picked up through the night, but I slept like a log, my tent almost flat, nevertheless, I could see the campfire burning, and if last night's chicken tea cooked via our driver, tasted absolutely delicious, I'm so looking forward to what is on offer for breakfast.

Soon packed away, and all neatly crammed inside the land cruiser, and on the roof rack too, with everything needed to survive for three days out here in the desert, hundreds of miles from anywhere.

Thinking how lucky I am, and at my age, still able to undergo this type of sightseeing holiday, rather than a lazy poolside five-star luxury type of break.

However, when weighing up all that I have seen so far on my trip, and the previous one, my itinerary, so different.

Now travelling for three days into the desert, with two guys I did not know, I am putting a lot of trust in my trip organisers, Tommy, Carolyn, and T&C tours for the arrangements to see, and feel, these mind-blowing experiences.

Onwards, to our next stop, the roads almost non-existent, as the winds had blown sand over, across and up to side, and central barriers, making it almost one-way on a normal two-way road.

Looking similar to country roads here in the UK, when after a snow storm, snow piled high at each side, leaving just enough room to drive in the middle.

Stopping off at a garage for fuel, more drinking water, and ice-creams all around, and a chat about what I will gaze upon in the next half hour or so.

The black desert, and gazing upon it, is actually black, a strange phenomenon, with volcano shaped hills capped with basalt, some over three-hundred feet high, giving them characteristic black tops, dating back to the Jurassic period, 180 million years ago.

Climbing to the very top of one, and taking a 360-degree video using my phone, our land cruiser looking like a dinky toy in the distance.

The heat, almost unbearable, but plenty of drinking water on hand, and even better, our stopover for lunch had a huge swimming pool, an oasis type café/motel, ideal for a swim, rehydrate, and cool down before eating our prepared food.

The owners appeared to know my driver and guide extremely well, obviously a regular stop over point for these trips, and good for picking up fallen tree branches, though out here in the desert a minority for our campfire, and evening meal cooking.

I must have dozed off in our cruiser on the way to the white desert, but over an hour had passed since leaving our lunchtime stopover, and now leaving the road/track to enter the White Desert National Park.

Yet another phenomenon, the sand, and white chalk formations whiter than white, looking like individually carved monuments, some over twenty feet high.

The park established as a protected region in 2002, and I can see why, as another tourist 4x4 land cruiser also joining us, parking a few hundred meters away, setting up camp for the night.

Our driver, doing all the work to set up ours, placing the vehicle at ninety degrees to a high rock formation, placing a wind break and thick woven rug on the sand, and setting up a fire, ready to cook our evening tea.

Most of our food preparation conducted at the rear of the 4x4, behind the windbreak, out of view of me and the guide, who continued chatting to me about what had transpired throughout the last two days.

His English exceptionally good, although my Yorkshire accent had him beat a few times, having to "posh" up my voice, to give out a clearer explanation of my questions, or what I asked or talked about.

Our tea delicious, chicken once again, with potatoes and veg, and a pudding of chocolate biscuits.

Drinking lots of hot tea, and from a teapot, delicious, however, not Tetley, Yorkshire Tea, PG tips, or Twinings, but nevertheless still a tea flavour, and a tasty drink.

Feeling rather full, and the same for my guide and driver, and just a little food left to put out, away from the camp as a treat for the wildlife that roam around these parts.

I had heard some yapping and howling noises the previous night, but assured that sand cats, jackals, and gazelle and anything else either walking or crawling, would not enter our camp.

Tonight's sunset, central to our campsite, an amazing view, as the sun slowly disappeared below the horizon, totally cloud free, and so much calmer than the previous night, in fact not even a slight breeze.

The campfire continued to burn after our tea, as I settled down for the night, still early, but so dark, blacker than black, no light pollution at all, and seeing so many stars and constellations, not sure I would get much sleep at all tonight.

I pointed out lots of constellations to my touring team last night, to little response, as they see this night sky four nights every week, and for over twenty years, so not the marvellous views to them, as for me.

A restless last night out here in the desert, constantly waking, staring up at the night sky, my driver asleep a few feet from me on the rug, while my guide tucked in the 4x4.

Attempting to sleep in over 20 degrees, my sleeping bag folded down to my waist, and no t-shirt, but must have got some sleep as hearing our driver preparing the fire for a cuppa and breakfast, just in time to see the sun rise, spectacular.

Arriving back at my hotel around 15.00hr, in between dozing, a day full of excitement, lots to see, other than desert, and a further stop over for yet another dip in freshly pumped chilly water.

This irrigation pumping station located in yet another oasis area, a location to prepare and eat lunch, and time to immerse myself in cold clear fresh water.

A sort of retaining pool, about eight feet long and six feet wide, and quite full above my waist, with water coming in as a waterfall at one end, and a valve at the other, allowing a constant stream of water to flow as irrigation onto the land, and apparently has done so for decades.

Reflecting on my almost three full day outing, while laid on my hotel bed, thinking about the relationship between me, the driver and guide, and all of those amazing things I had seen and done, a one off, maybe, but I am sure lots more to see and do in this amazing country.

And my flight to Luxor and Nile cruise to Aswan to look forward to.

CHAPTER TEN

Egypt – October - 2022

(Second Visit – Nile Cruise)

Another early rise, after a good night sleep on a comfortable bed, my driver waiting at the hotel main door to transfer me to Cairo airport, for my one-hour flight to Luxor.

No sooner taking off, and now time to land, and still only 07.30hr, and keeping my fingers crossed, but absolutely sure a taxi booked and waiting.

Instead of leaving my suitcase back at the hotel like my last visit, and taking just a rucksack packed with t-shirts, shorts, undies, and socks, with suncream, and my toiletry bag all squashed in, this time taking my suitcase and all it contained, making sure I had not forgotten anything for my four-day river Nile excursion.

Unfortunately, this also means I have got to go to baggage collections, instead of just walking with my rucksack directly through to passport control and outdoors.

However, not taking extraordinarily long to spot my case with the bright green florescent straps tightly around it, speedily heading towards me on the now fully loaded conveyor belt, and soon looking for the exit signs to leave the airport terminal.

My nice and light new suitcase packed to the required maximum weight, and with four working wheels helping to keep the case sturdy, and upright, and so easy to walk and push along side of me at the same time.

I did take just my rucksack for my desert trip, as not requiring lots of stuff, just a few things, factor 50 suncream a must.

Easily spotting my taxi driver amongst the throng of others waiting for exiting passengers, my name in black ink on white card clearly visible, holding up my hand, and frantically waving.

Unfortunately, this signal recognised for a baggage helper, to enthusiastically attempt to take my case to our waiting taxi that will undoubtedly result in a tip.

My refusal to immediately hand over my case meeting with more persistence, giving hand and verbal gestures, and grabbing the handle from me,, insisting he wanted to push it.

My driver, giving me a waving hand gesture to let him take it, saying a hundred Egyptian pounds (£4)all it will cost.

Reluctantly agreeing, and allowing this chap to walk alongside us, but keeping a close eye on my case during the fifty meters to the waiting taxi.

Handing over a folded Egyptian one-hundred-pound note, instantly putting it in his t-shirt top pocket, then running at a fast pace to command another unsuspecting traveller's case.

I had a few Egyptian notes of a low denomination in my mobile phone case, for such an emergency, as not wanting to take out my wallet, as who knows what the baggage carriers/wheelers would expect for a tip then.

The car journey only taking twenty or so minutes to reach the river Nile, where lots of boats moored at the quayside as far as the eye could see.

One after another for hundreds of yards, all waiting patiently for passengers to arrive, my driver picking out my boat, and soon booked in ready to start my four-day cruise upriver, although geographically south, to Aswan.

Luxor, a city built on the site of ancient Thebes, and the pharaohs capital at the height of their power, now full of tourists, hustle, and bustle on the key side, with sellers offering anything and everything, including water.

If my memory serves me right, all these boats moored along the shoreline, and in places three boats deep from the water's edge, interconnected side by side, all pulling up anchor, and leaving together.

A long flotilla, one behind the other, against the flow of water, unless a faster boat overtakes, usually to the sound of unified sirens and resounding horns, with passengers joining in whistling and waving at each other.

I think a while yet before sailing, tipping my taxi driver, with a customary one-hundred Egyptian pound note, and yet another tip required for the boats crew, once my case carried from the roadside, onboard my floating hotel, and to my room.

A quick look around my cabin, a speedy visit to the bathroom, then removing the strap and opening my case, taking out a few things, and hanging t-shirts in the wardrobe.

Now time for a tasty breakfast.

The boats dining room situated below deck, the waterline and river visible through large windows along the boats hull side, making sure I picked a table with a good view, rather than looking directly on to another boat moored alongside.

Deciding to have a full English breakfast from the self-service counter, making my way to a readily cleaned table, and looking at other crockery strewn tables, now partially cleared away, I appear the one last passenger to eat.

The late arrival of some passengers delayed some of the visits, dinner served and an opportunity to go onto the top deck, to take in amazing afternoon views, and a little bit more sun.

A planned visit to Luxor temple, taking place at 14.00hr, and so looking forward to enjoying a good look around, remembering the atmosphere from my previous visit, and it did not disappoint.

Looking at the now completed avenue of the sphinxes between Luxor temple and Karnak, work in progress and partly completed during my first visit, now fully opened in 2021, and available to walk the 2.7 miles from one temple to the other.

Walking not required, as a minibus taxi arranged to attend both temples for quite a few passengers embarking from our boat.

Our visit extending into the evening, both temples and avenue of the sphinxes looking amazing, with strategically placed spotlights lighting up the whole region giving maximum effect.

Spending the night on my boat, third boat from the quayside, with all the receptions from each boat joined together, my pass allowing access through the two other boats reception areas, to mine.

I am so pleased our boat not moored directly at the quayside, or the next boat, central connecting to the first and mine, as I have an incredible view of a clear night sky, with the moon shining bright, its reflection visible on the fast-flowing river.

This volume of water, the longest river in Africa, and historically, the river Nile considered the longest river in the world.

Heading north, the Blue Nile and White Nile, join together at Khartoum, forming the river Nile, and eventually making its way to the Mediterranean sea, flowing through eleven countries.

The Democratic Republic of the Congo, Tanzania, Burundi, Rwanda, Uganda, Kenya, Ethiopia, Eritrea, South Sudan, Republic of the Sudan, and finally Egypt.

My four-day, three-night snippet of the Nile from Luxor, located on the east bank of the Nile, to Aswan, would cover about one hundred and fifty miles, stopping off at a number of locations en-route, and attaching either behind, in front or alongside other boats each night.

Our first visit after breakfast, a mini-bus ride to the Temple of Hatshepsut, stopping off along the way to look at the amazing matching statues of the Colossi of Memnon.

Looking in amazing condition, considering their age, although the righthand one looking much better preserved than the other.

Evidence of archaeological works continuing to a location at the rear of these guarding statues, the Funeral Temple of Amenhotep III, and sure in the not-too-distant future, this complete site will become a visitor's attraction and open to the public.

I could see The temple of Queen Hatshepsut in the distance, and part of my itinerary during my last visit, but definitely worth a further look.

A strict security procedure in place to enter this ancient attraction, following a terrorist attack in November 1987, where fifty-eight tourists and four Egyptian people massacred on this very site.

Including six tourist from the UK, with a married couple living just a few miles away from my home, all tragically killed.

An amazing construction, built of limestone, sandstone, and granite, attracting hundreds of thousands of tourists each year, and plain to see why.

A fleet of open air ten-seater buggies taking sight-seeing passengers from the security entrance, or if you prefer to walk to the temple steps, but in this unprecedented heat, plenty of water, and shade required while in the buggy my preferred option.

Meeting another lone traveller, a chap called Ahmar, from California USA, on this trip, similar to my first meeting of Jim and Ann from Coventry in 2020.

Ahmar, born in Egypt, but leaving to continue his vocation in pharmaceuticals, and doing a sort of solo backpack tour of Egypt and Israel.

Booking destinations and individual tours on the go, whatever sites he had read up on, or takes his fancy, a fantastic way to travel and see this part of the world, and becoming a great asset during other destinations I would meet up with on my Nile cruise.

Walking around the temple and listening to our guide, giving an historical concise dialog, and pointing out artefacts and cartouches / pictographs on ceilings and walls.

Back to our mini-bus, and onto the Valley of the Kings, another equally fantastic ancient site to visit, and if anything like two years ago, one I cannot wait to see.

Once again, buggies used to ferry tourists from the security zone to the start of the tour, where I will descend down ramps and steps to see tombs of pharaohs.

Drinking water even more of a necessity when inside these extremely long, highly decorated tunnels, excavated using hand tools, leading to burial chambers set deep inside the cliffs.

It seems a bit macabre taking many photos of these access routes and burial chambers dating back thousands of years, but how else would today's society learn of the remarkable feats the Egyptian people would become renowned for.

Setting sail mid-afternoon, all boats leaving together with horns blurting out, forming an orderly queue centrally in the river, but some distance apart, and just as I thought, other faster boats soon coming along side, and passing us, taking up the lead.

All as if taking part in a hypothetical race to the next location, as now moored up far behind lots of others, and in my opinion, and to my advantage, once again secured to an outside position of three boats, and central to the whole flotilla.

Edfu temple, our next stop, my second visit to this temple, yet another amazing structure, taking my time to take in everything, no rush, or time given to get back to our boat, while this area packed with tourists, still a beautiful place to enjoy.

Our boat second to none, at least a five star plus accommodation, the ample size double bed cabins, as too the bathroom, and the choice and taste of food available on the palate, absolutely delicious.

Over the next couple of days, I would continue with my journey on the Nile, stopping off at yet another temple, and one steeped in ancient history, The Kom Ombo temple, before reaching our final destination, Aswan.

Not so lucky with mooring up this time around, the second boat from the quayside, and three further boats to the other, certainly no waterside of starry sky views tonight.

Heading out to Aswan high Dam, and already sat in my pre-arranged taxi, Ahmar.

He had booked to see the dam from his hotel, and the guide and driver procuring a two for one deal.

Ahmar had just returned from visiting Eilat in Israel, and Petra, located in Jordan, and as you can imagine, our constant chatting covered both of our last two days destinations, prior to reaching the High Dam of Aswan.

Our guide telling us of the construction of one of the world's largest embankment dams built across the Nile during the years 1960 to 1970, dwarfing the downstream low dam completed in 1902.

The almost three hundred mile long, nine mile wide, Lake Nasser, a reservoir, and huge, manufactured volume of water in place via the High Dam.

This crocodile infested body of water around four- hundred feet deep, and a possible later river boat tour, if Tommy and Caroline can convince me to book it.

Taking almost an hour, to walk and talk, our taxi waiting to take me back to my boat and Ahmar to his hotel.

Ahmar talking to our guide in Egyptian, asking if at all possible to stop off at the unfinished obelisk, just a few miles away, but only a few hundred yards from the main road.

I did recognise the word money as part of the conversation, and a fee of four hundred Egyptian pounds irreversibly agreed.

I had watched a few documentaries about the obelisk, and eager to have a physical look, and share the cost with Ahmar, who reluctantly accepted my offer, but giving a wink to say once out of the taxi he would talk about it.

Our trek up the quarry side on badly constructed ramps and steps, clearly in need of some maintenance and fortunately without incident as now nearing the top of the quarry.

Ahmar began to explain the conversation that had taken place in the taxi.

Ahmar, had certainly done his homework, knowing that this location only a few hundred yards from the main road to our destination, and asked the guide if possible to call here.

The guide and driver discussing a proposed cost between them, four hundred pounds agreed with Ahmar, however, certainly not a fifty-fifty split with driver and guide, on the contrary.

Once returned to the taxi, our guide taking three hundred pounds, leaving one hundred for the driver, fortunately, in this contactless phone and card era, I had a few one-hundred-pound notes tucked away in my phone case.

Cash in the form of notes, certainly the preferred method of payment here in Egypt, also a formidable tipping culture, so exchanging and bringing along lots of Egyptian pounds in various denominations exclusively for this use, as my sightseeing trip all-inclusive, with transport, food, and admissions all taken care of.

Nevertheless, for us, worth the insignificant cost, as seeing with my own eyes, the colossal unfinished obelisk, known as the Lateran Obelisk, still in position, with a commencement date of around 1508 -1458 BC.

Carved out of solid bedrock, measuring around one hundred and thirty-seven feet long, and estimated to weigh one thousand and ninety tons.

I would join Ahmar once again to the Philae temple and Nubian village later in the day, yet another surprise to see him, along with other tourists on our taxi boat.

The Philae temple complex built around 280BCE, and situated between the low and high dams on a small land mass, known as Agilkia island, and only accessible by small boat.

Dedicated to Isis, Osiris and Horus, another stunning structure, taking almost two hours of walking and talking with our guide to get around the whole island.

Back onboard our small boat, a short, powered sail to a Nubian village, a massive backlog of small boats all queuing in an attempt to either offload or pick up passengers from the quayside.

Once on shore, a flight of steps leading from the water side to the village entrance awaited us, and lots of locals and tourists in a busy, but colourful settlement.

Our guide and another tourist disappeared into a shop selling assorted spices, for what seemed ages, Ahmar informing me that he had a midnight flight to catch to Cairo, and could not stay much longer.

Taking a short walk to a café, where children actually holding baby crocodiles, wanting us to take photos for tips, even mums passing over small babies for photos and tips too.

Needless to say, Ahmar and I did not spend a lot of time in this establishment.

Everything coming at a cost if wanting to take photographs, hands reaching out for paper money as soon as a phone or camera becomes visible to the locals.

Finally, our guide and tourist from our party appeared, Ahmar giving him the news of his up-and-coming departure flight, also, the tourist with our guide said also booked on the same flight.

Making our way back to the waiting taxi boats, our observant guide spotting our boat and driver, using his mobile to call him over, a wave also helping.

Now on our way downstream, but not at a pace quick enough for Ahmar, he typed what he wanted to say in English, then chose the option to translate to Egyptian, pointing his phone to the driver, who instantly put his foot down, so to speak.

Ahmar smiling at me, saying that message did the trick, as our boat began to make headway, and considerably faster than our journey to the Nubian Village.

Our guide, me, and the tourist, disembarked to the quayside, leaving the taxi boats driver and Ahmar on board.

Ahmar saying the boat journey to his hotel much quicker on the river than ordering a taxi, or travelling using a car, saying our goodbyes, and exchanging phone numbers.

However not the last I would here from Ahmar tonight, receiving a text message as soon as I got to my cabin.

The boat driver attempting to hold Ahmar for extra cash, a ransom, until he paid for the guide and tripled taxifare, in anticipation of allowing him to leave the boat.

Ahmar's past time in Egypt, knowing the language, and living in this region came to fruition.

Now terribly angry, Ahmar, blurted out he would immediately call the police if not allowed to leave the boat, agreeing to only pay his own taxi fare, and explained to the taxi driver he should start with the booking agent responsible for the guides fee, and use of the river boat taxi.

Reluctantly, after paying the original agreed charge, Ahmar finally allowed to leave the boat, picking up his suitcase from the hotel, and after all this fuss, ended up sharing a taxi with the other tourist in our group, managing to arrive at the airport on time for their pre-arranged flight.

After spending my last night onboard ship, indulging in a delicious three course meal, and a bottle of wine, taking about a glass full back to my room for a nightcap, then a goodnights sleep.

An early rise to meet my taxi to the airport and flight back to Cairo, taking about one hour forty minutes, a further thirty minutes at the baggage carousel, and meeting my familiar waiting driver outside the arrivals entrance.

My calculations indicate I have given out over two-thousand Egyptian pounds,(eighty English pounds) in tips from the start of my Nile river cruise, an expense made aware of beforehand, and still two more days left of my holiday here in Cairo.

Arriving back at my hotel in time for lunch, and meeting Tommy and Caroline at cafe Antakh, and a birthday surprise for Tommy.

Two massive birthday cakes on show, one irrefutably Tommys, and the other cake, a celebration of one of Tommy and Carolines friends achieving excellent exam results.

Everyone present taking lots of photographs, mobile phones held at shoulder height, and also asked to take part, posing with Tommy and Caroline, including other invited guests.

Saying it didn't seem thirty months ago since celebrating my sixty-eighth birthday in the same café, a total surprise, definitely not expecting a huge cake, and customers who I had never met, singing happy birthday.

After Tommys birthday afternoon lunch, me and Caroline took a horse drawn buggy ride around central Cairo, looking impressive at dusk.

Hotels, bridges, monuments, and the free standing one-hundred-and eighty-metre-high concrete Cairo tower, with multi-coloured floodlights lighting them all up, an impressive skyline.

A table booked at the Seagull restaurant overlooking and at the very edge of the River Nile for our last meal together, then my early hours' departure from my hotel to the airport and flight home.

Yet another memorable, and at times exhausting, but definitely mind-blowing fourteen nights in Egypt, with an unquestionably thought out, and prepared itinerary, by Tommy and Caroline of T&C Tours.

Giving me the absolute best opportunities to travel and see as much as possible around Egypt during my stay.

My flight from Cairo, and car journey from Manchester airport to home without incident, and so pleased to see Lottie and Ted, waiting for me, babysat at my sister's home until earlier.

The kettle on, and just giving lots of thought about my holiday, and what I had experienced, my photos will bring back those memories for many a year.

However, also making me think and contemplate yet again.

If unknown civilisations existed on earth fifty-thousand or one-hundred thousand years ago, one of the few things that would survive this length of time, are stone buildings and objects.

Many things in our world, and especially those I have seen and touched in Egypt, that certainly do not fit into archaeologists' interpretation of known written history.

I, like others visiting these sites, astounded at what our ancestors accomplished in the distant past, and once again, my favourite saying comes to mind.

Every photograph worth a thousand words, and each and every photograph will raise a thousand or more questions.

CHAPTER ELEVEN

Jim's Birthday Bash

(Seventieth)

During our band rehearsals and live gigs, age and how much longer each of us still have the impetus, and continued enjoyment for our band to carry on playing in its current format, always high on the agenda.

In particular when an awkward trek for all our equipment, short narrow steps, and stairs, either internal or external always a tight squeeze, and an absolute nightmare.

Stage doors located such a long way from our parked truck, or clubs with a small stage, or nothing at all, all play on your mind, giving the impression of, "Is all this really worth the hassle."

However, "Mister Twister," now in its twenty-forth year, and originally saying only going to do our band thing for a few years way back in 1997, and still at it midway through 2022.

To continue all these years as a semi-professional outfit, hold down a full-time job, and the constraints of a family home life, has over the years, had its difficulties, but seems all worthwhile.

Our overall friendships have stood the test of time, regardless of issues that come our way, with little or no disagreements to call of, knowing each other's limits, just how far to push points of interest, and long before things could potentially turn nasty, folding at an uneasy but acceptable compromise.

Much the same with members from all my previous bands, when enthusiastic about your music, musician friendships remain cemented for life, and now to date, totalling more than fifty years.

Most of my present and former band mates, and musical acquaintances over the years able to join me at my seventieth birthday bash.

Conversation now centred around yet another big "do," our guitarist and one of two lead singers, Jim, Mr-Fix-it Trueman, and his up and coming seventieth birthday.

Jim the instigator of getting our band together following the demise of "Aircrew" in 1992, a 1997 regroup of four members, Jim, Dave, Martin, and me, and also our sound engineer, Barry, with the addition of Mick on Bass, hitting the working men's club scene once again.

My nickname for Jim, "Mr-fix-it Trueman," came about years ago, when anything failed for one reason or another, repaired, and working once again when delivered to Jim.

Especially my former bands troublesome sound mixer, taken to lots of different stores to fix, but not until taking it along to Jim did the problem finally get permanently resolved.

Not only our bands financial adviser and responsible for all things involving cash, but our Jim excellent at making things from scratch, in fact taking over a year to completely construct our bands huge PA system way back in 1997.

Purchasing all the electronic items required to put together bass, mid, and top sufficiently powered amplification units, and building eight speaker cabinets of assorted sizes using 25mm thick marine plywood.

All knowing it too, after unloading and loading our truck, with all of these cabinets, and wheeling, lifting, and carrying them in and out of clubs for the last twenty-five years or so, a wonder our backs, arms, fingers, legs, and toes all still intact.

Common knowledge has it, that if Jim made it, whatever "it" or "that," will last a lifetime, and to date, each large or small item Jim has made, built, or restored, all still with us, requiring no major repairs, and only little or no maintenance.

It appears Jim having the same dilemma as I did when starting to put together my birthday celebration party.

What to do, where to have it, who to invite, and when, and on what day, just for starters.

Happily, Jim's partner Angela lending a hand, giving some innovative ideas and suggestions, including using the same caterers as I did, saying the food at my birthday bash certainly plentiful, and tasted delicious, requesting the Bradford twosomes contact details from me.

A good start, particularly with food, with a date and venue now finalised, including our band engaged to play on the night, a Saturday night in July, Alverthorpe Working Men's Club, a local club around the corner from where my own seventieth birthday bash took place.

At least I know I have an invitation, and playing on home turf, as gigs coming our way wherever needing to travel following the many months of austere covid lockdown, now few and far between.

All of those well-established Working Men's Clubs of yesteryear that did engage the likes of our band, now in the minority.

The remainder of these clubs still nervous about opening up their large concert rooms, with additional staff required, then to heat, and light, with no guarantees of people coming for a night out to fill them.

So, artists, and predominantly expensive to employ groups, left high and dry, a constant remark from agents when the band ask why still no clubland gigs in our diary.

To think that throughout my playing days, I have missed so many family gatherings, a Saturday night curse, as more often than not, everything planned for a Saturday night.

I have given my apologies thousands of times, "sorry our band playing in South Yorkshire, or the North East," regardless of where, reluctantly, but a necessity in keeping a roof over my own household, not joining others in my larger family.

Nevertheless, onwards, and upwards towards this planned, private gig, along with added attractions, a selected audience, including some of my family, AND lots of delicious food.

Although a welcomed gig to play, it will not put any cash into our bands somewhat diminishing bank account, with escalating expenses such as fuel, road tax, insurance, and maintenance for our aging truck, that still require regular payments whether our band earn any money for gigs or not.

Alverthorpe club not known amongst artists for its easy load either, in particular bands, with lots of large heavy equipment, yes only a short walking distance directly from the main road, through the dressing room, and directly onto the stage.

Nonetheless, not exactly straightforward to manoeuvre all our weighty equipment through a single door at right-angles to the road, then taking three of us to lift most things up three narrow steps to the rear of a large corner stage.

Great planning when modernisations to the club took place, in hindsight, perhaps the clubs management team and architects should have asked the views of artists.

Because of this oversight, and the amount of equipment now placed at the rear of the stage, almost everything required moving or put in its place, so I could start to set up my drumkit.

Taking almost an hour to put all our equipment in place, and now on with our somewhat disturbing to some, sound check, in particular, my drum kit.

"You building a shed mate," a comment often made when audience early arrivals come into the concert room, while our soundcheck taking place.

However, a free from visitor's room so far, so quickly continuing, and not deterred until Baz completely satisfied with my drumkit sound, and tonight, all accomplished in record time.

Not a moan or groan on my part, as playing in premises of this calibre for over fifty years, I have seen it all.

From talking to unhappy committee men, or happy ones, good and bad audiences, carrying our equipment to a first-floor concert room, using rickety steel fire escapes, and in all weathers.

Also, using large or small lifts for equipment, usually with people in them other than us, vans, and trucks stuck on soddened grass, yards upon yards away from stage doors, trapped on motorways in snow drifts, you name it, all musicians have done it.

Playing together in bands for all of these years, our friendship circles almost the same, lots of recognised faces now appearing that had attended my birthday bash, except Jims close family, some of which I had not seen for more than a few years.

Unlike my birthday, Warren and partner Sommer not serving food tonight, and able to have a drink, and listen to our band, along with Ashley, their mum, and husband Martin, Ian, and Steve from Black Lace, Robin, two Mick's, Martin, and lots of other musician friends and acquaintances joining the select audience tonight.

While guaranteed to have a full house in the concert room, Jim speaking with the door attendant, also giving consent to allow members or others who normally frequent this club on a Saturday night, and wish to join us, can do so, with one major exception, the food for Jims invited guests only.

Jim and Angela arranged a professional photographer friend to take as many photos as possible of guests around tables, or posing in selected groups in front of a white screen, and taking lots of photos of our band while performing on stage.

Viewing lots of iPhone images and videos of my recent birthday bash, and some that inexplicably appeared on many social media platforms, making me smile, as really enjoying my birthday night.

On the other hand, what a great idea to ask a professional photographer to attend, and preserve lasting memories of tonight's special event.

All agreeing to open up the night with our usual first set, lasting around fifty minutes, including the "Happy Birthday" to you tune, and subsequent sing-along, allegedly composed by Patty Hill, and Mildred J Hill in 1893, then FOOD, and close off our evening's performance with a dance spot.

A typical working men's club timetable, but instead of playing numerous houses of bingo between our two sets, replacing this ever-popular numerical event with choosing and eating our food, lots of un-interrupted chatting, along with the photographer taking a plethora of memorable photos.

Apart from performing to an exclusive audience, and eating lots of hot and cold scrumptious food, our appearance no different from a normal Saturday night gig, except that an all-encompassing Redbeck breakfast special after our gig, certainly not required tonight.

Changing into my freshly washed, and ironed stage clothes, my in-ear headphones and headband in place, and now ready to go on stage, patiently waiting for our recorded opening music.

The same melodic tune since our first inaugural gig in a Dewsbury club, way back in 1998, and one tune that I never get fed up with hearing.

A Mike Oldfield composition taken from the album, "Songs of distant earth" released in 1995, "Let there be light" which uses audio from the Apollo 8, Genesis reading.

Jim editing this tune to reduce its length from almost five minutes to around two minutes, and all while retaining those immortal words.

"In the beginning God created the heaven and the earth."

Hearing those opening few tuneful seconds, instantly giving me a heart pounding thrill, now eager to get on stage, and not striking my cymbals or skins until hearing Jims distinguished pre-recorded announcement voice.

"Ladies and gentlemen, please welcome on stage, Mister Twister."

A loud count in from me, one, two, three, while hitting my sticks together at the identical time, bringing a start to our opening song, "The Boys of Summer," a Don Henley composition of The Eagles fame.

Our fifty-minute, ten-song set, finishing with U2's, "Streets with no Name," in a set completed in what appeared double quick time, and to a chosen over enthusiastic top-quality audience.

I did notice that throughout our somewhat quick set, Jim singing his tunes with passion, and added gusto, especially his personal favourite song.

The original version of MacArther Park, actor Richard Harris singing this in1968, reaching number 4 in the charts, and after performing our rendition tonight, receiving extraordinary applause.

I always think of the song as "cake" song.

"Someone left the cake out in the rain, I don't think that I can take it, cause it took so long to bake it, and I'll never have that recipe again, OH NO!!!!"

All in all, an impressive extremely well received first set, Dave singing his songs, playing his little heart out, and now really looking forward to tucking into a tasty, combined tea, and early supper.

My tastebuds now raring to go, looking to sample lots of choices, as the aroma of piping hot cooked food began to filter into our dressing room.

Quickly changing from my rather moist stage wear, drying off, a spray or two of deodorant, slipping into my jeans and t-shirt, heading quickly out into the concert room, feeling rather hot and sweaty.

However, that did not stop others from forcefully, although playfully, escorting me for some group photographs.

A "Black Lace" reunion photograph, with me Ian and Steve, and lots of other different permutations, friends, family, and anyone wanting to get involved.

My sons Warren and Ashley also joining in, and a full complement of all Jims musician friends too, hustle and bustle sorting out a baying throng, all eager to have images taken, and just about squeezing everyone in for a photograph covering almost fifty years of Jim's musical buddies.

Repeatedly, and shamelessly glancing at the now busy tables of food, lots and lots of our audience filling their large disposable paper plates with lots of mouth-watering goodies.

All while continuing my impatient stance, and forced smiles, and wondering if sufficient food remaining for band members, including me, once the photographer has finished.

The photographer gathering together all of Jim's, and our musician colleagues, for a memorable photo, some of which, I and others, have a long history of playing in bands together.

One chap I always enjoy having an all-encompassing chat with, Mick Linskey, the first driver from our bands conception, way back in 1970, who along with then girlfriend Angela, taking our band to gigs in their Morris Commercial J2 van.

A constant fight as to which of our Black Lace band sitting in the front seat next to Angela, from memory usually Alan Barton, and the reason, fashion at that time, a short mini-skirt, and gorgeous legs.

Ironically, both recalling the last time chatting in this club a few years ago, actually Micks seventieth birthday bash, with a similar audience present then, although sadly some not with us to day.

Micks wife Angela, and musician friends passing away, between then and now.

Received lots of compliments from family and friends, and musician colleagues about the bands overall sound, our choice of songs, good musicianship, and vocals.

Also, lots commenting on my impressive looking explosive sounding drum kit.

I always remark, "thank you, but I only hit them, its Baz, our sound engineer who produces what you hear."

I did have my fill of tasty food, not indulging that much, just a level plate, although full of tasty goodies.

More than enough to feel satisfied, and not bloated, as I still have a final fifty something minute second set to complete, depending on how many encores, then pack everything away, and the brief but ever so awkward journey to load up our truck.

Our last set tunes totally filling the dance floor, surprising after the food tables looked almost completely cleared, and I would imagine lots of over full tummy's jumping up and down, looking at the amount of food piled on their plates earlier.

Packing up my drum kit, and all the equipment away after a fantastic nights entertaining gig, taking much longer than usual, perhaps our own full tummies had something to do with it.

The insignificant amounts of food remaining after everyone had left for home, ended up in our tummies, with just two, quarter full stainless-steel tureens, one of chilly, the other rice, unexpectedly left over.

These put on the rear seats of my car, to pack and freeze, to share and eat later, meanwhile our truck still to load up.

Yet another successful birthday within our band, and overall, so pleased with the night, and my playing, and also our band, especially in front of other esteemed musician friends, and an appreciative audience of our families and other friends.

I had not given this much thought while on stage, as confident with playing our tunes, but then reflected on how Ian Howarth must have felt when performing at my birthday bash.

Perhaps a little nervous, concerned, or simply happy to play and do his thing, any worry or anxiety certainly did not show on what I witnessed on the night.

Also thinking when it comes along to Daves seventieth in a few years' time, will he want to do the same sort of thing.

Nevertheless, a steady, short drive home, and my bed, feeling totally shattered after loading our van, and certainly tired.

However, bed would not come as quickly as I thought.

My unflustered drive home, in control through the speed cameras in Alverthorpe, edging on to Kirkhamgate, through Wrenthorpe to my home, involving quite a few sharp corners, hills and manoeuvres, resulting in lukewarm chilly spilling from a tureen onto my rear seats.

I should have known earlier, but just thought what a pleasant aroma, not that pleasant though, chili con carne covering almost all the rear seating area, and on the backrest of my driver's seat too.

119

Taking almost an hour to scrape all the product from the seats, double wash, disinfect, and towel dry, leaving all windows open just a few inches until morning.

Not the "dream" I thought of ending the night with, nevertheless, both tureens now indoors and what leftovers of chilly and rice remain, put into plastic containers, and put in my somewhat empty freezer.

Placing both empty tureens in the dishwasher, alongside a few days' pots, pans, plates, and numerous utensils.

A blue tablet in its holder, sorting my desired program, pressing start, and snapping shut the door.

Taking Lottie and Ted outdoors for a tinkle, the outside light of our summerhouse shedding a tiny glow over the astroturf lawn.

The night sky looking good, sadly not in the mood to remain out for any length of time tonight after the previous hour of cleaning up.

Once back inside, giving Lottie and Ted a goodnight, or should I say, a one-thirty early morning food treat, and fresh water in their bowl.

Finally, my much-anticipated waiting bed.

CHAPTER TWELVE

Israel – May - 2023

(Almost)

Pondering about my next holiday, maybe a poolside trip, staying at an all-inclusive hotel, or yet another enjoyable, but exhausting sightseeing expedition.

I had really enjoyed both my last two Egypt holidays and last year's trip to Israel, some thirty-six days in total, pounding the desert sands of these far eastern countries.

Nonetheless, and almost certainly, my ten-days in Israel, undoubtedly the most enjoyable, spending my time with a twenty-seven strong party, all easy to get along with, and all lovely people.

My Egypt jaunts more often than not, a solo trip, with others joining me, or visa-versa, on various visits to look at artefacts, and ancient monuments, from my floating hotel on the Nile, or as a passenger with my guide and taxi driver from my hotel in Cairo.

Whilst last year's Israel trip more of a full-on tour, in as much as what the authorities allowed us to see, and safe to visit.

Incorporating every one of us in our party, our coach traveling from one location, and hotel to another, a different destination each day, throughout the land of milk and honey.

My fascination of Egypt now practically accomplished, and what I have observed with my own eyes, either there in the flesh, using the internet or watching documentaries on TV, almost to the point of what else to arrange, on a safe, secure, carefully planned sightseeing holiday.

As mentioned before, there is the possibility of a Lake Nassa, four-day boat tour, which tags along from a four-day river Nile trip, and as yet, I

121

have still to make up my mind whether to plan this sightseeing voyage of discovery, or not.

At this moment in time, more to see and do in the land of Israel, and will enable me to absorb the Jewish culture, and to this end, I have asked Julia if I could join a new group of sightseers currently in preparation for a fourth coming 2023 all-encompassing trip.

An insight into my thoughts, that while journeying on our expedition of discovery with a similar minded group, all in harmony with their beliefs, and all wanting to see and experience the same sights.

I cannot think of a better way to travel around Israel.

This can only add to my unpretentious verities gained on my last trip with Julia, and Da'vid, and once again getting involved.

Listening to captivating conversations that take place during mealtimes, travelling, room sharing, relaxation while in the hotel bar, and nightly readings.

A date for our holiday now confirmed as, 4th to 15th May 2023, and currently in Julias possession, a list containing names of forty-two would-be travellers wishing to take part.

As the only non-Christadelphian brother on the list, feeling privileged to have an opportunity to join Julia, brothers, and sisters, on a knowledgeable sightseeing adventure of a lifetime tour of Israel once again.

Nevertheless, my sightseeing tour in the land of milk and honey still away off, and anything can happen between now and then.

With my last Egypt trip now a memory, Christmas now almost upon us, just six weeks away, and as usual, what gifts to purchase for family and friends now on my mind.

In the scheme of things, this small but thoughtful undertaking seems to get harder each year, when in theory everyone seems to have everything they require anyway, or perhaps await more of the same.

Vouchers seem a promising idea, an ideal opportunity for loved ones to buy whatever needed, or perhaps giving money a better option.

To then build up a pot to add to cash from friends and relatives already given, and possibly purchase what they desire, or would like, or require.

My thoughts all over the place, what best to do that will no doubt please some, and perhaps not others, then again, would family and friends disclose if content or unhappy with your gifts anyway.

All of these thoughts did not seem to matter one bit after receiving a call from mums CareLink home welfare provider.

Mum had pressed her necklace emergency button, and when connected, informing the call centre that she had fallen in the living room, and still on the floor.

Mum, repeating in tremendous pain, and fearful that she had broken her hip, an ambulance required as soon as possible.

CareLink informing me of mums' current situation, and asking if I could immediately drive to mums' home, the call centre said they would ensure an ambulance would meet me there.

I have to say an arrangement with a care provider, a remarkable success, knowing that mum can instantly "call up" someone with her necklace emergency button, and get an immediate response.

A two-way conversation can then take place from anywhere in mums' apartment, using a high-tech speaker system.

A friendly person can offer help and advice, and inform family what has transpired, and remain in contact with the injured person, or person requiring help and assistance, until support arrives, what a great lifesaving service.

Arriving at mums at the same time as the ambulance, my short drive full of anticipation, and not sure what would face me and the ambulance paramedics once I unlocked the front door.

Tentatively, calling out, mum, "I'm in here love," replied mum, in an almost whisper, the living room door partly open, enabling me to see mum laid on her side with her back up against the sofa.

Feeling helpless as the paramedics instantly taking over, asking mum lots of questions, "how long have you been laid like this, have you tried to move, where does it hurt," then checking mums vital statistics and making her comfortable.

Bringing in a stretcher from the ambulance, the paramedics confirming that mum has a suspected broken hip, and would have to take her to the accident and emergency unit at our local hospital.

At 19.30hr, a night without any doubt, and a long one ahead, agreeing that I would inform other close family members, then drive to the hospital, park up, and meet mum, and close relatives in A&E.

Soon becoming clear following x-rays, that mum had indeed fractured her hip and would have to endure a major operation.

Firstly, to remove, and then replace a ball made from ceramic or metal alloy to her femoral head or hip, then attached to a metal stem, and inserted into the top of her femur.

Once this unthinkable operation has taken place, and given the all-clear, mum would have to tolerate months of structured daily rehabilitation.

On my mind at the time, saws, hammers, screwdrivers, tools of a joiner, not necessarily tools of a surgeon, but no doubt required to fulfil mums hip replacement, and getting her onto her feet once again.

For our family, this will mean lots of visiting hours at the hospital, giving mum constant assurances all now ok, nonetheless, requiring lots of family patience during the forthcoming weeks, and perhaps months.

Christmas this year undoubtedly not a planned family gathering as in previous years, instead, meeting at the hospital bedside over the whole festive period.

However, good to see mum remaining positive during her ten weeks stay in Pinderfields and Pontefract hospitals, and then requiring "home help" for a few weeks afterwards, getting her once more into a somewhat steady routine for making meals, using the toilet, and bedtime, with the help of a few services.

A zimmer frame for starters, helping mum to walk around her home unaided, also a four-wheeled stable trolly for putting food on, or anything else that will help manoeuvre things about, handrails at either side of the loo, and bed, along with a commode, all indispensable equipment.

Nevertheless, all seems just a bit too much for a ninety-one-year-old lady, who remarkably just a few months earlier, lived totally self-sufficient.

My family did joke after suffering two major falls in fifteen years, mum now almost bionic, requiring all-encompassing surgery for a broken wrist, collarbone, and two new hips, whatever next, optimistically nothing else that a few days' rest, and minimum recuperation cannot solve.

My seventy-first birthday on the horizon, no big party for this one, moreover, I cannot believe where the last year has gone, although I have had lots of things to do, reminding me that retirement not all that it is made out.

More to the point, my Israel sightseeing holiday now less than two months away, and seemingly Julia completing all the necessary planning, and the holiday company on track too.

I had made it a point to watch the late news as often as possible, just to ensure no current on-going troubles in Israel that could potentially put my holiday at risk.

However, so far so good, with no reports of anything taking place that could interrupt an uneasy peace.

I had purchased a few items of new clothing, t-shirts, a few pairs of swim and dress shorts, a lightweight jacket, cagoule, and along with other clothes bought for my last Egypt trip, all would fit snuggly into my suitcase.

While on my last Israel trip my previous suitcase becoming un-wheelable after pulling my case and Julia's from the airport to our hotel, and returning the following day to catch our flight.

Unbeknown to me, a stone had lodged in one of the wheels, stopping it from turning, and after a walk of almost one mile each way, the one wheel of four that became stuck fast, had worn flat, making it unbalanced and impossible to push or pull, without considerable effort.

I would look out for this when arriving once again at Luton airport in May, making sure that my suitcase wheels all working correctly and smoothly, so as not to hinder my protracted walk, and prevent the costly acquisition of yet another new suitcase.

Taking Lottie and Ted to my sister Marcia's homes, a doggy sitting partnership I had come to rely on for my last two Egypt trips, and previous Israel holiday, as not wanting to use a kennel service for almost two-weeks while away from home.

Stopping off at mums, who during the last few weeks has improved with her walking and general household duties no end, able to conduct most functions, maybe a little slower, but now confidently cooking meals, using the toilet, and putting herself to bed.

Certainly, a worry for us all, and more since mum discharged from hospital and at home.

Nevertheless, now confidently assured that mum, and Lottie and Ted, in great hands while I took yet another sightseeing holiday to Israel.

My youngest taxi-driver brother, John, dropping me off once again for an arranged 07.00hr meeting at Dewsbury bus station, along with Julia and two new travellers, Darren, and Kathy, to board a National Express coach, for an enduring, multiple stop, six-hour journey to Luton Airport, and hotel for the night.

Strangely enough, our footpath walk from the coach stop at Luton Airport to the Ibis hotel, did not appear to take anywhere near as long as my previous visit, and my case standing up to the fast pace, those small wheels on both my case and Julia's, all working to perfection.

The weather on our side, overcast, but no rain for the twenty or so minute walk, Julia, Darren, and Kathy following up the rear.

Checking in, and receiving my room key, and notification I would share a room with Clive, a brother from further south, although only for tonight, as while in Israel my roommate is Mark Guntrip, a brother from Barrow-in-Furness.

Already spotting two travellers sat in the lobby, whom I had spent my Israel holiday with last year, Lyndsay and Cathy, husband, and wife from Glasgow.

A hug and handshake positively received, and general chatter following, all about what our families had done, and got up to throughout last year, and what our new group expect to see on yet another amazing experience, in the land of Abraham, Isacc, and Jacob.

Our host, Julia, introducing me to Clive, and instantly "hitting it off," pushing our cases along the corridor and into the lift, and heading off to our second-floor room.

Clive informing me that he should have joined us on last year's trip to the Holy Land, however, following a major operation, and not intending to risk massive amounts of walking and hill climbing, inevitable with this type of sightseeing holiday, deciding best not to join the tour this time around.

Two large single beds becoming a place to put our suitcases on, in a cosy room, overlooking the main highway to the airport.

Julia had said to arrange our own evening meals, and to have eaten in plenty of time for a 20.00hr welcome meeting, and then hymns, prayers, and Bible readings.

Taking all this into account, quickly having a shower and a change of clothing, sorting out the TV while Clive followed suit, both of us on our way to the restaurant in plenty of time.

Introduced to Mark my Israel roommate, while in the foyer, and his daughter too, and other later arrivals joining us for tonight's meal and group meeting.

I did recognise Angela, and a husband-and-wife couple from Norway, who joined us on last year's trip, so making a quick deduction, and concluding thirty-two extra faces, and names I should take the time to remember, excluding the ones I have either travelled with last year, my room mates, or on our coach journey to Luton.

How would I ever put all these names to faces, instantly recalling them all, realising that taking a short cut, calling everyone "love," not necessarily the answer, and certainly not acceptable on this trip.

Our tour company provided name badges on lanyards at the time of booking, except in my experience, the ones I have previously worn never seem to remain name facing outwards, so a fun experience, and optimistically, not an embarrassing one.

Lots of chat taking place around the restaurant table, lots of questions, most of which I had answered on last year's Biblical trip.

How had I come to know Julia, have I visited a local ecclesia, and what I had come to know about the Bible, all helping to break the ice, with others I had only just met.

Julia had given brother Darren and sister Kathy who we had travelled with to Luton, and Mark and Clive, enough knowledge of who I am already, and how I had got to know her.

Others I travelled with last year all fully aware of my somewhat complicated, but nonetheless interesting, and thought-provoking past.

Undoubtedly, I will have plenty of inquisitive inoffensive conversations during the next twelve days, that will no doubt iron out any misconceptions of a stranger in their midst, namely me.

Last year's tour going extremely well, so confident this year's planned trip equally as good, and confident all will get along fine.

Our tour group welcome meeting taking place first, Julia giving instructions of our timetable, and requirements, a precursor to settling into our Bible meeting, incorporating hymns, readings, and prayers.

The Bible readings tonight from Deuteronomy, Song of Solomon, and Acts, all brothers and sisters in our party reading a number of verses in turn, including me, finishing just after 21.30hr.

All saying an early good night, and to see everyone in the hotel foyer at 06.00hr.

Once all the party numbers verified, and none left behind, then commence the start of our walk, or book a taxi if the preferred option, of course weather dependant, or capable of walking such a distance, and pulling along a suitcase.

Nevertheless, I did not mind walking at all, and pulling two large suitcases, as the aircraft seat now my comfort zone for over five hours, with little or no exercise until landing in Israel.

I am now so looking forward to my trip, and Clive too, as our conversation carried on for ages, also when in our respective beds, our bedtime tete-a-tete continuing into the early hours.

Taking turns to chat about what seemed never ending stories, covering many years, about anything and everything, including my past years and Clive's too, and all in the pitch black of our room.

Both laughing when thought our conversation had dried up, when either me, or Clive would once again ask a question, or say something, until finally dropping off to sleep.

In my opinion, Clive, now in retirement, had an amazing past, working with all of my favourite 70's and 80's popstars as a personal accountant, with names such as Freddy Mercury, Pink Floyd, The Who, and even meeting my drummer hero, Phil Collins, the list endless of who Clive had worked for and with.

Furthermore, Clive running a small holding for a number of years, a miniature farm containing lots of livestock, that in itself an arduous task, and all while dealing with his popstar clients.

Asking Clive if he had not already planned to sit on the almost full to capacity coach with anyone, would he sit next to me while touring around Israel, as I know so much more to learn about Christadelphians, Bible knowledge, and so much more about each other.

Arriving at the airport in plenty of time, the footpath looking more like a congested motorway, with over thirty adults, pulling cases, on a twenty-minute fast pace walk to the airport check-in desk.

Anyone travelling to Israel will endure lots of security checks, with passports, baggage, who knows who in our party, for how long, and why am I going on this holiday.

All of this attention, and after adding to all previous information already provided about ourselves, laborious, yet obviously fully understanding the reasons why, and just like last year, our security checks appearing to take forever.

Finally, everything required to travel, ratified, and all now through to the departure lounge, and another hour or so, before boarding the EL AL aircraft, and the start of our tour.

Although, as far as I am concerned, my holiday began the previous day, at the moment I locked my front door, and getting into my brother John's taxi for the short drive to Dewsbury bus station.

I do enjoy flying, and all that travelling in an aircraft entails, regardless of how long it takes to finally sit down in my assigned seat, and whatever else involved to get to the reserved destination.

Finding all the security checking prior to our preparation to board, and then finally getting comfortable, ready for take-off, not a problem at all, in fact enjoying this as part of my holiday get-a-way.

In addition to all of the other Christadelphian passengers in our group, I am looking forward to seeing our Israeli guide, Da'vid Beradt once again too.

Listening to a mountain of biblical and historical knowledge, and all spoken in excellent English, making my Israel tour, yet another sight-seeing tour I am unlikely to forget.

CHAPTER THIRTEEN

Israel – May – 2023

(Itinerary Tour)

Who would have thought that in just twelve months I have visited Israel in May 2022, Egypt in October 2022, and now in the hustle and bustle of Tel-Aviv airport Israel in May 2023.

Unbelievable for me, but all falling into place allowing me to enjoy more of the same sight-seeing experiences, especially with, and around lovely people.

The flight went without a hitch, my aircraft food tasted delicious, and although I had drunk a tea and a few soft drinks, thankfully not feeling a need to join the toilet queues.

As usual, the aircraft had only just come to a standstill, everyone sat in seats next to the aisle promptly standing up, and opening overhead lockers to remove luggage and other personal items.

The walkway now awash with passengers reaching across others, all eager to retrieve their stored hand luggage as soon as possible.

Organised chaos, but I too joining the throng, not wanting to hold up those passengers to the rear of me.

Pulling out Julias small case and my jacket from the overhead locker above her, and placing them between my feet.

Just to stand up and stretch my legs bringing instant relief, a little tight between each row of seats, a disadvantage of long legs and being rather tall.

My knees firmly pressed into the seat in front of me for most of the journey, but sat in an aisle seat enabled me to at least stretch out my legs now and then.

Slowly shuffling our way towards the cockpit end of the aircraft, airhostess bidding us farewell, and to have a pleasant stay.

Gradually leaving the aircraft to the awaiting passenger boarding bridge, with no steps to encounter, everything automated, lots of walkways, lifts, and escalators in this modern Tel-Aviv airport.

All our party of forty-two through the hi-tech automated passport checkout in record time, and immediately ushered to a meeting point, located directly above, and on the outside perimeter of an enormous circular eating and duty-free shopping expanse.

A huge balcony space awash with tourist arrivals, although our party certainly given V.I.P treatment, as a waiting chaperon, holding a large banner above everyone's head, saying "Julia Fentiman Holy Land Tour."

Our allocated airport operative eager to take us promptly through the remainder of the terminal to our awaiting coach, and a smiling Da'vid.

A few stragglers along the way, when leaving the airport terminal, not surprising in the evening heat, Julia making a beeline for a hug, and clear to all that Da'vid also pleased to see not only Julia, but the rest of us too.

A hot evening out in the carpark, and delighted to now board the coach, greeting our chauffeur for the next ten days, and taking a seat two seats behind the driver, against the window.

Clive sitting next to me in the aisle seat as the air conditioning, a must in this hot climate, immediately taking its rapid effect, and pleased to say the temperature on our coach, registering a cool 15C.

With-in minutes of becoming climatised, Clive commenting, saying a hot night if our rooms do not have air-conditioning in them.

Thankfully, as the coach pulled away from the airport terminal, Da'vid said during his welcome talk, that over 94% of all Israeli households and hotels have air-conditioning units as a standard feature, and confirmed our party would visit all the locations on our planned itinerary.

Great news, but our arrival time also coincided with hitting the Tel-Aviv rush hour traffic almost as soon as our coach joined the highway.

Lengthy tail backs, and congestion, just like home, and taking a look at one of the reasons, ongoing major civil engineering roadworks along our way.

Clearly a terribly busy area around the airport, but once these roadworks, and new bridges fully completed, they will undoubtedly complement existing lanes on the northbound motorway, no doubt in the interim, adding more problems with this rush hour traffic, again, also just like home.

I do not think Israel traffic as unmanageable as I encountered in Cairo, Egypt, with thousands of cars, HGV's and coaches causing utter chaos, and blatant disorder, with constant lane swapping, and the pipping of horns, surely not, regardless, they do all seem to get from A to B, eventually.

Looking at what is happening in front of us, not appearing quite as bad, orderly queues waiting patiently for temporary and permanent traffic lights to change, and not hearing one car horn as yet.

Our journey to Netanya, taking about thirty minutes longer than anticipated because of slow traffic, and our first hotel, the ten-floor high, one hundred and three roomed, King Soloman Hotel.

The very same first stop as last year, situated just a few metres from the Mediterranean coast, and arriving just as the setting sun disappeared from view.

Immediately bringing to mind last year's night of heavy rain and winds, my roommate then, Trevor, and tonight, Mark, and for the rest of our stay in Israel

Our cases soon off loaded and waiting for us in the hotel foyer, however, tea first, then sort out our room key, fingers crossed another high floor like last year, but with a much better clearer morning outlook over the Mediterranean Sea, than the previous year's cloudy, miserable showery view.

A buffet tea, with lots of tasty looking choices, as now honestly feeling so hungry and my need for food, now uppermost in my thoughts.

Meeting up with Mark after a delicious tea, and putting our cases in the lift, seventh floor, a good height, nonetheless, once opening the door to our room, a big problem faced us, not two single beds as expected, but just the one double bed.

As previously discussed, in my band days working away from home, I have shared a double bed with Alan more than a few times, however, just a bit reluctant to join my roommate in bed on this occasion, saying to Mark, I will go down to reception and get the matter sorted out.

The male receptionist understanding my comments and hand gestures, immediately making a few quick phone calls, and sounding a bit annoyed to me, putting down the phone and asking me to wait a few minutes.

A member of staff came to the reception, taking a key, and in my mind, going to inspect a possible room for us.

Returning in just a few minutes, handing the key to the receptionist, some words exchanged, as the receptionist held out the key for me to collect, with a nod and facial gesture to say, "there you go," and giving a verbal instruction to go to floor three.

Some of our party already making their way to the meeting room, now a bit of a rush to get back to the seventh floor to collect our cases and bring them to our third-floor new room.

Both lifts now in constant use, holding me up, and thinking in my younger days I would have run, no sprinted up the stairs, with my case in hand to the seventh floor.

Mark waiting patiently in the room for news, showing him the room key and saying, floor three, let us go.

Not exactly a palatial suite, but a much larger room than the one four floors above us.

A sort of L-shaped room, the double bed in the largest of the two areas, with the single bed pushed into the thin end, and a set of patio doors leading to a balcony between them.

Nevertheless at least a choice of beds, a double and a single, and no arguments who is sleeping where.

Mark promptly saying, "you take the double Terry, I'm fine sleeping here."

Now sorted, and a quick wash and brush up, and soon off to join others in our party for this evenings Bible readings, hymns, and prayers in the hotels meeting room, then to bed for an early night, and fingers crossed, a good night's sleep, ready for an early morning alarm for the official start of our Isreal tour.

A totally different weather greeting us this morning from last years through the night storm, lots of sunshine, and already ridiculously hot as I picked out my case for loading and joining Clive on a much cooler coach.

Only the one night at this hotel, and each individual in our party isolating their cases, and raising the handles, for the hotel staff and driver to load them onto our coach, a case with a handle not raised left until identified, before loading.

Our case identification process taking place each time our party change hotels, and understandable that everyone's case on board the coach, as such a long way to return for a case or anything left behind.

A brother giving an appropriate morning prayer, and then off on our travels, but not before Da'vid began to give a breakdown of the day's planned activities, and journey to our next hotel.

Also, and like last year, giving all our coach full of sightseeing participants an individual number to check everyone now present, prior to leaving the hotel forecourt for a short coastal route to our first stop of the day, Caesarea.

Clive given number one, me, number two, and after allocating everyone else on the coach a number, finishing with Julia, number forty-two, what could go wrong.

Da'vid saying to check the person sitting opposite you, as a second safeguard to establish all on board, and to sit in the same seats each time when boarding the coach, as best if the calling out of numbers becomes difficult to hear for those seated at the front of the coach.

On our way early so as to arrive at our first destination, and subsequent visits ahead of other tourists always the plan, and not feeling as though a rushed visit, with parties already there, and others following up our rear.

Unfortunately, today's first visit one of those days, yes, after a quickly eaten breakfast, way so early, but not what greeted us on our arrival.

Already half a dozen coaches parked up, and sightseers mingling all over the carpark, and just like our party, all evaluating their personal "whisper" headsets.

Caesarea, definitely the place to reach as early as possible, and clearly on this day, all of the same mind.

An amazing deja-vu moment came over me as I entered the colossal amphitheatre, taking my breath away.

Standing on this same spot last year, staring down at row upon row of descending steps, my gaze traversing the vast semi-circle seating area, and finally onto the stage way down below.

Yes, almost a year ago, but this time, sending shivers down my spine.

PA riggers hard at work preparing the stage for what is looking like a forthcoming concert.

Speaker cabinets hung from a huge gantry at either side of the stage and a vast amount of lighting, with a backdrop over a blue Mediterranean Sea, wow, what an amazing experience to set up my drum kit and play at a venue like this.

Descending slowly down the steep stairs and crossing to the front of the stage, lots more personnel working in this location, but no sign of any instruments or backline equipment just yet.

Our party leaving the amphitheatre, using a sort of back door, so to speak, heading in an orderly manner towards a palace ruins, and unprecedented views over the Mediterranean Sea.

The cloudless blue sky, meeting a blue sea, almost as one, with just a mild easterly breeze enhancing an already sweltering coastal climate.

Sat in our hotel bar, feeling full and content, with a glass of house red, and reflecting on all of today's visits.

Highly delighted, and thoroughly satisfied with what I have seen and done, and wanting the second morning of our stay to come around quickly so that I can see more.

Wondering if I would have the same experiences as I did today when visiting places I visited last year, with still more distinct locations presented on this year's itinerary.

I am sure that I will.

Really enjoying my visit to Caesarea, incorporating the national park, 2000-year-old synagogue, Nymphaeum, ruined palace, harbour, and walled city, taking over two hours to complete, with lots of things I did not see, or cannot recall seeing last year.

Da'vid saying only an estimated six percent of this complete site excavated, and confident even more to see in the near future, and I can fully understand why this former Roman capital city and its surroundings so popular.

A long walk from the amphitheatre along the beach promenade, with the Mediterranean Sea and harbour to our left, and hippodrome (chariot racing stadium) to the right of our party, all the way until reaching the walled city.

Our time-consuming walk taking quite a while, and gave an indication

135

to Da'vid as to who of our party the quickest, those slower, and in need of support, and those who knowingly delay our party in reaching its destination to take photographs.

Forty-two people all requiring a diplomatic solution in getting from A to B in the shortest time possible, but to remember that everyone has different strengths, and weaknesses, so allowing everyone to take things at their own pace, but not actually rushing anyone.

To listen intently to all Da'vids information of historic and biblical significance about our current location, what our group will see, and giving adequate time for those of our party being a tad slower, and individuals wishing to take more professional photographs of the sights.

A difficult scenario, for our party to fit in all the planned visits each day as per our scheduled ten-day itinerary, and considering all pre-paid admission arrival, and departure times, a situation that I am sure will take a few days to completely master, and optimistically way before our tour comes to an end.

Leaving Caesarea and heading to Mount Carmel, The Valley of Jezreel and Esdraelon plain, Tel Megiddo, and then arriving in Tiberias, on the sea of Galilee, and our hotel, The Restal, for our three-night stay.

Clive, Darren, and Kathy joining me, sharing a bottle of red wine, and not awfully long before others in our party joined our little get together at the hotel bar lounge.

All excitedly talking about our first day's events, including a tasty lunch, delicious tea, and an enjoyable meeting.

I am pleased to say that our room has two single beds, Mark picking the one closest to the window, overlooking, albeit at some distance, the Sea of Galilee.

Our room has lots of in-between floor space, plenty of capacity for our cases, two bedside tables, each with a bedside lamp, and adjacent electrical sockets for charging our mobile phones and my wrist watch, built-in wardrobe, a dressing table, and a huge flat screen wall mounted TV.

The hotel has an inviting kidney shaped pool, and patio area, both of which I am sure will get a visit from some of us tomorrow, before tea, that's if our innovative plan to keep everyone as close together as possible when returning to our coach after each visit, essentially works.

Simple really, as the tallest person in our group, and wearing the brightest of t-shirts, I will always bring up the rear, constantly checking our party heading back to the coach, from whichever itinerary location.

Not necessarily to quickly usher the less speedy walkers, but to ensure that Da'vid can see me when way up at the front of our party, with a wave or thumbs up from me ensures he keeps moving forward while discussing our place of interest, rather than continually waiting for everyone to catch up.

Not over late to bed, Mark not joining our little group at the bar, and already asleep, and thoughtfully had turned on my bedside lamp, not over bright, but enough to see without having to turn on the rooms more powerful centre light.

Why then the more you try to remain quiet, the worse it becomes.

Setting my mobile phone alarm for a 06.00hr wakeup call, it went off when attempting to adjust the volume, then when removing my shorts, some coins fell from my pocket, rattling along the tiled bedroom floor.

Next, habitually flushing the toilet when leaving the bathroom, what a disaster, fortunately Mark could not recall my clumsiness, when I explained what had transpired at breakfast, apologising profusely at first light.

Breakfast soon eaten, certainly hungry this morning, and eating such a lot at teatime, all of my daily exercise certainly giving me an appetite.

Walking such a lot from our coach carpark, to wherever our place of interest located, and back again, numerous times daily.

Exactly what I wanted to do, seeing, and hearing as much as possible about each place visited every day, and one of the main reasons I found last year's tour exactly to my liking, and so pleased I could join this year's Christadelphian group.

However, some of our party's brothers and sisters finding themselves worn out, and only the first day of our tour.

Perhaps our second day's visits will involve less walking, and more time to relax between places, but if last year's locations anything to compare with, I doubt that very much.

First stop, Beit She'an, one of the oldest towns in the world, located twelve miles south of the Sea of Galilee and four miles west of Jordan.

Beit She'an, history tells us occupied since 4000BC, where excavations have now exposed at least eighteen separate activity levels, suggesting that each successive conqueror destroyed the existing town, and built a new one on its predecessors ruins.

Attracting hundreds of thousands of visitors each year, this tourist site brough back memories of last year's visit.

However, this year some entertainment on the cards, when Da'vid said to follow him to the latrine (toilet) area.

Looking over a wall, to a much lower section of the site, sat Darren on one of a row of ancient loo's, a great big grin on his face and waving to us.

Now I mentioned lots of walking earlier, and this location no different, lots and lots of walking, and for a small splinter group leaving our party, also climbing up lots of steps to an elevated former stronghold location, atop of a high manmade hill or tel.

I declined last year, but when watching Julia set off up the steps like a spring chicken, and at ten years older than me, I did wish I had made the effort.

Though, not outdone this time around, duly setting off, one of the leaders to make it to the top, and in record time.

The views over the whole region below us looking amazing, certainly appreciating the excavations that have taken place to expose this former amazing city, reduced to a pile of rubble following an earthquake in AD-749.

Our downward journey much more relaxed, and as agreed the following day, I would follow up at the rear as our small party joined other members of our group heading towards the giftshop and a much-needed ice-cream.

All our group carried plenty of water, and lots of super chilled bottled water available daily on our coach at a much-reduced cost, and if like last year, I will drink gallons, perspiration constantly pouring out in this May heat, and exacerbated when walking, climbing, and descending lots of steps.

Heading to Harod Valley next, lunch and then to Ein Harod (Gideons spring) at the foot of Mount Gilboa.

The waters of this crystal-clear spring have continued relentlessly to run since long ago, and prior to Harod Gideon choosing three hundred men to fight the Midianites in 1050BC.

Nazareth next, and yet another hilly long walk, first through a large visitor's centre and then outdoors to a remake of a "living history" village, a first for me, and what an enjoyable experience.

Meeting a shepherd, weaver, and a carpenter, who took time to demonstrate their ancient skills, seeing sheep, goats, and of course donkeys, that equally as good then, as now, used for the transportation of goods and people.

Also sitting in a synagogue and listening to a local guide reading a passage from Luke 4: 16-20.

Next stop, Mount Arbel, between Magdala (home of Mary Magdalene) and Tiberias on the western shore of the Sea of Galilee.

Astonishing views from the lookout over Safed, Tiberias, the Golan Heights and on a noticeably cloudless day.

Mount Hermon in the north and Mount Tabor in the south and most of the sea of Galilee, what a view, this whole region declared a nature reserve in 1967.

Our final stop of the day, the plain of Gennesaret viewed from the heights of the Arbel cliffs, yet another amazing view across a vast fertile region of land on the northwest shore of the Sea of Galilee.

Lots of walking and climbing today, but our plan of me staying at the rear appears successful, with no stragglers per say.

A brother and sister stand out as obviously keen photographers, and usually both to the rear of me, but more fit and able than others to quickly catch up to our strewn-out group of sightseers, so not a worry for me or Da'vid, and all making the coach, without having to wait for anyone.

Nonetheless, still very tiring for some of our less able brothers and sisters, and not alerted of any complaints as yet.

Julia also appears to manage incredibly good at the tender age of eighty years old, or how Julia would say, eighty-years young.

I could see that I had caught the sun, even when using a factor 50 suncream, as others in our group looking a little red-faced, although not sure from the suns hot ray's, or simply through exhaustion.

Day two over, and looking forward to sailing on the Sea of Galilee in the morning, and then on to a new site for me, Nof Ginosar, a Hebrew pronunciation of the name of the ancient town of Gennesaret.

Little remaining of this town today, then a short drive to Capernaum, that tradition says named after Nahum the prophet in BC 713, reputedly buried there.

However, sleep first, everyone turning in early, but a quick glass of wine first in a rather busy boisterous lounge, all talking over loudly, echoing all around, and not all from our remaining small group.

A few of us enjoying each other's company over a bottle or two of quality vino, and conversations taking lots of twists and turns, a comprehensive view of all sorts of subjects.

Talking about religious themes, holidays, stargazing, former jobs, and in particular, my time as a professional musician in our band Black Lace, and Stormer, my time as a semi professional musician in bands, Aircrew, and Mister Twister, also my retirement hobbies at the Rosse observatory, or Supporting Music for All (SM4LL).

My time to retire to my room would not come quickly enough, remembering to hold back my yawns so as not to appear bored of other thought-provoking conversations, and knowing that my roommate, Mark, had retired to the bedroom almost two hours ago.

Nevertheless, no calamities this time around, preparing myself in advance, ensuring my phone alarm already set for my morning wake-up call, and checking I had no coins in my pocket in the lift while on the way up to my third-floor room.

Ensuring I did not turn on the bathroom light until firmly, but quietly shutting the door.

Bedtime ablutions quickly taking place, turning off the light and gently opening the bathroom door, and lastly tiptoeing to bed, turning off the bedside lamp, and not hearing anything until the sound of my six o'clock alarm, waking me from a deep sleep.

Little did I know at this time, but a ritual of sorts taking place every evening from now on.

Between the two of us, Mark always the first to call it a day, and going up to our room, preferring a quiet nightly read, before finally dropping to sleep.

Mark awake and up, already in the bathroom, just like Trevor last year, and silently taking place without waking me up.

Perhaps a little too much wine for an impromptu night cap, and I have to say a thoroughly enjoyed one, certainly helping me sleep, although I cannot remember indulging in any alcoholic beverages ahead of bedtime last year though, strange...

This year's group getting along great, to say all of forty-two of us, our last night in this particular hotel, bags packed, loaded onto our coach, and the next full day of visits ahead of us.

Scheduled visits to Tel Hazor, the Dan nature reserve, Tel Dan, Banias, The Sanctuary of Pan, Mount Bental, The Jorden Valley, and the Judean wilderness, a full day, and a hard slog.

What fantastic experiences though, all tired, but coped excellently in the heat, and upon our arrival at the Kalya Kibbutz for a two-night stay, and a definite dip required in the more than ample swimming pool.

Yesterday's swimming pool more than adequate for a few short lengths, but a huge pool by comparison, and a traditional oblong shape, ideal for swimming lengths or breadths if preferred.

Although a long hot exhausting day, I still managed double figures swimming lengths ahead of teatime.

Once again the warm friendly welcoming atmosphere of this superb kibbutz hitting all the right notes, the food, room cleanliness, and hospitality second to none, making our two-night stop-over an unforgettable experience.

More so, having two bottles of wine for our pre-bedtime get-together, and no available bottle opener, a disaster.

Clive making numerous efforts, along with using various utensils in an attempt to remove the cork stopper from a bottle of red, almost disintegrating the stopper, quickly realising this red fluid delight with bits of cork floating in a glass, definitely not an ideal tasty nightcap.

Abruptly stopping his attempt to open the bottle before that happening. What a dilemma.

However, I called at the onsite shop, and along with purchasing a bottle of red for the table, also taking the initiative to obtain a bottle opener, and using this item as a little inducement to raise a few laughs amongst our small splinter party.

A lovely enjoyable evening, under a clear night sky, and on this occasion Mark joining us, after taking a long walk around the kibbutz perimeter with his daughter.

Tonight, I am not worried about my bedtime ablutions and getting ready for sleep, as everyone continued to enjoy lots of jovial banter until just after midnight.

Sleeping remarkably sound until my alarm, noticing Mark already in the bathroom.

After breakfast, a coach ride to the Judean wilderness and Masada, Ein Gedi, named Davids's waterfall, both locations I visited last year, but so looking forward to seeing and taking part in the long uphill climb to David's waterfall, and taking a ride once again on the huge cable lift to the Masada summit.

Lots more walking, and for some sightseers, an opportunity to opt out, and sit in the welcoming shade, especially for those who have previously visited this location, spotting a few heading for the canopies and seating areas, with plenty of bottled water to hand.

Next stop, the Dead Sea, and now my third time at this location, 1979, 2022 and now 2023, and could not wait to experience total weightlessness.

Floating around for almost an hour, but as I explained in an earlier chapter, a changed occurrence from forty-four years ago in 1979, than witnessed today.

Heading back to Kalya Kibbutz after a much-needed lunch, with a few of us enjoying a sun catching, relaxing few hours beside the pool.

Taking to the pool once again, completing twenty-six lengths, and a restful sunbed nap, a shower and changed ahead of our 19.00hr tea.

Our itinerary now taking the form of last year, lots of visits while heading towards Jerusalem, and other locations over the next three-days, and all in and around this century's old city, often mentioned in the Bible.

Looking back over this year's sightseeing Israel holiday, I can only describe as yet another amazing once again experience, and for all sorts of reasons.

Yes, the itinerary, although similar in lots of ways to last year, however, seeing and hearing so much more, in particular from the unique people I have travelled and made lots of friends with.

The additional knowledge I have gained, as in biblical, historical and the Christadelphian faith, especially from my coach seat and room partners, Clive, Mark, and Julia.

They overheard lots of what Clive had discussed with me while travelling, and adding to, and confirming what conversations took place, and our guide, Da'vid doing what he does best.

Also, all our pre bedtime chats with our little group, especially Darren, Clive, Kathy, Lyndsay, and Cathy, and anyone else who joined us.

So much so, I have made a point to Julia that if cautiously mentioned a further trip organised for departure in November 2024, to count me in as a definite addition to the group.

CHAPTER FOURTEEN

My Dad

(A Complicated Synonym)

Not often one can boast, if this the correct way of describing what I am about to say in the imminent chapter.

All will become clear shortly.

My dad Jim passed away on March 31st, 1986, at just sixty-one years of age, after a brave, and courageous fight with throat cancer.

In remission after chemotherapy, following his diagnosis in 1982, and barely a year after taking early retirement as a coal miner, working his last years at the Manor colliery, and certainly not a great start to the retirement mum and dad had planned.

Cancer returning with a vengeance in late 1985, and with no hope of any treatment that would give him some quality of life in the time that remained.

Leaving mum, a widow at the age of fifty-five, with just my brother John still at home, myself, Brian, and Marcia all married, and in our own homes.

However, Jim, my dad, mums second husband, as mum's first marriage to Arthur Davis, ended in divorce.

My grandma, from mums side, told me that the man I had called dad for fourteen years, Jim, in fact my stepdad, my two brothers, and sister my stepsiblings.

This information corroborated according to my tatty looking, and somewhat crudely altered birth certificate, mums previous husband Arthur Davis, my father.

Laying my stepdad Jim to rest in 1986, and more than satisfied with my childhood, calling Jim dad all of these years, so not that interested at first in looking at discovering my "real dad" and producing an active "family tree."

My dad Jim always giving me good advice while as a youngster, incredibly supportive throughout my childhood, even getting me my first job from leaving school.

Jim knew Harry Robinson very well, often chatting over a pint in the Scarbough Arms pub.

Harry, a foreman at a building firm in Ossett, Raymond Horner Ltd, and the company looking to employ an apprentice joiner, to work alongside Harry and a chap called Fred Patterson in their joiners shop.

I had enjoyed joinery lessons in school, so an obvious ambition to become a carpenter, and took this opportunity with open arms.

Starting my job of work on the Monday after leaving school on the Friday, and only just a few months after my fifteenth birthday.

Following through over five years at building college, and obtaining professional qualifications, so a definite thank you to my dad Jim, and Harry for his confidence to employ me.

Jim an immensely proud dad, especially so when I represented the UK in the 1979 Eurovision Song Contest, held in Israel, as a drummer with our band Black Lace.

Lots of my family meeting in the Peacock Hotel pub, to watch the three-hour show, mum saying dad visibly moved throughout the whole performance.

Also, and while in remission, dad helping me decorate when moving to my new home on Balne Lane, lots of work to do, with four bedrooms, bathroom, a through lounge, hall, and kitchen, not putting him off one bit.

Dad proud of my sister and brothers, offering the same help, time and time again, always on hand whatever required of his services.

One big reason of many, why I did not feel the need to search for my blood father, but after a few weeks of constant banter from my work colleague Ken, eventually giving in, and making a start.

Obtaining mums birth certificate, a good place to begin, and two wedding certificates, mums parents at birth, and their wedding certificates, and of course a new unaltered long birth certificate for myself.

So far so good, nonetheless, things will get a little more complicated, as when putting together my family genealogy, the information I am starting to gather, will dramatically change one or two things.

Everything confirmed just as mum and grandma had explained to me, Arthur my "dad," including confirmation that mum the only child of a second marriage, something I had known for a few years.

My granddad's first wife died, grandma married granddad, and gave birth to mum, their only child, and mum having a stepbrother, James, from gradads first marriage.

Uncle James passing away on my birthday at the age of just fifty-five.

Mum married Arthur in 1949, divorced in1953, and mum then married to Jim in 1954, almost two years after giving birth to me, Brian born in 1955, Marcia 1960, and John in 1962.

Amazed at information no matter how sensitive, easily obtained from various websites these days, including family tree facts.

Quickly finding Arthur, including a second marriage to Doreen, grandparents, aunties, and uncles, but no blood brothers or sisters for me, so far.

When discussing my intentions with mum, and my progress to date, mum looked me in the eye, and dropped a further bombshell, saying with a smile.

Arthur, not my blood father either, that pleasure would fall to a man called Tom.

The plot thickens, and now giving me a headache putting all of this together in some sort of chronological order.

Ok, so Jim and Arthur definitely not my blood fathers, and no further information available at this point, other than Tom and mum, started an affair in 1951, while Tom lodged with Grandma and Granddad, and mums husband Arthur, serving in India as a corporal in the RAF.

Mum shedding a little more light on Tom, openly admitting she could not recall Toms surname after so many years, and further explaining that while expecting me, Arthur came home on leave, and after establishing mums now obvious pregnancy, a noisy fracas taking place between Arthur and Tom.

With so much fuss in Grandma and Granads front garden, it soon became inevitable that the police needed to intervene, arresting Tom, and taking him along to Wakefield Wood Street Police station.

Following my relentless on-line research, and with constant help from Ken, I currently have lots of incriminating information to hand, and now eager to continue with Ken to complete my family tree once and for all, as Ken the key instigator of starting my accurate family lineage in the first place.

Ken would constantly say that to "find" my dad, would bring an end to speculation, and with relatives alive or dead, you may get to know all of your recent family history, certainly the last one-hundred years, and possibly even further back in time, as on-line information frequently updated.

In an attempt to give me a pre-Christmas surprise, Ken telephoned the Wakefield Archive building, to seek information of Tom's arrest.

However, no information given to Ken, so obtaining my father's full name as a pre-works do Christmas present, came crashing down.

Instead, Ken passing on the telephone number for me to get in touch.

Giving the address of our former family home, and approximate dates in early 1952 of when this altercation between Arthur and Tom may have taken place, and an indication of Toms possible arrest, the lady officer advised me that this information if correct, recorded in a ledger.

The knowledge I had gained, proved accurate enough to find the full name of my biological father Tom.

Thomas James Kemp, Tom, for short, my blood father, and a copy of the ledger page where the information recorded given to me, but Tom not the name on my birth certificate.

Mum explained, soon after my birth, Tom, Arthur, and mum, all in total agreement that I should take Arthurs surname, because mum and Arthur, at this point in time, still married.

Complicated, absolutely, and taking a little time for all of this to penetrate my somewhat modest grey matter.

However, now fully understanding the complexity of mums life while in her late teens and early twenties, and not forgetting my Grandma and Grandad, and of course mum, who had held everything together in my early life.

After Jim, my step dads death, Mum leading a single life until meeting Peter Hammond on a "girls" night out, and would become mums partner in 1993, almost seven years after the death of her second husband, Jim.

147

All our family taking an instant liking to this lovely man, almost ten-years mums junior, nonetheless, fitting perfectly into our family life.

Bringing domestic bliss for mum once again, and no surprise when Peter gave notice on his single persons flat, to join mum and John, in our family home on Sycamore Avenue.

John engaged to Gill, and not long before he and Gill joined in matrimonial harmony, and fleeing the nest, leaving mum and Peter to get along as a couple.

Mum and Jim did not have a car during our childhood, although Jim could drive, even learning his brother-in-law John Bartram to drive and pass his test, this immediately changed when Peter eternally joined our family.

Mum and Peter, purchasing a two previous owner good condition, two-door Ford Fiesta in red, enabling them to visit us siblings for a change, rather than the other way around, and to drive to east and west coastal districts, and many other places of interest.

Mum thrilled to bits, and clearly enjoying their many journeys around beauty spots with-in a hundred mile or so radius from home.

Years and years since I caught a service bus in and around Wakefield, but had I done so, I may have come across Peter, as he served lots of years working for the old West Riding bus company as a bus driver.

Working the many neighbourhoods, and routes in and around Wakefield, and you would have thought fed up with driving with the amount of traffic on our roads these days, although retired from the busses when he met mum, now a security guard for a local firm.

Peter becoming our stepdad, and grandad to our children, in every sense, enjoying many outings to restaurants with all our family, joining mum at John and Gills wedding, also babysitting, dog sitting, house sitting, shopping for family, you name it, Peter always the first to volunteer to do whatever required, for each of our families.

Peter also loved his gardening, making an excellent job of everything botanical, while living with mum in our former family home.

However, when in the garden cutting the hedge, weeding, and cutting grass, Peter suffered a severe chest problem, requiring complete rest, and a heart pacemaker fitting, which forced his early retirement.

The garden had become demanding work for both Peter and mum, so a huge decision made to move from our three-bedroom family home, with a lovely south-west facing garden, where all of our family had enjoyed lots of outdoor time.

Their imminent relocation taking them to a first-floor, two-bedroom flat, set in communal gardens, just a few hundred yards away, and still on the Peacock Estate.

At the very least, the council's environmental services team maintains the lawns, shrubs, and flowerbeds, so that would offer some benefit, helping to prolong Peters ailing but controllable health.

May 1997, the day of the move, a sad time for me, and my sister and stepbrothers, since lots of our memories taking place in and around this house, and always enjoying our visits to see them both, and recalling what amazing occurrences took place there as kids.

Our neighbours Chris and Frank also upset at the move, as mum and Christine close friends, but would remain so even years after the move.

A new chapter for mum and Peter though, and one they grasped with both hands, and figuratively speaking, exactly what Peter did.

Thankfully, Peters garden spade, fork, and rake, not disposed of, as he began to use them once again in earnest, to make the bland open plan, front lawn garden, a sight to behold.

Forming boarder flower beds, fitting hanging baskets, and planting a rose tree, all with permission, winning prizes from their landlord for best kept front open plan garden, and picking up their awards following a lavish meal and presentation, at Wakefield's Cedar Court Hotel.

Peter had suffered constant pain, and a slight back disfigurement since childhood when he fell from a tree, but this did not appear to slow him down one bit.

Peter part-exchanged the red Fiesta for a similar model after a few years of trouble-free motoring, this time in a shade of white, and after a further year, and travelling many more miles around the country, this car a trade-in for yet another car.

Purchasing a brand new two door Suzuki, yet another red one, and far more economical for their extended journeys than the two fiesta's.

One of their favourite destinations to take the car to the seaside resort of Skegness, spending a few two-week holidays over a number of years at the same guest house, close to the sea front, making new friends, and acquaintances along the way.

When mum and Peter talked of these holidays, they brought back lots of memories of my Black Lace days while playing in Skegness during our lengthy summer season work.

In particular, Bottons Fun Park in the long sizzling summer of 1976, and Butlins Holiday resort in 1977, two great locations to learn our musical craft in the first two-years of becoming professional musicians.

The living room window from mum and Peters Gibson Avenue first floor flat, overlooked, at some distance, the rear of Lincoln Street, and coincidently, to the rear garden of my first home, 85 Lincoln Street, purchased some nine-months prior to my July 1973 marriage to Jacky.

Although at the time of this purchase, my own rear view from my Lincoln Street home, overlooked council allotments, and around three-years later when construction commenced to build these blocks of flats.

I do digress.

I now have a name, Thomas James Kemp, my blood father, and just about over that initial shock, and about time I took the initiative to locate my biological dad, and piece together my blood family.

Unknown at this time if Tom still alive, as according to his birth certificate, now around eighty-eight years old, and I could not find a death recorded for him, so feeling positive.

As I began to receive information connected to my family tree, I immediately added this on Genes Reunited, and almost as quickly, other genealogy research individuals started to get in touch.

Ironically, when adding Tom's name, his brothers, sisters, parents, and grandparents, after some painstaking research, instantly raised the number of emails received.

All asking for permission to look at my family tree, to check the possibility of me, or my newfound family members, relatives of theirs.

Quickly eliminating most of these early requests, leaving just two requiring a reply, and demanded a little more investigation, one family from York, and the other in Gravesend.

Both parties rejecting the York emails once Toms official birth date, and year confirmed, leaving just the Gravesend contact to endorse.

Hearing from John and Brenda in Gravesend began to put everything in place, Tom not only a relative of Brenda, but had also known John for over thirty years, and John actually worked with Tom for around twenty of those years.

John and Brenda making the arrangements following a family get together, Tom eager to meet, and wanting me to travel down to Gravesend.

Brenda picking up Tom from his home in Dartford, for a joint meeting at their Gravesend home.

Our meeting after almost fifty-six years an unforgettable experience, and with mums permission, bringing Tom at the age of eighty-eight, back to Yorkshire to stay with me for a few weeks, and meet mum once again.

Peter electing to drive mum to my home for a first meeting back in Wakefield, and Tom making the long journey and staying a few more times.

His age, and failing health, prevented him from travelling with me over the long distance between Wakefield and Dartford for further visits.

I met all my surviving relatives, and sadly attended funerals of others, making numerous regular visits, and in touch either via social media platforms, telephone, or letter with those still with us to this day.

Peter, a true gentleman throughout the three years Tom travelled with me to visit my family and friends in and around Wakefield.

Tom enjoying our trips to mum and Peters flat, everyone happy to listen to his many stories about the time spent in Wakefield in the early fifties.

Sadly, Tom passed away in Dartford hospital with bowel cancer on November 28th, 2014.

Travelling down to Dartford to help sort out his belongings, and clear his bungalow home, making it ready to hand back to the housing association.

I now have lots of my dad Toms belongings and memorabilia of my family, including some hand tools, and two mouthorgans, probably the same ones he used to play in pubs when living at grandma and granddads house in the early fifties.

Toms funeral taking place on December 18th, 2014, family members in attendance from far and wide, including many friends, and neighbours.

The Dart public house Dartford, relatives choosing this pub for Toms funeral wake, a regular band gig at the time, and where the Rolling

Stones rehearsed, long before the band became world superstars, all those years ago.

I am so pleased I did eventually acknowledge Ken's persistence, and take the initiative to search, and find Tom, and in hindsight perhaps should have made the effort some years earlier.

With Kens help, I did get to meet him and my blood relatives, those few years making a massive difference to my outlook, and bringing together my mum and dad, even for just a brief time, but a time I will never forget.

Peters health not that good either, requiring a second pacemaker after suffering a mild stroke, and spending almost three-weeks in Pinderfields hospital.

Mum thinking, he would not get better, as for the period in hospital, most of the time in a semi-conscious state, constantly fidgeting in bed, and I would think unaware he had visitors.

Thankfully, and to everyone's astonishment, Peter did recover, although mum knowing Peter not in good health, and saying when discharged from hospital, not seeming the same person as prior to his illness.

However, astounding everyone, quickly recovering, and back to our family, so much so, electing to become mums carer, providing for mums every day needs, including meals and bedtime necessities.

Not that mum had become disabled, although now fully recovered after a fall in the kitchen, and requiring a replacement hip, and surgery to her shoulder and wrist, on the contrary, Peter more the man who cares about mum, and wanted to do the absolute best for her.

All of our close family unit giving as much help as possible during this time, and all fully aware of the twenty-four-seven attention Peter gave to mum.

At one of my regular visits, mum pointed out an obituary notice in our weekly newspaper the Wakefield Express.

My dad, as written on my birth certificate, Arthur Davies, had passed away, and giving a time, date, and funeral location.

Mum saying she would like to attend, however still not one hundred percent with her health, acknowledging this, saying I would like to go, and represent the both of us.

The church and place of rest situated in Sharlston, just a few miles on the outskirts of Wakefield.

Only six people attended the funeral, including the local vicar, and my presence an obvious surprise to the mourners attending.

I did make myself known to a husband and wife, who Arthur had known for a few years, although none present, knew of my existence.

Mum told me that while married to Arthur, they had both taken fertility tests, and Arthur could not have children, this confirmed, as when married to Doreen, Arthurs second marriage, they had no children, either because of medical reasons, or choice.

Talking with Arthurs friends I learnt that he and Doreen had become great at ballroom dancing, winning lots of trophies during their time together, and told that upon his death, "things" may come to light.

That certainly coming true, with me turning up, although they all knew that Arthur had married previously, but did not know of me, laughingly saying, I had become the proverbial, skeleton in the cupboard.

Those mourners present at his funeral, said such a shame that I had not got to know him beforehand, as since the death of his wife Doreen, almost twenty-two years earlier, he had become lonely.

On my return from Arthurs funeral, telling mum what had transpired, and said no funeral wake had taking place to catch up on lots more about Arthur, the name in the fathers column of my birth certificate.

During our family visits, mum and Peter often reflecting on memories of their many day trips, and holidays in the car, also many Monday to Friday coach trips, to locations all over the country that they enjoyed, meeting similar likeminded holiday makers too.

Pointing out that their Christmas card list, getting ever longer, besides adding many names, and telephone numbers in their landline phone book, and to Peters mobile phone.

Mum and Peter enjoyed dog sitting, my mother and son, at times demanding Lhasa Apso's, often stayed over at our house, two-weeks at a time, living in our bungalow, our Abri.

Saying it felt like having an extra-long holiday, enjoying our large gardens, and open views across the valley towards the Pennines, usually while me, and my family appreciating some warmth in Spanish resorts, and of course some much-needed sun.

Lottie and Ted enjoying mum and Peters twenty-four-seven company, and of course getting regularly spoilt, with lots of doggy treats, love, and heaps of affection.

Peters health didn't improve, and as such he qualified for an invalidity car, preferring a make and model that suited mums ability to get in and out with ease.

Choosing a slightly better kerb hight SUV model, rather than a traditional almost sitting on the tarmac sort of low car.

Everything Peter did, always having mums abilities, and health in mind, rather than exclusively his own preference.

Peter enjoyed sitting at his P.C. located in the small second bedroom, messaging family, internet shopping, and uploading many photographs of their travels, also short holiday and family video clips, a hobby he took to like a duck to water.

One of Peter's most pleasurable talents, showing images of his love of wildlife, and everyone enjoying a particular Christmas treat, Peter using these images when making yearly calendars for all our family, and their many friends.

Starting around September, purchasing countless packs of A4 glossy paper, to personalise each front cover for whichever family member or friends that Peter made them for.

Always an enjoyable treat as each month expired, wondering which images he had chosen of a past party, family gathering or holiday, bringing those memories to life once again.

During covid lockdown, both mum and Peter had spent time in hospital with this dreaded sickness.

Mum in hospital for over a week, and a further two weeks in a care home to convalesce, Peter on the other hand, discharged from hospital after only a few days.

Certainly not fully recovered, and not looking his best, nevertheless, healthy enough to release his hospital bed for other desperately ill and needy patients.

Peter celebrated his eightieth birthday at home, and as a treat, and unbeknown to mum and Peter, all the family arranged to meet outside mum and Peters flat, while remaining socially distant from each other, to wish him all the absolute best.

Peter and mum opened up the patio doors to their Juliet balcony, clearly emotional, Peter began to take lots of photographs of us stood in the rain, singing our hearts out to this truly remarkable man.

Unable to enter their flat because of lockdown, but still a poignant time for everyone present, and a lasting memory of a loving couple.

Peter taking delivery of a new invalidity car, a dark blue Ford Kuga, slightly larger than his last Vauxhall SUV, and this new car possibly a little big for their garage.

Sadly, this would prove correct, as Peter struck the driver's side wheel arch, just a small dent, and scratch, and requiring a little work not only to the new car, but to the garage doorframe too.

Taking along a claw hammer and wrecking bar to straighten out the steel up-and-over doorframe, whilst a family friend taking the repairs in hand required to Peters car.

Following this incident, the new car remained on the road at the front of the flat from this day forward, Peter not attempting to put it in the garage.

All feeling that this particular incident, an unquestionable turning point in Peters health, regrettably for the worst.

Although not requiring a hospital bed, Peter becoming weak, and lethargic, necessitating treatment, and eventually home visits from care workers.

My sister, sister-in-law, me, and my stepbrothers all "mucking in," whenever possible, running errands for mum, furthermore, helping with Peters treatment for as long as possible, until others in the care industry, taking away that daily course of action from our family.

A nurse telling us that we had done as much as possible with Peter at home, nonetheless, his condition had deteriorated beyond our capabilities, and would necessitate admitting him to a hospice.

Making a telephone call from mum and Peters flat, the nurse informing us a place located for Peter at Pontefract Prince of Wales Hospice, and told an ambulance would arrive shortly.

A sad time, as Peter knew that this the last day spent together with mum at home, saying "it's much too soon," many, many times, as the paramedics carefully placed him on a stretcher.

Peters new car returned to the distributers, with little recorded mileage, certainly none for over two months, and the car in perfect condition, well almost.

Visiting Peter at the hospice, bringing tears to our eyes, although sat up in bed, and eating a yogurt, he looked healthy, and able to come home, sadly, all knowing just a minor reprieve on his last few days with us.

Mum also saying he looked healthy, certainly making her feel much better, sadly his best day, as from then on, Peter taking induced medication, until his passing.

Peters funeral taking place with all covid restrictions still in position, with only sixteen mourners allowed to attend.

That in itself would create a bit of tension, as some of Peters family, who Peter had not seen for years now in touch.

Despite knowing of Peters terminal illness, had not attended mums, the hospital or hospice while alive, now wanting to attend his funeral.

Our family taking up twelve places, as all of us constantly with him throughout mum and Peters almost twenty-nine-year relationship, leaving four places, Peters two sisters, a brother, and the youngest of two sons taking these.

Peter had a good association with this son, playing snooker once a week, however he had only visited a few times when mum and Peter moved to the flat, quite a lot of years ago.

My sister Marcia held Peters funeral wake at her home in Crigglestone, and all attended, even those that could not enter the crematorium chapel, earlier emotions put aside to help give Peter the send-off he justly deserved.

Peters ashes scatted under a huge tree on the front lawn of the crematorium grounds, and as Peter loved bird watching, taking hundreds of photographs, and having lots of books, a further memorial discussed.

All deciding to purchase a bird box, adding appropriate words on a small but readable disc, and having this fixed to the tree, along with a plaque close to the area where his scattered ashes lay.

Peter remembered with lots of love and affection, and constantly talked about.

Our family will always remember him.

♡ R.I.P. Dad ♡

James Richard DOBSON – March 31st, 1986.
Thomas James Kemp – November 28th, 2014.
Arthur DAVIES – April 30th, 2017.
Peter HAMMOND – April 24th, 2021.

AT THE END OF LIFE

In the end, it's not the years in your life that count.
It's the life in your years.

Abraham Lincoln

....

What really matters is not what we bought,
BUT - What we built.

Not what we have got,
BUT - What we shared.

Not our competence,
BUT - Our character.

Not our success,
BUT - Our significance.

Live a life that matters,
LIVE A LIFE OF LOVE.

Author unknown

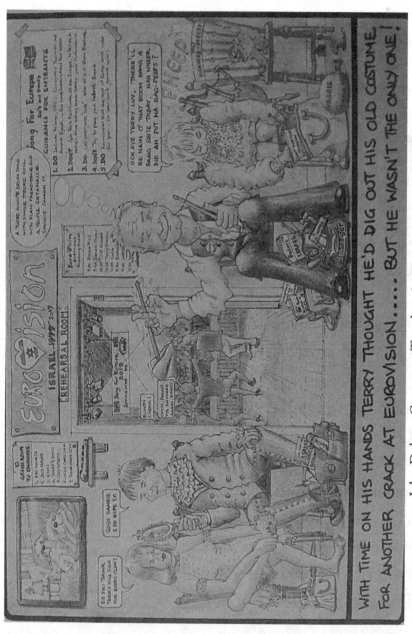

John Dales – Cartoon – Terry's retirememnt present – 2018

Terry & Julia – Amanda & Daves home - April 2022

Julia – Sea of Galilee - Israel - April 2023

Brian – John – Marcia – Mum – Peter – Terry

Terry – Mum – Dad Tom - 2010

Thomas James Kemp (Dad Tom)

Drummer Splash Back - 2024

Cooker Hob - splash back – 2024

Dead Sea - Israel – 2023

Jerusalem – Israel – 2023

Stepped Pyramid of Djoser -Egypt – 2022

River Nile Cruise – Egypt – 2022

Terry – Egypt – 2022

Space Shuttle Atlantis – Terry - Kennedy Space Centre – 2024

Warren – James H Newman – Terry – Kennedy Space Centre 2024

VAB – Space Coast – Florida – 2024

Rocket Garden – Kennedy Space Centre – 2024

West Yorkshire Astronomical Society –
(WYAS) - Outreach Gazebo 2024

West Yorkshire Astronomical Society – (WYAS) – The Observatory

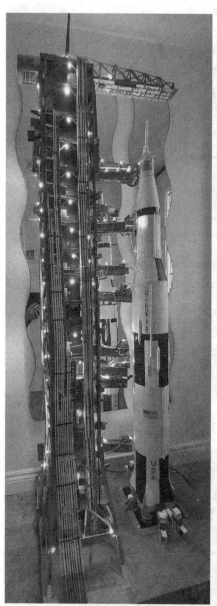

The Rocket – (Saturn Five - from Redcar) - 2024

Birthday Cake – March 2022

Liam – Band of the Irish Guards – Trooping the Colours 2024

Concorde – IWM Duxford 2024

John Dales Cartoon – 2024

WHAT A WEEKEND

I went to the doctors, I wasn't that ill, but he said that I ought to try this new pill.

Take it on a Friday, at teatime is right, and you'll get lots of pleasure all through the night.

I did what he said just after my tea, and notice my wife grinning at me.

A look of expectancy she tried not to show, I covered my lap as I started to grow.

We went to bed early we put out the light, we did a Rod Stewart all through the night.

The following morning, I looked with a stare, the pill was still working the bulge was still there.

"Why should we waste it" that's what my wife said, so we gulped down our breakfast and went back to bed.

We stayed there all day we couldn't do more; we then tried the kitchen the stairs and the floor.

On Sunday she said, "Let's go into town," I can't go out yet until it goes down, she said, "Please don't tell me you are still erect, I didn't know pills could have this effect.

We did it all day every which way and when, we finished all that we just started again, my wife got dressed up in Satin and lace, I thought, "Not again!" she could tell by my face.

175

We had a wonderful time and then had some soup, as the bulge in my trousers started to droop, I think I will miss it and my wife will too, though I'll not be embarrassed when I'm facing you.

Viagra on Fridays that'll do me,

BUT NEVER AGAIN WILL I EVER TAKE THREE!

Dennis Glossop (2019)

ALIVE AND KICKING

This expression first recorded, and sometimes shortened to:-

"Live and Kicking,"

Coastal fishmongers originally used this phrase when selling their wares, usually shouted out in full voice to attract and convince customers of the freshness of the fish they are selling.

Considered a cliché since 1850.

The variant used today:-
"Alive and Kicking"
originating in the 1960's as the repudiation of someone's reported demise.

CHAPTER FIFTEEN

End of an Era

My career or vocation, if you can call it that, of playing drums in bands a long one, over fifty-five years, of performing throughout the country in working men's clubs, private clubs, pubs, night, and variety clubs, and appearances on TV in the UK and abroad, has finally come to an end.

As mentioned time and time again, years have literally flown, with so many memories and lifelong friendships mostly conceived while performing and playing my drums in bands.

So much fun and laughter with other musicians either at rehearsals or on stage, or staying in pro-digs around the country.

Individuals, and families, from far and wide who had come along to see our shows, some of which required tickets, others either while on summer holidays while our band played lengthy summer seasons, or just present when our band booked to play in various establishments.

I remember the very start of my journey, spending time with my friend Freddy Pearson, recognising him as a good "air" drummer.

Miming to hits of the Shadows, and giving me the inspiration to try and become a little ambidextrous, attempting to copy him, knocking dust out of his mum's best room chair arms with super thick knitting needles.

My neighbour, Billy Blackburn, playing drums in a jazz trio, donating an old drum kit to me, my first, to tinker with, clean up, re skin and knock up a tune or two.

Annoying mum and dad to the point of me and the drumkit, permanently barred from ever setting up and playing in the house.

My presence behind a drum kit, totally through default, although always wanting to become a drummer in a band, but originally I had an aspiration of becoming a bass player.

However, in Ian's band, Raymond Bolland filling the post of a four-string bass guitar, his home in an off-licence shop next to Howarth Funeral Directors, on New Scarbrough, and just a few hundred yards from my home.

Derek Tucker sat in the drummers position, with Roger Haigh on guitar, (Roger sadly not with us anymore) all originally school mates at Thornes House school where this band started, including singer, Steve Scholey from Snapethorpe School.

Getting to know and watch Ian and the band in rehearsals, above Ian's dad's joinery workshop, and also performing at a few local venues more than a few times.

They finally folded, and with me already a long-time friend with Ian Howarth, an idea to form another band now a plan worth pursuing.

Our first band, named The Impact, becoming a reality after meeting Nigel Scott, via Neil Hardcastle, Alan Barton, and the return of Steve Scholey.

Beginning rehearsals as a five piece in earnest of a fast-approaching gig, a valentine's dance at Alan and Nigel's former school, Horbury secondary school.

A much-enthused gig that sadly did not amount to much, from a playing in a band point of view, only accomplishing half a set, as the schools PA system broke down, nonetheless, an initiation of what to come.

A name change to Penny Arcade, becoming more confident with our instruments and performances, and almost self-sufficient, with backline equipment and now the owners of a PA system, although still requiring a permanent driver with a van to get us to our booked venues.

Ian Bowden, a bass player, neighbour of Nigel, and the owner of a van, becoming our first driver for quite a few bookings, unless it clashed with one of his own band's gigs.

A support driver, and plan B, one of the most regular, Mick Linskey, and girlfriend Angela, taking us as far away as Doncaster to gigs, which at the time seemed a gig much too far, miles away from home.

Nigel acquired a rather old, decommissioned post office van, which the five of us hand painted in a bright orange, with black go faster stripes.

It lasted a measly four months, as the vast amounts of rust and holes took their toll, now deemed hazardous, and a dangerous risk to travel, waving it goodbye to the scrapyard.

Alans brother-in-law Ronnie, now our permanent driver for a good six-months, driving a new to us, second hand van.

That too becoming a trade-in to help purchase a twin wheeled Ford transit van, apparently, the preferred transport for most clubland groups and bands during the early to late seventies.

A relation of Mick Linskey also joined the band as a roady come driver, again for around six to nine months, but bringing about the need for one of us, namely me as the oldest group member, to take lessons and pass a driving test.

Finding it difficult to believe that our band fitted in all of the above in just two years, then a decision to change our band name yet again.

A name chosen that all thought mirrored the direction for our choice of music, "Love or Confusion."

Our chosen moniker, the title of a Jimmy Hendrix song, not that our music followed that perspective, however, our satin and lace stage dress sense did, as the five of us enjoyed a further eighteen months in this lineup.

What happened next now a bit of a blur, me leaving, then the band splitting up, getting a new drummer Neil Hardcastle, that not lasting long, just four months.

Two bands forming out of our band when joining other musicians, what a mess and upset, however, setting the scene in a local pub, the Flanshaw Hotel, for a reincarnation.

Four of us getting back together, Alan, Steve, me and Nigel, and a new name, "Badge," a name only lasting just one gig, at an audition night for an agent at Askern miners welfare club.

The agent liking us as a band, as individuals, and our choice of covers music, but not our identity name.

Not deterred, with-in a week the agents sending through a Saturday night gig at Armthorpe Miners club near Doncaster, with an attached caveat, "when you arrive at the club, whatever name you see written on the noticeboard, that is your band name from now on."

Our equipment almost set up, the sound also checked, before realising our band still did not have a name for the chairmen to announce, prompting us to enquire what's written on the notice board situated at the clubs front entrance.

The name on the weekly artists appearing noticeboard, and directly opposite Saturday night entertainment, "Black Lace" – "Harmony Band from Wakefield," a name that would stick, and now acknowledged for decades to come.

Nigel would leave the band to pursue his work and family business, Ian coming back in as replacement bass player, and bringing together our musical unit for a further eighteen months, including the acknowledgement of a summer season in Skegness to begin in May 1976.

Sadly, Ian would not remain with us for our summer season event, and bringing about other changes necessary for our band to progress further.

Introducing Colin Routh (Gibb) to our line-up for starters, all of us leaving our jobs, and turning professional, income from our band now our sole livelihood.

Steve the first of our little band of merry men to marry, and later with his first child, Samantha.

Alan, and me also married, and our wives expecting, Colin engaged to Sheila, a marriage date yet to set.

Not an ideal time to take the decision to all pack in our original day jobs, and all with mortgages, or paying rent, bank loans and other personal mounting debts to contend with.

All our parents at a loss with our seemingly reckless and irresponsible judgements, and apparent non-existent wisdom, bringing about an uneasy time until the start of our summer season.

I have a trade background, so able, when needed to do an odd job or two for cash in hand, not mega bucks, but a few pounds to help with escalating household bills.

Black lace, continued regardless of whatever came our way, van breakdowns, all over the country, new engines, repairs to, and new equipment.

Anything, and everything needed to keep us on the road earning money, a necessity in maintaining our family life, and all that they demanded, now the utmost priority.

At times, more money going out than coming in, nevertheless, a further summer season, and weeks and weeks on end, traveling, playing our music up and down the country, including gigs on the Shetland Isles, just about kept our heads above water.

And our dream alive...

One aspiration of ours disappearing almost immediately, following a drive to London in our group Van to meet the husband of female drummer from the band "The Honeycombs."

He owned a recording studio and had placed an advertisement in a music magazine for up-and-coming bands to record their own compositions.

The "deal," and studio not to our liking, a song composed by Alan Barton, "It's the little things you do," sounding awful, our playing and singing all respectable, just the mix, and overall sound, poor quality.

Even worse, the journey back home fraught with road blocks, diversions, and traffic queues on every turn.

Steve my co-pilot, managing extremely good, using a worn, well-thumbed Collins A to Z road atlas, and all prior to the M25 motorway ring road coming into existence around our capital.

Similarly, a further trip to London, to DECCA records, and a further audition that sadly did not go our way.

Although at the very same auditions The John Miles set, signed up with a recording deal.

John Miles, a name known throughout the music world for his song writing, singing, piano, and undisputable guitar playing abilities.

The song "Music," written and recorded in 1976, released from the album "Rebel," attaining the position of number three in the UK singles chart, winning an Ivor Novello award in the same year.

Born in Jarrow April 23rd, 1949, and died peacefully in his sleep with family at the bedside on December 5th, 2021, in Newcastle upon Tyne

Once again an opportunity came our way to travel down to our capital, seemingly the place to go for musical acknowledgement, this time to meet a singer songwriter from ATV music, Peter Morris.

Peter had lots of songs, but one in particular heading in our direction, a composition called "Mary Ann."

Peter liking the sound of Alans voice, on a "Smokie" track originally from Bradford, Oh Carol, after watching us perform on a clubland promotional video, filmed in St Helens.

Steve, our bands lead singer accepted this change immediately, and would carry out additional backing vocals with Colin, and occasionally my non-talented vocal chords on tracks too.

Mary Ann, a song transporting our band into the heights none of us would think possible.

Our tune picked to represent the UK from six-hundred hopefuls, in the twenty fourth Eurovision Song Contest, held in Israel, March 31st, 1979.

Our bands fifteen minutes of fame on UK television, taking the four of us to many parts of Europe, Denmark, Poland, the Sopot festival, Bulgaria, and the Golden Orpheus festival, to Spain, and East and West Germany, long before the Berlin wall, with a little help from hammers, crowbars and the like came crashing down.

Performing on stage with some of the greats of the time, Boney M, Demis Roussos, Paul Young, Susie Quatro, Patrick Hernandez, to name a few.

Flying now our preferred mode of transport, although short lived, but so enjoyable while it lasted.

Our Black Lace band, coming to an end on January 2nd, 1981, a date synonymous with the capture of the Yorkshire Ripper, Peter Sutcliffe.

I continued to perform and playing drums in another professional four-piece band called "Stormer," formally "Method," from Castleford.

Stormer, previously "signed" to Ringo Starr record label, drummer of The Beatles, continuing my playing with this brilliant band for a further three years, while also taking along our Black Lace roadie, Richard.

Richard remaining with me, John, and Steve, for the last two of those years, with Mick the lead singer leaving at Christmas 1982.

Our three-piece "Stormer" band coming to an end on New Years Eve 1984, at Woodseats working mens club, Sheffield.

I would take almost a year out, twiddling just my thumbs instead of my drumsticks.

A time for reflection, and an attempt to keep my hand in, as I had returned once again to full time employment as a maintenance joiner for the local authority.

During this time, enjoying the success of my former Black Lace band mates, Alan, and Colin, joining them in the recording studio, playing drums to songs penned via Alan and Colin (Barton & Routh) for potential "B sides."

Taking the band name, now a duo forward with present day known famous tunes, such as, Superman, Agadoo, Do the Conga, Music Man, and other party type good time songs and Party Albums.

After a few months lay off, a telephone call gave me the opportunity to help out musician friends in a band called "Aircrew," their full-time drummer taking ill, a Wednesday night at that, in a Dewsbury nightclub.

A session I would remember, not only that a job offer of becoming this local bands permanent drummer, but also for the speed of me listening to twenty songs, just the previous day, and then playing all of them the night after.

I am not saying for one minute I played them all perfectly, far from it, nevertheless a performance I felt proud to get through, after a layoff of playing live music for almost a year to an audience.

Joining the band for proper rehearsals at the home of Ian Bowden in Ossett, a rear bedroom set out with back line guitar amplifiers, PA system, and an acoustic drum kit.

Helping to use the best of our limited evenings rehearsal time, to learn new songs and bring them quickly into our shows, including hours transporting our equipment, instruments, setting up, then finally playing our two sets.

A few line-up changes over the following six years of a fabulous time together, saw me leaving the band in 1992, around the same time as the breakup of my second marriage.

The band did continue for a couple or more years, changing their name to "Hit the Silk" then finally folding in 1994.

I did keep in touch with Jim Mr Fix it Trueman, a few evenings each month to record a few of our own compositions, although nothing tangible from a finished song point of view.

Gaining lots of experience, and a bit of fun coming from those once weekly sessions, and the idea of possibly forming yet another band.

Jim wanting to build his own Public Address system from scratch, the speaker cabinets, and amplifiers all taking over a year to complete, but what a massive sound for the band to take onboard.

Getting in touch with former band mates, asking if interested in putting a band back together, all jumping at the chance, including our former sound man, Baz.

Dave, (Guitar, Vocals,) Martin (Keys,) Mick (Bass, Vocals,) me, on drumkit, and Jim, (guitar, vocals,) our first of many rehearsals taking place in earnest, and now ready for our first gig.

A work colleague offering his local working mens club in Dewsbury for our momentous gig to take place.

Jims PA system completed, and adding a lighting rig into the mix too.

A hire truck provisionally booked for our forthcoming weekend, that also included a local Sunday night gig in Horbury.

A two-night weekend in July 1998, certainly a good start to get us into performing and playing music to a clubland audience once again, and now looking forward to our first gig, and with a new name, "Mister Twister."

An early decision envisaged our new band to only survive a couple of years, however, strong musical friendships ensured that did not materialise at all.

Martin leaving our band first, requiring a few stand in keyboard players, Micks son, helping out first of all, Ann from my place of work helping out for over a year, then a friend of my managers daughter for a few weeks, adding Richard, my former roady with Black Lace and Stormer to the mix, and finally John joining us on a permanent basis.

John living in Hull, performed with us until his retirement from full time work, although having to step down for a few months due to an accident at home, his daughter helping out during this time.

A friend of Jim then taking on the challenge, James, becoming our keyboard player.

"Mister Twister" never stopped working weekends throughout, until March 2020, Coronavirus, (Covid 19,) quickly emerged that would put an immediate full stop to our gigs.

In limbo for over eighteen months, as clubland once again began to open its doors, however, certainly vastly different from before, and the war in Ukraine and the developing energy crisis not helping one bit.

Clubs could not afford to open up a large concert room, staff the bar, and have heating and lighting on, if no guarantee of a full concert room, necessary to pay the bands fee, and bar staff wages.

A dilemma for sure, as clubland committees having to make decisions that will change the whole clubland establishment forever.

Bands that carry lots of heavy equipment and stage lighting, who demand a huge amount of power, while also commanding large appearance fees will undoubtedly suffer.

Unquestionably, "going out" on a Saturday night, to see and listen to a band, and play a few houses of bingo, certainly not the same as the pre-covid period at all, as most punters now preferring to stay at home.

To perhaps drink alcohol purchased far cheaper from supermarkets, and watch whatever available on hundreds of channels on their supersized TV's.

Babysitters appear a thing of the past, those too almost redundant, as the knock on of clubs either cutting back, or closing altogether, the site and carpark areas becoming brownfield for sale building plots.

I feel that our era has had the best of times in clubland, from the first appearance of beat music in the sixties, bringing about, local theatre and variety clubs, such as Batley, Wakefield, and Sheffield, employing stars of stage, screen, film, and radio, always packed to the rafters.

Most of these venues seating over a thousand, tables full of drinks and all tucking into Chicken and Chips in a basket, prior to the top of the bill taking to the stage.

Holiday Camps, and working mens clubs, all booming during these times, as having artistes performing on stage seven nights a week, including Saturday, and Sunday lunch times.

I know, done it all, playing my kit in bands at all of these establishments during the seventies, eighties, nineties, and from memory, what wonderful times those days and nights performing our music, and playing my drums turned out.

However, noticing a deterioration of clubland in the mid-eighties, following the Miners' strike, the decline of the UK steel and mining industries, the smoking ban of 2007, the Covid epidemic, and finally the emerging energy crisis.

A sad and lean time for those artists who play and work at these venues to earn a living, as our band Black Lace once did.

However, there appears plenty of clubs and pubs around that employ single self-contained artists, duo's, trios, and of course bands, but not on as many mid-weeknights.

The weekend nights still the preferred working nights for artists, with few mid-week nights available, or where these venues inclined not to open the concert room, preferring the smaller best room or lounge as their entertainment area.

These rooms certainly small for our band's equipment, and a reluctance amongst us to reduce, or downsize anything and everything to do with stage, PA equipment, drum kit or lighting.

Our band is what it is, no compromise, as our twenty-six-year run Mister Twister has come to an end, and possibly the conclusion of me performing and playing my drums too.

Sadly, at seventy-one years old, I have thoroughly enjoyed what I and other clubland musicians that continued through these years to a ripe old age, will consider the last fifty years as being the best time of their lives.

Some of us climbing the ladder to further success, while other artists content in becoming a covers band, playing music of other artists material in the club and pub circuits.

Giving "punters" what they want, and especially in clubs, where at times these appearances just a complementary performance, sandwiched at either side of vast numbers of bingo games.

In my musical vocation, I feel extremely fortunate to accomplish both, to continue playing for all of these years in a semi-professional capacity, and as professional musician too, with just a few of those years off.

Where other musicians, and for whatever reasons, have given up playing music to an audience, and content to continue playing their instruments of choice in the confines of their own home.

Nevertheless, our decision to disband not as a result of a fall-out, or fisty cuffs, really a sign of the times, and of course our fourth coming old age, with all that it entails.

All culminating together in a short period of time, and I am sure we will keep in touch, and meet up for a beer or two, in due course.

CHAPTER SIXTEEN

First Men in the Moon

(Before Apollo and Beyond)

I remember as a young six-year-old while at Flanshaw Infants school, drawing and colouring space rockets, my artistic creations had me travelling the star filled universe in search of other habitable planets.

Not that I thought myself any good with a pencil, crayons, or paint brush, but my teacher must have thought acceptable, as a few of my depictions did end up on the classroom and corridor walls.

Our TV showing programs like Flash Gorden set in the year 3203, or Torchy the battery boy, Fireball XL5, Lost in Space, Thunderbirds, Star Trek, and other space themed series that would certainly get my imagination going.

Not until my first year at secondary school did my interest expand enough to actually go to the cinema to watch a space themed film.

My mum used to work at the Essaldo Cinema, (Formally Theatre Royal Wakefield) as an usherette, and if a little cheeky, and mentioning mums name, the lady in the pay kiosk would let me in for free.

Watching this film today more of a comedy science fact, than a science fiction movie, when as a twelve-year-old becoming glued to the large movie screen, visiting the cinema more than three times in less than a week to see this one film.

Enthralled in the film, as at the time a far-fetched amazing story, and even as an almost teenager, my "what if" imagination working overtime.

"First men in the Moon," an H.G. Wells classic, released in 1964 covered the story of a United Nations moon landing in modern times, which they think for the first time on our natural luna satellite.

The astronauts delight when landing on the moon's surface turns to shock, when just after leaving their craft they discover that a Victorian party had actually completed the precarious 240.000-mile journey from Earth to the moon in 1899.

The modern-day astronauts came across a small dust covered handkerchief size Union Jack flag, placed on a small rocky outcrop on the moon's surface, along with a document confirming that Victorian astronauts stood on this spot, claiming the moon on behalf of the United Kingdom, and Queen Victoria.

As this amazing news flashed back to a stunned world, the press and Government dignitaries begin the hunt to search for any 1899 crew members that may have survived the journey back to Earth, and still very much alive.

After searching archives, they discovered that indeed they had made it back, and the only remaining survivor, an Arnold Bedford, now in his nineties, living a solitary care home life.

Arnold begins to excitedly, but with some trepidation, tell the tale of how a new friendship and heroic journey, way back in 1899 to the moon began.

Arnold, along with girlfriend Kate Callendar, began a conversation with their neighbour, a Joseph Cavor, who went on to say he had developed a miracle substance.

Gold in colour, and when "painted" in its boiling red-hot state onto any surface, and cooled to become touch dry would resist gravity making the object, no matter how large or heavy, lighter than air, and rapidly rise to infinity.

The product proven to Arnold, when asked to sit on a chair, Cavor painting this amazing substance to the legs, and with-in a few seconds the chair rising along with Arnold, both the chair and Arnold becoming squished to the ceiling.

Some laughable conversation and panic ensued, until Cavor managed to get Arnold down to the floor.

Cavor had already built a spherical space craft, and other than test it out, prepared to make his unaccompanied flight to the moon.

However, on meeting Arnold, Cavor agreed a financial partnership that would ensure enough of this miracle formulated substance manufactured to send this spherical craft and both men, hurtling to the moon.

After applying a single coat of magical hot gooey liquid material aptly named "cavorite" to the retractable window blinds, that once dry, will cause the craft to rapidly rise.

Arnold and Cavor, waiting patiently inside the man-made craft for it to cool down and desiccate, enabling the sphere to defy gravity and "lift off" at a tremendous speed, crashing through the roof of Joseph Cavor's glazed summer house.

Not before pulling in Arnolds girlfriend, who had come looking for him, and dangerously close, into the moon bound sphere.

Speedily travelling to our nearest celestial object in Cavor's constructed space craft, with strategically placed train carriage buffers all around to cushion the intended bumpy landing, Kate now joining Arnold and Cavor in the crafts cockpit for its inaugural flight.

The moon touchdown became anything but, as the sphere hit the moon's surface at speed, and taking on a fast bumpy cushioned roll, until coming to an abrupt stop when abutting a small mountain range.

Although, a near catastrophe avoided shortly after leaving earth's atmosphere, when altering the spheres trajectory using the window blinds, one becoming stuck in the open position, hurtling the sphere towards the sun.

Once Arnold and Cavor had donned their makeshift space attire, former diving suits, and exited the craft, both now fully aware of Kate, having to leave stowaway girlfriend of Arnold behind, with no space "suit" for her to wear.

They came across an entrance to descend beneath the moon's dusty surface through a doorway in glass topped ventilation shaft.

After descending below the moon's surface on a purpose made stone staircase, they encountered a developed bee like four-foot-tall species, around four feet tall, living, and working in subterranean caves beneath the moon's exterior.

The Victorian space travellers captured, but not with-out a fight, in particular Arnold punching a few, and others falling to their deaths from a drawbridge over a deep cavity.

Both now prisoners of the bee people, Cavor coins the name "Selenites," after the Greek goddess of the moon, Selene.

These creatures living in the oxygen rich below ground advanced environment, and communicated with Cavor and Arnold through an innovative translating device.

Soon learning their spacecraft now underground with Kate, also held captive, as a group of Selenites beginning to slowly dismantle the spherical craft, preventing the astronauts from ever returning to their idyllic homes on earth.

A long story short, Arnold and Kate manage to put the few removed pieces back together on the sphere, with a little help from Cavor, while the bee creatures took a short hibernation.

An Earth Sun eclipse had cut off the sunlight driving the below ground oxygen forming generators, leaving the Selenites frozen on the spot for a brief time.

However, Cavor wished to remain behind to befriend and exchange knowledge with the bee creatures.

Arnold managed to guide the craft back to earth, and on their return in 1899, married Kate, but at the time, no one believed their cock and bull story, as the craft had sunk beneath the sea, and no other evidence of their amazing trip to the moon and back remained.

This latest moon expedition now unfolding on the TV in front of an excited but concerned Arnold.

The press and government officials, watching the care home TV, as the expedition crew found what remained of the Selenites former below the moon's surface existence.

Now in a derelict and collapsing state, the Selenites had long since perished.

The astronauts began to make the perilous journey back to the moon's surface, avoiding becoming trapped in the fast crumbling below ground level catacombs.

Cavor did have a terrible cold at the time of their moon adventure, always using his handkerchief, as sniffling and sneezing throughout the film.

Opinions grew that the Selenites probably all extinct as a result of the human microorganisms that Cavor passed on, way back in 1899.

A similar story to yet another H.G Wells classic story, War of the Worlds, an Earth invasion of Martians and their machines, and a story that Orson Welles captivated the radio listening USA public in 1938.

Directing and narrating his story and broadcasted on Halloween night, simulating a Martian invasion of New Jersey.

The broadcast included realistic sound effects and breaking news bulletins, with lots of listeners believing the invasion true and ongoing.

Orson Welles causing mass moral hysteria across the United States.

This story made into a successful film, Byron Haskin directing in 1953.

The film featured Gene Barry and Ann Robinson, who both made a cameo appearance almost at the end of an updated version in 2005, featuring Tom Cruise and Tim Robbins, with Steven Spielberg directing.

A book fantastically reproduced to film, ending in a similar way as First men in the Moon, when the Martian invaders also succumbed to Earths microorganisms, ending their take-over bid to conquer our wonderful planet, and all its inhabitants.

What I became drawn to in the 1964 space mission film, First men in the Moon, and how accurate the actual journey took, and how it mirrored NASA's 1969 moon landing.

Not that the astronauts encountered a bee like species when landing and exploring the moon's surface in 1969, but more of the technical knowledge the director, producers, film crew and technicians used to make this realistic1964 film in the first place.

The story board, film set, funding and actual filming, possibly in place years ahead of the films1964 release.

Many years before the actual 1969 moon landing mission, and perhaps just a year or so after President Kennedys inaugural promise, "we choose to go to the moon" speech, sending a man to the moon, before the end of this1960's decade.

The First men in the Moon opening frames, show a spacecraft orbiting the moon, a lander separates from the mother ship and descends to the moon's surface.

I remember watching this scenario as a possible solution to achieve the goal of a moon landing discussed in a documentary featuring Werner von Braun, a German rocket engineer who with his team, fled to the USA after World War 2 came to an end.

The graphics showing a three-stage rocket, a large booster first stage to leave the earths gravitational pull, leaving a second stage mother ship for the journey to the moon.

A separate lander would detach from the mother ship for its descent to the moon's surface, the very same format used for the July 1969 moon landing, and this idea evident in the 1964 film.

I think some inside information, perhaps a discrete collaboration between NASA and film producer, as the "Luna Orbit Rendezvous" option decision, becoming the most obvious, and least complicated way of three options, to travel to the moon and return safely back to earth, only established in1962.

This rocket and lander option making the 1964 film so believable for my young inquisitive mind at the time of first going to watch this film.

On Sunday July 20th, 1969, the huge Saturn 5 rocket completing the Apollo 11 mission to land a man on the moon before the 1960's decade is out.

The Apollo Lunar Module, named Eagle, has landed.

Neil Armstrong slowly climbing down the ladder of the Apollo Lunar Module, six hours after touch down, watched world-wide with over 650 million TV viewers tuned in.

Neil placing the first footprints onto a dusty moon surface, Buzz Aldrin following some twenty minutes later.

Michael Collins manned the "mother ship," located in moon orbit throughout the time Neil and Buzz remained on the moon, until time for the Eagle modules lift off, link up, and return to Earth.

When the crew boarded the mother ship, named "Columbia," the Eagle module then released, abandoned in luna orbit, its ultimate fate unknown, but theoretically still in orbit around our luna cousin, to this day.

Apollo 12, launched on November 14th, 1969, became the second successful mission to land two humans on to the moon's surface, and Apollo 13 soon followed, but did not quite make it to landing.

Launched on 11th April 1970, amid huge publicity, although the excitement of TV stations and viewers, had already diminished.

Commander Jim Lovell uttering those immortal words, "Houston we have a problem," when oxygen tanks exploded enroute to the moon, bringing TV crews and the viewing public around the world back in their droves, to watch this nail-biting development unfold on their TV sets.

Nevertheless, although Apollo13 failed to land on the moon's surface, it did complete a "free return trajectory" at an altitude of around one-hundred and fifty-eight miles above the surface of the moon.

Using the moons gravity as a sling shot for the journey back to Earth, captivating everyone who owned or could view a TV set.

Apollo 13 becoming a successful 2006 film depicting the failed, but deemed successful moon mission.

Astronauts James Lovell, Fred Haise, and Jack Swigert, Tom Hanks, Bill Paxton, and Ed Harris playing these real-life characters, and Gary Sinise acting as Ken Mattingly, the astronaut who failed his medical at the eleventh hour.

Jack Swigert now part of the three-man crew, replacing Ken Mattingly after exposed to German measles, medical experts thinking he would pass on the virus to crew members.

This did not happen, and possibly a good omen he did not go to the moon, as Jack became a massive co-worker at the NASA space centre in resolving all the issues Apollo 13 experienced during its journey.

The successful 2006 film Apollo13 directed by Ron Howard, capturing all of this truly remarkable historic event.

Not forgetting those earlier space pioneers who began the space race in the first place, Soviet cosmonaut, Yuri Gagarin, the first person in space, completing a single orbit on April 12th, 1961, and John Glenn, the first U.S. astronaut to orbit our earth, completing three orbits on February 20th, 1962.

The launch, and return of Apollo 17, taking place between December 7th to 19th 1972, bringing an immediate end to long duration manned space flight.

Apollo 18, 19, and 20 cancelled, with astronaut Gene Cernan the last person to date, to set foot on the moon.

Now fifty-two years and counting, bringing back a memory of watching a documentary with Gene Cernan actually stood on the moon, during the Apollo 17 mission, saying something like, "this trip had cost in the region of one-million dollars per man, per minute to get us here, it had better turn out ok".

With costs of that magnitude, make no wonder President Richard

Nixon cancelled the remaining three Apollo missions to the moon, not only to save money, concerns of safety, and many other factors too.

Although, some of the savings created funding for NASA to launch the Skylab space station, using the Saturn V rocket from the negated Apollo 20 mission.

The launch of the Space Shuttle "Columbia" on April 12th, 1981, returning to Earth on April 14th just fifty-four hours later, after completing thirty-seven Earth orbits, starting the next phase of low orbit f manned lights.

This amazing NASA Space Transport System – 1, STS-1, a marvellous technical engineering achievement, beginning space missions around Earth's orbit that would last for three decades.

On February 1st, 2003, after flying 28 missions, on its final approach, just minutes away from landing at the Kennedy Space Centre, "Columbia" would catastrophically break up over Texas.

All seven crew members perished as a result, at an altitude of around forty miles after successfully completing their orbital STS- 07 objective.

On January 28th, 1986, The "Challenger" space shuttle exploded just 73 seconds after take-off, disintegrating 46000 feet above the Atlantic ocean, just away from the Cape Canaveral launch site in Florida, all seven crew members on board perished as a result.

Stunned spectators and a TV audience of millions, witnessed the disaster as it unfolded, however, the TV stations cutaway seconds later, leaving the viewing public unaware of what actually happened, until news bulletins would broadcast the catastrophic event afterwards.

This particular STS-51L mission had the first non-astronaut on board, a schoolteacher called Christa McAuliffe.

NASA arranged for a satellite broadcast directly to schools, and many children watching, becoming extremely upset and hysterical, as "Challenger" appeared to explode.

The direct line to numerous tv channels instantly disconnected to prevent further panic and upset, although films exist showing the full catastrophic event as it unfolded.

Space shuttle "Discovery" launched on April 24th, 1990, to take the Hubble Space Telescope into an orbit 326 miles above earth's atmosphere, ready to peer into the vast unknown of space, however, a problem with Hubble's primary mirror an issue, and required repairs.

Space shuttle "Endeavour" became the shuttle that would "save" the Hubble telescope, after seven crew members undertook extensive training to carry out repairs and replacements.

Astronauts Steven Smith, and John Gunsfeld carried out this complicated, and extremely tedious work on December 22nd, 1999.

Five further missions taking place between 1993 and 2009, to repair, improve, and update the Hubble telescope, and still in use to this day, following over thirty years of sending back amazing data to earth.

The shuttle crafts now the main workhorse space vehicles used in the construction of the International Space Station (ISS).

Although a Russian proton rocket delivered the first segment on November 20th,1998.

The first U.S. segment, Unity Node 1 module, tucked away in the cargo bay of space shuttle Endeavour, mission STS-88, and launched on December 4th, 1998, from launch complex 39A at Kennedy Space Centre.

Linking the unity module to the Russian Zarya module, initiating the first ISS assembly sequence, and taking another ten years, and over thirty missions to fully assemble.

Five space agencies, representing fifteen countries involved in the manufacture and supply of modules.

The circumnavigating space station about the size of a football field when finished, completes one earth orbit approximately every ninety minutes, equalling sixteen orbits per day, traveling through sixteen sun rises and sunsets.

Weighing approximately four hundred and sixty tons, 250 miles above Earth, the ISS circles Earth travelling at an incredible speed of around 17,500 m.p.h.(2800km/h,) hypothetically covering a distance to the moon and back each day.

The first crew "moved in" on November 2nd, 2000, with NASA astronaut Bill Shepherd, and cosmonauts Yuri Gidzenko and Sergi Krikalev, instigating four months of demanding internal and external work to bring the space station to "life."

The first long-duration mission involved a three-person crew, lasting 136 days from November 2000 to March 2001, and beginning an uninterrupted human presence on the ISS from November 2nd, 2000, to this day.

Sadly, the completion of the ISS, also brought about the retirement of the thirty-year Space Shuttle program, at a 2011 cost of 196 billion dollars.

STS-135 "Atlantis" left launch pad 39A, Merritt Island, Kennedy Space Centre Florida on July 8th, 2011, completing its mission to deliver a payload of supplies to the International Space Station (ISS).

Landing on runway 15 KSC, for the last time on the morning of Thursday July 21st, 2011.

"Atlantis," first launched in October 1985, and one of four remaining space shuttles, with 33 missions completed, taking 207 astronauts over 126 million miles, and spending a total of 307 days in space.

Achieving the highest orbital inclination ever reached by a shuttle craft at 62 degrees, and the first to dock with the Russian Mir space station.

A purpose made, one hundred million dollar building to show off "Atlantis," displayed in ideal surroundings for everyone to see, and admire at the Kennedy Space Centre visitor complex Florida.

The Space Shuttle "Discovery" returned to Earth on the morning of March 9th, 2011, becoming the world's longest running most travelled spaceship.

STS – 133, the last assignment of "Discovery" after flying 39 missions, spending 365 days in space, and flying an incredible 148,221,675 miles.

The "Discovery" on display at The Smithsonian Institution National Air and Space Museum, Chantilly, Virginia USA.

Space Shuttle, "Endeavour" on display at the California Science Centre, and the Space Shuttle "Enterprise" located at the Intrepid Sea, Air and Space Museum.

The space shuttle design features numerous times in various films since its conception, such as "Moonraker 1979," "Space camp 1986," "Armageddon 1998," "The Core 2003," and "Superman Returns 2006," ana a plethora of documentary movies.

I am sure not the last of a similar designed space craft in the development stage for future luna and planetary journeys.

Over a decade later, space flight once again on the NASA and private enterprise agenda, and a sure possibility of the return of astronauts to the moon's surface, and maybe a journey to our second nearest planet, Mars, in the not-too-distant future.

SpaceX, and founder Elon Musk, appears ahead of this latest "race" to the moon and beyond, amongst other countries, private entrepreneurs, and of course NASA.

Not forgetting Blue Origin, when in 2021, William Shatner, (Captain James T kirk, of Star Trek fame,) becoming the oldest person at ninety years, to fly onboard the New Shepard rocket, travelling just beyond the Karmen Line, or boundary of space.

Lasting about ten minutes, other passengers on this momentous flight included, Audrey Powers, Blue Origin's vice president of flight operations, Glen de Vries, a tech supremo, and Dr Chris Boshuizen, former NASA engineer.

The new age of re-usable booster rockets, that can actually take-off, accurately and gently land, then prepared for a quick turnaround for a repeat mission, directly from science fiction, and rapidly becoming a routine science fact.

I eagerly await viewing the up-and-coming instalment of the next moon landing, and journeys beyond, and whoever becomes "first," in this new chapter of innovative prolonged manned space flight.

Maybe, just maybe, I will visit Kennedy Space Centre in Florida to see the many rockets that made history, and not forgetting the shuttle program, and an opportunity to look at space shuttle Atlantis for myself.

One day...

CHAPTER SEVENTEEN

———⟫•⟪———

Back to the Future

(Shattered Dreams)

My third marriage now well and truly over, coming to an end in May 2002.

What started as an affair, leading to a courtship that failed after four years, and some thought irreversible.

However, a protracted reconciliation taking place leading to marriage, sadly this matrimonial twosome lasting a mere forty-five months, our what seemed a more off than on relationship, prevailing about nine years in total.

Divorce, not an easy pill to swallow, an extended period of upset, prolonged sadness, a feeling of complete failure, and at an age of almost fifty years old.

With four children from two previous marriages, and this, a third heartbreaking permanent dissolution for me, making everything difficult to comprehend.

Fortunately, no children planned or otherwise during my third marriage, which could add to even more virtuous upset, and further complications with parental rights, and supportive maintenance payments.

Whatever next, join a singles club, I think not, perhaps an internet dating site, a bit of a cattle market approach.

Maybe not…

Perhaps go out and about a little more often, again, after a few not so memorable drinking sprees, definitely not for me.

I need time to come to terms with my past nonconformist endeavours, to look forward, and as sad as it seems, consider a single life for the foreseeable future.

To focus on my day job, my band rehearsals, and performances, and possibly decide what appropriate alterations, if any, or what allowed to do with my local authority rented first floor home.

So much for concentration, a typical Piscean, gazing out through the living room window from my two-seater sofa, a quiet period of contemplation taking me back to 1988, now almost thirteen years ago.

While visiting a new housing development with my then manager to look at four blocks of flats, each having four flats in each block, now almost fully complete, and ready to hand over to the local housing allocations department.

College Grove, a district of Wakefield, now part of a property clearance zone, lots of back-to-back terraced properties demolished, and cobbled roads removed to make way for new social housing flats.

All with open-plan communal gardens, seating areas, enclosed clothes drying facilities, and secure off-street car parking.

The council works department apprentices built these flats, situated close to Marsh Way ring road, the new bus terminal, Lightwaves swimming and sports centre, and Wakefield city centre.

I remember saying to my manager that I like this roadside first-floor flat, having a good look around at the workmanship, the main reason invited here, my eagle eyes looking for any minor snagging jobs that maybe required prior to handover.

Two reasonably large bedrooms, bathroom, kitchen, store, living room, and entrance staircase, a central hallway separating these rooms.

These flats situated in an improvement region, and with-in close proximity, and walking distance to town, definitely a convenient location.

Taking a closer look through the living room bay window, up and down the street, admiring all the local amenities with some interest.

My voice echoing around the unoccupied living room and flat, indicating each observation with some exhilaration to my manager.

A building firm, a fish and chip shop, a public house at either side of the road, a leisure centre, Wakefield central bus station, an off-licence shop, and all with-in a less than two-minute on foot distance, perfect.

Packing my few belongings into plastic bags, and leaving Jane in her flat on Bradford Road, moving in with mum, on a temporary basis until the local authority offered me a home.

I did not have to wait long, as I received a message to pick up a set of keys to have a look at a flat in town.

A definite and somewhat happy deja-vu moment, as who would have thought that nine years later, here in this very same living room, looking at the very same local amenities, where nine years earlier I stood here with my manager.

Fate or what, instantly making my decision to take the tenancy of this flat in July 1997, and I could not wait to move in, quickly planning to purchase modern furniture, paint, and emulsion, and start decorating, and perhaps enjoy a few of these local facilities.

However, after a few months of living alone, a reconciliation would see Jane moving into my Lower York Street flat, and our quickly arranged marriage taking place.

After just three years and a few months of not so matrimonial bliss, asking Jane to leave, and divorce proceedings now taking place.

Back here in 2001, my somewhat happy and sad contemplation over, and back to a form of reality, my thoughts returning to my here and now.

Following the departure of my imminent third ex-wife, and with no change to the way I currently feel, perhaps a single life an intention worth pursuing.

Just me, and what has now become my cats, Bud and Scrumpy, with no clashes or disagreements whatsoever over possession rights, or maintenance payments.

A quiet life, just my day job at Wakefield council, and my band, "Mister Twister," and other more important "things" on my mind.

One "thing" I do need to resolve, and quite quickly, to bring about an opportunity to cease paying a monthly rental fee to my council landlord.

Placing a Right-to-Buy application to Wakefield council to purchase my first-floor flat, an aspiration to own my home once again, and as a sitting tenant, should not take long to complete.

When Margaret Thatcher became Prime Minister in May 1979, the Conservative Government passed a legislation Scheme in 1980 to implement the Right to Buy, granting the desire of home ownership to millions of tenants living in state owned properties.

Starting my path to flat ownership with designing and fitting a new kitchen, including built in appliances, a new bathroom, boarding out the loft, including a retractable ladder, and because of all my clearly disruptive work, the flat requiring decoration throughout.

Lots of extra hours needed to carry out these alterations, above and beyond my day job, keeping me busy on evenings and weekends, and every attempt not to make much noise in the process.

In particular, drilling, sawing, and banging, an extraordinary amount of prolonged DIY work, and with elderly neighbours at one side, and also those living directly underneath me.

Certainly not an ideal environment when trying to retain a good long-lasting relationship with the other tenants in my block, my immediate neighbours, and all much more mature than my fifty years.

My alterations taking shape, and rather than sleeping all day long, Bud and Scrumpy enjoying their time messing about with rubble, bits, and pieces of wood and broken tiles.

I must remember to bag up all of these off-cuts and fragments, when bringing my DIY work to a close each evening.

Taking almost six months of challenging work to complete all my planned ideas, and decorations throughout, my first floor flat finally looking good, and feeling like a home once again.

My home, a first floor flat, now with a fifteen-year mortgage, and a one-hundred-and-ten-year lease, all in place.

Asking my band mate, Jim Mr-fix-it-Trueman to build me a computer, a first home PC for me, other than those I use daily while in work.

My PC will have a large screen, keyboard, mouse, pair of speakers, bass woofer, hard drive, and a desk unit to contain it all.

All items quickly purchased and personally delivered to my door, methodically put together.

Jim setting up all the IT equipment and testing, all working fine and connected to the internet, but where to locate it so as not a central attraction.

Not wanting this unit in the living room, certainly not in the second bedroom come dining room, if wanting to work on the PC when the kids stay over, so a dilemma for sure.

Removing a bedside cabinet and customary reading lamp from the righthand side of my bed, and placing them in my new storage space.

The loft, now a massive boarded out floor space, and becoming a beneficial useful storage alteration to my flat.

My new computer desk unit, replacing the bedside cabinet, ideal, out of sight from the rest of the house, and when fed up with typing late at night, straight into bed.

Once again, reflecting on what had transpired over these last six months, and hypothetically speaking over the last fifteen years.

A nuptial agreement for life, what could have existed in a wholesome loving marriage, had at least one of those of three marital agreements survived the test of time.

Now at a brusque cessation, divorce papers finally signed, once more for a third time, positive feelings of onwards and upwards.

Deep-seated thoughts, a saying regularly getting used to, as sadly my two previous connubial failures, undoubtedly all my responsibility, nonetheless, my third time in marriage, and in a comparable situation, I plead not guilty.

Nevertheless, an undisputable feeling of what goes around, comes around, and do not do to others, what you do not want doing to you...

Oh well...

Absolutely shattered, feeling lethargic, and totally drained as I arrived home on the last working day of the week.

Flu like symptoms getting the better of me, and certainly not in the mood for cooking tea, retiring immediately to bed, after taking half a dozen paracetamol, and a Beecham powder, a definite cold coming on.

A bit of an overdose to say the least, but nevertheless having a good night's sleep, and thankfully no gig in the diary for our band on this particular Saturday night.

Deciding to spend the entire day and night, between my now saturated cotton sheets, and duvet cover.

Talk about sweating it out, I feel worse now than I did while in work on Friday...

An extended early Sunday morning hot shower, and starting to wake up and feel much improved, following the previous two nights and a full day of sleeping and prolific sweating.

My usual arrangement to pick up Warren and Ashley from their mums in Ossett, just about feasible, as earlier, thinking a cancelation telephone call to their mum more appropriate.

Even more water covering my body, a very cold alternative though, visiting Lightwaves leisure centre swimming pool for a bit of fun.

Enjoying our customary play about on the slide, a further shower under elevated jets of water, and in the pools wave machine.

Warren and Ashley becoming good confident swimmers, and having lots of enjoyment at the same time too, certainly a worthwhile experience on what had become a regular Sunday morning in the pool sessions.

A two-minute walk home, quickly putting together a kids favourite cottage pie lunch, and spending all afternoon in the flat.

Filling the washing machine, putting clean fresh sheets on my bed, curling up on the sofa with Bud and Scrumpy and watching whatever on TV.

Not feeling 100% yet, but now certainly much better than I did during Friday night, and all-day Saturday.

Warren, Ashley, and Kerry as good as gold, amusing themselves for the remainder of the day, as not going to the park or visiting mum and Peter, deciding best to keep away, feeling like I do with these cold flu-like symptoms.

No running nose or sore throat, just feeling lacklustre, and a little unapproachable, but still managing to fit a few pieces into a mammoth jigsaw puzzle, while waiting patiently for Mandy (my second ex-wife) to pick up our kids at 18.00hr.

Broken marriages no fun at all, especially when family children involved.

However, throughout our positive lengthy parental discussions, with all our help, our children have gotten used to these regular weekends, and alternate midweek evenings visiting or staying with me, to enjoy our limited, but rewarding special times together.

Although today anything but special, especially with me feeling groggy, and an attitude not normally reserved for these typically amusing fun filled days.

Predictably, and once again, another early night for me, back to my freshly changed bed, more pills, and a further Beecham's powder.

Optimistically, my "man-flu" much better for a 07.00hr Monday morning rise and shine alarm, and the start of a new working week.

Over the last few days, I had not made any effort to turn on my new PC either, purchased and installed for the sole purpose of progressing with a university degree.

A bit late in life going back to "school," but my course at Huddersfield University, a crucial step in furthering my day job career.

These days my work takes me to two different but reasonably placed local offices each working week, Wood Street in central Wakefield, and Eastmoor estate, usually alternating between both each day of the week.

After a breakfast of toast and mug of tea, setting off to walk the short distance, through the new bus station to my central Wakefield office, located next to the Museum on Wood Street.

Formally a car showroom, then becoming offices and showroom for the Yorkshire Electric Board (YEB) before extensive alterations taking place to become a central Wakefield Housing office.

Although feeling much better, my Monday morning and those in our office not starting good at all, firstly, after unlocking and opening the main front door, the public entrance security shutter would not open.

A good firm kick and bang later, it began to noisily rise, ever so slowly at first, but finally progressing enough to allow our waiting customers to enter.

Not wanting to test the security shutters operation any further just in case it remains wedged in a halfway position, immediately placing a telephone call to our works department to resolve this issue before closing time arrived.

And secondly, notified of a late afternoons unwelcome guest sat on a chair in our office reception.

Urgently coming downstairs from my first-floor office in an attempt to rectify the situation, and prior to a possible telephone call required to the police station across the road.

Not the first time summoned to carry out this particular task, but now becoming a more frequent, after lunch event...

Much darker afternoons now, progressing ever closer to putting our clocks back one hour, and long dark nights ahead for everyone in the UK for another six-months.

The brainchild of a builder called William Willett, who suggested that clocks should advance for summertime, and reversed for the coming winter.

Claimed a positive wartime production boosting device under the Defence of the Realm Act, and subsequently other countries adopting the adjustment of time too.

Sadly, William Willett did not live to see daylight saving become law, as he died of influenza in 1915 at the age of 58.

William Willett, none other than the great, great, grandfather of Chris Martin, lead singer, of the celebrated band Coldplay, one of my favourite bands, and a few songs our band Mister Twister reproduce and play.

My somewhat regular, and unwelcome reception guest, none other than Paul Sykes, a Wakefield author, and renowned former heavyweight boxer.

Completing just ten fights, amid a culmination of six wins, four knockouts, three losses, and one draw, with books and documentaries to his name.

Sadly, a shadow of his former self, not exactly sitting, but slumped over, the top of his head pointing towards the reception counter while sat in one of half a dozen customer chairs.

Paul's fully clad body doubled up, and head between his thighs, arms at either side of both legs, with both hands placed palms down on the floor, and as fit as I think I am, a position I would find extremely difficult to put myself in.

Looking a sorry state, this onetime favourite man of Wakefield, now appearing worse for wear, scruffy, smelling of alcohol, obviously fast asleep, and at any second, could end up in an untidy bundle on the floor, but what to do with this former giant of a man.

"Paul, Paul, wake up," my question spoken in a moderate none-authoritarian tone, and not wanting to touch him, with timely skills of attacking and punching he may still possess, even for his age, sat in an unorthodox, and clearly comatose condition, certainly not wanting to aggravate him.

"What, what do YOU want," came a just about audible but muffled response.

"Paul, I would like to close reception, and I need you to wake up and leave," almost a plea, rather than a stern request, but it did the trick.

Slowly, and somewhat confidently, Paul sat up in the chair, steadily, with support from the backs of other chairs, began to rise to his feet.

Standing almost upright, and giving me a good look up and down through half open glazed eyes, "I thought you were the coppers," said Paul.

"I'm going," repeating over and over again, his voice a bit of a drawl, nevertheless coherent, as he made an unsteady manoeuvre, gripping anything to assist him, as he just about stood upright.

Offering me his right hand, no gentle squeeze today, giving as firm a grip as possible, and not the slightest wince from Paul, as he shuffled through the automatic opening door.

A terribly slow but fairly safe exit onto Wood Street followed, and certainly not like the many confident steps Paul would have taken in a boxing ring or while in training.

Now making his unsteady way, leisurely walking towards the centre of town.

Feeling somewhat relieved that this matter did not escalate, and the Police not required to move him, and in no doubt he would have probably caused a dreadful embarrassing scene.

Possibly ending with Paul bundled into the back of a black maria, or paddy wagon van, and locking him up, and perhaps a warm bed in a cell for the night, more than likely what he may have wanted.

Sadly, after spending many more years in a similar condition, never reverting to the man he once had become in those early years, Paul would pass away on March 7th, 2007, in Pinderfields Hospital.

The security shutter issues resolved just after lunch, its downward movement much smoother, and virtually noise free, as I ensured everything locked up and made my way home.

Walking once again through a busy bus station, past Lightwaves, and fish and chip shop, still not feeling hungry, but the inviting smell coming from the chippy certainly a temptation, just the long queue putting me off.

After a cuppa, taking a couple of paracetamols, and a further Beecham's powder, possibly another early night.

Bud and Scrumpy looking at a loss as to why so many premature nights to bed, as usually both on the sofa with me until almost midnight, and then both at the bottom of my bed, until wake up time.

My extended time in bed absolutely necessary, if I am to get back to feeling completely fit and healthy once again.

A slice of toast smothered in raspberry jam, and cuppa for my Tuesday morning breakfast, and a short drive to the Eastmoor office, taking all of five-minutes, and not the first into work today, already other staff cars parked up.

My black XJS four litre Jaguar car, a bit thirsty on these short runs, the heater and radiator not even reaching temperature, but with meetings and visits to attend, my car a necessity today.

I prefer using the cars cruise control for motorway driving, in particular when using the car to our band gigs, usually around a hundred-mile radius, where I get a much better miles per gallon performance, especially at this time with the price of fuel.

Kettle already boiled as I made yet another cuppa, and logging on to my PC, to have a look at what has transpired overnight.

Lots of emails today, no change there, and one in particular catching my eye.

Party at O'Donoghue's tonight, Dave's fortieth birthday bash, Dave playing with his band, 19.30hr sharp, all welcome.

Dave, one of the caretakers responsible for two city-centre high-rise multi-story flats, or apartments, and the bass player of a popular pub band, "Doctor Blue," a gig and party I should not miss.

However, still not feeling one hundred percent, and rather than attending a great night with colleagues from work, I am more in favour of taking additional medication, and yet another early night.

Eastmoor area staff all up for tonight's "gig", but I am still not feeling my old self.

After receiving numerous telephone calls, text messages, and emails from staff, encouraging me to attend, what actually materialised as a result of this unprecedented attention, would become a night that brought about a life changing experience.

Reluctantly, eating yet more slices of toast, needing some food no matter how trivial it seems, taking a long hot bath, a change of clothes, and walking to O'Donohue's at the bottom of town.

Located next to Glad Tidings Hall, a residence I visited in my before teens years to Sunday school, feeling a little pressure from some school friends to attend, but not taking to it at all, just two mornings, and then handing in my notice.

Capitulating to the inevitable, unable to refuse listening to a good rock band, and perhaps a taste of some buffet food, no matter how off-colour I felt, and for once in over three months, an actual night out, other than when playing with my band.

Meeting work colleagues, and of course our caretaker, Dave Elcoate, for what I am sure will turn out a great musical party night.

The band had only played a few elongated songs, guitar solos amazing, when Dave called me on stage, announcing a "star" in the audience, wanting me to play a few tunes on drums with his band.

A little embarrassing at first, nevertheless I thoroughly enjoyed playing drums with great musicians.

Lots of add-lib drumming on my part, loved the long guitar solos, and also fitting in a few bars of a drum solo.

Afterwards while stood at the bar, Dave introduced me to a few of his guests, and one invitee I took particular attention to, a lady called Tricia, who began our conversation asking how I knew Dave.

That in part helped to get what turned out a lengthy conversation, almost ignoring everyone else around us, until "Doctor Blue" struck up once again.

Secretly hoping Dave would not ask me to play drums in their second, and last spot of the night, as extremely content, settled, and feeling somewhat fortunate in our little twosome environment.

So pleased that I had made the effort to attend Dave's party, regardless of all the attention, and my earlier, although now almost fully recovered infirmity.

Who would have thought that after just ten weeks of "courting," Tricia making an announcement, a declaration certainly not expected.

Our first Christmas Eve together, enjoying lovely food and company in Tricia's home, and just after eleven-thirty, both making our way to bed.

I had turned on the bedside lights earlier, and placed a present on the bed, but who would have thought what would take place next.

Having a bit of fun on, and under the sheets, when Tricia calmly announced she is having our baby, a lovely joint Christmas present, a gift of this calibre certainly not predicted.

Saying a shock for the both of us, an understatement, especially when Tricia married to her previous husband, and preceding partner, pregnancy had eluded them.

So much so, preventative measures not considered at all, both having a sincere opinion that pregnancy, would never become a likely proposition.

Total disbelief, nonetheless, after three home pregnancy tests, confirmation, that pregnancy indeed a possibility, regardless of past actions and activities.

Tricia fully aware for a few weeks now, and on reflection, no wonder, with missed periods, no contraception, and over these past ten weeks, most of our time together, either in bed, or finding ourselves in other alluring salubrious locations.

Our baby born via caesarean section at Pontefract Maternity unit, at the end of July 2002, a son, and following lots of deliberation, naming him Liam Benjamin.

The next three years would see him growing into a fine little boy, taking to nursery and pre-school like a duck to water, nothing appearing that difficult or hard to grasp, absorbing anything and everything delivered to him like an enormous sponge.

Sadly, just days prior to Liams fourth birthday, Tricia would leave us, losing her life as a result of a severe asthma attack, in the early hours of Monday July 17th, 2006.

All our immediate plans scuttled, no sandwich shop business, a joint acquisition so close to completion at the time of her sudden heartbreaking death, our ten-day summer holiday to Malta cancelled, and everything jet-propelled into an unenviable distressing turmoil.

Moving permanently out of my flat, and into our Valley Drive home, and an emotional decision not to take my cats, instead a lady friend of my younger brother adopting them.

Taking full responsibility for my son Liam, a formidable task for a fifty-four-year-old, but a totally accepted challenge I could not renounce.

Father and son, albeit with a huge age difference, beginning a life together, that during these next few years would prove not exactly a harmonious one.

Nevertheless, between the two of us, making the absolute best of an unpleasant, and still haunting situation.

Everything changing for the better when taking on what turned out to become a gigantic task, the renovation of an almost dilapidated four-bedroom bungalow, situated in a huge field that would eventually become our home.

Taking almost four whole months of demanding challenging work, to turn this former dilapidated structure, into a magnificent home to enjoy.

Liam helping me almost every night, and weekends, now a perfectionist in sweeping floors and mopping up afterwards, also an accomplished gardener, assisting with the rejuvenation of two huge lawns, numerous flower beds, and dense unkempt large shrub patches.

All while Liam taking part in a number of activities requiring dads taxi to take him everywhere, pre-school, weekend football, and cricket, including weekly training sessions.

Showing more than an interest in table magic, illusions, music, his drum kit, including tuned percussion, and of course his X-box, obtaining a profound set of unimaginable skills in all of them.

Liam winning a "Britain's got talent" junior school show while competing as a dancer, yet another attribute he became particularly good at.

Moving into our bungalow, our Abri, on a short-term lease just weeks prior to Christmas 2011, a definitive celebration, but knowing full well our home, appropriately named "Abri, My Oasis," would not become our permanent residence.

Just a father and son, two devoted guardians of an architecturally designed family dwelling, until its planned demolition, and the land sold to build eighty-eight homes.

During our time living at the bungalow, also taking time while empty, to carry out, and complete a number of alterations, to our main home on Valley Drive.

This work will ensure that our permanent home, remains in a good state of repair, and will offer a sizable accommodation for our future when the inevitable becomes a reality.

Only five years had transpired, before the agents acting on behalf of the property owners and developers, serving notice to leave our bungalow home, our Abri.

My mum and Peter, sister Marcia and husband David, enjoyed their brief times staying over while dog sitting, my biological dad, Tom loving his many visits here too, and of course me and Liam living in these ideal picturesque surroundings.

Oh well…

Receiving an instruction from the agents to remove all fixtures, and numerous fittings that I had purchased, to make further use of these, if I so desired, or to sell on, but to leave the property in a secure state.

A sad day indeed, April 15th, 2015, when handing over keys of our home to a person from the agents, but not before an announcement of sorts.

I am giving you what I never had when commencing required work to make this former derelict building a habitable home.

A set of keys…

All windows and doors boarded up for over four years, and no other way of entering other than taking off boarding, and removing and fitting new security locks.

The property empty once again, standing for a further two years, a period of one-hundred and four further weeks that the bungalow could have remained our home.

However, during all this time, the property continually vandalised, and certainly not remaining secure.

I feel the last straw for the developers to finally demolish, came when two fire engines and crews in attendance putting out a huge fire.

The lounge and bedrooms totally gutted, and a concern for everyone that a blaze of this magnitude could have killed the trespasses that started it.

Such a sad end to a distinctive family home, built for the McCauley family in 1957, at a cost of around seven-thousand pounds, that had stood in an isolated, yet elevated picturesque Wrenthorpe location.

For over sixty years, the McCauley family known for growing rhubarb, either on open fields or forcing sheds, and instigators of the Rhubarb Triangle in the Wakefield district.

Onwards and upwards, our welcoming Valley Drive home certainly not in any way ready for demolition, in fact all happy with the improvements I had carried out while vacant.

Liam once again helping whenever free from his other activities.

Liams many percussion lessons now helping him to become an accomplished percussionist in the Wakefield Metropolitan Brass Band, and taking part in lots of concerts at Outwood Grange school.

I enjoyed attending these, in particular getting involved with selling raffle tickets, and helping out behind the counter, serving hot drinks, and lots of home-made confectionary.

Amanda making trays full of cakes and buns of every description, mum-in-law Jennifer offering lots of help too, all these tasty titbits handed out for just a small donation.

Monies received helping to purchase sundry items for the schools bands and orchestras.

Liams percussion playing with brass bands, taking him all over the country, performing in the "areas," and finals, giving him a wealth of performance experience.

Also, taking part in a drum ensemble, Liam's drum teacher Rhodri putting this group together, with music pupils of similar ages attending Manygates, and other Wakefield music hubs.

The national Music for Youth heats held country wide, our local one held at St Thomas-a-Becket catholic school.

Their on-stage performance, sealing a second presentation, held in Birmingham, success here too, giving the ensemble a place to perform at the Royal Albert Hall in London.

All parents travelling down to witness a superb show, with school children from all over the country, playing instruments, dancing, and singing, obviously our kids performing the best, an amazing accomplishment, and making everyone proud.

After sixth-form, Liam leaving Outwood School to pursue a career in the Army, joining a six-month training session at the 299 Parachute Squadron Royal Engineers on George Street Wakefield.

Following completion of his course, Liams army career somewhat stalled, instead, taking six-months "off," then choosing to carry on with his education, opting to attend Pontefract College to take "A" levels.

Two years of travelling on the bus to Pontefract and back most of the time, unless sleeping in, then relying on dads taxi to get him to college on time.

Liam taking many practical, theory percussion examinations, and playing drums with a pop band "The Jarrs" at many locations during time between his college work, Brass Band rehearsals, and many concerts.

A busy active life from an early age to his teenage years, and a life I too thoroughly enjoyed.

Playing in our band during my semi and professional years, and a career worth pursuing, if Liam eventually decides to do the same.

My eldest son Warren, settling into his paramedic duties, now fully qualified, me and Liam attending the celebrated end of his academic studies in Sheffield.

A cap and gown "do," and an immensely proud day for everyone there, that included me, Liam, Warrens mum, and Warrens partner Sommer.

Warren and Sommer, both receiving news they had passed a selection process to enable them to travel to Qatar as paramedics, to work alongside other paramedics as part of the 2022 FIFA football World Cup.

Almost three months of living, travelling, and working at football stadiums throughout the length of the tournament, bringing about an amazing end to a wonderful year for both of them.

Saturday December 10th, Warren actually on duty at the stadium where England failed in the quarter final stage, and not reaching the World Cup semi-final, France winning 2-1 at the Bayt Stadium, Doha.

On the other hand, Liam concluding his two-year "A" level period at Pontefract College, and also army training at Winchester, and offered a position as percussionist in the Band of the Irish Guards.

Along with his position, Liam about to live in a two-bedroom semi-detached army residence in Hounslow, near London, sharing with a fellow musician, but he does not play in the same band.

Moving most of his belongings to his new residence, a home for the foreseeable future, and not long before an abrupt realisation of its location becoming apparent.

A half-moon shape of a number of semi-detached dwellings, the army owning and managing these properties, situated at the very end of the runway for Heathrow airport.

Britain's busiest airport, opened in March 1946, with over eighty-nine airline companies using this airport, flying to two-hundred and fourteen destinations, in eighty-four countries, dealing with nineteen million passengers every year, or the equivalent of 128,178 passengers per day.

Aircraft of all sizes, from the wide-bodied Airbus A380, and Jumbo Jets, to single engine light aircraft, passing directly over his bedroom to land, on one of two runways, and at what seems only a few hundred feet above the roof, every thirty seconds.

Surprisingly, not appearing very loud once inside, and thankfully time restrictions during the night, allowing for a good night's sleep.

Liam settling into his daily duties quickly, with changing of the guard at Buckingham Palace, St James Palace, and Windsor Castle, and playing percussion at other prestigious locations and events too.

Also, appearing on TV numerous times, while performing at the coronation of King Charles third, and Trooping the Colour as part of the Kings birthday celebrations at Horse Guards Parade

Wanting to see a Trooping the Colour spectacle for myself, rather than watching edited versions on TV, making the decision to see it "live," as it happens with Warren.

Leaving home at 01.30hr, and taking my car along with Warren, to drive the one-hundred and ninety miles, on the M1 and M25 motorways to Liams home first.

Taking a twenty-minute walk to the nearest station, and all using the tube to travel into London, a walk and journey Liam takes both ways, every working day.

Leaving Liam at the barracks to get ready, and having a look at my family ancestors statue, Lord Nelson.

Walking around the vicinity of Buckingham Palace, The Mall, and finally taking our seat at Horse Guards Parade ground, waiting patiently for the 10.00hr proceedings to start.

This rehearsal, the second, taking place a week before the actual performance, on what turned out one of the hottest Saturdays in June, unlike the previous Saturdays first rehearsal.

A sell-out first rehearsal Saturday at Horse Guards Parade, rained continuously throughout the performance, everyone taking part soaked to the skin, including instruments, rifles, gun carriages, and uniforms, and of course the audience too, the parade ground awash with lots of puddles.

After these second rehearsals came to an end, meeting up with Liam to enjoy lunch in a packed local Wetherspoons, then catching the tube back to Liams home.

A long drive ahead for me and Warren north to Wakefield, thoroughly enjoying our full day with Liam in London.

Celebrating Liams 21st birthday in July, and the engagement of Warren and Sommer, and Liam completing almost a year in this celebrated band of excellent musician's, a massive achievement for my youngest son, and with some anticipation, many more years ahead of him.

A brief resume of twenty-one fast paced years, and a reflective 2023 year, remembered for all sorts of uplifting and self-effacing reasons.

CHAPTER EIGHTEEN

Fit as a Fiddle

From an early age, my parents often said to take care, and look after myself, when leaving for work, or later years when travelling with my band.

Clearly an expression of concern for my well-being, a suggestion that I should stay safe and healthy.

At times taking this further, informed to eat good fresh food when possible, plenty of fruit and vegetables, and stay away from pre-packed ready meals, this advice will all help in enabling me to stay in good health and feeling fit.

Close family and friends often making this same remark directly to me, making me wonder, do they see or know something I don't...

I have looked upon my physical weight in relation to my height as reasonably good, regardless of what decade I find myself in.

Although over many years I have fluctuated quite a bit, remembering my weight around twelve stone with a waistline of between twenty-eight and thirty inches wet through for a number of years, while working as a joiner, and playing drums in our band.

Now after eight years as a professional musician and some thirty years in management positions, and five years and counting in retirement, I now weigh in at around seventeen stone ten pounds, with currently a thirty-eight inch, and fast-growing waist line.

A saying that having a cuddly body an asset, nevertheless, in my own opinion I feel the need to lose a few pounds, more of a benefit to my aging body, although never refusing a cuddle.

I wouldn't say that I am overweight, but you can imagine my shock when putting my age, height, and weight into an on-line screening app, only to discover the generated statistics pointed out that I have a high Body

Mass Index (BMI), of over twenty-five, and alarmingly classed as not one bit overweight, but fundamentally obese.

Looking at my reflection through a full height mirror, I do have a bit of a podgy tummy, and protruding squishy "love handles," but in my eyes, certainly not looking or feeling obese.

While in my school years and throughout my teens, I would say I have never seen myself as having an athletic type of body, more likely because I did not like taking part in sports at school, but involved in lots of exercise outside school hours.

For instance, riding my bike to Ings Road senior school every day, over a mile and a half each way, also working for a milkman most mornings before attending school for over two years, also undertaking the usual paper rounds.

Furthermore, taking on a Saturday job the previous year while still at school, assisting with the delivery of bread and assorted cakes around the Batley and Cleckheaton districts for a local bakery.

All of these youthful pastimes required lots of corporeal agility, and in my opinion, had I regularly taken part in school sports, and with a greater amount of enthusiasm and determination, perhaps I may have remained in a much better physical shape than I am today.

However, the school sports that I did reluctantly take part in, such as gym fitness, running, rugby, five-a-side football, and cricket, sort of enjoying all at the time, until frequent injuries put me off taking part in all of the above.

These injuries, only minor, although on one occasion requiring stitches, not obtained as a result of an individual excessive performance, more in the wrong place at the wrong time, or not paying attention to my teacher during each activity.

For example, having a distinct lack of ability as a footballer, and always put out of harm's way in goal, which as a collaborator absolutely fine with a good defence, or if no corner kicks awarded, or the goal mouth not full of water, or goalposts made of harmless foam.

Predictably, I would never become a Gordon Banks or Peter Shilton, as at the end of each one-sided high scoring game, I would come off the field totally despondent with blood emerging from some orifice or other.

Much the same with each and every other school sport I took part in, grass burns on my elbows and knees, burst nose, bruises in abundance, and receiving burns to my hands while sliding down the rope after a hurried climb towards the gym ceiling.

Although, what I consider as the least physical sport where I required stitches to a gaping head wound.

Would you believe, cricket, put in the position of deep forward, stood out on the fields perimeter, and possibly the furthest from the stump, undeniably out of harm's way, or so thought our sports teacher.

Cricket, definitely not one of my favourite sports to take part in, and the least likely I could observe with any degree of enjoyment, so most of the time my attention span extremely limited to say the least, finding the whole experience boring, especially this particular game of cricket.

Who would have thought that one of the schools best batsman, and a big hitter, repeatedly hitting sixes, would connect perfectly with the now assaulted looking cork ball once again, sending it hurtling at the speed of light directly towards me.

Had I paid some attention to what a cricket game is all about, this may have become the catch of the century, boosting my self-esteem and that of my school mates to the highest level.

As I have said, finding the game of cricket rather boring, and for over half of the game I had not even touched the ball, so not even looking towards the wicket, and unaware a former glossy well-thrashed red cork and leather shod ball heading in my direction, and at a tremendous speed.

I recall watching a passenger train with many carriages heading towards Westgate Station over the elevated "ninety-nine arches," and hearing someone shouting, "Dobbo, catch," but far too late, just as I began to turned to face the batsman, "whack," the ball hitting the back of my head...

I have talked about seeing stars in a number of my chapters and books, but never feeling a pain like I did on this day, a sensation more like a whack on the head via a cricket bat, rather than a cricket ball.

The rules of the game, in principle, quite easy to understand, but I cannot recall one such rule saying each, and every man fielding should give 100% attention throughout this uninspiring game.

A trip to the outpatients at Clayton Hospital required, and three stitches to a bloody hair-soaked head wound.

It did heal quickly, but my head sore to the touch, and even after having umpteen stitches removed, the pain lingered on for a few weeks.

An exaggeration with umpteen, exactly three stitches, but feeling like the nurse had removed lots more.

I cannot remember ever playing the game of cricket again at school, but did get cajoled into playing for fun with an inter-team challenge at work, a few years later.

Ironically, while recently attending the funeral of a former colleague, most of the eulogy based around the theme of cricket, as Bob not only a good maintenance manager, but to learn a brilliant cricketer and captain too.

During the many depictions of Bobs working days at Wakefield Council and Wakefield and District Housing (WDH), and now his playing cricket days, a former teammate reading out a poem making everyone in the crematorium laugh.

Triggering those thoughts about my minimal experience of the game, but even though accurate in my case, I had never thought of cricket as this.

"You have two sides, one out in the field, and one in.

Each man that's in the side that goes out, and when he's out, he comes in, and the next man goes in, until he is out.

When they are all out, the side that is out comes in, and the side that has been in, then goes out, and tries to get those coming in, out.

Sometimes you get men still in, and not out.

When a man goes out to go in, the men who are out, try to get him out, and when he is out, he goes in, and the next man in, goes out, and goes in.

There are two men called umpires who stay out all the time, and they decide when the men who are in are out.

When both sides have been in, and all the men have been out, and both sides have been out, and both sides have been out twice after all the men have been in, including those who are not out, that is the end of the game."

Simple...

Where am I...

A little confused after reading that.

Oh yes, physical fitness, and why I feel like I am today...

Thinking back to my joinery and band days, in fact, two jobs on the go at once for over eight years.

Joinery during the day, our band during the night, none stop seven days a week.

Unloading timber wagons, making, and lifting wood window frames, hardwood external doors, making, lifting, and stacking staircases in a joiners shop, or on a building site, Monday through to Friday each week with my apprentice companion Gary Shaw.

After tea each night, traveling all over the country, unloading our van of musical equipment, carrying everything into working mens clubs and placing it on countless stages, setting up, and playing our tunes to at times sublime audiences, until all hours.

Then loading the van and returning home, including weekends, and in most cases, a Sunday lunchtime show thrown in for good measure.

A definite déjà vu, or groundhog day, every single day, so quite easy to explain my physical appearance at that time.

Looking more like a six-foot two-inch bean pole, straight up and down, muscles like nots in cotton, with a full head of permed curly hair, and if wearing my Cuban heeled shoes, even taller.

I remained in this "shape" for many years, and not really noticing how much I had changed until into my late fifties.

Recalling a few years during the early eighties when attending Shapers Gym, located on the corner of Westgate and Smyth Street in the former Co-op building, Unity House.

Working out three times every week, Monday, Wednesdays and Friday's, men only days, following a designed plan of working with weights and on a variety of apparatus, and consuming gallons of protein drinks, all to give me muscles and a toned "shape."

The gyms owner often made comments about all my hard work, saying that as having a magnanimous nature, I should attend the gym more often, train a good deal harder, using a more active plan that will improve and develop my body even more.

The final coup de grace statement…

I should seriously take up body building, and attend shows and competitions on behalf of the gym.

WHAT!!!

During this time, I played drums professionally in a band called "Stormer," so out most nights touring the many working mens clubs around a hundred or so miles radius of home, perhaps no time to even contemplate showing off my body.

My Stagewear consisting of blue wet-look shorts, white t-shirt and trainers while playing my drumkit, and maintaining an all over tan as a result of a thirty-minute sunbed session after each training period at the gym.

I suppose already showing off a little more body than I should, but saying that, and drummers always placed behind with the drumkit central at the rear of the stage, so not exactly a "front" man in full view of an audience.

Apparently, my developed shape partly the result of having "big" bones, and with the help of continuous training, bringing about increasingly large arms, legs, neck, and chest bicep measurements, loosely resembling, or similar to an Arnold Schwarzenegger class body…

Nevertheless, the ever-expanding changes to my physique I did not like, and becoming less and less familiar with a reflection that looked back at me while training in the gym.

Now becoming increasingly difficult to purchase smart looking trousers where my thighs or bottom did not split the seams, or shirts with a neck measurement of over 20 inches, one measurement I felt too far.

Understandable now why most, if not all bodybuilders wear track suits and t-shirts at all times of the day, a realisation for me that enough is enough.

Cancelling my membership and aiming to get my body shape back to some "normality" as soon as possible.

That easier said than done, taking more than a few years to "shrink" my form back to looking like a kind of typical bloke, although I seriously think a marriage breakdown and divorce had a lot to do with it.

I did think about taking a long walk, in fact, quite long, covering a distance of 22,387Km or 13911 miles, from Cape Town South Africa to Magadan in Russia.

This "walk" taking all of one-hundred and eighty-seven days non-stop, 4,492 hours, or five-hundred and sixty-one days, walking 8 hours a day.

The route would take in seventeen countries, six time zones, crossing lots of bridges, and in no particular order, encounter all the seasons of the year.

Obviously, soon putting that walk to one side, and permanently on the back burner, instead, deciding on staying local, with walks into town or to mums home.

However, in just a short period of time I can once again purchase jeans, trousers, and shirts with a reasonable size neck, with no fear of all of these garments splitting at the seams.

No more gulping down protein drinks, lifting or using weights to manipulate muscle building, or anything remotely involving any form of exercise, other than walking.

That said, I still had equipment to carry into clubs, as part of playing in our band, but minimal in comparison.

There you have it, simple, however, a distinct lack of any form of exercise has resulted in me piling on weight, and despondently not a single muscle of any kind.

I do consider myself as an active retired pensioner, and certainly not a couch potato glued to the TV, in fact on the go most days.

I will just have to up my activities, and maybe exercise with lots more walking, swimming, eat less, or eat food that does not help in putting on weight.

Taking all of the above into consideration, perhaps a clever idea to join a gym once again, but not to take my age and abilities seriously.

An induction session booked to bring me up to speed with all this new-fangled high-tech apparatus, and a plan of action for exercises to take place over a three day a week morning attendance.

Not that it matters when I attend, mornings much better for me after getting up after a night's sleep just after 06.00hr for the last ten years, my body clock accustomed to an early start.

My 08.00hr Monday induction going extremely well, with no mishaps, the apparatus easy to use, even for me, and a much-improved specification than when training for over three-years at Shapers, and the occasional visit to Tops health centre in Outwood.

Taking to cycling and rowing, working up a profound sweat while reaching my daily training targets, but without a great deal of muscle effort, not ideal if wanting to burn of lots of inches from my waist and tummy.

Sticking to a similar routine on each visit, and getting to know a few regulars that attend around the same time as me, although not noticing a significant difference in my "shape" at all.

Still the same podgy tummy and squishy "Love handles," and after almost a year of three times per week training.

Then along came the covid epidemic, so taking to walking, along with Lottie and Ted, although reluctantly at first, that's Lottie and Ted, my Lhasa Apso dogs.

Lottie, the mum of Ted now in her fourteenth year, while Ted coming up to twelve years old, walked miles and miles throughout the pandemic, registering over eight hundred miles in total on my walking app, ambling along around all our neighbourhood, more than not, covering over five miles each day.

Going back to the gym did not bring about any further change at all, even after another year of constant three day a week activity, perhaps a different approach needed.

Almost a joint decision between Amanda and me, to take a trial swim at Minsthorpe leisure centre.

I will explain.

My youngest son Liam, and Amandas youngest daughter, Rosie, both at rehearsals for Carlton and Frickley Brass Band in the next village of South Elmsal, and with-in five minutes of the pool.

Swimming a perfect resolution to fill in the time, and get fit, as driving twelve miles just to sit in the car for over two hours waiting for our children's rehearsal to conclude, nonsense.

Alternatively, drive there and drop off our kids, drive back home, only on arrival with just a fifteen-minute break, having to about turn, drive the twelve miles to pick them both up and return home once again, further nonsense.

A forty-eight-mile extravagant journey for just over two-hour rehearsal, so a few lengths in a local pool making a difference to not only our bodies, but the environment, perfect.

Our regular swims started with completing twenty-four lengths, an achievement for me, as not a strong swimmer at all.

However, Amanda much stronger, and if not waiting for me to catch up at each end, would have probably completed thirty lengths in the same period.

The slight delay did more often than not, result in a chat, as that few minutes interruption helped me to get some air into my lungs instead of an abundance of chlorine tasting pool water.

Amanda and I have continued with these once-a-week swimming sessions long after Liam and Rosie left our respective homes to go to London and university.

Now accomplishing up to sixty-four lengths of Sun Lane's twenty-five-meter swimming pool, equating to a mile in just a few minutes past an hour, integrating ample chatting about various subjects too.

An achievement for me, as swimming not high on my agenda at the best of times, but I do really enjoy swimming with a partner or other friends.

As at times, Amandas daughters Holly and Rosie, and Liam have joined us when on leave or mid-term break, with plenty of chatting and laughter and not much swimming on those occasions.

Usually, an attempt made to defer our chatting until after our swim, when enjoying a drink either in the pools café, or to include a snack with a drink at Muffin Break.

Sadly, even with all this effort, I still have the very same "shape," and my weight has not fluctuated much either.

I have found it difficult to keep away from chocolate and large helpings of tasty food, so I have only myself to blame, although since purchasing an all singing and dancing watch, I can see results already.

Perhaps my self-imposed diet, working afterall, and with more patience, at long last my health watch assisting with notifications of weight loss, sleep patterns, counting of steps and general daily exercise helping no end.

So, who knows, in the next few months my body shape and weight may become reasonable for my height afterall.

I have a partner in crime to assist me with all these weight watch shenanigans, as Amanda my stargazing companion, has the very same health watch, so we can exchange our daily statistics, and our swimming day results.

Onwards and downwards!!!!

CHAPTER NINETEEN

The Kings Birthday Celebrations

(Trooping of the Colours)

Car journeys on Britain's motorways have become a bit of a nightmare, and not an ideal way to travel, unless an absolute necessity.

Continual road works, full road and lane closures, breakdowns, millions of top hat red and white traffic cones, flashing speed restriction lights, and speed cameras galore.

Huge information screens, above and at the side of motorways, abundant traffic lights, and still incidents and accidents aplenty.

A 2021 survey pointing out all of the above, and saying an everyday occurrence when travelling on Britain's ailing roads.

An incredible 247,800 miles of roads in the UK, consisting of 31,900 miles of major roads, and 2,300 miles of motorways, the rest made up of dual carriageways, and "A" and "B" roads, and dirt tracks.

Over the many years in our band days, I have travelled many miles on all of these roads, even the dirt tracks, regardless of sat-nav instrumentation.

Our A-to-Z road maps useful in taking us everywhere to our gigs, some numerous times, in particular, along the A1, M1, M6, M8, M60 and M62 motorways to name a few, and more recently my personal journeys on the A1, A14, M11, M20 and M25.

From passing my driving test in 1969, I have covered many miles in various vehicles, on new highways as constructed and opened, and many older roads throughout the UK.

Travelling from club to club, venue to venue, hotels and digs, airports, for work and pleasure, and in all weathers, or during my musical and working career.

Fortunately, during my many years of travelling hundreds of thousands of miles I have suffered very few breakdowns, and not involved in any accidents requiring rescue vehicles, the police, or an ambulance for recovery.

Although I have seen plenty involving all of these, and the subsequent results and consequences of them.

Recently I have made quite a few trips to London, a journey I travelled often some forty-five years ago, as part of our exhilarating Black Lace band days, and umpteen times again around fifteen years ago, mainly to visit my newfound biological father, and an abundance of relatives I knew nothing of.

Since my biological dad Tom's passing in November 2014, these trips to our capitol have only taken place a few times, until now.

As mentioned in a previous chapter, my youngest son Liam, now an army musician, playing in the Band of the Irish Guards, working from Wellington Barracks.

Liam commuting daily from his second home in Hounslow into London each day, taking a brisk twenty-minute walk to the local tube station, and around the same to his barracks.

When taking up his post, and given living quarters it became my job to move the remainder of Liams belongings from our home in Wrenthorpe to Hounslow, a distance of 195 miles, and taking almost four hours to get there, regardless of traffic.

Liams new home a convenient location to park my car, and just the same short but invigorating twenty-minute walk to the nearest station to catch the tube for visits into London.

Mostly driving on my own, and taking place a few times during January, also in the month of May, and one particular time when meeting up with Liam after a drive down to London with my eldest son Warren.

On this occasion using my car, as the last time making the same journey using Warrens fully electric Audi etron, brought about a bit of a standstill at one of the many service stations on the M1.

A long queue had formed, all waiting to recharge their cars on six available charging stations, and looking at the cars to the front of us, clearly some time remaining before our turn.

A hot cuppa and cooked breakfast helping to reduce our frustration, but even after eating, still a further forty-minute delay in waiting for a vacant charging point, and then another thirty minutes to "fill up," not an ideal situation if in a rush.

If for business or pleasure, currently no comparison between filling up your car, van, bus or wagon with diesel or petrol fuel, much better than having to join a queue for an unknown length of time to "fill up" at a charging point.

Although no messy and potentially hazardous fluids to worry about, almost as simple as plugging in a kettle or toaster, when using Warrens all electric car to drive to Winchester on April 28th, 2022, to attend Liam's pass out parade, the following day.

Staying overnight in a nearby hotel for an early 08.00hr start, thankfully ideal weather for a special all outdoor morning event, Princess Ann, our Queens daughter, also in attendance.

Me and Ashley sharing a room, but first tucking into a delicious evening meal, and not late to hit the sack, for our early morning start.

I did become emotional at the thought of Liam finally passing out as a fully-fledged soldier, and about to embark on his musical career within the army.

A further six months of training based at HMS Nelson in Portsmouth prior to posting, and coincidentally, this venue one of a few in the location our band Black Lace performed at during the late seventies.

Such a proud moment to see Liam and the rest of his company marching onto the parade ground, with an army band leading the way.

Princess Ann in attendance to take the salute, and give out individual awards to recruits that had achieved a high standard during training.

Liam given an award for the fittest recruit in his squad, a surprise for us, and a rather lengthy one-to-one chat with Princess Ann on the parade ground in the process.

Liam had a number of photographs taken in doors with Princess Ann prior to the ceremony start, unfortunately, these images seem to have disappeared, as despite numerous enquiries, not yet located for Liam to purchase.

Spending the next few hours on and around the parade ground with Liam, Warren, Sommer, and Ash, and meeting lots of Liams fellow soldier friends before all heading back home to Wakefield.

After just one hour of driving, the need to "fill up," and yet again, meeting with another queue in the services on the northbound carriageway of the M1, directly opposite the service station used as on our way south the previous day.

Unfortunately, only two charging points available at this station, with two cars on charge and four cars waiting, giving the impression of yet another lengthy tea break.

All enjoying a tasty KFC, Liam choosing a vegan option of food, and once on our way again, I became the nominated driver, and what an experience.

Sat in the front seat as a passenger for most of the journey, until now taking the helm, adjusting my seat, and then "starting" up the electric "engine."

Super-fast acceleration for such a large heavy car, with lots of luggage, four passengers, and me adding to the weight, although not appearing to make any difference at all.

Thoroughly enjoying this driving experience, and with-in minutes everyone fast asleep, so all noticeably confident to let me take the wheel to drive a top of the range all electric zoom machine.

Or perhaps everyone so worn out, and obviously extremely tired, I became the only other option.

A day to remember, for all sorts of reasons, and confident I will hear more of Liams training exploits when eventually arriving home.

I do like to hear of innovative technologies, and in particular fully eco-friendly electric or hybrid cars, but still a long way to go with lithium-ion car battery development.

The duration in miles for each maximum charge, would benefit a major increase in electric car purchases, and the infrastructure required to enable a much quicker charging capability for busy on the go motorists, a further essential bonus.

I do diversify...

Oh yes, my recently acquired VW Tiguan R-Line TDi S-A, statistically a much-improved economical diesel SUV car from my last Tiguan model, using less than half a tank of fuel to make this, my second journey to London in my new car.

With an adaptive cruise control (ACC) fitted as standard, making driving this car all the more relaxing.

Not to worry about speeding as when I have activated the ACC, this gizmo takes over all the usual tedious decision-making objectives.

It has speed limit indication that automatically slows to each speed limit on A roads, dual carriageways, and motorways, and increases accordingly, without the need to touch the accelerator or breaks, in fact just to steer the car required, even that controlled to a point.

A definite bonus when on "smart" motorways, with speed limits constantly changing due to traffic conditions, my car dutifully obliging, adjusting its forward motion, matching the speed indicated on the overhead gantries.

The ACC also judges speed and distance of the car or vehicle in front of you, slowing or accelerating as required, so much more than a conventional cruise control system, enabling a more stress-free motorway driving experience.

I would think this addition to motoring, making yet another massive step towards enabling driverless cars in the near future.

Filling up the previous day prior to leaving home at 02.00hr to pick up Warren, driving on the M1 all the way south until reaching the M25, taking an anticlockwise direction, and all lanes reasonably quiet at this unearthly hour.

Making a scheduled stop, two miles from Liams home at a 24-hour MacDonalds, for a much-needed break.

A quick dash to the loo, thankfully, both able to hold our bladders, until the very last minute.

Using a huge touch screen to place our order, and soon drinking a 06.00hr cuppa and tucking into a breakfast treat of a bacon and egg bap.

Feeling refreshed and rejuvenated after our long uninterrupted drive from Wakefield, now driving the few remaining miles to Liams home, where he patiently waited for our arrival.

Leaving my car in an on-street parking spot opposite Liams home, then taking a short but hurried walk to Hounslow tube station for our rush-hour trip into the capitol.

Saying our "see you later" to Liam as he entered Wellington Barracks to change into uniform, and prepare for his second rehearsal of King Charles 3rd, birthday celebrations at Horse Guards Parade.

Still reasonably early, giving me and Warren an opportunity to have a look around the immediate vicinity of Wellington Barracks.

Finding time for a coffee, and taking in a look at one of my ancestors atop a huge stone column, Lord Horatio Nelson, in Trafalgar Square.

10 Downing Street, The Cenotaph, Buckingham Palace, and The Mall, finally finding and taking our seat at Horse Guards Parade.

Already the London temperature into double figures, and today's forecast predicting a hot cloud free sweltering day.

A far cry from the first rehearsal last Saturday week, a complete washout, raining most of the day, although that did not stop the first of two Saturday rehearsals taking place.

Finding our block and seat numbers, the very top row facing Buckingham Palace, just visible way in the distance, a pair of excellent seats, sitting comfortably for a precise10.00hr start, to view a finely tuned spectacle, the second dummy run for the Kings birthday celebrations.

Although locating them did not come without a telling off .

Walking up the Mall, and turning right towards the parade ground and finding ourselves at the wrong side of security barriers, although not knowing this at the time.

Continuing on foot, chatting, and laughing, until two stern faced looking Police Officers approached us.

Clearly aggrieved, pointing out their concerns, and wanting to know how and why the both of us had entered a restricted area, and what of our intentions.

Explaining our apparent wrong turning, and offering genuine apologies.

Showing our entrance, and seating tickets, the police officers then pointing to a manned gate, giving advice and guidance, of how to safely reach the main entrance and enter the parade ground.

Lots of security personnel, some armed, a bit of an eyeopener when living in our home city of Wakefield Yorkshire, a sight seldom seen.

Showing our e-tickets from my phone, and purchasing two programs, and then heading with other invited guests beneath an ornate stone archway onto the parade ground.

Men and women in formal dress, and noticing most wearing military medals, and sun hats, sat all around as far as the eye could see.

As Warren and I climbed the steps in our stand, and instantly spotting I am somewhat underdressed compared to others.

Both Warren and I did have a collar and tie, (I borrowed a tie from Liams home,) trousers, and polished shoes, looking reasonably smart.

Putting our dress code aside, feeling positively privileged and so proud to sit amongst serving and retired military personnel, family, and friends.

Taking our seats and enjoying the view across the parade ground, commenting that Liam had done exceptionally well in purchasing these tickets in an ideal location to watch the up-and-coming celebrations, and an attempt to spot Liam amongst all the other military musicians too.

I began looking through the program photographs and order of service in an exceptionally produced and printed schedule, when a buzz of conversation erupted around the parade ground as the distant sound of band music broke the hot and getting hotter still air.

Sat at the opposite side of Warren, a lady commenting to her teenage daughter, that daddy on his way marching up The Mall, and playing in the first band to come into view.

Talk about heart in your mouth time, what a spectacle as the first band entered the parade ground.

The drum major leading the way, dressed in a unique uniform, including bearskin, with bands crest, an ornate sash, or baldric, and mace used to signal commands.

A multitude of soldiers followed close behind the band, all marching in complete unison to the amazing sounds of the foremost band.

With the amount of foot traffic about to enter and march on the parade grounds fine gravel surface, and the horses and gun carriages yet to appear, no wonder vehicles pulled water sprinklers back and forth over the gravel surface.

An obvious good soaking in lots of time prior to the celebrations commencement to prevent lots of dust blowing around.

Saying to Warren, that sprinklers not required at all at last week's first rehearsal with all the rain about.

The lady sitting next to Warren, began pointing and giving an indication to her daughter how to spot her father, counting down the line of bandsmen heading across the far side of the parade ground.

Excitement an understatement as she identified her dad, pointing him out, just as the second drum major and band, with soldiers following, all arriving at the parade ground, marching just a few minutes behind the lead band and soldiers.

The band of the Irish Guards next, the third band of four to arrive at the parade ground, and my turn to point out and spot Liam, and hopefully before Warren.

Hearing the band of the Irish guards brought a tear to my eyes, feeling so proud as they started to emerge from the spectator lined Mall.

An Irish Wolfhound mascot (Turlough Mor) named Seamus, with dog handler leading in the band.

Finally, the last of four marching bands and soldiers entered the ground, all now creating that formidable crunching sound as they began to get into formation, and looking picture perfect to me.

Then again, what do I know about what has gone on when creating an amazing spectacle of this magnitude.

Constant band rehearsals, not only playing their respective instruments, but marching in precise formation, criss-crossing, about turns, and circular marching.

You name it, all the bands did it, and all without bumping into fellow musicians, potentially causing embarrassing chaos in front of thousands of spectators, including esteemed guests, royalty, and of course the TV cameras.

Although saying this, the rising heat becoming almost unbearable, and as for the standing armed soldiers, mounted soldiers, and musicians, had now started to take effect.

Soldiers standing at arms began to faint, toppling over, full length, and musicians too, a trombonist fainting whilst still playing, and continued to play while laid on the ground, as stretcher bearing personal ran to their aid.

I had wondered how everyone had coped so far without incident, dressed in their smart tunics and bearskin fur hats, as other paid guests all around, including Warren and me, just sat down doing nothing, had begun to perspire.

Out in the open with no shade for protection from this incredible heat, with not a hint of cooling breeze across the parade ground, most spectators using programs as fans to help keep cool.

To our left, spectators clearly in the shade as overhanging deciduous tree branches sheltering them from the sun, unlike the majority watching and taking part as the spectacle progressed.

Talk about extremes from one week to another, pouring rain and cold temperatures on the first rehearsal, and unbearable heat on the second.

What would the weather forecast predict next Saturday, when the celebrations proper would take place, anyone's guess.

More than a little worried about Liam, wondering if he had drunk plenty of water before the start of his bands long march up The Mall, and would he last throughout the duration of this rather overheated, and clearly gruelling second rehearsal.

To see it all happening on the parade ground bringing about gasps from the capacity audience, as one two-man team after another, ran to help those succumbing to increasing heat.

The fallen trombonist did get to his feet and continued to play to thunderous applause, but once again after just a few minutes, capitulating to the ever-increasing morning heat.

Crumpling to the gravel surface once again, just as the stretcher bearers got to him.

Gently lifting him and his trombone onto the stretcher and a quick dash towards the parade ground perimeter, meanwhile the show continued, with the household cavalry now joining everyone else on the parade ground.

Even though the water bowsers had thoroughly soaked the gravel, dust started to rise and form a cloudy haze, as the mounted horses began to pull gun carriages at a steady canter around this enormous ground.

Our programs becoming even more of a needy fan, wafting away not only the sweltering heat, but also the rising dust.

Nothing changed at all on the parade ground, soldiers at ease, the bands playing, horses pulling gun carriages circulating the parade ground as if everything going to plan.

Prince William joining the parade on horseback, following an immaculate horse drawn carriage that in just seven days' time will contain King Charles 3rd.

Overall, at least a dozen soldiers and musicians overcome in today's developing rising heat, the stretcher bearers certainly needed on one of the hottest May days in years.

Thankfully the both of us attending this week's rehearsal and not last Saturdays overcast damp rainy one, preferring heat rather than rain.

The show obviously over as the bands, marching soldiers and mounted sections all started to leave the parade ground, all marching or riding to the amazing sound of each of the four bands.

Leaving the way they came, across the parade ground and down a ten deep spectator full Mall, towards Victoria Memorial and Buckingham Palace.

Warren and I getting to our feet and joining other spectators leaving the seating areas, some making their way across the parade ground, certainly a short cut if heading down The Mall.

Warren suggesting a good route to take and should go the same way to join others along what appears a short cut avoiding the busy Mall.

A steady walk over Horse Guards Road, and heading through St James Park, past the terribly busy St James Café, across The Blue bridge, after standing back to allow a dozen or so marching soldiers priority access.

Finally, onto Birdcage Walk to meet up with Liam at Wellington Barracks, and to find somewhere for a bite to eat.

Liam emerging in casual clothes after a further twenty-minutes, looking none the worse for wear, saying he did get rather hot and sweaty in his Busby and uniform, and felt a little faint while marching, playing, and stood for prolonged periods of time on the parade ground.

However, he had drunk plenty of water beforehand, and above all else, the toilet desperately needed as soon as the band arrived back at the barracks.

Liam knows the location around the vicinity of the barracks, and it shows, as the three of us heading towards the nearest Weatherspoon's for some lunch.

Everywhere heaving with locals and tourists, everyone enjoying todays rather hot climate, in most cases sat outside to eat and drink.

All the café open-air areas packed, and no doubt our preferred lunchtime venue just the same.

Arriving home just after eleven o'clock, a full twenty-one hours from locking my front door, to putting my key in the door and opening it once again, but what a day, and so pleased I made the effort, Warren agreeing with me.

Taking just four hours to drive from Liams Hounslow home, and with a short toilet and cuppa stop too, although still feeling rather stuffed following our appetising lunch at Weatherspoon's.

I thought with all the walking to the tube from Weatherspoon's, and then walking from the tube station to Liams I could have walked a bit off...

Although, while travelling, a bit of excitement taking place at one of the tube station stops.

The train had come to a halt, but did not leave as quickly when leaving at the previous stop, when suddenly, armed railway police ran past us in the carriage, asking us to leave the train, but to remain on the platform.

Over ten mystifying minutes chatting amongst ourselves, when suddenly police emerged from the train with a young man, handcuffed to an officer, but attempting to struggle free, lashing out with his legs and shouting abuse.

A distressed young lady just behind this apparent free for all, also leaving the train, other officers now surrounding her, and all heading our way.

No idea what had transpired while on the train, a few carriages to the rear of ours, and no time to find out, as the guard blowing his whistle for everyone to re-board our respective carriages, and soon back on our way.

To think, Liam uses the tube for his journey into London to his place of work and home again every day, and for over a year, with no reported incidents of this nature, and after today's skirmish, I am keeping everything crossed it was an isolated incident.

Soon to bed, alarm set for 07.15, and after a good night's sleep, yet another exciting day awaits.

Perhaps not.

CHAPTER TWENTY

A Billion Miles From Earth

My interest in astronomy only a few years in the making, but from an early age always looking skyward, and wondered what lies beyond our visual understanding.

An enduring curiosity continuously around viewing the heavens, space travel, the technology, infrastructure and the many men and women behind these amazing achievements, and voyages into our solar system.

From the era of rockets, the space shuttles, and building of the International Space Station, also putting the Hubble and James Webb Space Telescopes, and many satellites into orbit.

The new era of private enterprise such as SpaceX, Blue Origin, Virgin Galactic, and of course NASA, and ESA, also many others, all either preparing or achieving the aim to launch rockets into space.

Most containing satellites, men, women, and mechanical robots, into orbit, to the International Space Station (ISS) circling around Mother Earth.

Or even further into space, as mentioned, the James Webb Space telescope, orbiting the Sun at the second Lagrange point, about one-million miles from Earth in a halo orbit, allowing the telescope to maintain a roughly constant distance with the Sun, Earth, and Moon.

Also, a unique collection of remarkable scientists and engineers in building crafts and machines to journey, and land robots on planets or asteroids within our solar system, and travel far beyond, sending back utterly amazing images, all in my lifetime.

To me, the Apollo program of rockets, definitely the most famous of these incredible sky bound machines, Apollo 8 in particular.

Speeding three astronauts, Frank Borman, Jim Lovell, and Bill Anders,

240,000 miles to the moon and back in late1968, early 69, signified with using the number 8 on all publications, becoming the first humans to orbit another world and return safely home.

Since the retirement of the space shuttle program or Space Transportation System (STS) the last of which Atlantis, completing mission STS135, and landing for the last time on July 21ˢᵗ, 2011.

Powerful two and three stage rockets have now become the "shuttles" of the future for procuring anything and everything into the gravity free blackness of space.

Elon Musk, and Space X capturing my imagination, watching each and every launch from conception to the current initiatives of this amazing organisation.

To observe a two-hundred-ton first stage booster rocket return from blast-off, and land safely on a flat surface, amazing genius, but to see the same returning booster "caught" in mid-air by "chopsticks," located from a four-hundred-and-eighty-foot tower (the highest launch tower in the world) directly above the launch pad, yet another truly mind-blowing feat.

Who would have thought that science fiction from yesteryear, now becoming science fact, as these huge rockets with up to thirty or more engines propel enormous three-hundred-and-ninety-seven-feet high structures into space, and the boosters actually returning for re-use.

As a result of my earlier interest in space and space travel, becoming a paid-up member of West Yorkshire Astronomical Society, based at a local observatory in Pontefract, to help further my knowledge.

Although, my visit and membership would not have taken place without the friendship of Amanda, the mum of Rosie, who attended music lessons, rehearsals, and playing in concerts with my youngest son Liam, in various music ensembles.

I will explain…

As parents and regular chauffeurs for our children, me and Amanda taking them here there and everywhere, and over many years, cementing our continuing friendship.

Unbeknown to me at the time, Amanda already a keen stargazer, and familiar with what a clear night sky has to offer, having occupied a steamer chair in their family homes rear garden, and looking skyward over many years.

Sitting there, with many layers of clothing, and donning a hat scarf and gloves, effective insulation required during many a cloud free dark chilly night gazing into the heavens.

Using a star map to identify the many visible stars, planets of our solar system, constellations, and locations of deep sky objects in our northern hemisphere, and all with just the naked eye.

Our friendship would take a different approach, when chatting over a coffee waiting for our children to finish music lessons or rehearsals, when mentioning her knowledge of the night sky, as I too had wonderment, but not done anything about it.

A little embarrassing when mentioning my involvement and limited awareness of the night sky.

Just a glance now and then, or perhaps more of a long panoramic gaze when in dark sky regions, amazed at the many stars in my view, dumbfounded, but not taking time to find out what I had actually looked at.

Our discussions over many hours in the Manygates music hub café, covered lots of topics, but always coming back to the visible wonders of the night sky.

You can imagine my surprise when chatting once again at the café, Amanda saying she had searched the internet many times, seeking for observatories or astronomical societies in our location, and one in particular looking promising, and with-in a forty-five-minute drive from our village.

The Rosse observatory in Pontefract, open every Tuesday evening, and about to launch a regular Friday night for beginners to astronomy.

Amanda making all the necessary arrangements for a joint visit, to experience looking at the night sky through a professional telescope, and to add to knowledge Amanda already has, and an absolute start from the beginning for me.

Our first of two visits over a month, taking place in October/November 2017, and I could say the rest now history.

So much has transpired since those early visits, and talked about in other publications of mine, nevertheless, I feel some explanation as to where the observatory, and what its members and visitors are presently doing.

Our regular Friday night visits continued after inauguration of our first few beginners evenings, getting involved with other members and visitors, becoming part of this amazing hub of keen and knowledgeable astronomers.

At times an infuriating hobby, as always weather dependant, clear skies a must, whether viewing the night sky, or solar viewing during the day, however, our meteorological conditions not giving as many clear cloud free Friday nights as expected.

Owning two identical pairs of binoculars, a pair purchased for use when in employment, and my biological dad giving me the second pair, so offering my purchased binoculars to Amanda, to keep and use whenever at home on holidays or while at the observatory.

Each other's homes on clear nights becoming an option, as and when time permitted, and other than Friday nights at the observatory, to scan the night sky.

Both having a different celestial view from our rear gardens, regardless of light pollution from neighbours outside security illuminations, or streetlights.

A good East and South view from my rear garden, but with some obstructions, and Amanda with an East, West, and Northern view from her homes rear garden.

Although Amandas telescope quickly moved to the driveway to capture a South view, sadly encountering lots of light pollution from nearby homes and street lights in this location.

Remembering one occasion when Liam joined us at Amandas home, and with the fourth planet of our solar system almost in view.

Mars, hiding just below the opposite roofline of properties directly across the road.

Without hesitation, Liam picking up Amandas recently purchased Christmas present, a six-inch Dobsonian telescope, and running down the street with it held firmly in his arms.

Built of strong materials, and not just Liams arms and legs, these scopes not lightweight at all, but Liam handling the scope as though light as a feather, running at a good pace almost fifty meters away, before gently setting down the telescope on the pavement.

Pointing the scope immediately skyward between the rooftops of two houses to capture a magnified view, and once the rest of us had caught up, and with a little adjustment to height and location, all of us enjoying an amazing observation of the red planet Mars.

A sigh of relief from my point of view, Liam making the short but emphatic run without falling or dropping Amandas telescope, and what Amandas neighbours must have thought, I have no idea.

A much better and clearer view some fifty meters down the road, than when the telescope placed on Amandas light polluted front driveway.

On a normal clear night would see us picking out individual stars, star clusters, constellations, planets, and smudgy exceptionally deep sky objects, Amandas knowledge of the night sky aiding me no end.

Our standing at the observatory taking a turn for the better, as both of us elected to the committee, then at the next Annual General Meeting, Amanda chosen as secretary, a position she has confidently held for over six years.

Lots of other changes taking place at the observatory, including the introduction of a last Friday of the month Young Astronomers evening.

Children from four years of age to twelve, along with parents, invited to book at a small cost to take part in an organised night, consisting of a presentation talk, stargazing, arts, and crafts.

Both me and Amanda taking to these nights like ducks to water, thoroughly enjoying the last Friday of the month events.

As numbers of children with parents gradually increased each month, from tens to twenties, and clearly no need to advertise, as all the committee extremely happy with a constant monthly increase.

Children provided with a drink and snack at the half-time change over, from Arts and Crafts to the observatory, and visa-versa, also personal cards stamped at each attendance, and when full, will grant children and accompanying parents a cost-free visit.

Nevertheless, remembering one particular Young Astronomers Friday night, when numbers jumped from around twenty-five, to a phenomenal ninety children.

All accompanied with parents, grandparents, aunties, and uncles, descending on gobsmacked observatory volunteers.

Absolute mayhem ensued, as the queue to sign-in grew ever longer, and with a carpark already full, cars filling up the kerb along the main road as far as the eye could see.

Far too many adults and children, for the number of current volunteers to proficiently manage with-in the confines of our observatory, and grounds.

All children attending good from an educational point of view, and in aiding a great Friday night financial turnover, but significantly too many people and cars, becoming a children, parents, and traffic management nightmare.

However, our volunteers on the night managing exceptionally well, a full on exhaustive two and a half hours.

Running out of everything, from arts and craft materials to all drinks and snacks, and at times, our stamina and patience pushed to the limit.

Our volunteers giving out a massive sigh of relief when this unforeseen momentous Young Astronomers evening ended, and everyone finally departing from our premises and surrounding parts.

Complete silence, a sort of shock coming over everyone, as discussions began to take place covering the magnitude of the evening, and so pleased all proceeded as best as it could, because no doubt catastrophic consequences for the volunteers had things gone wrong.

A much-needed cuppa and an extra-large slice of cake, finally bringing about home time.

As a charitable organisation, our many functions involve outreach groups, such as cubs, scouts, beavers, school classes, and private visits, where everyone attending keen to learn more about our solar system and the universe.

Nonetheless, on a single Young Astronomers evening visit, the numbers on this particular Friday night at the observatory, far too many to comfortably manage with the number of available volunteers.

Clearly the "word of mouth" and internet jungle drums had certainly worked, but having a more sustainable number of children and family members requires addressing, and quickly, prior to our next month's Young Astronomers last Friday of the month when it comes around.

As it happened, the committee members did not have to do anything urgently at all, as the shock covid pandemic brought about the immediate closure of the observatory, and almost the rest of the country.

Meeting in numbers now against the law, everyone house bound, unless the Government deems attendance at your place of work a necessity.

My recently purchased ten-inch Dobsonian telescope finally getting a bit of use, as too Amandas six-inch version of the same make of scope, but sadly not in each other's company.

Instead, reliant on numerous WhatsApp messages as to what objects each of us could find, and clearly see.

Now a little more familiar and knowledgeable of what and where to look in the night sky, although reliant to some degree on Google, night sky Apps and of course Amanda.

Amandas knowledge, and astronomy intellect, aside from the rest of our members an uppermost requirement of what's needed during our weekly "open" nights, as visitors of all ages come to look at the night sky, and accomplish whatever else on the theme of astronomy at our observatory.

Lots of questions requiring answers, discussions around visible stars and planets for the time of year, what best to use to view these celestial objects, and general knowledge of our universe, all helping to bring about an enjoyable evening, regardless of the many interrogations and our unpredictable climate.

During the period of a lock-down reprieve, lots of alterations and decorations taking place at the observatory, all our committee and members involved in some regeneration ideas to bring our building and equipment up to date.

Decorations throughout the observatory, new easy clean floorcoverings fitted, lighting and electrical sockets installed to the external store, the dome repainted inside and out, that in itself a momentous task.

A mat black paint used on the inside of the dome, but not before a lengthy preparation and painting of the outside, a task that me and Amanda volunteered to do, not realising the immensity of the project, and time involved.

Removing countless layers of paint previously applied over many years, a self-adhesive webbing material used on all the aluminium joints, and some minor repairs to woodwork, and a final sanding in preparation for two coats of smooth white "Hammerite" metal paint.

The sixteen feet diameter, ten-foot-high dome had certainly stood the test of its forty-year age, predominantly sound, with no major maintenance work required, and once painted, should survive a comparable amount of time.

Taking on this particular challenging job with open arms, me and Amanda attending on many a day, while focusing on extensive preparations.

Each with a paintbrush in hand, to give the dome a first coat, using a purpose made ladder, curved to meet the domes half a sphere shape, making my part of our twosome team much easier.

Precariously climbing an odd-shaped ladder after fitting extended feet for additional support, taking on the task of painting from the top-down, with Amanda stood on the flat roof of the observatory, painting bottom upwards to the dome, meeting in the middle, or thereabouts.

The tapered curved panels, sort of half a "Terry's chocolate orange" segment shape, much quicker for me to paint from the top narrow pointed panels while moving down the ladder.

One rung at a time, until our paint brushes vigorously combatting to complete the last little bits, at our just below central meeting point.

Painting one panel at a time, the first coat taking many afternoons to complete the entire circumference of the dome, although enjoying many a transitional roof top chat with a prepared drink and snack during the process.

The second, and final coat of paint much easier to apply, possibly taking half of the time as the first, with the end result looking an amazing blotch and run free sparkling white.

Standing back and admiring our "work," and the many paint splodges on our clothes, face, hands, and also on the flat roof of the observatory.

The both of us should have good muscle strength in our arms and wrists, a workout and a half, a job long overdue.

Now complete, and looking extremely good, our three-inch brushes almost threadbare, with over five hundred square feet of painting with each coat.

Completely weather tight and possibly looking as good as when first erected way back in 1973, and a welcoming sight from the main road.

As things began to get back to some normality after the covid pandemic, a trip out proposed for members to visit an Astronomical show, placed on the forthcoming meeting agenda for consideration.

Taking an enjoyable mini-bus ride south to a location close to Warwick for this annual event.

Twenty committee and observatory members travelling to look at a variety of current and forthcoming merchandise, always on show, and available to purchase.

The huge premises containing the latest obtainable astronomical equipment on a few spacious floors, a full day that included fee paying talks and presentations about various space related subjects.

Always a good day, and an opportunity to see, touch, and maybe spend a little or lots of our hard-earned cash on amazing products for the continuation of our hobby.

Prior to one such event, the committee unanimously agreeing to purchase a variety of lenses for our telescope located in the dome, and furthermore, some palm size meteorites.

These meteorites to add to others, although much smaller wafer-thin encased ones already owned, this time, much larger, certainly big enough for children to physically handle.

A task to purchase these becoming the responsibility of two of our long-term knowledgeable members, who would track-down the best possible "deal" using our limited fast depleting observatory funds.

A few of us attending presentations and enjoying the café food court, furthermore, trying out, and admiring a variety of gadgets that clearly had pound signs above our individual spending limits.

However, parting freely with money allocated for the observatory lenses, and two rocks from outer space.

Purchasing three assorted 50mm lenses at a bargain affordable price, and two palm sized meteorites.

These space rocks purchased from a reputable dealer for the sum of £300 each, and will fit in perfectly with tutorials for the Young Astronomers, including our additional outreach and open nights at the observatory.

To test the authenticity of each rock, a full explanation sheet and certificate supplied, and applying a magnet demonstrates the strength and "pull" of each one, revealing the amount of magnetic products they contain.

One of which clearly showing the strongest pull, as appears almost all metal and quite heavy, with most of the rock burnt away as it entered the Earth's atmosphere, while the other a much weaker "pull," remained mostly rock and almost as weighty as the other.

Meteorites come in various sizes, usually pieces of naturally formed space debris blasted from the surface of an asteroid or planet by much larger celestial objects.

These chunks of space rock vary in size and weight, and occasionally intersect with our Earth's orbit, and if not fully burning up as they make their descent through our atmosphere, they will form a speedy fiery bright flash across the night sky, prior to impacting the ground.

Thankfully most of what remains of these meteorites after speeding through our atmosphere "land" in uninhabitable regions, although over many years a few have created a spectacle for all to see.

One such Earth-bound object, known as the Middlesbrough Meteorite, hitting the ground close to this England town on March 14th, 1881, at 15.35. close to a railway siding.

Burying itself in the railway embankment just yards away from active workmen, who immediately reported this once in a lifetime incident.

A famous astronomer, Alexanda Herschel recognising its importance, as other respected artifact personnel carefully excavating, and placing it in a box.

An argument unfolding as to who the rightful owner of this well-travelled ancient interstellar object, and where it should "live."

The British Museum apparently wanted it to add to their collection of artifacts, however, Northeast Railway deemed it "lost property," because it fell from the sky onto their land, insisting it stays within Yorkshire.

This meteorite, about 4,500 billion years old, formed at the same time as our Earth and solar system, classed as Chondrite, approximately six inches in diameter and weighing about three pound nine ounces, now located in the Yorkshire museum in the grounds of St Mary's Abby, York.

Our recently purchased meteorites may not have travelled the same distance, or quite as old, although one of the two an ordinary Chondrite, although unclassified, and possibly found in Northwest Africa.

While the other meteorite a genuine fragment of the much larger Campo Del Cielo iron meteorite, found in Argentina by Spanish explorers in 1576.

Iron meteorites, pieces of a once molten core of large asteroids or other planetary bodies, at some point in time, violent impacts blasting them apart.

Our observatory so proud to become owners of these meteorites, and looking forward to showing them off to all who want to see and hold them.

The first of these events came around quickly, another Young Astronomers night, and one of the first using our new "booking" system.

A Young Astronomers email soon set up to allow control of how parents could book their children to join us, and information limiting the number of attending parents.

Preferably, one parent per child, helping to keep overall numbers to a controllable amount within our premises, and to aid with our volunteers available at any one time.

The email responses, and spreadsheet becoming my responsibility, also arranging for payment for places, when issuing an invoice.

The completed invoice sent via PayPal following an email request for a child place, or places, and to date, all working exceptionally well.

I remember taking great delight in explaining where these meteorites originated from, while the children held them while handling a small magnet to test the "pull" or magnetism of each of them, and to compare.

Explaining the possible distance travelled, and the age of each, adding that what they have in their hands, possibly the oldest items they will ever hold during their lifetime.

For a number of years these meteorites have formed part of all our educational outreach gatherings, and usually me who enjoys this part of the presentation.

However, recently a group of children and parents attended where things did not go exactly to plan.

Beginning my little session by removing the meteorites from our locked illuminated glass display cabinets, along with two small magnets in preparation to start a handling session with the kids.

Always giving an explanation as to the origins of both these space rocks, before handing the least magnetic one to the first child, and passing over a magnet to test its magnetism strength.

Then passing on to the second child to test, while I present the other space rock to the first child, along with a second magnet to test its magnetism.

This particular metal looking one has the strongest "pull," as each child takes hold of each in turn, holding and testing each for magnetism potency.

During my presentation, all going to plan, as it has done for the last group, and lots of groups and individuals before that, when suddenly a large bang, as the most rocky of the two meteorites hitting the floor, a large chunk instantly breaking away.

A piece about the size of a 50p coin, spinning wildly on the timber floor a few feet away from the now larger meteorite, a calamity for sure, as the child who dropped it picking up the broken smaller piece, and handing it to me.

An unlikely not foreseen incident, however, wherever children become involved, always that possibility.

Who would have thought, a chunk of rock possibly millions of years old, that had travelled millions If not billions of miles throughout our universe, penetrating the Earth's protective atmosphere.

Finally arriving for safe keeping, and a viewing experience for visitors at our observatory, and when dropped from less than two feet onto a wooden floor, would break on impact.

Carefully examining the two pieces, and soon becoming clear the meteorite had broken on an existing flaw, and a clean break at that, so should not be difficult to bond the two pieces together with a strong transparent glue.

Oh well…

Our valued piece of space rock has hit the wooden floor when dropped a few times, so possibly weakened a visible flaw line for it to break this time around.

Using a clear impact glue, the two pieces of meteorite now back in one piece, the breakage almost invisible.

Considering how I show off our meteorites in future, certainly more careful, although not quite the same when describing our ancient rocks fragility to future generations of children at the observatory, but may raise a few nervous laughs in the process.

CHAPTER TWENTY- ONE

The Light Room

(Coal Drops Yard London)

I have often talked about, and published my thoughts about space travel, and none more than the July 1969 Apollo eleven mission, to land a man on the moon.

From my teenage years I have read books, magazines, and watched countless documentaries on the subject, and written a recent chapter about the classic HG Wells film, First Men in the Moon.

So, you can imagine my surprise when reading a Facebook advertisement about an immersive short film that has started a run of daily showings every hour in London.

No ordinary film presentation, taking place in a huge square room with little seating arrangements, in fact almost saying in the advertising blurb, best viewed while laid or sat on the floor.

Reading the article with interest, about how the famous actor Tom Hanks became involved, and actually co-writing and delivering most of the narration for this epic, almost hour-long historic experience.

A larger-than-life film covering the Apollo missions, including the 1969 moon landing and interviews with astronauts involved with the Artimis program and a return to our closest celestial object, The Moon.

The aptly titled "Moon Walkers" film, definitely a right "up my street" sort of event, but to travel down to London on my own just to see this one-hour film seems a little extravagant.

Although ticket prices for the show inexpensive, it still seems such a long way to drive there and back in a day, but as you have read earlier, not the first time driving south to our capitol city on my own.

Maybe a possibility of spending a couple of days with Liam, if I could find a dog sitter, but then even more arrangements, not only for our dogs, but especially if Liam at work or fitting me in with any free time to make it all a worthwhile visit.

Looking at my trainline app, train ticket prices reasonable, perhaps a same day return train journey a much better option.

Especially as the venue, and location for this somewhat summarised celebrated film show, The Light Room, just an insignificant eight minutes' paced walk away from London's Kings Cross Station.

Nevertheless, a newly added bucket list item slowly beginning to become a reality, and optimistically in the extremely near future.

All the same, what best to do, do I make the three-to-four-hour challenging drive on busy motorways, or travel almost from my doorstep in a relaxed atmosphere, on a train taking just two hours to make the journey to London.

Seems a no brainer to me, as according to advertisements, tickets for this event selling fast, so I do need to decide, and quickly.

At a 10.00hr show start, and then every hour until 19.00hr each day, with busy times around lunch to mid-afternoon, my train departure and arrival times will need to reflect this, and after a long day, to reach home at a reasonable hour.

The location of The Light Room positioned with-in a recently refurbished neighbourhood called Coal Drops Yard, in the N1C location of London.

Exploring Google Earth, a canal, and grassed seating area, with-in a nature reserve and visitors centre, and plenty of shops and places to eat, all located in this compact setting of our capital.

Getting better by the hour, and still a possibility of meeting up with Liam for a late breakfast or light lunch, even for just a few hours an added bonus.

Chatting about this nonlocal event to Amanda, my stargazing companion while on our way to a regular Friday night visit to the observatory, dropping a large hint to see if this show of some interest, and the slightest possibility she might like to experience an event of this space theme calibre.

The two of us have attended numerous other space themed excursions that have resulted in some great memories.

251

One in particular, going to see Helen Sharman, the first British women in space, along with other members from the observatory, at a small but intimate venue in Leeds.

Helen, born in Sheffield and at just twenty-seven years old, taking part in Project Juno, a private British space program, disbursing the Soviet Union for a seat to join a mission to the Soviet modular space station Mir, in May 1991.

Also, joining Amanda, husband Dave, and children, Holly, and Rosie, to visit the Space Centre in Leicester.

A full day with lots to see and do, an unforgettable interactive experience, with an amazing all singing and dancing planetarium, great company and of course tasty food outlets, a visit I would recommend for all astronomy and space lovers.

Me and Amanda also joining Rhod, (Liam and Rosies drum and percussion teacher,) for a night with Brian Cox along with comedy side kick and The Infinite Monkey Cage partner, Robin Ince, at the First Direct arena in Leeds.

Starting off our arranged get together with a delicious Italian meal at Prezzo, with-in The Light carpark complex, close to the Direct Arena.

Other members from the observatory had booked seats to see Brian and Robin too, and all sitting just a few rows in front of us.

Yet another amazing unforgettable experience, so much so, booking once again to see an updated performance of Brian's at the same venue two years later.

Similarly, ordering tickets to see Tim Peake, (Major Timothy Nigel Peake), first at Leeds town Hall and enjoying his show so much, re-booking some eighteen months later, to see him once again at the Doncaster dome.

Tim, a British ESA astronaut, military officer, and author, and the first British astronaut to travel into space for over twenty years, joining other astronauts and cosmonauts on the International Space Station, where he carried out over two hundred and fifty scientific experiments for ESA and international partners, during his six-months on board.

Making his journey on a Soyuz rocket on December 15th, 2015, returning to Russia on June 18th, 2016.

During Tim's shows, he delivers a fantastic rendition of his time in space and how he learned the "ropes" to become an astronaut, including learning the Russian language.

The both of us enjoying these amazing visual and narrative events, so much so, a further third visit booked to see Tim and his updated show in the coming months at Sheffield City Hall.

A further bucket list item for me having read the book, watched the first film made in 1953 featuring Gene Barry, and the remake of this film in 2005, featuring Tom Cruise, with Steven Spielberg directing.

I own a double CD, and I now want to see Jeff Wayne's live musical of War of the Worlds, featuring Justin Hayward and Liam Neeson narrating using a hologram effect, an extravagance of immense proportions, complete with a fire spitting alien machine.

Asking Amanda if she could accompany me to see the show, and so pleased she could, although some distance away, taking place in the Manchester O2.

Deciding to take a short car journey to Dewsbury Train Station, rather than tackle the M62 teatime rush hour, and then a cross Pennine train to Manchester Victoria Station, situated beneath the actual arena, to see this spectacular space themed amazing musical and visual experience.

It did not disappoint, hearing all these amazing double album tunes live, a massive more than capable orchestra playing the music, individual musicians excelling with their craft, and the man himself Jeff Wayne, conducting.

The visuals, and overall sound truly awe-inspiring and beyond belief, and understandable why this show attracts sell out audience's wherever performed.

Just a short delay on the station platform, an hours train journey, then fifteen minutes in the car from Dewsbury, arriving home just after midnight, with no hold ups or anything, a much better way to travel, in my opinion, to see a concert at Manchester O2.

Becoming hooked on finding other space themed events, this time the Aurora Borealis (Northern Lights) as I had heard so much about this spectacle, but located in the central West Yorkshire area I had never seen them.

Others at the observatory booking a five-day cruise to sail around the Norwegian fjords to capture a glimpse, almost on the last day, before they appeared, but doubtful my stargazing partner Amanda could join me on an excursion of this magnitude.

Making further interrogations of the internet, I spotted flights to the north from airports around the UK, offering a fully immersive flight, including accompanying guest speakers.

A one-hour briefing presentation taking place prior to take-off at a local hotel of what to expect when airborne.

A more likely option of the two, and only away from home a matter of five to six hours.

Quickly discussing this option on yet another journey to the observatory, and once again so pleased that Amanda said she would also like to see the Northern Lights spectacle, and accompany me on a three-hour round-trip flight.

Explaining that I have viewed many an image that others have supplied of this event, and in my opinion, the most cost effective and easiest way to do it, and much better I now have a like-minded friend and companion to join me.

The overall experience yet another unforgettable occurrence, as the two of us joined over a hundred and thirty like-minded passengers.

Firstly, all to meet up at a local hotel with guest speaker Pete Lawrence, from the Sky at Night magazine, who gave a narrative and slide show of what the audience might, or likely view on our three-hour Jet 2 flight from Leeds Bradford airport.

The aircraft circling over the Shetland Isles, with the inside of the wide-bodied aeroplane in total darkness, but for small LED foot lights, a strange experience, but worth it to have the views on offer.

Our eyes soon getting accustomed to the darkness, making it easy to take part in pre-arranged seat swapping, all to get the best possible view of the above cloud star filled clear night sky.

A light snack and drink short break, and back to our porthole viewing, swapping seats numerous times, crossing the aisle and back, and even using un-booked vacant seats where the passengers did not occupy a full window not centrally located to the seats.

However, not a deterrent, as using these un-occupied seats as an arm rest while crouching on the floor, giving a spectacular almost vertical view of the millions of visible stars and constellations from above any clouds at the altitude of thirty-five thousand feet.

As a natural occurring event, on this occasion the active Northern Lights phenomenon eluded us, all the passengers could make out a solid green band on the distant horizon, but the clear night sky at thirty-five thousand feet a truly remarkable sight, and yet another amazing experience.

Whatever next, as you have probably guessed, the train tickets and Lightroom experience now booked after Amanda said she would like to see this once in a lifetime part film part documentary, one-hour long 360-degree historic film show.

An early 07.00hr start, picking up Amanda from home, and parking my car in Westgate's multi-story carpark adjoining the station.

This multi-story car park has existed for quite a few years, and the first time I have need to use it, as on our return to Wakefield, a quick turnaround, then immediately driving to a committee meeting at the observatory in Pontefract.

Our two-hour train journey, and one my son Liam uses time and time again, when traveling between home here in Wrenthorpe, and his second home in Hounslow, a suburban area of West London.

I can understand why, so pleasant a journey, with a refreshments carriage placed amid first and second class, although a variety of snacks already in our rucksacks, just in case this mobile refreshment carriage not readily available.

Looking at the immediate locale just north of Kings cross station on Google Earth, one thing, but actually treading the cobbles heading for The Light Room premises, another.

What a lovely place, and vibrant, lots of people of all ages milling around a variety of buildings, on different levels, and typically aged to look like the whole expanse from a Victorian era.

Crossing a canal bridge heading towards the shops and cafés, the google maps app on my phone helping to locate The lightroom premises, following asking directions from a railway worker who said to just put it on my phone.

The advertisement for this show correct, as it did take just eight minutes quickly walking once leaving Kings Cross Station to get there, and both the train and our walk getting us there on time.

Technology, utterly amazing, everything from the train to the event entrance all booked using my phone, marvellous, and even more so, when entering The Lightroom.

Our quick response code (QR code) displayed on my phone granting access, and after a quick bag check, shown to a steel staircase leading down two floors to what I can only describe as a huge basement location.

A space that resembles a vast cube, with a slightly raised section from the floor, with few strategically placed seats, not set out in rows, as a traditional seating plan.

A large, carpeted central floor area especially for the audience to sit or lay down, bench seats on the raised platform, and others located around the floor space, all set at different angles, unique for a cinema type audience.

A fully immersive experience, and the show certainly did not disappoint.

All four walls becoming a wrap-around screen, a full 360-degree show, with re-digitised film from the Apollo missions, including the 1969 moon landing, and interviews with the astronauts that will take part in the up-and-coming Artimis missions.

Tom Hanks delivered an exemplary narration throughout the hour-long film, with a surround sound experience second to none, making you feel actually present, and experiencing the excitement at pad 39A, at the Kennedy Space Centre's Launch Complex.

Woefully, the one-hour show over far too quickly, leaving you feeling wanting much more, and with the next hour audience already descending the staircase, now the time to leave.

A souvenir shop located part way up the exit staircase, lots of things on offer, purchasing two colour magazines full of the images seen in the film, great to look back on at a later date.

Sending a text message to Liam to let him know that me and Amanda had watched this amazing show, and on our way for something tasty to eat.

In my text saying he should book tickets, along with his girlfriend, Alice, to see this amazing show, and as he works not that far from here, as soon as he can, before the show comes to an end.

Liam responding almost immediately, saying he had forgotten that Amanda and I had made the earlier journey to London, and he would meet us in around twenty minutes.

Our breakfast order already taken, and food on its way, and saying to Amanda, Liam will definitely enjoy the vegan breakfast offer when he arrives.

Almost halfway through our breakfasts when Liam arrived, and not having long to wait before he began to tuck into his vegan breakfast.

Liam apologising, but then commenting he had finished work early, so only able to join us on the off chance.

Liam soon on his way to his second home in Hounslow, to meet up with Alice, however, having to use the bus to travel part of the way, as some sections of the London underground workforce electing to take a strike day, so no trains heading west from St Pancras station today.

Me and Amanda headed over the canal to a grassy stretch, and the nature reserve visitors centre, to walk off our breakfast, then heading back towards Kings Cross to the London Canal museum.

Sadly, on this day of all days closed, but still further local things to see.

Our homeward bound train leaving Kings Cross Station at 16.00hr, arriving at Wakefield Westgate at 18.05hr, although a slight delay near Peterborough holding up our train for around ten minutes.

Calling at our local KFC for a quick bite to eat, and then heading over to the observatory for a scheduled committee meeting starting 19.30hr.

All in all, an excellent full day, nonetheless, I wish that also said for the committee meeting that took place at the observatory.

Although our arranged get together started on time at 19.30hr, everyone attending faced with a detour around the village of Carleton because of road works.

In the end, my drive brought us back to the beginning, now ignoring the diversion sign, and driving direct to the observatory.

The warning signage should have said "No through traffic - except for access," instead taking a good twenty minutes driving my car nowhere but in a huge circle and back, and others attending the meeting, all doing just the same.

Nevertheless, making good progress in the meeting, each agenda item getting a tick of completion, and looking forward to a mid-way break, when a further committee member arrived.

Clearly looking distressed at coming to our meeting over forty minutes late, however, all enjoying our tea and cake break, and all going as our agenda until time for the late arrival to give feedback on her committee duties.

What happened next became a talking point for the next few weeks, and certainly not anything I would want to elaborate on further, other than to expand a little of what a likeminded group of people really enjoy undertaking for the observatory.

In a nutshell, as an elected committee member, our responsibility to ensure that the observatory obligations all carried out in good faith.

To maintain our constitution and policies, and finally observing all the charity commission rules, and not forgetting that all of the above duties carried out on a totally voluntary basis.

Oh well…

Onwards and upwards…

Looking forward to yet another space/astronomy themed outing that I am sure one, or more waiting just around the corner for me and perhaps a stargazing friend, to book tickets and attend.

CHAPTER TWENTY-TWO

A Heavenly 70th Birthday Celebration

(St Georges Hall Bradford)

I would like to think that all my family, friends and relatives never forgotten when they pass away, memories preserved of those wonderful times spent together in person, or while looking at photographs, and videos.

Always raising plenty of smiles of those past experiences or circumstances that remain in our thoughts, regardless of how many years have passed us by.

Recalling those times with fondness, a recollection of close friendships that have remained strong, an alliance endured during lean hard times, and through extremely rewarding prosperous periods.

Although, I still to this day find it difficult to believe that one such close friend should die as a result of a road traffic accident in Germany, March 23rd 1995.

Over twenty-eight years ago, those memories flooding back when I first met Alan Barton, way back in the summer of 1969, up until that tragic time remain as vivid today as then, and all while in my early teens when our friendship and little musical ensemble came into existence.

Five young men, all just about completed our education in comprehensive or high school, or attending college as part of our apprenticeships.

All passionately wanting to become good musicians and eventual popstars, performing, and selling our music to the masses.

Non more than one of our five, Alan Barton, who had a profound determination, ambition, and desire way above anything the rest of us had, and our friends and families thought absolutely nonsensical.

However, the somewhat fragmented pieces would fall into place when all leaving our day jobs, and becoming professional musicians in March 1976.

Three of the former five, and a new member, Colin, all now in a privileged position to transport our band Black Lace, to achieve heights in the entertainment world, that only a few novice clubland groups of our calibre would ever dream of reaching.

Our band known on the circuit as a valued club and pub band, representing the United Kingdom in the twenty-fourth Eurovision Song Contest, held in Israel during March 1979.

As the competition drew to a close, the eventual winners Milk and Honey from Israel, and a second Spain, our band Black Lace finishing in a respectable seventh position,

Our name now on the lips of many, with performances and appearances on TV and throughout the UK and Europe, with top of the bill appearances, tours, and hit singles to our name.

Nevertheless, during the summer of 1980, our four band members decided to part company, split up our group, and go our separate ways.

A heart-breaking decision fuelled by the Polish Government cancelling our fourteen-day tour, as the ongoing debilitating strikes and unrest, continuing throughout the time our tour should start.

Fulfilling all our diary bookings throughout the UK until January 1981, the finale taking place on a cold winters night at Newton House working mens club, Wakefield, a night to remember.

Following this night, Alan, and Colin, remaining as a duo, keeping our Black Lace name, and would accomplish even more success during the following three years.

Hit singles, Superman, Agadoo and Do the Conga, to name but a few, and successful party vinyl and CD albums, one of which, Party-Party, attaining double platinum status.

I auditioned and joined a band from Castleford called "Stormer," playing at local clubs and Army Naval bases, until New Years Eve 1984, and throughout this time continued recording with Black Lace, until late1985.

Then becoming part of a local band, playing drums in "Aircrew," until 1992, and finally "Mister Twister", a rename of "Aircrew" from 1997 until the present day, with just a few years of "rest" between the launch of each band.

Alan leaving Black Lace duo, to reform the successful Bradford band "Smokie" in 1988, until Alan's untimely, and ever so sad death in March 1995, as a result of a traffic accident while on tour in Germany.

The consequence of which would knock the stuffing out from everyone.

Alans funeral arrangements would include a service at Wakefield Cathedral, and then a close family gathering taking place at Wakefield crematorium.

A fitting "send-off" for a son, brother, husband, dad, and friend to many, leaving a musical legacy remembered with affection for years and years to come.

I attended a gathering to inter Alan's ashes at a cemetery close to his Heckmondwike home, with family, fellow Smokie band mates, Terry Utterly, Alan Silsden, and manager John Wagstaff, and a few close friends.

A low-key sombre affair, with poignant words spoken by our close friend, funeral director, and co-founder member of Black Lace, Ian Howarth.

Rounding off this subdued occasion with a meal, and an enjoyable reminiscing session at a local restaurant, not that far from the Heckmondwike cemetery, bringing together a compilation of everlasting memories that will live on for everyone present.

Moving on four years to March 1999, and I had an idea to arrange a celebratory concert in collaboration with former Black Lace band members.

The show planned and held at Balne Lane working mens club, in celebration of twenty years from the time of our 1979 Eurovision Song Contest appearance in Israel.

BBC and ITV outside broadcast units attended the club during our mid-afternoon set up and sound check time, to interview me, and Colin about our bands previous successes, and the untimely death of Alan, four years earlier.

An interview and our Eurovision song "Mary Ann" played live, and the recording appeared on the local evening news channels, between the hours of 18.00hr and 18.30hr on the evening of March 31st, 1999.

My band Mister Twister taking to the stage to open up this memorable night, with a set of rock/pop anthems, getting everyone in the mood for the night to come, including a much-anticipated mid-way raffle and auction.

Alan's eldest son, Dean, taking centre stage in lead singer position, with me on drums, Colin on bass guitar, and Ian Howarth on lead guitar, to perform our Black Lace Eurovision song, Mary Ann.

Other song covers followed in our set, especially the summer of 69, a Brian Adams hit from 1984, and a memory of when in our teens, our band first got together, a great tune to complete our middle band, thirty-minute set.

Black Lace duo, featuring Rob and Colin ending a fantastic fun filled event with top tunes, Agadoo, Superman, Do the Conga, Music Man, and hit tunes of the eighties and nineties, the successful night raising several thousand pounds for charity.

Winding the clock of time forward a further sixteen years, and another celebration planned that will bring our Black Lace band and many musician friends together once again, this time Alans eldest son, Dean Barton arranging the show.

March 20th, 2015, yet another night to remember, although a sad and emotional night, as this show organised in remembrance of twenty years since Alan left us.

The venue, St Georges Hall, Bradford, a fantastic location, and not the usual working mens club venue, me and our band had grown up to know.

I had visited St Georges Hall more than a few times to see the top bands of yesteryear, in particular Whitesnake, of "Here I go Again" fame, and in later years with my son Liam as part of his highly competitive Brass Band competitions.

This extremely well organised gig would once again bring together previous members of our Black Lace band, a former band manager from our youthful days, Mick McGinley, as compare for the evening.

Me and Ian Howarth, Robin Vickers, a long-time friend and former band mate, a relation of Ian playing bass guitar, and Chris, front man from The Troggs fame, all joining together on stage for one night only, to re-ignite the sounds of our Black Lace band.

Colin, resident in Tenerife unable to join us, although a long way to travel, and at great expense when playing just three songs to an almost sold-out appreciative audience.

One of Alan's former partners of the Black Lace duo, Dene Micheal, would take to the stage to perform hit songs, Superman and Agadoo, two of the most remembered tunes from the early eighties.

Dean Barton, now fronting "Spirit of Smokie," a tribute band of the highest quality, performing covers of this amazing 70's band from Bradford, and including drummer, Ron Kelly.

Ron, currently Dean Bartons drummer, but formally a member of the late sixties band "The Elizabethans," a name change to "Kindness," and Ron then leaving in the early 70's, as a further name change to "Smokie," taking place, and the band becoming mega famous.

Always great to catch up with everyone, a night of reminiscing, playing music to a more than abundant appreciative audience, and raising lots of money for a charitable cause at the same time.

During the 2020 covid epidemic, me, Ian, Colin, and Dean Barton, would once again perform together, although this time, and uniquely, from the comforts of our own homes.

Ian the instigator, had an idea to plan a recording session of our 1979 Eurovision song, Mary Ann, and put together a video, with no other reason, just for the hell of it, but to do something musical when the Government prohibited people from meeting in numbers, a fantastic suggestion.

Colin residing in Tenerife, Dean Barton on the Mediterranean island of Gozo, Ian in Ossett, and me just a few miles away in Wrenthorpe, four musician friends as near, or as far apart as one could imagine, and no mean feat in organising.

Yes, definitely a challenge, putting the tune of our 1979 Eurovision song together, with various stringed instruments, and my electronic drum kit, including lead vocals and harmonies.

Nonetheless, with current technology, our years of experience working together, and in whatever format, a sound and video created with a difference, fully compatible for radio and TV.

Technology once again playing its part, as all band members appeared on our local news program, Calendar, via zoom.

Taking part in a pre-recorded interview with a difference, linking everyone simultaneously from thousands of miles apart, bringing our band together on screen.

What an experience…

A seven-minute slot of early evening TV time on this news program, our 1979 Eurovision song getting a further airing on TV once again after our "live "broadcast in Balne Lane club, almost twenty-three years ago.

Who would have thought that three and a bit years following the making of our video, a further concert at St Georges Hall would take place.

Dean Barton, once again arranging this show, a full eight years after the last one, again to raise money for charity, and in celebration of his dad, Alan Bartons heavenly seventieth birthday.

Ian Howarth, once again the organiser of our band reunion, enlisting a few fresh faces, swelling our numbers to form a rather large musical conglomerate.

Regrettably, Robin Vickers unable to join us on this occasion as currently unwell, and for some time, all wishing him a speedy recovery.

A collaboration required to put together a set list, a minimum of ten songs, creating a forty something minute set, that would involve a few hours of resolute individual and band rehearsal time.

Our band consisting of the following musician's:-

Ian Howarth, lead guitar, lead vocals.
Terry Dobson (me), drums.
Steve Scholey, lead vocals.
Mick Linskey, twelve string guitar, vocals. (our former driver roady from the early 70's)
Stuart Duffy, guitar, vocals, (former Ossett music centre owner, and ex sound man of Black Lace whilst in Demark).
Neil Hardcastle, drums, (long-time friend and former drummer with Black Lace for three months in 1973).
Richard Black, guitar, vocals, (originally from Ossett, then moved to South Africa, returning to live in Wakefield).
Chris Gibson-Allen, bass guitar, vocals(lead singer and front man of the Troggs, and played bass during our 2015 concert).
Bernie Odell-Lowery, guitar, and lead vocals as Alan Barton, singing Mary Ann, and Mr Tambourine man, also sang in our 2015 concert)

Not all on stage at the same time, although when I complete playing kit on the first five tunes, Neil then taking over to sit on the kit for the remaining five tunes.

I will stay on stage playing something or other, and everyone together on stage to perform the last song of our set, Chris singing the Troggs tune, "Wild Thing."

A name mentioned in our put together band that until my own seventieth birthday had become a bit of a recluse, as far as meeting up concerned, Steve Scholey, our Black Lace band mate from 1969 until our reluctantly arranged January 1981 split.

Ian had invited Steve to join us for the last two get togethers, Balne Lane Club reunion in March1999, and the 2015 concert at St Georges Hall, but sadly declined.

However, knowing that Ian had agreed to perform two solo sets at my birthday, I invited Steve along to celebrate the night with me, family, and friends in the Conservative club in Alverthorpe, and an absolute pleasure for me when he attended.

Seeing and talking to Steve after almost forty years became an absolute pleasure, three of our early Black Lace band together for the first time in over forty years.

Steve also attended my "Mister Twister" band mate Jim mister fix it Trueman's seventieth birthday bash, so really happy when Steve agreeing to also join us for our September 2023 St Georges Hall gig.

The rest of our assembled band all so happy to see and work alongside our Steve once again.

Band rehearsals would commence as soon as possible, but unlike last time, Ian's rear room at his former home on Alverthorpe Road not available.

Mick volunteering his ground floor front room studio to assist in getting our band on the road, so to speak.

A list of tunes quickly agreed amongst our band, and compiled to take around forty minutes playing time.

Consisting of a variety of songs that would suit the vocal range and playing abilities and memories of each member of our formidable band.

Final Set List

St Georges Hall Bradford, September 12th, 2023.

- ➤ Take it Easy – vocals - Ian
- ➤ Walk in the Room – vocals - Ian
- ➤ So long Susie Baby – vocals - Steve
- ➤ Mary Ann – vocals - Bernie
- ➤ Crazy little thing called love – vocals - Steve
- ➤ The way we were – vocals - Steve
- ➤ Mr Tambourine Man – vocals - Bernie
- ➤ Honky Tonk Women – vocals - Steve
- ➤ Jonny B good – vocals - Stuart
- ➤ Wild Thing – vocals - Chris

These songs purposely picked, as they have some nostalgic meaning to each of us, a celebration of our professional and semi-professional careers during the many years of playing in each of our bands in clubland and beyond.

A few hours ahead of me to learn them all, in my case, just the first five songs playing drums, no vocal harmonies this time around, thankfully, Neil will learn drum parts for the remaining five songs to complete our set.

On my part, home rehearsals made so much easier when shouting out, "Alexa," play "Take it Easy," and picking up my sticks to play along to this track, and to familiarise other song titles while playing on Liams electronic drum kit.

All of "my" tracks familiar tunes, some of which I know, and others requiring just a little more practice before our first "all together" rehearsals begin.

I would have liked to perform the Rolling Stones song, Honky Tonk Women, the first ever tune Ian played in the Horbury Bridge family home of Alan Barton.

Alan's dad and sister also present, as guitars strummed away, and happy meeting them all for the very first time, while sat in the terrace property front room in early 1969.

Neil will play his tunes in the second section of our opening set;

however, I will stay on stage playing cowbell for one song, Honky Tonk Woman, so at least playing something on this memorable song, and tambourine in the remaining four tunes.

For as long as I can remember, until his death, Alan always remaining a massive Rolling Stones fan, with a collection of all their singles, and LP records since the time of our first meeting, and almost instantly becoming lifelong friends, and the rest shall I say, history.

Our rehearsal day and times planned to perfection, as not all band members required on every occasion, and with six weeks to go until our show, ample time to get the arrangements tight, and of course correct.

Organising rehearsal nights in such a way as to give an opportunity for some time off for certain band members who have to travel a long distance, and during busy rush-hour traffic for our 18.00hr start time.

Neil, currently living and working in Hornsea on the east coast, Bernie also on the east coast, but much further north in Redcar, Steve travelling from Selby, and Chris travelling from his home near Manchester, these band members living some distance apart, and thankfully just a one-off gig.

Ian setting up a WhatsApp group, to help with collating these up-and-coming rehearsal sessions, as each and every one of us spending as much time as needed to learn our agreed parts.

My drum parts played on Liams electronic kit in our small front bedroom, and with the use of "Alexa," an extremely useful time prior to these looming pre-band get-together rehearsal nights.

One thing for sure, this gig will not follow the same footprint as when setting off on the road for a normal clubland gig.

Where band members spend an outrageous amount of time packing lots of heavy equipment, driving, setting up, tearing down, packing the van, and driving home, than the band actually do playing music on stage.

All of our so-called work appears worthwhile from an entertaining point of view, certainly not from our accepted fee for all of these unearthly hours.

However, a bit of tasty sustenance at an all-night café, or preferred place for a late supper or early breakfast helps to conclude a long full night, and I would not change a thing of doing the same night after night, even after all of these years.

267

Common knowledge amongst musicians that you never forget time spent in a band, a choir, or part of an orchestra or other musical ensembles.

Friendships cemented for life, the many feelings, laughter, emotions, and a sense of belonging while staying in digs, at rehearsals, and gigs you perform while making music with other like musicians.

As a now "semi-retired" musician, I am already constantly recalling all of those years on the road, as you have no doubt read, and use the term retired loosely, as confirmed I will have an opportunity to play an acoustic drum kit "live" once again in the not-too-distant future.

A date in September agreed when I will pick up my sticks to play an acoustic kit live on stage in front of a sell-out audience once again.

In the meantime, our first rehearsal also in our diaries, a two-hour practice session that I am so looking forward to.

Mick ever so welcoming, inviting us to use his home for these much-needed musical get-togethers, more so for me, as over seven months since I last appeared on stage, and not given any thought about future band rehearsals.

Told often, you never forget how to ride a bike, no matter how long, thanks to muscle memory, as once you have learned your craft, unlikely you will forget.

Usually the case, all the long hours put aside to rehearse our chosen songs, and our bands part of this remembrance gig, over in a flash, however, a time that I will remember for my remaining years.

Looking back over the last two months brought musician friends back in contact with one another once again, after a period of over forty years, that in itself something to celebrate and recollect.

The concert becoming an evening for all in attendance to remember, each having their own reasons to purchase tickets to see and listen to this amazing remembrance charity show.

From my point of view, I found the night so emotional from a playing perspective, with band members from a bygone era, and more so with my youngest son, Liam, making a surprise train journey from London to join me on the night.

A busy schedule with all his work commitments playing percussion in the band of the Irish Guards, a circle ticket purchased for him, just in case he could make it.

Liam recording such a lot of our set on his iPhone, which I had the pleasure of watching and listening to once at home, back in Wakefield.

Dean Barton, and Spirit of Smokie giving an amazing unforgettable hour and ten-minutes long performance, and sure many more to come in the UK and Europe in the not-too-distant future.

Recalling the events of just a few hours ago, and thoroughly enjoying taking part in the very last song of the night.

All the nights performers joining together on stage for one last time to sing a rendition of a fitting emotional song, "With a little help from my friends."

Originally a Lennon and McCartney song from The Beatles 1967 Sgt Pepper Lonely Hearts Club Band album, drummer Ringo Starr the singer, but on our night in Bradford, in the arrangement and voice of Joe Cocker.

Everyone in the auditorium, including stage musicians and invited singers and musicians joining in with the words, and bringing an end to an absolutely amazing poignant evening.

Meeting up next to St George Hall for an after-gig drink in the Great Victoria Hotel, and chatting to Elaine Barton, Alans first wife and lifelong friend of mine, also her sister Diane and mum Brenda.

Liam also enjoying meeting them, even when Elaine mentioned changing his soiled nappy while visiting her Mirfield family home, some twenty years previous.

Saying goodbye to everyone around midnight before driving a fourteen-mile journey to our home, and a welcoming bed.

A go fund me page on Facebook, and this concert in Bradford raising a substantial amount of money for two charity organisations, the children's Heart surgery fund, and auto-immune arthritis fund.

My brief car journey to drop Liam at Westgate Station for his 10.00hr train back to London made all the more shorter when talking about the previous night's concert.

The both of us agreeing, all over much too quickly, as Liam boarding his train after spending just fourteen hours with me while in Bradford the previous night, and a few hours at home, nevertheless, on leave for seven days in just a few weeks' time.

I began to wonder if an occasion may arise ever again, when all our musician friends will get the opportunity to play together once again.

To perform a similar variety of songs on stage, wherever or whatever that will entail, or at the very least keep in touch with each other, via social media, or WhatsApp.

Fingers crossed…

CHAPTER TWENTY-THREE

The Space Coast

(Cocoa Beach Florida)

Not often in one's life, the phrase, "it feels like a dream come true," does actually come true, but on this occasion, it really did.

A dream that reminds me so much of ELO's, Hold on Tight, released in 1981, and always makes me smile when listening to this on the radio, and just recently with Bob Harris, on Sunday afternoons Radio two show.

Especially the French bit, and in particular Accroches-toi a ton reve, translated to "You hang on to your dream," and I think on this occasion, I have hung onto mine long enough.

I have talked and written about lots of stories in relation to space themes over many years, but never in a million of those years did I think I would visit the Kennedy Space Centre, Florida.

My trip to view an engineering marvel of a monster space flying-machine close up, and in person.

To actually stand alongside the retired space shuttle Atlantis, one of six manned crafts like no other, (the Russian Buran copy an exception)or the test vehicle Enterprise, that never flew in space.

The others, Columbia, Challenger, Discovery, Atlantis, and Endeavour, all launched like a rocket, and landing like a glider, transporting astronauts into space and back for over thirty years.

During this time, Atlantis covered an amazing 125,935,769 miles while involved in thirty-three space transport (STS) missions into low Earth orbit, just absolutely phenomenal.

However, my seven-day amazing holiday experience, only came to mind just a few weeks ago, and did not take place without a few trials and tribulations along the way, mainly due to me, and not my organiser son, Warren.

Having occupied more than a few hours researching my holiday, with locations, flights, car hire, hotel accommodation and places to visit while there, my original idea to make this trip on my own, soon becoming a traveling threesome.

My son Warren first to say he would like to realise this rememberable trip with me, asking if he also could come along.

Liam, likewise, saying he too would like to join the two of us in making a three-thousand-mile, eight-hour west bound flight, over the Atlantic ocean.

Not a problem at all, in fact welcoming the companionship of my eldest and youngest sons, with an adventure of a lifetime that awaits all of us.

Regrettably, my youngest son Liam, having to give backword almost as soon as the date for our departure became apparent.

Engagements already in his diary for the weeks leading up to the end of April, and first week of May, taking up many days during this time.

Liams regular playing duties for his daily work in The Band of the Irish Guards, involving changing of the guard at Buckingham Palace, St James Palace, and Winsor Castle and other prestigious undertakings.

Also, two further extended gigs, not connected to his band, one a little envious of myself, playing at London's O2 arena located on Peninsula Square, south of the River Thames.

Liam performing on each of a four-day run of concerts with the amazing Take That, although Liam not actually on the O2 stage, but in the entrance lobby, playing snare drum prior to the concert start.

Performing all Take That tunes, along with a number of other musicians, all dressed in white naval style service uniforms.

Remembering taking my daughter Kerry, to a Take That gig at the Manchester arena, way back in 1994, D:Ream, being the more than adequate support band, with their hit single, "Things can only get better," high in the charts around the same time.

Little did I know on this occasion, and a total surprise when finding out, but the well-known TV personality and astrophysicist Professor Brian Cox on stage playing keyboards for the band.

I have viewed many an astronomical documentary on TV featuring Brian Cox, and actually seen him live at the Leeds O2 twice, both amazing shows.

A comment from Brian Cox certainly blowing my mind when talking about the vastness of our universe.

The size and scale beyond our imagination, with an estimated two-trillion galaxies, with around four-hundred billion stars in our milky way, that would take one-hundred thousand years to cross at the speed of light, (186,000miles per SECOND.)

To put this on a more understandable level, seven and a half times around the Earths equator, in one second.

Similar to the1978 Superman: The Movie, when at the time, a grown-up Superman (Christoper Reeve,) far exceeding this speed, circling the equator, pushing back time to save Loise Lane (Margot Kidder,) following an Earthquake that crushed her car.

Mind blowing...

Take That, and D:Ream on the same bill, a memorable night all around, and the last full Take That tour before band member Robbie Williams, left mid-tour in 1995, Take That disbanding in 1996, reforming in 2005 with-out Robbie, producing a hit single "Patience," now in the archives of music history.

The other of Liams gigs, a theatre show, playing drums along with a recently formed mini orchestra and conductor for a further four evenings, including a Saturday matinee.

The performance called, "Roles we'll *probably* Never Play," Liam sat in the theatres orchestra pit for the production company WAOS-MT.

Our departure date, Friday April 26th, 2024, on a 13.25 Virgin Atlantic flight from Manchester Airport, but not before a 06.30hr train journey from Wakefield Westgate station, to Leeds, and a change of train direct to Manchester Airport.

My decision to take this holiday come sightseeing tour of Cocoa Beach, much sooner rather than later, all due to the predicted weather patterns of this region of America.

The transition periods of dry and rainy seasons between May to October, with April usually a dry month, picking the end of the month just into May, to avoid any troublesome weather patterns, namely an early HURRICANE...

Wanting to avoid this season at all costs, as watching these past experiences live on TV of devastating twisters and weather patterns, leading to catastrophes unheard of here in the United Kingdom.

I had forgotten just how much I enjoy travelling on a train, these carriages far more comfortable than I remember, and with Wi-Fi and charging facilities for mobile phones and laptops available too.

Both outward bound train journeys not over busy at all, lots of vacant seats, and during what I would think "rush hour."

Possibly commuters looking for something more dependable, at least until this three-year long fiasco of continual rail strikes for a pay increase and worker conditions finally resolved.

A private lounge awaited us once checked in at Terminal two, Manchester Airport, Warren pre-booking this for a cooked help yourself breakfast ahead of our flight.

Scrambled eggs, sausage, bacon, baked beans, and a slice of toast, optimistically just how I like to see it, burnt.

Our breakfast eaten in organised relaxed tranquillity, overlooking the runway prior to boarding our aircraft.

However, while tucking into our gastronomic delight, discussion centred around the earlier events that had transpired while weaving our way through security after checking in our suitcase.

A security officer removing my hand luggage case from the roller conveyor track, as informed requiring further checks, and beckoning me to a counter to open it.

The security officer saying that the x-ray device had identified something suspicious located inside my case.

Asking if I had packed the case myself, constantly in my possession the whole time, and if I had received, or offered to carry something for someone, either from home, or while at the airport.

Giving my answers a resounding yes, and a firm no to the last question, although fully implicating myself, and me only, for whatever I had packed, and now identified as looking dubious while travelling through the state-of-the-art X-ray machine.

One of two rather large black zips confronted me, one to enlarge the overall volume of my small case, the other to fully open, and trust me, nervously picking the wrong zip as a start.

Both heavy duty zips not the easiest to slide open, especially with someone in authority looking intently over me, and also a worried looking son.

The instant my case opened, the security officer delved in with disposable gloved hands, moving items and clothing around, finally pulling out two plastic containers of sun cream.

Carefully scrutinising both cartons, then taking them behind a screen just a few yards away, leaving me stood at the counter with an anxious, but patient Warren looking on.

Returning after a few minutes, saying the diagnostics machine did not like, or could not identify the liquid contents, and announcing I could not take these with me, depositing both in a nearby bin.

I did not mind, anything to get moving quickly to the lounge area, and something to eat, however, my dilemma not yet over, as then asked to return to the walk-through X-ray machine, for yet another body check.

Removing my fleece, shoes, leather belt, watch, wallet, phone and change from my pockets and placing them in a waiting tray, to begin the security process amongst other eager passengers once again.

Gingerly walking through the archway metal detector (AMD) with no beeps, or ominous sounds, and clearly not satisfied with the results, as then giving me a further thorough body check with a handheld device.

Under each arm pit, between and around my legs, my back and full front, what a palaver.

Had I packed those two containers of recently purchased Aldi sun cream in our collective luggage, and possibly in the aircraft hold all safely tucked away, and the both of us eating a delicious breakfast much sooner.

Having previously encountered issues with sun cream, as on last year's trip to Israel, when some fluid escaped in my case, ruining a few of my t-shirts and shorts.

A costly reminder, I should have taken advice to pack the sun cream in a sealable bag, and putting it in our main suitcase.

Thankfully Warren confirmed he had packed plenty of sun protection, and in sealable bags, as finally the security officer handing back my case, and giving the all-clear to continue through to the departures lounge.

The both of us certainly looking forward to a drink, and some tasty food, as now almost 10.30hr, and neither of us had eaten anything from waking at 05.00hr.

An eight-hour flight awaiting us, arriving at 17.25hr in Orlando Florida, and with a five-hour time difference, lots of fun when sending messages at teatime from Florida, and everyone in bed fast asleep back home.

Warren had booked a window, and middle seat, in a row of three, in a 3-4-3 configuration on this wide-bodied Airbus A330 – 300 jet, aptly named "Ruby Rebel," Virgin's latest acquisition.

Everyone appeared seated, seat belts clicking away, and as luck would have it, the flight captain gave the instruction for the cabin crew to close the doors, leaving the aisle seat next to us vacant, so lots of room to spread out.

Listening to the cabin crew announcements from the small tv screen on the rear of the seat directly in front of me, eager for them to finish so that I can peruse a variety of available films to watch.

Almost immediately after the announcements had ceased, a young child in the row directly to the front of ours, clearly upset and began to cry, a shrill annoying scream, and with eight hours to go, not an ideal fellow traveller.

Thankfully Warren had packed a pair of noise cancelling headphones, besides a pair of in-ear ones, passing the larger headphones, with a knowing broad smile, over to me.

Just two days ago, making a car journey to Manchester Airport to pick up Warren and partner Sommer, after completing yet another two-week working period in Qatar, and Warren using these headphones to enable him to have a good few hours' sleep on his return flight.

I must admit, doing the job exceptionally well, instantly reducing the ear-splitting vocal level of the young child, and even better once I had sussed out how to work the aircrafts tv screen volume.

Flicking through a variety of recently released films, and older gems, but what to watch first, so many choices.

Some of which I have seen previously, and lots I haven't, and with eight-hours ahead of us, I am sure I can fit in at least three good films during the cross Atlantic flight.

Choosing Denzil Washingtons latest Equalizer 3 film for starters, as the aircraft began to pick up speed and thunder down the runway.

Warren, sat next to me for a good hour at the start of our flight, with the third isle seat free, that all well and good, but a passenger from another isle, moved some of our belongings to sit down while talking to members of a larger party.

This group of travellers also included the small, still crying child, and not one word asking if they could sit here, next to us on our row of seats for five minutes.

After a short while the passenger moved, Warren instantly shifting over to the aisle seat, putting his rucksack and other bits and pieces on the seat between us, tuning in the central TV to track our aircrafts journey.

Our flight path taking us from Manchester, over Liverpool, Northern Island, across the Atlantic Ocean, and all the way down the coast of eastern America, to Florida, almost a straight three-thousand-mile line.

I had watched Equaliser 1 and 2 on terrestrial TV quite a while ago, and thankful for a bit of a breather when our mid-afternoon tea arrived, as this third rendition just as intense, and on the edge of your seat stuff, as the first two films.

My seatbelt thankfully remaining tightly fastened around my waist, otherwise with some of the more vigorous blood-soaked scenes, I may have hit my head a few times on the overhead lockers.

Certainly, much of the same as the two previous films, but as usual, Robert McCall (Denzil Washington) playing an amazing part as a former US marine vigilante, righting the wrongs of Camorra members on location in Italy.

The body count had already started to mount up, as an air hostess, and food trolly appeared.

Lots of choice put in front of us for our first of two in-flight meals, and feeling quite hungry, as over five hours since eating our self-service breakfast, and believe it or not, the young child still continuing with crying tantrums.

Pausing my film, and leaving the headphones on, just removing my right ear pad slightly, enabling me to have a conversation with Warren.

Both enjoying a chicken dinner, a blueberry muffin, two crackers with a lump of cheese, and a cup of tea, a further chat and then restarting our respective films.

Eight hours flown by already, pardon the pun, as I began to pack away Warrens headphones, and as an air stewardess passed from row to row, managed to deposit all our food cartons and rubbish in a bin liner.

Thinking, had I not retired and worked a nine till five job for a living, perhaps a full day completed in the office, travelled the short distance home, prepared, cooked, and eaten my tea by now.

Or maybe during this flying time, playing my drums in shows with my band mates in working men's clubs, perhaps travelling some distance to a gig, set up, sound checked and completed at least one fifty-minute spot, and possibly played a game or two of Bingo.

Maybe not the Bingo, a quiet drink with the band in a Bingo free lounge would suffice.

During our long and somewhat relaxed eight-hour flight, I had watched three great films, Equalizer 3, Meg 2, and Interstellar, had a few chats with Warren, eaten acceptable tasty food, also a bit of shut eye during and in-between these high-octane, fast moving blockbuster movies.

To think in just seven days, Warren and I will have the same opportunities to do this all over again on our return journey home, and with any luck, our aircraft seats offered with no crying children sat in close proximity.

Orlando airport huge, making our way from the arrival gate through security, showing our passports and visitor's visa, quite detailed questions followed, but swiftly completed, and with a little frivolity, finally onto the luggage carousel.

Our single case with an illuminous bright green strap quickly identified, and with a little navigation around this massive airport building, taking the lift downward a few floors to find and sort out our hire car.

Warren quickly dealing with this, with all the information stored on his mobile phone, giving the impression just a formality, as I overheard, "your car has only a few thousand miles on the clock."

Staff giving directions to the ground floor storage expanse of a carpark, just across an airport service road to pick up our practically new hire car.

A necessary transport for our initial forty-five-mile journey to the east coast, and our hotel situated on the Space Coast of Cocoa Beach, to begin our adventure week of fun and frivolity, and I am sure, driving here there and everywhere to see amazing sights.

All in all, carried out rather quickly considering the security elements and baggage pick up, now out in the open, with clear blue skies above, and the start of our seven-day trip.

Still kicking myself, actually here as a passenger in a hire car travelling with Warren, my chauffeur, and three-thousand miles away from home, at the other side of the Atlantic Ocean, in Florida, USA.

A country that in all my seventy-two years, I have never had the inclination or desire to visit for any reason, either for a theme park holiday, a sightseeing holiday, or just a lazy pool type holiday, and catch a bit of Sun.

Until now…

Our forty-five-mile journey not taking long on these extra wide not over busy motorway roads, and with my chauffeur having lots of practice driving on the "other side" in Spain, Dubai, Qatar, and during his army career, Warren an excellent driver.

However, our four door Nissan saloon, the first car in years, and an almost new one at that, to have no built-in satnav as standard equipment, making our eastbound journey to Cocoa Beach totally reliant on motorway, and dual carriageway signage.

Travelling from the airport on the A1A motorway, unknowingly missing our turn-off, only realising our mistake, when spotting a sign for Avon by the Sea, lots of miles further south-east, than our intended destination.

Turning right at the next set of lights, doing an about turn, then taking a left back onto the A1A and heading back north.

After just fifteen-minutes, spotting our hotel signage on the lefthand side of the road, pulling into the carpark, and laughing that neither had noticed such a prominent larger than life hotel sign, and at the time, on our side of the road, some thirty-minutes earlier.

Warren organized and checking in, no porter handy, a bit of a relief, as at this point no idea of taxes, and how to deal with tips.

An extremely large room on the fifth floor, with two massive queen size beds, a huge bathroom, and incredible all-around views.

Looking over the Royal Caribbean Port Canaveral to the north, with two huge cruise boats in port, the Banana River to the west, with the North Atlantic Ocean just to the east.

A perfect location for what Warren has in mind for our as yet non-existent daily itinerary.

Unpacked and settled into our room, already checked the weather forecast for the next seven days on a typically super massive flat screen tv, matching everything else here in the USA.

An evening meal on the cards, preferring somewhere local, certainly with-in walking distance, remembering seeing a restaurant on the main road a few metres ahead of our hotel turning.

Warren confirming an Italian restaurant, a pizza outlet, and McDonalds, all within a hundred yards from our hotel, re Google Maps or the Waze app.

For our first evening in Cocoa Beach, Zarrella's Italian wood fired pizza picked for our meal, and it did not disappoint, the food and atmosphere second to none, clearly understanding why available tables and seats in the minority.

Our reasonably priced tasty meal good value for money too, even with tax and gratuity added.

Something of a shock when seeing the menu or ticket price, and then noticing other costs added when presented with the bill, but now fully aware what to expect while enjoying our stay here in the USA.

Taking a steady walk back to our hotel, the warm air breeze blowing in our faces, quite relaxing, however, both feeling shattered and absolutely stuffed, the long journey starting to take its toll, bedtime would not come soon enough.

Ready for sleep at 21.00hr, unheard of, although 02.00hr back home, and after a full day of travelling since waking at 05.00hr UK time, feeling exhausted.

Not hearing a single sound until my 07.00hr alarm, definitely a much-needed solid night's ten-hour sleep behind us, on these extremely large comfy beds.

I could not hold back my anticipation any longer, certainly not until Monday, eager to get there as soon as finishing our tasty complimentary breakfast.

Soon sorted, and on our way to the Kennedy Space Centre, just nine miles from our hotel, and on an uncrowded multi lane motorway almost to the carpark and entrance.

WOW…what a sight to behold, and not yet set foot out of our hire car.

Instantly spotting the home of Space Shuttle Atlantis over to my right, two huge white solid rocket boosters, and the infamous massive central orange fuel tank, piercing the almost clear blue skyline.

An array of various size rockets, again pointing skyward to my left, what an amazing welcoming sight to the Kennedy Space Centre.

Excitement beyond belief, and so pleased our decision to attend on the Saturday, just a few sleeping hours after our arrival on Cocoa Beach, rather than wait until Monday.

Our doubts about the space centre being full to capacity over the weekend instantly dashed, when seeing the size of the car park and centre itself just ahead, like everything else in Florida, HUGE.

The vehicle queues not too long at a line of pay booth entrances, just a dozen or so cars at each.

Warren handing over ten-dollars car parking charge, and filtering into traffic, making our way some distance to a vacant space, closer to the park entrance.

Already I could see the bus parking lot almost full, also a few hundred cars, including lots of pick-up type trucks, of all makes and sizes, filling a few rows ahead of us.

These popular trucks look like making up over fifty percent of cars already parked up, lots of Ford, Maxus, Isuzu, Ram, all looking rather expensive vehicles.

Taking a quick snapshot of our cars location, section D, and parked in the fourth row, as cars began to pull up alongside and behind ours, with kids and grownups everywhere, and without a doubt, all as eager to get inside the Space Centre as Warren and me.

However, now questioning our last night's decision to attend on a weekend afterall, as looking extremely active at the main entrance.

Long queues at a number of entrance stations, checking tickets and baggage, clearly safety and security topmost at this location.

Nevertheless, these backlogs quickly reducing, as staff efficiency also topmost.

Excited visitors, me and Warren included, soon making our way to the information centre, and through yet another additional line of security protection still to take on board.

Apprehension getting the better of me, as so much visible directly in front of us, almost like a piece of cake on a plate, staring up at you, wetting your lips, but not allowed to eat it...

Well, not just yet.

CHAPTER TWENTY-FOUR

The Space Coast

(Kennedy Space Centre)
(Day One)

My chauffeur driven journey taking just over thirty-five minutes, and what a sight before me and Warren.

Totally unreal, my eyes cannot take in all of this panoramic view, where to look, or go to first, as absolutely sure, everything relating to space here in this amazing location to view, and maybe including some interactive stuff to try out too.

Once through all the security checks, heading over to the Information and gift shop building for a location plan and timetable of all the shows, and eyeing up those huge rockets just in front of us.

Almost wanting to ignore Warren, and make a dash some fifty metres for a close-up view at these monsters.

I suppose small in comparison to the huge space rockets currently leaving launch pads throughout the world, but not taking my eyes off them all the way to the information centre.

Nipping into the entrance, slightly ahead of those waiting at security, but alas, yet another queue, not too long though.

Lots of ideas for friends and family presents in here, having a quick look around, careful not to lose our place as Warren already looking at a plan of the centre, and making suggestions of where to go first.

"Hello love," my typical greeting of anyone female, and occasionally male, Warren butting in to ask one of a number of receptionists for a good place to start our tour.

An elderly lady behind the counter giving good advice as to what to do and where to go, highlighting venues on Warrens location plan.

Additionally, underlining approximate times of the forthcoming shows, but not before saying you two have strong broad accents, do you come from the UK.

Both giving a smile and firm nod, Warren saying just arrived here a few hours ago, booking into our hotel on the Space Coast Cocoa Beach, late yesterday afternoon.

I commented that my son Warren has joined me to become my tour guide and chaperone for our seven-day trip, and the both of us so looking forward to seeing as much as possible today.

The lady remarked, believe me you will both see plenty of attractions, and some you can get physically involved in here.

Also, believe me I know, she commented, that at ninety-two years old, she had worked at NASA for more than fifty years.

Wow, she certainly held her age, excellent at her job, undoubtedly sharp and knowledgeable about what's on here at the Kennedy Space centre.

Her smiling face lighting up the whole room, even with a lengthy queue amassing behind the both of us, and the information centre in general.

Remembering a conversation back home saying to leave out the NASA bus tours on your first day, just stick to the main space centre, to see and get involved in anything and everything throughout your day.

A return visit then required, maybe on Monday, to include a coach trip out to the many launch pads and Saturn Rocket building, and of course the massive Vehicle Assembly Building, (VAB).

Iconic...

To stand and see the VAB close up, after seeing this image on TV for most of my life, I'm sure an experience in itself, and yet another item to knock off my bucket list.

Completed in 1966, the VAB has a floor area of 32,000 square meters, and so vast it has its own climate, also recognised as the eighth largest single-story building in the world.

Additionally, to see all the famous launch pads, in particular, 39A and 39B, and looking forward to looking at the SpaceX tower located on 39A, a replica of the one located at Elon Musk's Starbase complex close to Brownville, Texas.

All these attractions on our agenda from the outset, not, discussed over breakfast just this morning, and following a chat with a SpaceX employee.

Receiving confirmation, a must to incorporate all of the above in a minimum of two daily visits, regardless of entrance fees and additional costs.

To travel all of three-thousand miles, specifically to visit the Kennedy Space Centre, and miss things, not an option.

Both agreeing, if more visits required to see absolutely everything, then that's ok too, and not forgetting, this whole region never stops.

The coastal region to the east of the KSC now a 24/7 working environment, with preparation and regular launching of rockets taking place frequently these days.

To think, lots of history made on this Atlantic coastal location, a Saturn rocket launched from pad 39A, SpaceX currently leasing this, and just a few miles from here, for man's journey in July 1969 to land a man on the moon.

This whole coastal expanse a hive of activity, where NASA, SpaceX, Blue Origin, and other companies, plan to send rockets including astronauts to the moon, deep space and beyond.

It could become an exciting few days, as Warren keeping an eye open for those recently viewed (TBA)comments on the Cape Canaveral webpage, to see if they change to actual launch times during our stay.

Almost reluctant to leave a cool air-conditioned building for the hot outdoors, as the temperature at least twenty-six degrees about now.

A slight queue at our first stop, a further security check at the main centre entrance, and then finally onwards to the rocket garden.

The indoors Heros and Legends centre, looks a good facility too, the rockets positively our first option, regardless of this ever-increasing heat.

You cannot help looking in amazement at the sight of these enormous manmade structures, rockets towering high above the garden area, pointing to clear blue skies and aptly named a walk among the giants in the booklet.

The Mercury-Redstone, Mercury-Atlas, and Titan II, all launching astronauts into space, while the Juno1 and Juno 2, Thor-Delta, Atlas-Agena, all involved in delivering satellites into space from the many Cape Canaveral launch sites.

The Saturn 1B rocket, and only rocket mounted on its side, with this and all of these engineering marvels constructed, and taking part at the very start of the USA's contribution to the space race.

My phone on hand to take more than a few photographs, Warren posing first, before exchanging places, the sheer size of these manufactured wonders dwarfing everything around, then making our way to join yet another queue at the entrance to the Heros and Legends centre, and no doubt, much cooler air...

All the exhibitions and attractions grouped in each chronological era and area, from the dawn of space exploration to the actual latest missions, the reception staff highlighted our paper program clearly showing this, and so easy to follow.

The first of our many indoor attractions, and what amazing things to see, clearly no expense spared, as each display bringing everything from a past space age, and currently happening, to "life."

All the astronauts from Alan Shepard, who became the first American in space on May 5th, 1961, launched atop of a Mercury-Redstone rocket, flying at an altitude of one-hundred and sixteen statute miles, during a fifteen-minute suborbital flight.

Alan Shepards spacecraft named Freedom 7, and other further flights planned for 1961 and 1963, both cancelled for reasons unknown.

Walking around and reading details of further astronauts, in the U.S. Astronaut Hall of Fame, heroes and legends of the day, most sadly not with us now, but gave humanity its first steps into space, and to what has transpired thereafter.

Taking over an hour walking around the insides of this amazingly laid out building, far too much on display to take in, photographing everything and anything, to look at later.

A short walk to the Gateway building next, massive from the outside, and no queues at the entrances, looking great so far.

The structure contains many of the innovative ideas for future space travel, and it did not disappoint.

So many forms of space craft, my eyes wide open at each of the exhibits, The Dream Chaser, Boeing Starliner, a full-size SpaceX cargo dragon, and a SpaceX Falcon 9 booster, Orion capsule, so much to see, including a space flight simulator.

Me and Warren booked to take part on this ride, just a thirty-minute wait, more time to look around.

Arriving back to the simulator just in time for our slot, and what an experience it turned out, wearing 360-degree goggles and strapped firmly into our seats, the rocket about to take off...

My 360-view taking me from the launch pad into the darkness of space, looking around and back towards our blue Earth.

Even looking up at the parachutes as I slowly descended in the capsule towards the sea, some ride and a half, and so realistic.

Absolutely blown away with the quality of the exhibits, and so pleased Warren and I did not leave without a go on the flight simulator, taking off from Cape Canaveral, a must for anyone wanting to experience sound, vibration, and 360-degree views, the lot.

Warren confirming the same, even saying he would like more information to perhaps purchase a pair of these technically amazing goggles.

My phone never out of my hands, taking photo after photo, space suits, rocket engines, space habitat, and information about James Webb Space Telescope, a full immersive experience.

Lunch time, and both of us starving, picking a take-away burger bar, not too long a queue, and not over expensive.

These massive burgers taste delicious, a meal deal enjoyed outdoors, and in shade, under a huge canopy, still warm, but bearable.

Discussing our next stop between bites of burger and chips, and the timetable for up-and-coming live shows.

Our next stop, the IMAX theatre, yet another huge building and whatever else to see in there.

MASSIVE, like everything else here, a screen bigger than any I have seen, bringing you up close to past space missions, and to the new frontier of space, including images from Hubble and the James Webb Space Telescope (JWST).

Quite a few in front of us, but while in an airconditioned building, who cares, admission and seating taking place like clockwork, picking an elevated couple of seats, central to the huge slightly concave screen.

The auditorium filling up quickly, as snap shots of various space related vehicles flicked across the enormous screen, wetting the appetite for the film show yet to begin.

The sound quality second to none, a huge full sound, equalisation perfect, and set at an ideal volume for all to enjoy, I cannot wait for the movies to get started.

I have to say, the Imax film experience should become countrywide here in the UK, and that maybe the case already, I should check, as this sight and sound encounter, bringing me right back to visiting the Light Room show in London, just a few months ago.

A film show taking you right there in space, from the Apollo rocket launch, and July 69' moon landing.

A bygone era that still raises the eyebrows of some doubters, but ensures these times not forgotten by us elders, and an amazing insight to those memorable, exciting, and challenging periods for our youngsters visiting centres of these genres.

Technology has progressed beyond my wildest dreams since those times, and what appeared laughable as science fiction in earlier low budget black and white films.

These at times low budget B films, now in most cases rapidly becoming science fact, and bringing me and my imagination to look enthusiastically forward to the next chapter of space exploration.

Onwards to our next indoor experience, already my mind awash with what the both of us have seen and touched already.

Stopping at the Space Mirror Memorial, a huge highly polished black granite memorial to all NASA's fallen heroes, astronauts who gave the ultimate sacrifice in pursuit of knowledge that lies beyond Earth.

Looking intently at all the names, most coming to mind from the Apollo1, STS-51L Challenger and STS-107 Columbia shuttle missions, twenty-four astronauts in all.

An ultimate reminder that space exploration still requires lots of faith, regardless of improved technology in those who design and build these remarkable flying machines.

Journey to Mars exhibition next on our list, and the information underlined by centre staff as a building not to ignore or leave out.

Once again the exhibits did not disappoint, lots to see, such as replicas of Mars rovers, interactive stuff, and simulators, plans to explore deep space, including asteroids, the Moon, what's happening at NASA right now, and a look at missions of the future, and all it will entail.

Both Warren and I deciding to omit a couple of buildings to visit, one particular attraction, to train like an Astronaut.

Looking a little too challenging for a man of my age, the Astronaut Training Experience (ATX) certainly not for me.

More for the younger children, although showing images of adults getting involved, possibly parents of children doing the training.

Watching a "street performer" conduct an experiment using "dry ice," interesting in the covered outdoor seating area, and commanding a large family audience.

The experiment to quick freeze an item, and then bring it back to "life," a complete success, raising lots of applause from the enthralled open-air audience.

Also bringing back memories of my time while performing in our band, using dry-ice material to create a low cloud stage effect for certain tunes, but after just a few months consistently using this product, all agreeing more trouble than its worth.

The purchased dry ice block, about one-foot cubed, and transported in a huge almost three-feet cubed wooden thermally lined container.

My job to break it into small manageable pieces, in preparation to drop a measured amount into boiling water, while sat at my drum kit.

No health and safety issues here, however precarious to say the least, the effect lasting all of thirty seconds, as a low-lying "fog" dispersed over the stage area onto the dance floor.

Moving on to Mars Base One, an attraction with virtual simulators on hand to help with your physical training to become astronauts, perhaps a visit at another time.

Also, the Planet Play centre, aimed at children between 4 and 12 years of age, reminiscent of our observatories Young Astronomers Evenings, although the attractions here far superior to anything our volunteers can emulate.

Such as spending time in the interactive area, climbing through a wormhole, walk on Saturn's rings, slide through an asteroid field, although sat at the bar with a cold refreshing drink while watching your child explorers, sounds a much better idea.

All the while when outdoors, the huge orange fuel tank and accompanying boosters that took the space shuttles into space, constantly in our view.

Towering skyward above all the buildings, and getting closer all of the time, as the attractions to view on our plan getting fewer and fewer.

As for me, seeing the shuttle Atlantis close up, the sole reason I wanted to take this trip west over the Atlantic in the first place.

Obviously in my opinion, saving the absolute best attraction in this location, until last.

Reading a few more statistics about this beast of a machine before turning into bed last night, as the figures never cease to amaze.

Totally mesmerised, to learn that at lift-off each space shuttle weighs in at around four and a half million pounds, slowly accelerating over a period of eight seconds, reaching 100mph, and has already consumed one and a half million pounds of weight in fuel.

Once in orbit the shuttle reaches an astounding speed of 17,180 mph, equivalent to Mach 23 at sea level.

Also, unaware, the black coated heat-resistant silicon tiles on the underside of each shuttle, can withstand up to two-thousand three hundred degrees Fahrenheit.

This amazing lightweight product prevents the whole craft from burning up, as it descends at a re-entry speed of 16,700mph through the Earth's atmosphere, with red-hot plasma shooting past the shuttle windows.

Remembering this particular view shown on TV, as a crew member commented, "they wouldn't like to find themselves on the outside of the craft at this time."

With just seconds remaining before the space shuttle Columbia disastrously broke up on Saturday February 1st, 2023, all seven of the crew lost their lives, as the space shuttle disintegrated upon re-entry.

A sad time, for the whole space world, everyone concerned, most of all the family, friends, and work associates of all the crew members.

However, my tiny brain finding all this hard to fathom, as upon take-off the shuttle reaches speeds of around 25,000 mph, with virtually no heat at all.

Most of the shuttle missions touched down on runway 15-33 at Cape

Canaveral Spaceport on Merritt Island, returning from missions in space where each craft takes around 11360 feet (2.1 miles) to come to a standstill, certainly gliders of immense proportions.

Next on our route, another huge building, and more space attractions of past present and future, and more things to see and do.

FINALLY, the last attraction of a highly informative day, and sole reason for my visit, to see and behold one of four remaining amazing technological wonder machines, space shuttle Atlantis.

Standing directly beneath the three external fuel tanks, the huge orange central fuel tank and white solid booster rockets at either side, towering one-hundred and eighty-four feet skyward above me.

Me and Warren taking turns in becoming part of these monsters, photo after photo from every angle, a perfect reproduction of the original boosters and fuel tank that assisted each shuttle, powering them into low earth orbit.

Making our way up a slight incline and into yet another huge building, not a long queue, thankfully, my feet have done lots of standing and walking already, in fact, my watch giving statistics I'm proud of.

Over fifteen thousand steps, and the day not yet over.

The queue winding its way steadily upward, spiralling around a central pillar towards the first floor, walking all of the time, and not long before confronted with closed double doors, and a centre guide saying just a few minutes until our turn.

Taking in amazing views across the space centre through huge glass walling, the crowds earlier queuing at the entrance to the site still visible, lots walking from one building to another, even the carpark looking full too.

I would imagine if everyone felt like Warren and me, reluctant to leave when closing time finally arrives.

Anticipation beyond belief, as the doors automatically opened to reveal a large room with seating around the perimeter, and floor area for standing, as all facing an elevated screen.

The show bursting into life as everyone began to view a film/ documentary of the early stages of a design needed for a reusable vehicle, required to ferry various objects into space.

On the film, a paper glider thrown from a balcony as unsuspecting designers and engineers watch on, and a narration describing the need for a returnable craft powered into orbit, but can glide back to earth.

Everyone present on the film told to get to work immediately, and to come up with an acceptable design that can do this, and quickly.

This short ten-minute film fading out, as numerous pairs of doors below the screen opened up, the audience filtering through into yet another large room.

So much higher, a much larger screen, and fantastic sound system, as the audience entered this "space," the space shuttle image we have come to know blasts off on the screen.

Bringing back that date of the first shuttle mission, April 12th, 1981, at mid-day, from Pad A, launch complex 39, Kennedy Space Centre, Cape Canaveral.

Some of the audience present may have witnessed this launch first-hand, but not a view and sound like this, truly thunderous as the shuttle powered its way into orbit.

The whole building felt as though involved in an earthquake as the film continued, showing lots of STS missions, and centred around one space shuttle, Atlantis.

The visual and sound system experience second to none, impressive, you bet, the music bringing out emotions in me I didn't think existed, as one mission after another came into view.

Finally ending with just the silhouette of Atlantis, appearing on a star clad black screen, as though in space, pointing nose first to a breathless and emotional audience.

The music composer and artists certainly knew how to capture feelings and reactions, as both took over me in a second, shedding a tear or two in the process.

Attempting to hide my obvious emotional state, looking anywhere but towards Warren, and thinking he may feel the same, however my efforts to say a few words giving the game away.

Just about to say, "fantastic," when suddenly the whole cinema screen ascended in one quick movement into the hall ceiling, revealing the space shuttle Atlantis in all its glory, right there in front of us, just a few feet to walk, and I could almost touch it.

What a sight to behold, I never thought I would feel emotions like this just looking at a now redundant flying machine, impressive, a word that somehow not quite enough to describe what faced me, totally overwhelmed.

Truly magnificent, and shell shocked, taking in all in front of me, slowly walking the full length of the mounted shuttle as though in orbit.

The bay doors fully open to reveal a huge cargo hold, capable of carrying a massive payload, in particular the Columbus Laboratory, the largest single contribution to the International Space Station (ISS) in February 2008.

The STS-122 ISS assembly mission a complete success, as others too, to deliver truss segments and Solar arrays to the ISS.

As spoke of in earlier chapters, one amazing machine, achieving phenomenal results for NASA, the ISS construction, and other important missions.

Our guide explaining that Atlantis set on display at a specific angle, elevated over eleven metres to uppermost wing tip from the ground floor, and slightly above the first floor to enable optimum views from below and all around.

Atlantis, mounted at a 43.21- degree angle, simulating the T-minus 4,3,2,1 countdown, suspended by massive steel horizontal and vertical beams and hardware, that once held the shuttle atop of a special Jumbo 747 while in transit, in an amazing $100million-dollar, 90,000 square foot location.

This building also incorporates over sixty other artifacts, rides and exhibits placed all around, above and below this fantastic centre piece of space hardware.

Taking best part of an hour to fully appreciate this space craft, walking all around on the first floor, before descending via a ramp to the ground floor, a visual experience, taking in even more of this superb vehicle.

So much more to see and do, but finding it difficult to tear myself away and explore the remainder of what's in this huge building.

At this time in the afternoon, not over long queues, so a decision to take a trip in the shuttle hold, a space trip with a difference.

Joining other "space travellers" for the ride, sitting in rows of six, and some ten deep in a mock-up of the shuttle's cargo bay for a space shuttle launch experience.

Tightly strapped in, although not sure why, as a fixed ride, and not going anywhere like a loop the loop or inverted ride as I have previously endured, some years ago now.

However, me and Warren both agreeing, it did feel like eight and a half minutes of actual space flight, including take off vibrations, seat tilting, and a feeling of weightlessness, not that the pair of us have ever flown into space to compare.

The "ride" made all the more special when the bay doors slowly opened to reveal a star studded beyond Earth's atmosphere, infinite black outer space, in total silence other than mutterings of wow, or amazing.

Everyone that I could see all taking photos, including Warren and me, yet another impressive realistic "ride."

Taking in all of the other attractions in this vast size building, looking at the actual vehicle used to transport the astronauts to the Apollo rockets, an actual front wheel from the space shuttle, and screen after screen showing various mission footage.

Also, a poignant memorial section to the two shuttles, The Challenger in 1986, and Columbia in 2003 their crews of seven in each shuttle, all of which fourteen astronauts perished.

Warren and I joined our last queue of the day, to meet and hopefully chat to an astronaut, today being James H Newman, who flew as part of crews of seven, on various shuttle missions.

The STS-51(Discovery), STS-69 (Endeavour), STS-88 (Endeavour, first shuttle to the ISS), and finally STS-109 (Columbia, serviced the Hubble Space Telescope).

To me, one amazing resume, four iconic missions out of a total of 135 carried out during the space shuttle program, and what a lovely chap too.

To say that James had time to talk to the both of us, utterly amazing, considering he had stood in the same spot for over an hour to my knowledge, chatting and posing for photographs, to an endless stream of excited visitors, us included, and still others behind patiently waiting.

Purchasing two personally signed photographs, one for Warren and me, the other to display in our Pontefract observatory, also other images captured on our phones of this lovely chap that included Warren and me too.

Making our way reluctantly to the Atlantis building exit, both excitedly talking about the day's events and of course the space shuttle Atlantis.

Commenting that I had probably run out of "space" on my phone with all the images I had taken, and couldn't wait to return to our hotel and sort through them all.

Some will require editing, trimming here and there, and mentioning to Warren that these images would look great in a photo album.

Discussing what the both of us would like to eat for tea, and where to go visit tomorrow.

The return journey to our hotel taking a little longer than first thing this morning, rush hour no doubt, but Warren fully in control as I took in the scenery around us.

Knowing that just a few miles from our hotel, when spotting two huge ocean liners moored at the Cape Canaveral docks, just a quick walk away once parked up at our hotel.

I had drunk quite a few litres of water during the day, a must in this climate, but definitely a much stronger drink required with our Italian meal later.

CHAPTER TWENTY-FIVE

Cocoa Beach

(Florida)

Our Sunday morning up early once again, a full breakfast and just a short car journey to the Sands Space History Centre, located on Space Port Way, in the dockland part of Cape Canaveral.

I could not miss two huge ocean liners moored up, towering hundreds of feet into the air, with deck upon deck of cabins, row up on row, looking like thousands, and that's just the port side, no doubt a mirror image on the starboard too.

This museum a first, free admission, and no additional fees whatsoever, and what a great centre, with hundreds of exhibits dedicated to the history of space exploration.

Enjoying a good three hours in a building not much larger than your average corner shop, looking at the many exhibits and information about each Launch Complex, (LC) constructed over many years, now mostly redundant.

Also, chatting to an elderly former NASA volunteer staff member, about their own experiences while involved in the space race, and where he informed us, a launch to take place this very evening.

Definitely a talking point, as Warren had kept a look out for any changes to the TBA posts on the NASA website.

In past years, a rocket launch only occurring every few months, whereas now they seem to take place every other day, and something to look forward to after tea.

Buying quite a few space themed souvenirs from the gift shop, some odds and ends for the observatory display cabinets before saying goodbye to the few, exceptionally busy, and informative friendly staff.

Taking in the one-time SpaceX control centre situated right next door, all the signage indicating their former "home," removed, but the wording still clearly visible against white painted external walls of the single storey building.

A further twenty-five-mile car journey north to yet another small museum, The American Space Museum and Walk of Fame, located in the city of Titusville.

Downheartedly, on our arrival the place looking a little deserted, and soon finding out why, this museum not opening on Sundays, however, not exactly a wasted journey.

As thinking about our car journey to Titusville, had things not taken a turn for the better, a definite "we're gonna die" moment averted.

Warren taking a left turn out of the carpark, only to find that our car now travelling the wrong way on a one-way main road.

Headlights flashing in our faces, giving Warren a stark warning of our imminent dilemma, and quickly taking evasive action.

The next available right turn from a thankfully not over busy road, did not come soon enough, immediately turning onto a much quieter, virtually car free side street.

Warren gathering his wits and consulting Waze maps from his phone, saying "a close shave," although on reflection, I did not think the both of us in any real danger.

Now heading the correct way, and on the right side of the road, towards the coast and memorial gardens, and views across the Indian River towards the Kennedy Space Centre and launch expanse.

Instantly spotting what looked like a rocket on the launch pad, but at a distance of some eight miles, anything but a rocket stuck up in the air.

Wishing I had packed a pair of binoculars, although our phones do have a zoom lens, so the possibility of spotting the launch when eventually dark.

Titusville became a treasured gem of a city due to the growth of Cape Canaveral and arrival of NASA, way back in the late fifties, early sixties.

Located in an ideal position on the opposite banks of the Indian River, Titusville known as "Miracle City, " or "Space City," with a motto of "Gateway to Nature and Space."

A fantastic location, where over the past years, thousands watching rockets and space shuttle launches, now having a further lease of life with what seems a rocket every few days lifting off.

Parking up and taking a walk to visit space related memorial gardens, a location Warren and I have spent the last hour or so walking and looking around.

Spotting a group of Manatees, swimming and playing close to the shore, attracting quite a bit of attention from locals and holiday makers alike.

Taking over two hours to walk through, read and photograph the many structures, images, and floral displays, set in this beautiful park.

The only park of its kind that honours Americas astronauts, and men and women behind the scenes, who after a shaky beginning, helped America lead the world in space exploration.

In this location, every space mission that had taken place since the first rocket launch, all fully recorded and itemised in stunning surroundings.

Titusville also became home to astronauts and NASA workers alike, most locating in a lovely strategically placed city.

Taking the Max Brewer bridge over the Indian River onto Merritt Island, for a drive south towards the Kennedy Space Centre, thinking it may take a few minutes from our journey back to our hotel.

That did not work out, as after driving some twenty minutes, the through road now closed, possibly due to this evenings planned launch window.

Heading back over the bridge, and along the road that Warren had taken the wrong turning a few hours ago, soon back at our hotel, a quick shower, change of clothes, and out for tea.

Heading back to the docks area for our meal, sat in the evening sunshine, and still warm enough for t-shirts and shorts.

Choosing a roast chicken dish, and once again the food did not disappoint, enough for a shared meal, never mind all to myself.

Heading back up to Titusville, for the planned SpaceX launch, the countdown had already commenced for a 21.30hr lift-off, as Warren pulled into an east facing carpark looking across the Indian river towards the launch site.

Looking pretty gloomy, and a few spots of rain evident as quite a few dark clouds rolling in a westerly direction from over the Atlantic ocean, beginning to disappointedly descend over the whole district.

With another twenty minutes still to go to lift-off, as a few other car drivers, passengers, and onlookers, doubting the launch would take place.

All vehicle spaces and pavements around us full to capacity, as these regular launches can obviously still pull in the crowds, even after over sixty years of rocket and shuttle liftoffs from this amazing location.

The dark looking storm clouds sitting quite low on the horizon, as I set my phone to record, pointing it over the river, to who knows where, as I overheard the car passengers closest to us comment with excitement, that the countdown just ten seconds to liftoff.

The dark sky lit up, a huge flash of fire and feeling of tremendous power as the rocket lifted off, about a mile south to where I had my phone set to capture all on offer, but seeing the marvel of a live rocket launch, exhilarating for the both of us.

Yes I had seen hundreds on TV, but neither of us had watched a live one.

Then sound hitting us, a huge thunder resonating all around us, but much deeper in tone, raising a few "wow's" from those stood around us, and the sound from over eight miles away, still so loud.

Unfortunately, seeing our first launch not the spectacle either of us had hoped for, instead, just a rolling sound of thunder, a few visible seconds of flames, disappearing into the clouds, appearing briefly a few times, finally vanishing all together.

Back to our hotel for just after 21.30hr, and yet another early night, but not before discussing the day's events.

One thing for sure, the both of us should have caught up with our lack of sleep during the long journey here.

Monday morning, and after a healthy breakfast of cereal, scrambled eggs on toast, fruit, and black coffee, on our way once again to the Kennedy Space Centre, and our planned coach tour.

Once again Warren taking the initiative, booking our seats on-line before dropping to sleep the night before, at least pre-booking will avoid any queues for buses.

The carpark just as full as the weekend, no difference at all, even for a normal working week.

Again, taking note of where our car located, using the rockets to give us a clue in what direction to head when leaving the space centre.

My shorts, t-shirts, and an abundance of suncream becoming the norm in this hot and humid Florida weather, making no wonder I found it difficult finding a hoody to purchase to replace the one I misplaced in the airport...

It seems that everywhere you look, and everyone of all ages, wearing shorts and t-shirts, so the both of us fitting in with the American public.

Not much of a tan, so far, as the both of us seem to spend more time INDOORS, looking at anything space related, however, today a different story, as according to the itinerary, outdoors most of the time.

The QR codes on our mobile phones working perfectly at the space centre entrance, and making our way directly to the bus station entry point, to begin our launch pad tour.

You just can't help looking around at the rocket garden, pointing skyward, and the Atlantis building directly in front of us.

Bringing back those amazing recollections of just two days ago, maybe a little time left before the park closes, to visit some of the attractions once again, when our anticipated bus tour comes to an end.

Warren purchasing cold drinks to take on our bus, already filling up with passengers as eager as Warren and me to see the launch pads, and the Apollo building, and whatever delights these have to offer.

The airconditioned coach heading out of the complex via a back road towards the coast, with the huge Vehicle Assembly Building (VAB) appearing just a stone's throw away.

Our coach pulling up alongside a perimeter fence, and all told to carefully exit for a closer look.

Enormous does not exactly cover the description of the VAB, towering high into the clear blue sky.

Taking in the enormous size of this building constructed in the sixties, and still very much in use with the current wave of blast-off's planned to take place.

All welcoming the cool sea breeze as Warren and I, and others from the coach, listened intently to our guides continuing vocal presentation about the VAB, and items in close proximity to us.

One item in particular, an actual launch escape rocket, normally attached atop the rocket capsule, should things not go according to plan at the time of launch.

Also, an actual gantry that astronauts walk across from the lift at the very top of the gantry, and into the white room, before assisted into the rocket capsule or Shuttle vehicles.

Gazing at the largest American stars and stripes flag on the VAB, huge, measuring a massive two hundred and nine feet high, and one hundred and ten feet wide.

An exact replica of a partial flag painted on the concrete, where you can stand and take-in the vast size of each of the red or white stripes and stars.

Each stripe approximately nine feet wide, with the white painted stars, over six feet across.

Our guide also pointing out a crawler-transporter, stood patiently waiting for its next assignment.

The crawler slowly carried rockets and shuttles from the VAB, to the launch pads for over fifty years, and retired in 2011, at the end of the space shuttle program.

This enormous machine, one of two built by Rockwell International at a 2022 cost of around 14 million US$, and consists of two tracked vehicles joined together by a huge platform.

The central platform measures approximately ninety feet square, with a load capacity and ability to transport, 18 million pounds of weight at a top speed of just one mile per hour.

It has an overall measurement of one hundred and thirty-one feet long, and one hundred and fourteen feet wide, standing at its loaded maximum height of twenty-six feet.

Crawler 2 now in operation and used to transport the Space Launch System with Orion space craft, and used for the first time in November 2022, and over eleven years since a crawler used to take a space vehicle to the launch pads since 2011.

Back on the coach and cool air-conditioned air circulating around, our considerate driver keeping the doors closed and a welcoming cold inside temperature greeting us all.

Heading out to the famous 39A and 39B launch pads, where the

Apollo moon launch programs, the shuttles, and now SpaceX and Artemis missions take off, all interesting commentary from our tour guide.

Parking up, and exiting the coach, making our way up quite a few steps to an elevated viewing platform.

Our backs to the Atlantic ocean, overlooking launch pads 39A and 39B, as far as the eye can see, to the North and South, on the eastern coastal area, and over to the VAB building, and not a hill in sight, so flat.

Two large display boards showing images of all the space vehicles that launched from these two iconic pads, and SpaceX now using pad 39A with its tell-tale umbilical black launch and catch tower, complete with chopsticks, a mirror image of Starbase in Texas.

The other SpaceX tower located at Starbase, Boca Chica, Brownsville, Texas, stands at an impressive four hundred and eighty feet high, and the tallest launch tower in the world.

NASA currently use pad 39B, for the Artemis moon rocket system.

To stand here, and rotate 360 degrees looking over the Atlantic Ocean, and over towards the launch pads absolutely amazing, and to know that almost every American rocket, and shuttle missions, launched from this location during the space race, and years afterwards.

Taking a last look down the length of the three-and-a half-mile long crawler road from the pads and launch towers to the VAB building, before heading down the steps and back to our air-conditioned coach.

Next stop, the Saturn V Rocket building.

Yet another vast impressive structure, housing a complete full size Saturn V Rocket, and other awe-inspiring displays and shows.

Not before spotting a SpaceX rocket atop a transporter, making its way to launch pad 39B, our guide unperturbed and commenting, all amazing, but just a normal working day for employees in and around the vicinity.

Quite a few bus loads already at this location, and the inevitable long queues waiting to enter.

Not taking too long before moving into the auditorium, and taking-in a short but informative movie about the Saturn Rocket and Apollo moon missions.

Once the entrance doors opened, everyone looking directly into five twelve-foot circular black holes, positioned in a two, one and two format.

The enormous five F-1 engines, attached to the first stage of the Saturn 5 launch vehicle, a definite wow factor, hitting everyone smack in the face.

The whole Saturn V rocket, showing a cut-a-way of its stages, one, two, and three, all suspended from the ceiling as though separated in flight, and just fifteen feet from the floor, giving an almost all-around view of this amazing machine, a sight to behold.

The information plaques located beneath the Saturn V rocket giving out some impressive details.

The first stage lifts the rocket to a height of around forty-two miles, the second stage almost into orbit, and the third stage sending the Apollo space craft into orbit around the Earth, before heading the 230,000 miles or so, towards the moon.

Next to the moon landing show, actually coming to watching this show twice.

A constantly crying child sat close to us hampered the first showing, obliterating most of the narration throughout.

The visuals so impressive, both Warren and I, returned sometime later for our second viewing.

To watch the Lunar Excursion Module (LEM) appearing from the ceiling once again, and softly landing on a prepared moonscape.

A space suited Neil Armstrong, or physical model of, ascending from beneath the stage, with the American flag in hand, sound, lights, and mirrors, making this show as realistic as possible.

Looking around the other exhibits, a replica of the lunar roving vehicle, that Commander David Scott drove, making history as the first person to drive a vehicle on the Moon, July 31st, 1971.

Accompanied by Lunar Module pilot James Irwin, using the rover on the Apollo 15 mission to explore Hadley Rille, collecting one-hundred and seventy pounds of lunar materials.

A variety of space suits, including the Apollo 14 extravehicular space suit worn by Alan Shepard, and a piece of Apollo 13's luna module returned by the astronauts, famed in the Apollo 13 film.

Also, a mini detailed version of the complete Saturn V rocket, although not exactly small, when over fifty feet long.

An actual piece of moonrock that you can touch, and other lunar samples from the Apollo 15 and 17 space missions.

The crew module for all Apollo missions looked impressive, heat stained with the hatch open, although not quite as large as I imagined, and I would think a tad claustrophobic when travelling to the Moon and back.

A full-size replica of the 1969 LEM lander certainly looking impressive on a Moon scape, complete with a space suited mannequin of Neil Armstrong, holding an American flag, all in its own glass surrounded display, and so much more of other flabbergasting memorabilia to look at too.

I can now understand why sightseers and tourists should visit the Kennedy Space Centre at least twice in quick succession, the space centre first, and then a coach tour second.

In my opinion, definitely two visits needed so as not to miss anything, to take in what's on offer, all totally mind-blowing for any serious space enthusiast, regardless of knowledge, rather than cram in as much as possible during a one-day visit.

Taking a walk outside, to look at the seated observation gantry, a viewing area, overlooking the launching sites, although still quite some miles away, but told tickets usually all sold out weeks in advance of each published launch date.

This particular seating section looking familiar on documentaries I have seen, even Warren commenting the same, but a sign on the perimeter fence giving some alarm.

"DANGER, Alligators and Snakes in area, stay away from the water, do not feed the wildlife."

Walking around the beautiful well-attended gardens to look at various memorials of astronauts, again, yet another eye-opening experience.

The return bus ride to the Kennedy Space Centre not taking too long, our guide giving a commentary about low rise buildings on the way, and what goes on in each of them.

What a fantastic day, and just about time to take in another viewing of Space Shuttle Atlantis before closing time.

No queues, just a handful of visitors making a much better experience for the few remaining, and almost a personal tour as Warren and I taking it all in once again.

The perfect end to two exceptionally full and exciting days at the Kennedy Space Centre.

Who would have thought that just over one-hundred years from the first engine powered airplane flight, when Wilbur and Orvill Wright flew for twelve-seconds on December 17th, 1903, a short but historic flight, above the sand dunes of Kitty Hawk North Carolina.

Then on April 19th, 2021, NASA's Ingenuity Helicopter made history when it completed its first controlled powered flight on another planet, the red planet, Mars.

What will the human race have accomplished in the next one-hundred years beggars belief, but what an exciting time for our children's children to become part of.

Yet another early and our last night on Cocoa Beach, feeling stuffed after a delicious meal, and absolutely sure I will sleep like a log.

My 07.00hr watch alarm startling me, Warren already wide awake, and in the shower, and looking to his bed, the lower part of our shared suitcase already packed and ready to go.

Breakfast first, after my shower, then put my clothes and toiletries from drawers, wardrobe, and bathroom, in the top half of our case, before heading north to Titusville and once again visit the American Space Museum and Walk of Fame.

What an amazing place, and so pleased Warren and I did return following Sundays anti-climax.

Talk about an Aladdin's Cave, so much to see, and with the help of yet another former NASA technician.

Our elderly guide began a long informative conversation revealing how he actually worked on the complicated preparation and testing of the USA/ Russian docking/birthing connection, when the capsules and astronauts from the two nations met in space.

The NASA Apollo spacecraft and Russian Soyuz space craft docked together in July 1975, in an historic first international space mission, with millions watching on TV around the world.

Giving the two of us an insight of those early days of his time working for NASA, all the while showing us around the many exhibits of a bygone space age.

Our guide Introduced me to the manager when explaining my hobby as a stargazer, and chairman of our local observatory.

He too now a member of our Facebook observatory page.

Another gem of a place, and even though a small rabbit warren of a building packed with exhibits, taking us almost four hours to absorb all on offer for likeminded visitors.

Warren fully aware of the traffic flow from the carpark, taking an immediate RIGHT, making our way back to Cocoa Beach and a visit to a restaurant on the Cape Canaveral Dock.

Two different huge ocean-going liners moored up, to either take on more passengers or disembarking travellers visiting the locality.

Heading back to Cocoa Beach for an evening meal, choosing an Italian restaurant, not too far away from our hotel, and hopefully the NASA App informing us, to maybe catch another early evening rocket launch.

After yet another delicious meal, driving towards a local viewing area.

However, and so disappointing, this particular viewing spot now full of cars, and hundreds of eager spectators and still over an hour before the advertised launch time.

The ticket booth operatives turning cars around, indicating a "full house," at a favoured Cocoa beach location for blast-off regulars.

Returning to the docks car park, looking to find a further location to look north towards the launching area, perhaps from between the two docked ocean liners.

The passengers will certainly have an uninterrupted on deck, or star side cabin view of today's rocket launch.

Parking up, almost in the same space as twenty minutes ago, when spying a multi-story car park, just a few hundred yards away.

An external concrete stairway leading to each of the two floors, and an open top roof parking area, what an open invitation.

A perfect viewing location, however, aware a possible private carpark, maybe for the ocean liner passengers or crew vehicles, although no warning signage, perimeter fencing, or locked gate installed to the stairs.

Warren commenting, if spotted on the top floor roof parking area, a possibility the both of us asked to leave, or even worse, the police or security guards could turn up, but not wanting to miss anything, deciding to risk it anyway,

However, neither of these transpired, and just the two of us on the top floor, an amazing location to view a rocket launch in perfect clear sky conditions.

Both commenting numerous times why others had not joined us to use what seems a "free" facility, especially on a day like today, with umpteen cars turned away from the local Cocoa beach viewing area.

Perhaps that is the reason, everyone driving and not walking, as this rooftop location ideal, and maybe the owners missing out on a lucrative income when a launching takes place, just a small charge for viewing generating a worthwhile income, for this text-book position to observe future rocket launches.

Warren and I had the whole enormous carpark roof to ourselves, uninterrupted, and spending a good thirty-minutes prior to the launch, enabling the taking of many photographs and video of the whole experience.

Amazing...

Although looking over our shoulders numerous times, expecting to see a police vehicle or security guard to move us on, as not fully believing our luck at having such a wonderful vantage point, when others possibly still driving around looking for somewhere to park up, and view todays spectacle.

Heading back to our hire car, more than fully satisfied that the both of us had witnessed the launch of a rocket until out of sight, and have recorded evidence to prove it.

Driving inland to Orlando, talking about our days on the Cocoa Beach, and looking forward to the remainder of our stay here in Florida, and wondering what other exciting things on offer.

Perhaps other stimulating places to eat, to visit a theme park, or two, or three, and confident that Warren has already got things in mind for the two of us to do...

CHAPTER TWENTY-SIX

Orlando

(Florida)

Arriving at the Hyatt Regency Hotel on International Drive, Orlando, during the afternoon became a further experience of how things "work" in Florida, and once again exposing just how naive the both of us really are.

I can say for my age, I would think a seasoned traveller, accustomed to coming up against or across most things, but clearly unaware of how these certainly high-class 5/6 star looking hotels function.

A smartly dressed concierge stood at the hotels huge glass entrance doors, promptly coming across to our car to welcome us.

Immediately offering help to unload our limited luggage cases from the boot, placing our large case, my small case, along with my limp looking rucksack on the pavement.

Then taking the driving seat, and moving our hire car just a few meters away from the hotel entrance.

Warren booking this hotel the previous day, now making his way to check in, while I sorted out our minimalist luggage, taking them into a matching our cars cool temperate foyer, and waiting patiently for his arrival.

Although, on his return, looking a tad thoughtful, and a little serious.

Asking if everything all ok, Warren instantly saying "of course, no problems, I just need to park up our car in a multi-storey carpark about a hundred metres away."

Taking just five-minutes to return, Warren commenting with some exasperation, "$30 a night to park our hire car in the carpark, and had I taken up the offer of a valet service, a further $20 per night."

A huge financial difference in a plush area of Orlando compared to the Space Coast just forty miles away, where our hire car parked for free.

Although once settled in our room, the difference all too obvious, certainly much larger, and improved facilities all around, with a room price per night certainly reflecting the added bit of luxury.

The same huge Queen size beds, and I suppose a TV, is a TV, of course a much larger screen than our space coast hotel.

Also, two bathrooms, a walk-in wardrobe, and views from the eleventh floor overlooking northern Orlando, and that's about it.

Not that much difference for the additional costly price per night fee, and a further shock, the extortionate tariff did not include breakfast or an evening meal.

Although both positive, plenty of good restaurants with-in a few minutes walking distance, and even more to see, and to do in this central region of Florida, other than space related themes on Cocoa Beach.

These remaining days not planned as part of our holiday, but definitely the correct decision to vacate our east coast hotel, and travel inland to Orlando for the remainder of our stay.

Taking the next hour or so to reflect on our last two full days on the space coast, our Sunday and Monday both busy days, Sunday in particular catching the afternoon SpaceX launch, fitting in as much as possible while on the coastal region of Florida.

Showered and ready for a walk for our tea, Warren locating an Italian restaurant about a mile north of our hotel.

The roads remarkably busy, in particular International Drive, unlike the footpaths, not passing or seeing anyone walking, other than us.

Already feeling hot and sweaty in this heat, perhaps that's the reason why everyone appearing to drive, rather than walk, conceivably their need for air-conditioning uppermost on their minds.

Definitely a must in Florida, and certainly pleased when arriving at our place to eat, and the welcoming cool environment, air-conditioning on full.

Our chosen food delicious, and now fully aware of how our bill presented, so no shocks with the bottom line.

A much cooler walk back to our hotel, not a cold evening as described in the UK, and viewing an almost clear night sky.

Not many visible stars about though, far too much light pollution in this built-up part of Orlando.

Stopping at the Wonderworld upside down building, having passed the attraction on our way to tonight's restaurant of choice.

A strange mindboggling structure founded by John Morgan, and as the story goes, once a top-secret laboratory located in the Bermuda Triangle.

After an experiment performed in the building went disastrously wrong, the whole structure appeared, upside down on International Drive Orlando.

A unique experience once inside, as you can imagine everything attached, such as window frames, doors, doorframes, staircase, and landings all upside down, other than the attractions and exhibits added to make it an adventure.

As a former joiner and carpenter, a visual illusion difficult to comprehend, as nothing appears plum and level, everything at acute mind-boggling angles, although if constructed on a level site, sure all perfect.

Bemusing to say the least, and certainly worth a look, and try out the interactive stuff, "edutainment," at its best.

A combination of education and entertainment, however, not staying too long in there at such a late hour.

Taking around forty minutes' to walk back to our hotel, at a steady pace, and still not seeing or meeting anyone actually walking on the pavement.

Plenty of people in bars and restaurants, and carparks briming, one thing for sure, my step count will have certainly exceeded ten thousand by the end of the day.

Not bothering with a night-cap, both agreeing to take the lift straight to our room, and settle in for the night, although not over late, just 21.30hr.

I did wonder if Warren pacifying me during our stay, as confident had I mentioned staying at the restaurant for further after meal drinks, or perhaps having a drink at the hotel bar, he would certainly have joined me.

However, further drinks not appealing to me or Warren right now, as both highly satisfied with the tasty food, feeling enjoyably stuffed, our drinks, and final bill at the restaurant, also to our liking.

My phone alarm waking me at 07.30hr, and Warren already in the shower, and both in agreement, these comfortable beds helping both of us to have a good night's sleep.

Although Warren saying he woke up over an hour earlier, taking time to look on the internet for a venue to eat breakfast, other than the hotel dining room, and perhaps visit a theme park.

I had mentioned Sea World, as not bothered about scary G-force type rides, at other parks.

Warren confirming only a forty-minute walk in the opposite direction from last night to Sea World, and able to take in a McDonald's midway for our breakfast.

Preferring to leave the car in the carpark, exercise favoured, to walk off the abundance of delicious food, so much better to take in the locality, and if early enough, miss the rising Sun and heat.

SeaWorld today then, and a McDonalds breakfast beforehand, a little sustenance needed during our walk.

The footpaths, verges and garden areas all maintained to a high standard, considering just the two of us heading south as far as the eye could see, although International Drive terribly busy with traffic.

Make no wonder the footpaths look good, certainly no wear and tear from foot traffic, and no litter about either, a lovely district.

With all our walking, feeling ready for a tasty breakfast as spotting the famous McDonalds sign in the distance, now coming into view.

A bit of a contradiction when discussing "junk food" but I have to say, needs must, and as the inside poster pointed out, indeed a tasty meal.

Arriving at the SeaWorld attraction, just after its 10.00hr opening time, taking about eighty minutes, incorporating a stopover at McDonalds for a tasty and not over expensive breakfast, of a sausage egg and cheese McGriddle, with a few Hash browns.

One thing for sure, the equivalent breakfast I ate at McDonalds, including unlimited drinks, more than likely, twice the price at our hotel dining room, and gained a few thousand extra steps into the bargain too.

Full of energy and ready to take on anything, although spotting an already packed themed attraction ride high above us, giving me the goosebumps.

Definitely not sure about going on these white-knuckle G-Force inflicting sort of rides, but then again, never say never.

Warren commenting that I am an elderly wuss, and I should take a ride on at least one of these many ride attractions here at Sea World.

Thinking a ploy for the two of us to sample one ride, as Warren doesn't want to have a go on his own.

Putting that comment to the back of my mind as on our way to visit the dolphin nursery, and looking at these amazing agile creatures zooming around a huge tank, clearly enjoying seeing the presence of us humans looking on.

Warren has the timings of all todays shows and events already programmed from the colourful leaflet he picked up at the entrance.

Our route taking us beneath a section of the Manta rollercoaster ride, way up above us and the excited viewing public.

Sending shivers down my spine, everyone on this super-fast ride, upside down, facing us, and by the look on their faces between us and a "catch all" safety net, said it all, total horror.

Making our way to the first show of the day, The Beluga Whale habitat.

These sea creatures look amazing, and so large, not sure I would like to come across one of these if out for an ocean swim.

The presenters making this an enjoyable show, clearly a "full house," all enjoying the merriment, and amazing "tricks," these undoubtedly happy looking and joyful creatures trained to do.

Taking a long walk to the next show on our itinerary, sticking to shaded tree lined areas, purchasing an ice-cream along the way to offset the increasing heat.

Entering the Dolphin arena for what I am sure a well-rehearsed and prepared entertaining show, and it did not disappoint, amazing what these creatures of the sea, and the SeaWorld company can do.

Raising lots of laughs and appreciation for the Dolphins and their trainers during the forty or so minute show.

Leaving this location, and heading for a snack, feeling hungry, and after midday already.

Deciding on a cheese burger for me, although not my favourite snack, but when in America, why not try one out for size.

Size means everything, my burger huge by comparison to those purchased in the UK, and rather tasty, however, not convinced about eating more of these so called "junk food" snacks, or after eating my extra-large burger, feeling like a full meal.

Onwards to the Orca arena, SeaWorld exceptionally busy, as once again the both of us walking under another elevated high fast ride.

Everyone screaming as the full ride passing at some speed, way above our heads.

All certainly looking in a happy mood, undoubtedly enjoying the ride, both commenting that this ride, although exciting, not for us.

What I have seen, I have enjoyed so far, and once sat down in the Orcas arena spotting these huge creatures in a secondary tank, awaiting release into the much larger pool and the start of the show.

I remember reading an article quite a few years ago now, that told the story of this very SeaWorld arena, where during one of these shows held in 1991, an Orca whale named Tilikum, dragging Dawn Brancheau, a trainer into the pool, tragically dying as a result of her injuries.

Clearly a dangerous and perilous place of work, nonetheless, during today's show, I did not see a trainer enter the same pool as the Orcas, and once again an entertaining lively show, even for the first few rows of seats, packed with spectators.

All getting soaked numerous times during the show, as the Orcas purposely "wagged" their tails at a given time, forcing pool water over the transparent barriers.

Applause and laughter, and an apparent pleased Orcas too, as they circled and "waved" at the audience, on the face of it, clearly enjoying themselves too.

Making our way to have a look at the shark encounter pool, for a close-up view of a number of species of shark.

The Sand Tiger shark, Epaulette shark, White spotted Bamboo shark to name a few, and these although captive, as near to their natural habitat, no games, or trainers present, just sharks swimming around, but still entertaining in their own right.

Again, looking up as yet another packed roller coaster rocketing along overhead, thrilling, yes, I expect dangerous, perhaps, and my thoughts of you will never get me on one of those rides, now a permanent fixture in my mind.

Sea lions next, almost at the other end of the theme park, great, lots of steps today, and still the walk back to our hotel yet.

The sealions gave an hilarious performance, so funny, and clearly enjoying their time on "stage" to yet another full house.

All in all, a fantastic time, and our day not yet over, and already discussing where to go for tea, when an attraction entrance came into view, and with no queues.

Already in hot sweats as Warren said to come all of this way, and not go on a ride, criminal, and the both of us should experience at least one ride on a Seaworld rollercoaster.

Doubts, you bet, and so much for you will never get me on one those.

Nonetheless, succumbing to Warren's "come on Dad" jibes, as he headed way below ground and beneath the water level of tanks, enabling a look at a variety of fish species, certainly a good distraction if queuing for this ride.

Not much time to take in what's in the tank, as only one person ahead of us, and reaching the ride carriages in double quick time, giving no time for hesitation as the ride assistants helping Warren and me to our seats.

Seats, not too sure about that, yes, almost immediately something to sit in, but not exactly sat in them, as the whole rows of seats on the ride tilting forward, almost laid flat, fully facing the ground.

What have I done...

One assurance, a girl aged around twelve or thirteen sat to my right, not showing one iota of fear, her face instantly lighting up, when the ride began to move forward.

Quickly picking up speed, as the carriages aimed skyward, then a fifty-eight second blur, as the ride twisted and turned, one way then another, inverted, and upside-down, our laid-down position giving the extreme effect of flying through the air.

Superman here I come, great if I could have kept my eyes wide open for most of the ride.

Bend after bend, up and down, to the left, to the right, almost on our sides, what a ride, the Manta certainly doing its job of scaring me half to death.

A first ride of this type in years, remembering taking Warren and Ashley when in childhood along with their step mum, Jane, to Alton Towers, both kids looking on as I took to the then scary ride called Oblivion.

That particular ride did not seem anywhere near as terrifying as this one, although not appearing to bother the girl sat at my righthand side, even Warren looking drained and a little shaken.

The both of us still chatting about various rides of this type on our long walk back to our hotel, and raising the subject once again, in particular about safety aspects, while eating in tonight's restaurant of choice.

The following morning yet another long walk planned, to the Titanic museum, on the northern end of International Drive, with an obvious midway stop at yet another McDonalds for breakfast.

Warren placing the order at a self-service touch screen port, confirming my food, and picking up a table number for staff to deliver to our seats.

Once again Warren sorting out the entrance fee for this attraction on-line the night before, and yet another exhibition that did not disappoint.

Lots of original artifacts plucked from the wreck some 12,500ft, or 2.4 miles below sea level, and some labelled replica's that gave a full perspective of the few short weeks passengers enjoyed onboard ahead of its time, renowned ocean liner.

Our boarding tickets given at the entrance in the names of two passengers that embarked on the SS Titanic on that fateful day, and looking for our given names on the passenger list with-in the museum.

Realising the both of us had actually survived the terrible 1912 seagoing disaster, RMS Carpathia plucking us as survivors from the freezing Atlantic Ocean.

The SS Titanic took all of sixty-two seconds to launch from dry dock into the River Lagan in Belfast Northern Island.

No modern-day champagne bottle christening broken on the hull taking place, however, J.P Morgan, J. Bruce Ismay, and Lord William Pirrie witnessed the event, along with over one-hundred thousand onlookers.

I have seen quite a few films about the SS Titanic, also many documentaries, so to visit a museum of the same name, yet another bucket list item now fulfilled.

Back at our hotel just after lunch, and making for the pool area, a first during our Florida stay, and a welcomed relaxing time to perhaps achieve a bit of a tan.

Fully sun-creamed up, and spending a good few hours either on poolside chairs, or in the pool, and spending some time beneath a larger than average waterfall, the force of which ideal for giving the two of us a good shoulder and back massage.

However, the power of this manipulating water, had, unbeknown to us, washed off our generous layer of sun cream.

Both of us looking quite red, and other parts of our anatomy a little sore by the time of going out for our last evening meal, yet again, an Italian restaurant, on International Drive.

Italian food our preferred option on our holiday, and as yet nothing to complain about, all delicious and filling, complimented with a few ice-cold beers.

Arriving at the airport in plenty of time, a good hour before allowed to check in, as dropping off our hire car a shorter than expected task, all our belongings removed, just a quick examination all-around the vehicle, taking just ten-minutes.

A form to sign and then on our way, taking a short walk to the super-fast monorail system whisking us directly into the huge airport terminal.

Finding a café area for a drink of tea, not like a cuppa at home, but will suffice until boarding the aircraft, and some much-needed food.

The afternoon after checking out of our hotel taken up with Warren driving to a few out-of-town shopping outlets, all much larger than our local Meadow Hall Sheffield, and White Rose centre Leeds, to look for family presents.

I wanted a new fleece to replace mine that I lost somewhere between leaving the airport and picking up our hire car, finding one, seems an almost non-existent commodity here in Orlando.

Racks upon racks of t-shirts, shorts, dress and sports socks, and undies galore, and not a fleece or hoody in sight.

Finally coming across a rail in the clothes section in last of four shopping centres, except only one choice of style, and just two colours, blue and grey.

Choosing a grey one, as my former blue fleece attracting thousands of miniscule hairs from my Lhasa Apso dogs, making it a ten-minute job of removing them every time I put it on!!!

Not that they continually moult, on the contrary, these hairs appear from nowhere.

Also, lots of small kiosks set on the outside walkways, selling an inviting choice of drink commodities, choosing a mixed fruit drink on ice, delicious, and refreshing.

Alarmingly, at another kiosk, spotting a sign for cut price tickets to the Space Coast and Kennedy Space Centre, and considerably cheaper than Warren paid when booking on-line for our two-day visit.

Boarding our flight and getting comfortable for the eight-hour flight home.

Taking the window seat once again, Warren sitting in the middle seat, with the aisle seat appearing vacant, as other seats quickly filling up around us.

A huge sigh of relief when the stewardess announced that all passengers had now boarded, and to prepare for take-off, leaving the aisle seat free, for around two-seconds.

Not giving anyone chance to provisionally claim the spare seat during our flight, as the extremely boisterous incident on the first half of our outbound journey.

Warren instantly shuffling across to the aisle seat, and placing our holdall containing headphones and snacks in the central vacant seat.

Setting the central screen to show our homeward bound journey, Warren saying it doesn't seem like seven days since doing the very same.

Feeling a little sleepy, and may try and get a few hours' shut eye, although looking at the film selection, I might watch a few further blockbuster movies first.

Choosing "A Million Miles Away," for starters, quite apt considering where the both of us had spent the first three days of our sightseeing holiday.

A film about Jose, a migrant farmworker that aspired to become an astronaut, and fly on the Space Shuttle, and he actually succeeds, against all odds.

A heart-warming two-hour fictional family story, full of challengers, upset, disappointments, and finally success.

Jose, ultimately overcoming everything to finally become an astronaut, flying shuttle missions and visiting the International Space Station (ISS).

Choosing a second film, just as supper arrived, smelling delicious, and not complaining as I devoured a hot spicy chicken meal, completed with a piece of cake and hot drink, rather quickly.

Warren getting comfortable, clearly looking to settle down and get some sleep, placing a pillow under his head, and my new hoody fleece over his upper body.

Making sure that Warren's headphones firmly placed over both my ears, and not set too loud, but enough volume to cancel out jet engine and background noise, as my selected film began.

Ironically my chosen film, "A quiet place," the second film about human survivors of planet Earth after gruesome looking Aliens invaded our planet.

The Aliens did not have eyes, or any type of vision, as an alternative, using their acute sensitive hearing to locate and kill for food, taking out anything and everything that moved or made a sound, almost all living creatures, in particular humans.

Our survivors from the first film began a search for other survivors, crossing vast areas of desolate and destroyed towns and cities, and while having to remain excruciatingly silent throughout their journey.

Definitely worth another watch when this film appears on our terrestrial TV screens in the not-too-distant future.

I did manage a few hours' sleep between films, eating food and chatting to Warren during his awake times.

A good idea to book our return flight through the night, although too many distractions to get as much sleep as when tucked up in my own bed.

Almost straight through passport control, and baggage collection, and on our way to the ground floor at Manchester Airport, in much less than an hour, reasonably quiet at this unearthly time.

Warrens partner Sommer, confirming just a few minutes away from meeting the two of us at the pick-up point of the terminal carpark.

Taking just an hour to drive home, our eastbound M62 journey not that busy at this time of the morning.

Sommer dropping me off, hugs all around, and even Lottie and Ted more than pleased to see me, fussy beyond belief.

My brother John and stargazing friend Amanda, looking after Lottie and Ted for the first three days of my holiday.

Repeatedly calling in to my home to check they have enough food and water, and to ensure both spend some time outdoors.

I am sure, both dogs spoilt with treats in abundance while away, not only by John and Amanda, but also my sister Marcia and husband Dave too, as they stayed at mine for the last four days of dog sitting, following their own return from a ten-day Tenerife holiday.

No doubt, Marcia and David pleased to get home to their own beds after almost three weeks away.

It goes without saying, and remiss of me not to thank my son Warren for being so attentive during our stay here in Florida.

I am so proud of how he organised everything, from flights to hotels, pre-paid tickets to attractions, chauffeured me around to all prearranged day-to-day visits and restaurants, and renumerated all of the above on a single debit card, of which my share addressed when home.

Precious quality time catching up on all sorts of subjects and issues, from Warrens early school days, playing junior rugby, his years in the army cadets, and from sixteen years of age when enlisting to join the Army.

Warren, a former soldier with the Royal Engineers, commonly known as a sapper, traveling to the Falkland Islands, two tours of Afghanistan, and Gibraltar, to name a few, and I'm sure lots of other destinations before electing to take retirement from the military due to reorganisation.

His later role as a fully qualified paramedic, and all that job entails, in particular jetting off to Qatar to assist paramedics in the mens football World Cup, and further working visits to that region afterwards.

Also, chatting to Warren about my somewhat lengthy past endeavours, and what I am currently up to, raising eyebrows numerous times.

Especially thinking I had thought of this being a solo trip to Florida, to book a return flight and hotel, just to gaze in wonder at the space shuttle Atlantis, and not much else.

To think that my six-thousand-mile round trip holiday could have gone perfectly as a solo traveller, beyond me.

In hindsight, such a stupid thought…

I am so pleased I did not follow my original pursuit, after having such a wonderful father and son time.

To my son Warren, for making my recently added bucket list item, a fabulous exceptional time for the both of us.

Thank you XX

CHAPTER TWENTY-SEVEN

"Family Reunion"

(Swaffham Norfolk)

To think almost sixty years since grandma told me that the person I have always referred to as my dad, in fact not my father at all, but my step dad.

Mum marrying James Dobson (Jim) after a divorce from first husband Arthur Davis in 1954.

Arthurs name appears on my birth certificate as my father, this too not the case, most of which you will have read my somewhat complicated explanation in chapter fourteen, My Dad.

My brothers Brian and John, and sister Marcia my younger step siblings.

This in its self not that unusual, as lots of families have suffered a marital or partnership breakup, and children from that relationship now the responsibility of devolved parents, either mum or dad, or both, and perhaps a third person, man, or woman.

Our family much the same from 1954, although not knowing any different until I reached the age of fourteen, when grandma, mums mum, spilled the beans.

Jim, my step dad, always my dad until his sad and untimely death at the age of sixty-one in 1986 due to throat cancer.

Meeting my Biological dad for the first time at dads relations John and Brenda in Gravesend, for the first time in January 2009, and thereafter traveling to this southern location, and to homes of other relatives that live locally to London, until dads funeral almost ten years ago.

Just a few visits to meet with family thereafter, mainly funerals of my new found relations, and regretfully within just a few years of meeting them.

All remarking that Tom had kept his son, me, close to his chest and not saying anything to anyone, other than in confidence to his elder brother, Maurice, sworn to absolute secrecy.

So, you can imagine everyone's surprise when I appeared on the scene, this fifty-seven-year-old only son of Tom, all the way from Wakefield, Yorkshire.

Introduced to my biological family, during a gathering at the home of Jenny, at Reeves Farm, Tickhill, near Swaffham Norfolk.

Everyone present pleased to meet me, commenting I am almost his double, my firm hand shaking grip, raising a few laughs to all my remaining uncles, and receiving lots of hugs from my enduring elderly aunties.

All continually asking how I managed to find Tom after all these years, about my past endeavours, and what I am currently doing.

Some of my newfound family remembering Tom had spent some of his time in Yorkshire, between the years1950 to1954, before setting up a permanent residence in Dartford, close to some of his family.

Also, Hillary, Toms niece, taking me the short distance to the local cemetery in Ashill to view the headstones of other relatives whom I sadly didn't get to meet in the flesh.

Reading the text on each of the memorials, most living to a grand old age, except Toms parents, my grandma and grandad, passing away in their early fifties.

Two grandchildren perishing at a young age while working on local farm land, ever so sad.

Lots of comments on our return to Reeves Farm, saying, "shame you didn't discover Tom sooner, as those, your relations in the cemetery, all-lovely people."

Hillary bringing Tom from his Dartford home to Tickhill, both travelling a similar distance to me, as chatting continued while tucking into a huge, tasty buffet put on for all my relatives and visitors.

Hillary driving from Sittingbourne along the M2, through the Dartford tunnel, some one-hundred, and thirty-miles, and me, travelling down the A1 from Wakefield, to our almost central meeting point of Ashill near Swaffham, around one-hundred and thirty-three miles.

A day I will always remember, and one I am to do yet again, some fifteen years later, invited to Jennys home at Reeves Farm for another belated, and long overdue family re-union.

Throughout these years, Jenny and Hillary keeping in touch, with regular emails and social media stories, including photographs, giving me information of what my relatives that remain are doing.

One of which I received from Jenny, telling of a virous that had robbed her of walking abilities, now using a wheelchair, and attending rehabilitation sessions in an attempt to get back on her feet and fully mobile once again.

Also receiving regular updates of her progress via social media, and immediate family posts too, so almost up to date with all goings on at Reeves Farm.

However, my direct journey to Ashill Norfolk not on the cards today, taking a one-hundred- and forty-seven-mile detour instead.

In the first instance, driving much further south on the A1 motorway to Duxford, and a long overdue visit to the Imperial War Museum.

My visit coming about after watching a repeat episode of the 2016 Car SOS TV show, featuring Tim and Fuzz.

On the show they restored a 1934 Singer Le Mans two-seater sports car, registration BBB 140, stored in a Cambridgeshire barn, covered in dust, following a wedding that took place in 1998, and not used since, returning the car to its former glory.

A total surprise for the car owner, as always, with just a few of his family in on the secret, and on this show, using the back drop of the Imperial War Museum (IWM) to return a now completed amazing looking like new car, to its clearly surprised rightful owner.

During the pre-car handover filming sequence, Tim, and Fuzz walking around the huge IWM display hangers, lots of aircraft either on the hanger floor, or suspended from the hanger ceiling.

One aircraft in particular catching my eye, Tim and Fuzz walking while talking beneath the huge wings of Concorde, giving me the initial idea to visit.

I had watched quite a few TV documentaries about the development of the supersonic passenger aircraft "Concorde," and actually observed and heard the unique engine sound of this amazing aircraft flying overhead a few times on its rare visits to Leeds Bradford Airport.

On occasions also seeing it landing and taking off at Heathrow Airport when in London with my band Black Lace in the late seventies early eighties, and aspiring to have a close-up and personal view of this disappointingly redundant aircraft.

Remembering taking my then in-laws to Leeds Bradford Airport for a pre-booked tourist flight over the North Sea on Concorde, one of its last flights before retirement, concluding on November 26th, 2003.

British Airways withdrew Concorde BAOO2, on October 24th, 2003, with a final scheduled commercial flight from JFK airport, landing at Heathrow.

The very last time a commercial passenger aircraft of this calibre would complete the supersonic flight across the Atlantic Ocean in three-hours-thirty-minutes or less.

Concorde Alpha Foxtrot G-BOAF, flew into Filton, the last of the supersonic passenger aircraft to fly.

The documentary mentioned the locations of each Concorde aircraft, and quickly noticed Concorde 101, located in the IWM, Duxford, with others positioned and displayed in locations around the UK, France, and USA.

> - 001 - Bourget, France.
> - 002 - Yeovilton, UK.
> - 101 - Duxford, UK. (test aircraft)
> - 102 - Paris, France
> - 201 - Toulouse, France
> - 202 - Weybridge, UK.
> - 203 - Destroyed in crash, Paris, France.
> - 204 - Manchester – UK.
> - 205 - Chantilly, USA.
> - 206 - Lothian, Scotland.
> - 207 - Sinsheim, Germany.
> - 208 - Heathrow, UK.
> - 209 - Toulouse, France.
> - 210 - New York, USA.
> - 211 - Scrapped in 1994.
> - 212 - Barbados.

> ➤ 213 - Bourget, France.
> ➤ 214 - Seattle, USA.
> ➤ 215 - Charles de Gaulle, Paris, France.
> ➤ 216 - Bristol, UK.

All of these amazing engineering marvels produced between the British Aircraft Corporation (BAC) England, and the state-owned Sud Aviation, France.

The slender streamline shape of Concorde distinguishes this aircraft from any other during its thirty-year commercial lifespan, only taking time out for a full refurbishment following the Air France flight 4590 disaster on July 25th, 2000.

The four Rolls Royce Snecma Olympus 593 turbojet engines, produce an amazing 152,000 pounds of thrust, eating fuel at the rate of around one ton per passenger seat, and when the afterburners engaged, boosting thrust by a further twenty percent.

Accounting for around twelve-thousand dollars per person, per return trip from the UK to America.

An expensive ticket price, but for the customers, worth the time saving cost, actually landing in the USA before setting off from the UK due to the time difference between destinations.

Twenty of these aircraft constructed, built in France and the UK, six of these used as prototype and development aircraft.

One of these on show prototypes in a hangar at IWM Duxford, and the one I am traveling down the M1 to look at, close-up and personal.

Also, whatever else to see afterwards, and all thanks to Tim and Fuzz of Car SOS fame.

Leaving home around 06.30hr, my journey driving south on the M1 motorway, remarkably quiet for this time on a clear, rain free Saturday morning.

Pulling up outside the entrance to IWM building around 09.45, with the carpark moderately full, and a long queue already forming at the entrance.

Clearly, others also deciding on an early get-a-way to look around what I have read as an amazing aircraft museum.

Deciding to book my entrance ticket on-line, filling in the requested details on the IWM website, while sat in my car and listening to Romesh Ranganathan on Radio Two.

Easy, when you know how, Warren sorting this task out numerous times just a few weeks ago during our Florida trip, and appearing to look easy to me.

Joining the queue, my phone open at the obtained QR code page, not taking too long before ushered to a waiting assistant.

Pointing my phone as directed to a receiver, a slight pause, and a confused look from the chap at the back of the counter.

While looking at his computer monitor, he politely asked when had I made the booking, as I had arrived a full seven-days early, inadvertently booking my attendance for the following Saturday instead of today.

What an embarrassing predicament, explaining when seeing the long queues, booked my entrance ticket just a few moments ago while in the carpark.

The assistance saying not to worry, he would quickly sort it out once he had received approval from his section head.

A few visitors in the queue patiently waiting behind me, although only taking a few minutes to alter my ticket date, and then allowed to continue into the museum.

To think, I had originally planned to take my recent trip to Florida to view space shuttle Atlantis at the Kennedy Space centre on my own.

Upon reflection, what a complete mess I may have made, had Warren not taken the initiative, and joined me, sorting out everything.

After my somewhat funny museum mishap, and in hindsight, such a relief.

Oh well…

Taking over three-hours to look around and take numerous photographs of various aircraft memorabilia, on this amazing busy airfield.

Of course, the icing on the cake, and sole reason for my journey, to actually look around the outside, and walk onboard Concorde.

Joining other eager aircraft enthusiasts to enter the fuselage at a rear entrance of Concorde, and slowly walking the length of the aircraft towards the cockpit.

Taking in as much as possible, including photographs, noticing just a few rows of seats to the righthand side for test crew, and occasional VIP guests, positive these seats rather less luxurious looking, than ones on commercial aircraft.

Most of the remaining space taken up with various monitoring equipment, with some room for manoeuvring around other visitors taking longer than expected to read and view various information sheets.

I fit nicely into that category, taking my time to fully appreciate this engineering marvel.

Interestingly, all the electrics "live," with various dials and coloured flashing lights, showing details as though the aircraft in flight.

Also, a short informative on-board back-to-back video, giving an insight into what the crews work entailed while on test flights.

This particular Concorde, the third built by BAC in Filton near Bristol, never carried commercial passengers, being a pre-production aircraft.

Instead, carrying over twelve tons of equipment for in-flight testing.

One notable achievement of this aircraft, becoming the fastest ever Concorde, reaching a speed of Mach 2.23, or one-thousand-four hundred and fifty miles per hour.

Of course, lots of other aircraft on display, including helicopters, light aircraft, jet aircraft, a Boeing B-17G Flying Fortress, named Memphis Belle, including helicopters, a variety of engines, and the list goes on and on.

Also, lots of other privately owned flying aircraft, frequently taking off and landing with fare paying passengers.

Quickly realising that my scheduled three-hours almost up, and certainly not enough time to take in everything the IWM has on show.

No doubt missing out on lots of other displays in other large hangers dotted around this vast museum airfield.

One thing I did not miss, a tasty all-day full breakfast lunch in the IWM café area, tasty, reasonably priced, and needed, absolutely starving following my banana, and fresh orange drink breakfast at 06.00hr.

Setting my sat-nav for the fifty-five-mile drive from Duxford to Ashill Swaffham, taking just over the hour.

My planned earlier arrival, and the greeting no different from all those years ago, although this time around, Jenny in a wheelchair, but still with a smiling face and open arms.

Visiting our local Aldi supermarket the previous day to purchase a variety of goodies, my addition to the prearranged buffet tea, and already lots of tasty looking morsels filling up the large refectory table.

A variety of sandwiches, skilfully placed on trays, lots of cocktail sausages, sausage rolls, pork pies, scotch eggs, crisps, homemade cake, and a selection of fruit, just a mention what instantly caught my eye, and lots of my relations still to arrive for the15.00hr family gathering.

Adding pringles from my carrier bag, Mr Kipling cakes, breadsticks, twists, and soft drinks to a plethora amount of food.

Jenny did say she had invited twenty-five relatives for the afternoon, and if all turn up, now wondering if they too will bring food to add to an already overflowing full table.

Where would it all fit...

One of Jennys daughters arriving on Friday after work, bringing along a large family and two lively retriever dogs.

Using a rather generous enclosed paddock area of garden to the rear of Jenny's Reeves Farm home to pitch their huge tent, staying for the whole weekend until late Sunday evening.

Although Reeves Farm now just a large bungalow, with many rooms, but limited space, as Jenny needs to access most of these rooms, including the house bathroom in a wheelchair.

The remaining spare bedrooms taken up with Jennys other daughter, husband and two children.

Years ago, Reeves Farm, a working farm with acres and acres of tendered farm land, growing a variety of crops, however, all this land either sold or leased to other farmers.

At the righthand side of the bungalow, a large section of land containing a huge garage, large enough to keep coach's for a travel company that Jenny's husband owned and managed before his untimely death, this demolished and containing a selection of new build family detached properties.

Jenny's younger daughter has now taken over the role of driving luxury buses, although the family do not own them anymore, instead leasing a coach for pre-booked trips into London, the east coast, or other destinations.

At this time though, currently making still more sandwiches, and sorting any available space on the table, putting paper plates and cutlery on the worktop, for starters.

Hillary appearing in the kitchen, just as I had asked Jenny if Hillary and husband Steve on their way.

Steve not with her on this occasion, but one of two daughters instead, making the three-hour journey from Sittingbourne Kent.

Mentioning the Dartford tunnels and QE2 bridge, a severe bottleneck for traffic travelling either way.

Stuck in slow moving cars and wagons, with quite a few miles still ahead, as Hillary entered one of the two, two lane northbound tunnels beneath the River Thames.

Bringing to mind the last time while here at Reeves Farm talking about this very same bottleneck, and the recommended new planned motorway route.

The proposal to bypass the Dartford crossing, that also incorporates the QE2 bridge, and double tunnels mentioned by Tom when first meeting him in 2009.

The Lower Thames Crossing proposal would see an easterly route from the M25, clockwise heading in a southerly direction, towards east Tilbury.

A new tunnel constructed under the river Thames, emerging to the east of Gravesend, with junctions onto the A2 and M2 towards Dover, that will, according to surveys, reduce the continual Dartford crossing constrictions.

However, after all these years of decision making around four proposed routes, planning approval still not granted, although with just one preferred route that may speed things up, and not before time.

The costs amounting to hundreds of millions, and increasing daily, and as yet, not one shovel entered into the ground.

Other relatives living local by comparison, and not taking long to drive the short distance to Jenny's bungalow home, also beginning to arrive.

Ample parking available, either in the front courtyard area or the road directly in front of the bungalow.

All the neatly laid out empty chairs soon starting to fill up, some in the dining room, others in the adjoining conservatory, and some preferring chairs in the fresh garden air.

More of my relatives started to arrive, bringing even more food, primarily homemade cake.

I can see lots of rather large doggy bags required at the conclusion of this somewhat generous teatime feast.

Not feeling as though I could eat anything just now, as my tummy feeling rather full of my relatively large lunchtime tasty all-day breakfast.

Eaten just three hours earlier, however the sight and aroma of delicious looking food making my mouth water, thinking I may at least taste a few fragments once the kettle has boiled.

Lots of conversation about my distant ancestral relations, in particular when my family lived in Wells next to the Sea, a former seaside town predominantly known for fishing, before moving to the farm land of Ashill.

Reminding me that Admiral Horatio Nelson born on September 29th, 1758, a famous ancestral relative of ours, actually lived, and raised, about six miles away from Wells, in the next nearby village of Burnham Thorpe Norfolk.

Also, the chicken drum stick king, Bernard Mathews, founder of Bernard Mathews Food, the home of bootiful food, a more recent relative, born on January 24th, 1930, in Brooke, Norfolk.

Not that I had forgotten, and needed reminding of these two famous relatives, as when prompted about distant relatives in any conversation, I can always summon up these stories, told to me in the first instance, and in this very location some fifteen years ago.

Not forgetting other distant relatives living in Spain's Hall, Essex, an Elizabethan country house, and former ancestral home of the Kemp family, purchased in January 2019 by TV chef, author, and former drummer, Jamie Oliver.

One of my relatives actually knighted in this building by Oliver Cromwell.

I am embarrassed to say, I did return to my outdoor seat with a full plate, taking at least one item of food from all the platters and dishes.

Feeling a bit of a glutton, as I had managed to lose almost twenty pounds in weight, over a period of around four months, and now tucking into this tasty looking lot.

Needing a refill of tea, as the milky hot fluid helping to wash down the abundance of pastries, crisps and of course, a huge piece of homemade lemon drizzle cake.

I could do with a nap after eating all of this food, never mind a three-hour drive yet to do before finally reaching home.

Rather warm today, ideal for sitting in the garden, and watching Jenny's daughters two dogs being so well behaved.

Most of the time both in a rather large cage, and not allowed to run around while everyone eating, but the right time to let them out for the rich tasty pickings remaining on plates.

Sadly, I have nothing left over to give them on my plate, however, seeing how they reacted when offered food, I suppose down to their training from being young puppies.

Told to leave, both staring at loose morsels placed on the grass, when told ok to eat, both instantly reacting, and everything eaten in two seconds.

A quick sniff around, then obediently returning to their cage.

I can see Lottie and Ted reacting just the same... NOT.

Some relatives that arrived after me, now leaving for home, and an early night.

Our goodbyes resulting in yet more handshakes, hugs, and kisses, difficult to believe I still hardly know most of them, apart from my visit in 2009, and attending funerals thereafter.

Nevertheless, all warm hearted towards me, and certainly making me feel I am part of the same family, regardless of my somewhat late arrival to the flock.

I had thought about leaving Reeves Farm around 19.00hr, this time came and went, before finally saying my goodbyes to those remaining at the bungalow around 19.45hr.

More handshakes, hugs and kisses and a promise of keeping in touch, and perhaps a further gathering of my relatives before Christmas.

Leaving Ashill and heading north west for the A1, and soon coming back to me how "slow" a journey when driving on this section of road.

Caravans, cars, and wagons on single "A" roads, with only short sections of dual carriage ways popping up, allowing for a quick foot down overtaking spell.

Arriving home just after 10.45, making up quite a bit of time when on the A1, and feeling absolutely shattered.

Certainly not hungry after all the food I had eaten for what appeared all day long.

Bedtime not coming soon enough, once I had taken Lottie and Ted out for their nighttime ablutions, and perhaps a glass of red wine, Jammy Red Rue to help my tired sleepy body relax.

Thoroughly enjoying my time at the Imperial War Museum, and afternoon and part evening with my relatives.

My six-thirty am start of my journey, arriving back home some seventeen hours later, certainly a full day, similar hours to the ones I experienced with my band in the seventies, and eighties, but so much younger and fitter then.

Sending an I'm home message, saying goodnight and a massive thankyou to Jenny.

Thanking her in the first instance for the invite, and for the hospitality throughout my time at Reeves Farm.

Until the next time...

CHAPTER TWENTY-EIGHT

"Queenie"

(Our Mum)

Remembering my nickname from many years in school and college, DOBBO, an exaggeration of my second name Dobson, although Tez, Tud, and quite a few others less appropriate names mentioned, no doubt some under friends and acquaintances breath.

Mum always acknowledges me when asking or in conversation with others, by saying Terry, other than when in trouble for some misdemeanour.

My full first name then used, and said with some mild hostility, TERENCE, of course all depending on the scale of naughtiness, then perhaps a little more venomous.

Dad and his quickly removed belt, used as a deterrent to help prohibit any further incidents of this nature.

These so-called belt incidents taking place more than once, and all because of a repeat of the self- same episode, so the belt and associated lingering pain, not working that good as an immediate deterrence.

Our local railway line typically the cause of my chastisement, less than fifty yards away from our home, an attraction that I could quite easily see from mums bedroom window, and just a skip and jump away.

The regular steam trains traveling from Wakefield Westgate stations, to Dewsbury, via the long gone Alverthorpe and Ossett stations, a railway line requiring my regular attendance at the track edge.

Sometimes a little too close, raising concerns from neighbours and more seriously the Railway Police.

Taken home twice by these uniformed officers, and twice receiving a backside belting from my dad.

Thankfully a family house move from my Peacock Avenue birthplace prevented me from attempting further visits to this possible life-threatening attraction.

With new neighbours, and school friends on Sycamore Avenue, not that far away from our previous home, but far enough, and with so much more to do while at play, far less precarious.

Mum and Dad no doubt pleased about my transformation of while at play childhood too, no mischief or potential harm to call of, and enjoying playtime as an up-and-coming teen while on the "street."

The latest edition to our family, my younger brother John, born in our new Sycamore Avenue home, bringing our now complete little family brothers and sister unit of four, to a close.

Not aware that dad had opted for a vasectomy, or using contraceptives, but no more additions after John's birth, so Brian, Marcia, John the youngest, and of course me, the eldest, in our three-bedroom council house.

Mum definitely a nurturer of the highest quality, ensuring that the four of us always suitably dressed, regularly fed and watered, and all while working unsociable hours at the new Balne Lane library.

A formidable steel and glass structure, built on former allotment land, to the south side of Wakefield's high security prison perimeter wall.

Up at 05.00hr, Monday to Saturday, walking the mile or so to start work as a cleaner at 06.00hr, finishing at 10.00hr, and home around 10.30hr.

Always waving to mum when taking the footpath from Balne Lane, and the full length of the prison walls and side entrance gate, on my way to Ings Road secondary school.

Mum working these weekly hours as a part-time "charlady," and then cleaning, cooking, washing and everything else required at home looking after our family.

Mums wages, although not what I would call substantial, adding to the pay of our coalminer dad, giving a certain amount of security, and our family not seeming "underprivileged" in comparison to other families living close by.

Our family unit did not seem to want for anything, all the mod cons for the time in our home, and not to my knowledge, in debt or having a financial liability to anyone, except our council landlord and utility companies.

Mum always insisted on paying the weekly rent to WMDC, never missing, saying "as long as you have a roof over your head, nobody sees what's on the table," a thought-provoking comment sticking with me throughout my adult life.

Mums pantry always stocked up, so never a worry about what's on our table at meal times.

An assortment of food in tins upon tins, short round ones, flat round ones, tall, and oblong, even tapered, all neatly stacked on shelves or on the pantry "stone."

Never in all my years living at home did I see mums pantry full of quality tinned food, dwindle.

As soon as tins opened, cooked, and eaten, immediately replaced when on mums weekly shopping trip.

The amount of tinned food available in mums pantry would fill many of today's supermarket shelves.

Also, an under-worktop fridge, again always looking full, containing an assortment of fresh food and bottles of red top milk for our breakfast cereal.

I still wonder how our family retained a slim build, all as thin as sticks, straight up and down, with the vast quantity, and quality of food mum frequently put on our kitchen table.

Family meal times always a treat, and even better when I started working, yet lots more food placed on my plate, as I now paid "upkeep" or board money.

Apparently a common practice at the time, to pay a small monetary sum to parents, and in my case taken from my weekly apprentice joinery wages.

Not many of the fast-food, take-a-way food shops, or supermarkets selling readymade frozen meals, meal deals, packaged frozen food in the quantities available these days, all our meals prepared at home, and cooked as required on the day.

The only food I remember as being prepared to eat the following day, being rabbit stew, a food not to my liking at all, even the smell when on the boil putting me off, never mind thinking of a herd of furry bunny's running around our local fields.

A shock for me in seeing these bunny's, pheasants and other furry or feathered livestock, hung outside a butchers shop in town, always making a detour to avoid.

However, this cuisine aside, I do remember the lovely smell of not only cooking, but mums baking too, although grandmas baking on our former homes "range," always a tasty delight.

Especially her scones, baked to perfection, crispy burnt bits around the edges to those placed closest to the open fire, ensuring a butter melting mouthwatering after tea treat.

Not to mention mums Yorkshire Puddings, they too, a gastronomic delight, when made in bun trays and piled high in a dish with lots of tasty thick gravy.

Our preferred local fish and chip shop expanding what they had to offer, by introducing curry sauce, a revelation of sorts, and adding battered sausages too, bringing that bit extra to an affordable alternative to a former fish, chips, and mushy peas meal.

A bag of chips and curry sauce a regular treat when leaving the Balne Lane Youth Club, the fish shop becoming an outdoor meeting and eating location, along with "Perrys" off-licence store.

Our mid-week after school childhood playtimes established with-in our local area, until the street lights came on, and then a short walk home, alleviating any worry for my mum and dad.

Obviously loving the summer months, as then needing a timekeeping mechanism if staying out, and to arrive home at the specified time, although confusing when going to bed, and still daylight outside.

Giving the illusion of missing out on lots more fun, and enjoyable playing out time.

My childhood by comparison of today's so-called fun, sounds a little boring, but a time when exploring the local fields, playing outdoor games on the "street," and friends to talk to face to face, brought about so much more streetwise experience.

Mum always the worrier if not home at the time she stated, and remembering one such occasion in the summer months when the whole street out looking for two missing children, in the dark.

Locating me and Lenny climbing over a scrapyard gate after falling asleep with a great Dane, a so-called guard dog.

Of course, not trespassing, the yard belonging to Lennys dad, so the dog, called Timber, quite happy to play, and sleep with us in the hay.

Not a pleasant time for mum and dad, and Lennys parents too, and a late night for everyone else concerned about our wellbeing, taking time out of their evening looking for us.

Needless to say, both given a good telling off, repeatedly told of the dangers when out playing this late, and as a punishment, grounded for the foreseeable future.

Having then to amuse ourselves at home after school, with listening to radio, or watching teatime programs on our black and white TV comes to mind, and little else, however, lots of paper and crayons to hand, so drawing on the kitchen table.

Sleeping, the only time spent in our bedroom, certainly not like children and teenagers of today, their bedroom a place of sanctuary and sleeping, not emerging for hours, or even days.

Colour TV's, laptops, game consoles, keep fit apparatus, and of course something to sleep on, all crammed into a former bedroom, becoming more of a "living" space.

A space that usually includes, drinking glasses, dirty plates, take-a-way left overs, you name it, and you will come across them at some point, lurking beneath beds, drawers or under soggy towels, sweaty socks, or underwear.

Bringing about an indescribable odour that anyone would think I have experienced at some time or other.

Mum still finding it difficult to comprehend, as my childhood involved lots of parent/child communication, and none of the above.

Our family, when all together at home, all in the same room, either watching whatever on the two or three channel TV, or just chatting about the day's events, or all sitting and eating our meals collectively at the table.

How these times have changed, and more so for me when leaving school and working as an apprentice joiner, then adding my band and playing music, and out until all hours to the mix.

To say mum and dad concerned about this musical pastime of mine, an understatement.

Mum always pleased when hearing our van pull up outside when dropping me off, and the front door quietly closing, usually after midnight, disturbing mums pre-midnight sleep, and then fully awake at 05.00hr for work.

How mum managed to get up at an unthinkable early hour for over twenty-five years, and doing her char lady job, as well as keeping a home, beyond me.

To this day mum often comments about how much she enjoyed working with the other ladies in Balne Lane Library.

Ironically, the dad of Gary, my friend and apprentice joiner work colleague, became mums boss, until mum retired from working at the library, around the time when all the remaining cleaners taken on by a private company, rather than employed directly by the Council.

Sadly, the library building and all its memories, now demolished, replaced with two-and three-bedroom housing.

Throughout this time my dad working regular nights as a coalminer at Walton pit, most weeks, and not fully aware of the ins and outs of my midweek "late" nights, or early mornings before I finally get into bed.

Although mum keeping dad regularly informed of my musical adventures while playing drums in working mens clubs and pubs.

Mum always ready to talk about anything, often talking about her own childhood and teenage days, and more so when I left the family home, making a home of my own.

Engaged to Jacky Herbert, and purchasing my first house, visits to our family home becoming less and far fewer as weeks and months rolled on by, and other priorities gradually began to take over.

My daily work, and band nights almost merging into Monday to Friday twenty-hour days, as arriving home from work, a quick tea then out with our band, home, a few hours' sleep, then back to my joinery job, and then repeat, day after day.

Apparently told by others, teenagers do not need too much sleep, and can survive on extraordinarily little shut eye.

Nevertheless, while in my twenties, and explaining what my day job entailed, and then performing each and every evening in our band, and with just a few hours' sleep, their appeared no time for rest and recuperation.

337

Weekends my only respite, and even those fraught with other issues, but usually finding time to visit my mum, brothers and sister, and in-laws, rather than just a quick landline, "hope everyone ok" type of telephone call.

Certainly, distressing both sets of parents, and even more so when each member of our band also made the decision to turn professional.

The four of us handing in our notice to quit our bread-and-butter day time employment, with just the income from our nightly band gigs to survive on.

I can still see the expressions on mum and dads faces when announcing my exciting bulletin for me and our band, but devastating news to hear for mum and dad.

"How can you make this announcement when you have a mortgage, household bills to pay, and Jacky, your wife, three-months pregnant" came mums initial response, dad nodding in full agreement.

My marriage, birth of our daughter Helen, home alterations, my soon to end day job, and of course most nights out playing music with our band, all taking up a considerable amount of my time.

Mum definitely concerned, and often visiting our home, usually, just Jacky and Helen present, no matter what time of day or night.

On the face of it, leaving my day job should give more available quality time when not working during the day, leaving lots of time for immediate family, and visiting mum and dad, brothers, Brian, John, and sister Marcia.

Although financially speaking, perhaps becoming a problem, as money earned just from our band, will not equate to what each of us earned when working through the day, and playing our music each night.

As professional musicians our nightly band fees did gradually increase, giving more money to pay ourselves a living wage, relieving some immediate tension, and as I have a joinery trade background to fall back on, I could always carry out some cash in hand jobs, should times become difficult.

Dad had moved from Walton pit to a local coalmine, only there a few years, and taking retirement when the Manor Road mine permanently closed.

Shortly afterwards diagnosed with throat cancer, possibly caused by chewing tobacco laced with coal dust during his work, when opening up new coal seams hundreds of feet below ground.

Awfully sad news, obviously hitting the whole family hard, but after many sessions of targeted radiation and chemotherapy, dad making a miraculous recovery.

Even choosing to help me decorate the living room in my new four-bedroom Balne Lane family home, one of two, built on land that previously contained a Methodist church hall, raised to the ground, after a former school class friend, set the building alight.

Our new home just a few yards from the youth club where I spent many a happy hour during my youth, and later band days, where an upstairs room became a place to rehearse our groups music.

However, dads remission period short lived, cancer coming back with a vengeance, totally destroying his will to live.

Dad needed an operation, and fast, to remove his trachea, and a replacement plastic tube inserted into his stomach, invasive to say the least, but at least prolonging our dads life a while longer.

Our family Christmas day gathering not the usual happy and jolly day as in previous years, a sad affair, as dad could not eat solid food, his Christmas dinner blended, resembling more of a thick soup.

Dad passing away at home after just a short time as a result of his throat cancer, on January 31st, 1986, exactly one month after his younger brother, uncle John to us, bringing an end to a sad Christmas, and now also a miserable start to a New Year.

Mum a widow at fifty-five years of age, still quite young by today's standards, and just my younger brother John, remaining at home for the next few years.

Mum taking a holiday to Cyprus with husband-and-wife friends, just what the doctor ordered, however, mum spending half of the holiday in hospital, overcome by the overwhelming heat, and collapsing, short of breath.

When mum arrived home at the end of the holiday period, further hospitalisation in Pinderfields Wakefield required, as diagnosed with pulmonary emphysema.

Instantly giving up smoking, not ever a heavy addiction, just a few, perhaps ten to fifteen cigarettes a day, but over the period of forty-some years, enough to cause this debilitating life-threatening illness.

As usual, mum pulling through, positively good stock, looking none the worse, and getting on with everyday life in the fast lane, taking their dog, a springer spaniel called Nell, most mornings onto the very fields I used to play on.

Following a few nights out with friends, and after six-years a widow after dads passing, our mum met Peter, and not long before they became a couple.

After a whirlwind romance, Peter handing keys to his rented flat back to the council landlord, and moving in with our mum, and brother John in our Sycamore Avenue family home.

All our family highly delighted with this loving partnership, and Peter too, enjoying regular family gatherings, either at our homes or local restaurants.

Peter accompanying mum to John and partner Gills wedding, looking every part the happy couple, just as the new bride and groom.

Peter loving our family homes large garden, turning both front and back areas into lawns with flower boarders, and keeping the front privet hedge neatly cut, Peter looking every bit like a professional gardener, with all the correct tools and clothes.

Sadly, Peter had a heart attack while gardening, and required a battery powered pacemaker fitted to help keep his heart beating regularly, and at a normal rhythm.

Gardening then becoming a low priority for both mum and Peter, and bringing about a decision to vacate our family home for a first floor flat, with council-maintained gardens and lawns, located just a few hundred yards away.

As always, mum turning their flat into a lovely home for her and Peter, and about this time earning the nickname "Queenie."

I think some reference as to how she liked their home to look, with good quality carpets and furniture, matching curtains and cushion covers, looking every bit palatial.

Buying their first car, much better for supermarket shopping, and daily and weekly outings, mum loving it, thoroughly enjoying these trips out.

Prior to meeting Peter, our family did not own a car, or go on family holidays, as individuals my brothers and sister all owning at least one car, but never mum and dad.

Peter taking mum regularly to destinations on the East coast of

Yorkshire, and occasionally venturing over to the West coast of Lancashire, but preferring Monday to Friday coach trips, staying over four nights if travelling much further North or South.

All our family so pleased for mum and Peter, but all would come crashing down, literally, when mum fell in the kitchen.

Mum had got up from bed in the early hours for a drink of cold refreshing lemonade from the fridge, only when removing the bottle top, dropping it, and stepping on it, losing her balance.

Falling to the concrete kitchen floor with a loud bang, waking Peter who immediately rushed to mums aid.

Mum insistent that Peter should help her back to bed, as she appeared virtually pain free.

However, Peter had other thoughts, telling mum to stay put, and not to move a muscle, as he telephoned for an ambulance.

Paramedics attending, carefully placing mum on a stretcher, and taking her to Pinderfields hospital, where when x-rayed, mum had fractured umpteen bones, and all on her left side.

Her hip, wrist, and shoulder blade, requiring major operations, plaster casts, a supportive sling, and terrible bruising everywhere, resulting in weeks upon weeks laid on a hospital bed in Pinderfields Hospital.

So much for mum wanting Peter to help put her back in bed at the time of her fall.

Our mum, "Queenie," at seventy-five years old, leaving hospital in a wheelchair, but looking much better following this worrying dilemma.

Now called "Bionic Queenie" with her new hip, although noticing not as confident when finally capable to courageously stand to her feet, and able to walk, clearly mums self-assurance had taken a big hit.

Nevertheless, not a detriment for this strong-willed woman, getting to her feet in due course, and continuing as near normal a life as possible.

Peter, not a particularly healthy man himself, elected to become mums carer, expertly taking on the role of cook, cleaner, and bottle washer for the foreseeable future.

Mum would see the four walls of a hospital ward once again, her pulmonary emphysema, coming to a head, making it difficult to breathe.

Peter and family all there to offer support once mum allowed home, and once again mum being mum, pulled through.

So much so, a further coach holiday booked to one of their favourite destinations, Llandudno.

Peter taking along mums recently purchased battery powered wheelchair, making the long walks along the beach front so much easier for the both of them, especially Peter.

Peters ongoing heart problems would also surface once again, and with the onset of covid, his health in serious decline.

Both mum and Peter would spend over two weeks in hospital when contracting covid, Peter allowed home first, mum needing convalescence in a Hemsworth care facility, before fully discharged and allowed to return home.

Both in each other's company once again, but everyone else in the country isolated, the government's policy of two meters apart, and only when outdoors still in force, making help with recovery so hard.

Our family gathered together outside mum and Peters home, to bring a little joy, by singing happy birthday to Peter, celebrating his eightieth birthday.

Sadly, Peter would not fully recover from both covid and his on-going heart problem, requiring lots of support from our family members, and also regular visits from care assistants.

Mums partner of almost thirty years, would leave their home for the last time, when admitted to Pontefract Hospice, where just a week later he slipped away from us all.

Devastated to say the least, and still in covid lockdown, the implications of which indicating that a minimum of sixteen mourners allowed to attend Peters funeral, with a family get together held afterwards at Marcia's home.

Would you believe it, mum had a fall in the living room, my brother John telephoning me to say mum had contacted the care-link operative by pressing the pendant hung around her neck, and could I join him at mums flat immediately.

I have to say these pendants a fantastic idea, and by pressing the fob, mum not only had me, but John, and an ambulance crew to her home within minutes, rather than hours, or the next day, or when the next person visiting mum, if not having a contact device around her neck.

Mum confident she had broken her other hip as in tremendous pain, and saying she should have left the living room reading light on, instead of bending down to turn it off at the switch, losing her balance.

Once in hospital, an x-ray confirming mum had indeed broken her right hip, and thankfully, although horrendous for mum, no other fractures or bruising.

A major operation, and convalescence and rehabilitation once again, different to Pontefract hospital, a care home in Horbury, Dovecote Lodge.

Mum sort of enjoying three weeks in this facility, staff, and food all brilliant, however mums only complaint, always too hot, although now the middle of summer and high temperatures outdoors too.

Arriving home once again in top form, not giving in for sure, definitely bionic, with both her hips renewed with titanium joints, and a determination and resilience that equals the same strength.

Once again, our "Queenie" pulling through, although even more cautious than before, and requiring a zimmer, or walking frame to get about the flat.

On reflection I will say mum has never got over the loss of her partner, Peter, and the same for the rest of us, as no doubt in our minds he had given mum lots and lots of happy times.

Mum would fall again, twice in fact, the last of which required a further stay in Pinderfields hospital, now becoming mums second home.

Needing a three-week prolonged session of rehabilitation, discharging mum from hospital after two weeks, and sending her to the same care home, Dovecote Lodge, in Horbury.

A period of some buoyancy with mum as she began to progress reasonably good, although not that much rehabilitation going on, as mum not able to stand on her feet un-supported for too long, requiring lots of assistance.

Mum returning home once again, after a three-week stay in Dovecote Lodge, clearly looking and starting to feel much better.

Becoming acclimatised at home, making her own meals as before, and generally getting about with the aid of her friendly Zimmer frame, when our family heard of some devastating news that knocked mum for six...

Mums former next-door neighbour, and friend for over fifty-years when living on Sycamore Avenue, and when moving to her flat, passed away after a prolonged illness.

Deciding not to tell mum of Christines death until the following day, and that awful message of her passing, given me to deliver.

My two-mile walk across the meadows full of how I should tell mum this distressing news, silently practicing of how to deliver my upsetting message, all to no avail, instead, just blurting it out, "mum, Christine has died."

A moment of silence, and then mum beginning to cry, saying, " I thought something wrong, as I had not heard from her in over a week."

To say mum devastated an understatement, so upset at hearing this awful news, pointing out that all her friends, except Iris Noble, have passed away.

I think mums further fall, a direct result of hearing this news, although a few days afterwards, and almost a repeat of the first fall, just a few months ago.

Another three-weeks in Pinderfields Hospital, two-weeks in Dewsbury Hospital and then moved to a Pontefract nursing home.

"Stella House," located to the rear of a huge popular eating pub called "The Cobbler," in the eastern area of Pontefract, and around thirty-two-mile round trip for me, and our immediate family to visit.

Not exactly home from home, but mum settling in well, enjoying the company of other patients here for rehabilitation, and the thoughtful, attentive caring staff.

Mum repeating, they have tasty food three times daily, and always plenty to eat, including lashings of gravy, a favourite of mum's on any meal.

Also, mum saying that all the staff help by cutting up plated items of food, such as steak, or chicken, enabling mum to clear her plate, ready for a pudding.

Still upset about Christine, and saying that the last two of her friends, Stella, and now Christine no longer with us, and with mum in a care home, just all getting too much for her.

In a flash, I said, "mum, they are both obviously thinking about you, look where you are, STELLA House, and your room number, 11, the same number as Christines home, what a remarkable coincidence, but serving its purpose, mum instantly coming around.

I attended Christines funeral on behalf of mum, with John and wife Gill accompanying me.

The crematorium at Kettlethorpe almost full, attended by family and many friends.

A thought-provoking service given by a lovely lady celebrant, recalling Christines life, and mentioning the long and caring friendship of mum and our family.

A funeral wake taking place at Alverthorpe Working Mens Club, giving everyone chance to catch up on both families current news, and reflecting on fun times while living as neighbours for a great many years.

Also, a remark as to the last time I had visited this club, recalling our band Mister Twister performing here for our singer/guitarists seventieth birthday, in July 2022.

The stage looking much bigger from an audience level, than when placing and setting up all our equipment, and of course my over large drum kit.

Mum upset that she could not attend her long-time friends funeral, due to her own health concerns at this time, and happy to receive a resumé of how the service took place from me.

Mum settling in to Stella House, enjoying the camaraderie and atmosphere remarkably well, all seeing a change in her demeaner, smiling such a lot more, and generally much happier.

So much so, after just five-days "living" in Stella House, mum issued some devastating news of her own.

Saying she did not want to return home to her flat, but to remain here, in a lovely care home of mums choice.

A shock for all of us, but taking the bull by the horns, Marcia, and John, taking her at her word, and beginning the process for mum to stay at Stella House.

Speaking to the manager and discussing requirements, as mums wish to live at Stella House permanently, to stay here for the remaining days of her life.

Mum already giving out orders as to who should get what from her home, John and Gill, sister in-law Gill, myself, Warren, and Ashley, all getting stuck in, to sort out all mums belongings.

Our close family retaining a lot, and heaps of quality furniture and belongings taken away by Wakefield Hospice, while other not required items given away to friends of friends, and a small amount from the loft taken to the local refuse centre.

Not enjoying this process at all, with mum still very much alive and kicking, constantly dispensing instructions, and frequently enquiring as to who is doing what, how things progressing, and what she would like to see in her new room with-in the care home.

Then the unthinkable happened...

Mum has another fall in her bedroom, reminiscent of all the previous falls, a further admittance to her second home Pinderfields Hospital, and told that mum had broken her pelvis in two places.

The breakage, around the pelvic ring and pubic bone area, causing mum excruciating pain and immeasurable discomfort.

Mum finding it difficult using bed pans, so much so a catheter inserted, her medication increased to help with pain relief, and unable to stand, requiring a protracted stay on a hospital bed.

You could imagine our thoughts at this point, what now, and what is mums future prognosis.

Our brother Brian, a porter at Pinderfields Hospital for over forty-years, becoming our go to person, as able to enquire face to face about all the if's but's and maybe's of mums lengthy recovery period.

Mum would descend rapidly into despair, her health deteriorating, so much so, all of us believing mum would not last until the end of the week, and enquiring about end-of-life care.

Spending two weeks in Pinderfields, and a further two weeks in Dewsbury hospitals, mum astounding us all, as once again making a near miraculous recovery.

A temporary room set up at Stella House, to allow mums discharge from Dewsbury Hospital, mainly due to acute bed shortages, and to take place sooner than later, but not without its problems.

Apparatus required for mum to move to Stella House not delivered, following a computer malfunction, leaving our mum on tenterhooks, still on her designated ward in Bronte Tower at Dewsbury Hospital for two further days.

Finally, all the pieces in place, and mum back at Stella House, her home for the foreseeable future.

Mums permanent room becoming available in three-day's time,

bringing an end to almost six-weeks of an emotional upheaval, not only for mum, but our family too.

Onwards and upwards...

Taking all of the above into consideration, and perhaps describing the next chapter of what time remains of mums exciting life, as a challenge, for all to enjoy.

Fingers crossed...

CHAPTER TWENTY-NINE

Right Place – Right Time

(Perhaps)

Over the years, I feel that at times "things" happen for a reason, no matter how small or insignificant, it or they, or whatever, constantly making me wonder.

Unexplainable instances that occur, but only when reminiscing do they appear to make any sense, bringing about a thought provoking "what if" scenario.

Perhaps fate stepping in, to remind me that in all my years I appear either lucky, fortunate, blessed, fluky or just jammy to arrive in this favourable, although at my time of life, somewhat limited position.

For all those earlier years of my misgivings and calamities, to survive almost intact at the age of seventy-two, without any known ailments, a marvel in itself.

On the face of it, I have spent virtually no time at all sitting in my doctors waiting room, or at hospitals, or chemists, save for inoculations for trips abroad, covid, or the well-man clinic for blood pressure, weight, and height.

I do however take a 2.5 milligram daily dose of Ramipril, a single pill taken for over five-years now, and required following a CT scan carried out by my paramedic son, Warren.

Brought about after others around me, noticed that I appeared out of breath when lifting items, or involved with not over strenuous workouts.

Not aware of anything different myself, and still refusing to believe anything wrong with how I breathe, when doing anything or nothing energetic.

Though told umpteen times about a bad habit of mine, holding my breath when lifting and walking with heavy objects, and taking larger than normal strides until reaching my expectantly close destination.

Then, and only then, do I feel out of breath, taking huge gulps of air to revitalise me, much needed oxygen pumped into my depleted blood stream and air-starved exhausted lungs.

All this aside, I do like to do lots of things, anything that in the interim, keeps me reasonably fit and active, walking, running, or swimming not a problem.

During my "down time," listening to news either on TV or radio, or a soak in Hector, where at times, most of my outlandish thoughts take place, lots of which you will have already had the pleasure of reading.

Also, I have not discussed my latest fixation, where I can "switch off," and for a considerable length of time, takes little or no energy in doing, in fact, I can have a coffee during the process.

If I mention, facial or body cleansing, what would you think that involves.

A face wash in warm water, using a moist impregnated tissue, loofah, an exfoliating product, a super sticky fascial mask, a peel, or all of the above, and more.

Well…

Coming across a YouTube video called "pimple poppers" where clients have Acne, resulting in lots of blackheads, spots, and other facial and body skin disorders, or cutaneous.

Patients individually taken care of, to help improve skin health and its overall appearance.

This highly magnified ultra-clear screen view, showing hundreds of singular blackheads gently removed by clinical staff, inserting a hollow sharp needle not much thicker than a human hair, or other razor-sharp implements probing directly into the skin pores.

Then either prizing or squeezing out bacteria product with a gloved finger and thumb, progressively immerging in the form of a long "string," or yukky gross thick looking custard fluid, or puss, from each distinct individual skin pore.

In lots of cases, bacteria certainly popping out, and blood too, but instantly wiped away with cotton wool or cleansing tissues.

Some operatives use two cotton buds to gently squeeze or ease them out, even plyers, yes plyers.

Not the typical bulky looking ones, used in various trade or DIY backgrounds, but made from either stainless steel or chromium, with extra sharp gripping jaws, more akin to a posh pair of wire cutters.

These utensils used to grasp a protruding thread like substance, following a slight amount of pressure given by the operative, and then gently easing out two-millimetre-long rice size semi-solids from each of hundreds of individual facial pores.

I would envisage this unorthodox, and perhaps costly procedure, taking a considerable length of time, depending on the severity and perhaps pain and suffering of the acne sufferer.

Most importantly the speed and tenderness of the usually female technicians while carrying out this face, or body cleansing process.

Revolting to some, and I don't know why, but to me, and what appears many thousands of other regular on-line viewers, clearly popular of this somewhat grotesk and perhaps evasive, repulsive form of a relaxing entertainment pastime.

Of course, not wanting to confess I enjoy watching these to anyone, but I do admit viewing these short, somewhat addictive videos in a pleasant, dare I say satisfying, and "relaxing" sort of way.

However, not a new experience for me, as I remember umpteen years ago, my stepdad Jim a miner, would often take an extra-long hot bath when home from work, and asking if I could do the honours of removing some blackheads from his back.

Obviously, a gross suggestion, nonetheless jumping at the opportunity to remove debris from his many inflamed skin pores, even recommending my services should take place weekly, and an increase in pocket money for my skills.

These days, my preferred option to watch rather than get physically involved.

I do ramble on…

However, and quickly changing the subject to my original "What if" scenario.

For instance, just the other week, when on my way on the M1 travelling to Duxford, hearing of a motorway pileup involving lots of vehicles, closing the southbound carriageway on my cars radio at the very same time that I had planned to set off.

However, as I left home fifteen minutes earlier than originally planned, I had avoided me and my car, stuck in endless hours of traffic, all of this turmoil now behind me.

Just lucky or jammy, perhaps…

Fate, unsure…

Also, you have read about me meeting Tricia, the mum of my youngest son, in previous paragraphs, and all that assignation entailed.

Never in a million years did I ever think I would become a dad again at the age of fifty years old, and a short but ever so happy relationship, and all brought about by a "chance" meeting when going to a birthday party.

Once again, fate…

Or, for example, both our youngest children engaged in music lessons at Manygates Music Hub, and meeting Amanda in the Manygates café while waiting for their drumming tuition to come to an end.

Discussing amongst other topics, my many years playing in a band, especially while competing in the 1979 Eurovision Song Contest, held in Israel.

Saying to return one day, a high priority on my imaginary bucket list, although after some forty years and counting, looking less likely as time passes.

Who would have thought that Amanda actually knows a lady called Julia in their religious ecclesia, who has organised Holy land trips for Christadelphian believers for over twenty-five years.

Amanda saying she will speak to her and ask if any places become available, to add me to the list for her next trip.

Sadly, I had to wait a few years before a place became available, finally accomplishing a forty-three-year desire of mine to return to this amazing country.

Not once, but twice over two years, fulfilling twenty days of site seeing and gaining far more historical and biblical knowledge of this region, creating amazing friendships in the process.

So much so, putting my name down for yet another October 2024 visit to this amazing land of Milk and Honey.

Unfortunately, because of the recent troubles involving what appears the whole region, Lebanon to the north, Syria to the north east, Jorden south east and the Gaza strip, my visit and that of other travellers scuppered for the foreseeable future.

Fate, or just luck…

Maybe, just maybe, the meeting of a singer song writer, living and working in London, who just happened to visit his home town of Bolton, and by chance meeting our Lancashire agent for a pint in his local pub.

Their chatting resulted in our band Black Lace invited to travel to London to record a song called Mary Ann.

Just by coincidence our song and Peters composition, entered into the Song for Europe to pick a song to represent the UK in the twenty-fourth Eurovision Song Contest held in Israel, March 1979.

Luckily a BBC strike took place during rehearsals at the Royal Albert Hall, and the televised show cancelled, leaving the jury to pick a song on sound alone, and on my birthday too.

Fortunately, our tune, Mary Ann, chosen to represent the United Kingdom, and probably still the only song to date, picked to represent the UK, on a tune and lyrics alone, an unknown faceless band, and without a prior appearance on TV.

Finishing the competition in 7th place, lucky for some, destiny appearing on our side from then on.

I know, not exactly earth-shattering revelations, and I am sure lots of people can tell similar stories of what may have happened, if only they had taken a different path, and at a different time.

I can recall lots of other events that in the echoes of hindsight, could have turned out so differently, had "fate" or other unknown help or assistance taken place.

Most of which I have covered in my previous four publications, but I feel this admission still needs more analysis, just to put my own mind to rest.

My "what if" thoughts constantly raising more than likely absurd questions, not only to myself, but to others.

Answers then received, or answers that perhaps I can establish for myself, not quite what I expected.

Confusing…

For instance, constantly having thoughts and affections raising numerous questions and possibilities about anything and everything in no particular order, concerning all of the following, and many, many more in reserve.

My lovely Mum, many close friends and associates, my bands and musical colleagues, my ex-wives, my children, Helen, Kerry, Warren, Ashley and Liam, grandchildren, Ethan and Violet, past in-laws and intimate companions, Tricia, and friends past and present from Liverpool.

My stargazing partner, Amanda, Christadelphian Ecclesia, the observatory, Supporting Music For All, Julia, my step dad, my work colleague Ken, helping me in finding my biological dad, Gary and work apprenticeship, school, college, university, all my years and acquaintances while working at Wakefield Council, and WDH.

All of my own, and other DIY projects, past, present, and in my mind yet to start, not only for myself, but for close acquaintances too.

Holidays, and my ever-increasing bucket list, all of the above bringing about a currently un-prioritised mental directory that appears to go on and on and on, certainly since just before my retirement.

Arguably, not a "quiet" retirement life, my mind awash with thoughts of past endeavours, my possible future, and those of family and friends, "what if" scenarios accumulating by the minute.

"Switching off" becoming a hard task, with so many contemplations of my past and constantly emerging present situations.

My nightly sleep pattern, daily walking, exercise, heart rate, stress levels and blood pressure, all monitored by my Huawei watch and Huawei Health phone App.

Not that I consider myself paranoid, not at all, but having a good guide in managing my daily routine, all helping to keep me on my toes.

With all of my innermost thoughts constantly flashing around, I do not appear to lose any sleep, as the app also gives a breakdown of my somewhat nondescript nighttime activities.

Deep sleep, Light sleep, Rem sleep, and Sleep breathing awareness, also how many times awake, if any, and giving a daily analysis and recommendations for a better night's sleep, if required, for the following night.

However, as I had three unexpectantly awake sessions during a previous night's sleep, an amazing app that also provides information to suggest if my pattern of fragmented sleep continues, can actually put more stress on my whole body.

Lack of sleep can weaken my immune system, and lead to neurasthenia and gastrointestinal illness.

Trigger problems with my heart, which may also initiate high blood pressure, a-fib, coronary heart disease, and other cardiovascular diseases.

Even worse, the lack of deep sleep can slow down my metabolism and accelerate aging process, also catching a cold or experience gastrointestinal issues, such as obesity and once again, high blood pressure...

What a frightening dilemma, but how do I rectify my fragmented sleep pattern, turning my time in bed fully around so that I can sleep more soundly.

Perhaps as instructed by the app, in particular, soaking my feet in warm water, or taking a bath before tucking into bed, or try not to smoke close to my bedtime, as the intake of nicotine can last for hours, decreasing my deep sleep duration.

Not that I smoke, or ever have done, so not a useful comment at all.

A reduction in deep sleep can also have an effect on the balance of my Leptin and ghrelin, leaving me feeling tired and lethargic, and affecting my memory.

WHAT!!!

On a helpful note, when told I have had a good night's sleep, I am assured that my immune system, cognitive performance, and creativity has taken a massive boost.

To add to all of this information, my skin cell turnover more efficient, helping to keep my skin elastic and glowing, enabling me to look much younger than my years.

All in all, giving me options that I perhaps do not or would not necessarily know, if not wearing my super-duper wrist watch.

Of course, providing that all these informative statistics in fact, reasonably accurate.

Planning and preparation has formed part of all my working and social life, regardless of my newfangled watch.

Years in preparing capital, and yearly maintenance programs, while in my day job, learning songs, rehearsals, arranging for band mates to pick up for our gigs, playing our music and the same in reverse, preparation and attending observatory and Supporting Music for All meetings, the list endless.

Although, known to recklessly "jump in," both feet first on some occasions, with little, or no planning, or limited preparation to hand.

A back of a cig packet approach, that at times has almost led to many a disaster of sorts.

However, these days in my retirement, and somewhat settled in my daily routines, I tend to "think" about things so much more, and actually prepare for most day-to-day "things," when needed, ahead of the time.

Sometimes thinking about the film "What Women Want," starring Mel Gibson and Helen Hunt, and after a thunderstorm and flash of lightning, Mel, or his character Nick, can suddenly "hear" the thoughts of women around him.

A hilariously funny film, Mel, or Nick then finally leading to romance with Helen, or her character Darcy.

Mel finally returning to "normal," after yet another electrically charged thunderstorm.

I could do with a brain and ears like that, if just for two minutes in the right location, I am sure a benefit of sorts.

In particular, when in meetings, to "hear" thoughts of others a definite advantage.

Nevertheless, back to planning, and specifically our Young Astronomer sessions at the observatory, where preparation essential to ensure the smooth running of these somewhat hectic evenings.

Admission fees charged in advance to cover costs for these events, taken on a payment website, giving a full account of how many children and parents are due to attend, so everything fervently organised as near perfect as possible.

Also, if expecting a large audience for a Heritage Talk or the like, where attendance to the observatory free of charge, or perhaps a small donation, organised so as not to allow an embarrassing or awkward situation to arise.

I have volunteered on a number of occasions to take these talks, one of which not my preparation, but that of a lifelong member of the observatory.

A specific talk carried out last year as part of a week-long Pontefract Heritage event, where members of the public can visit various locations in and around Pontefract, free of charge, or by submitting a donation.

With permission, I reduced this already prepared PowerPoint talk from around two hours long, to just over forty minutes, allowing visitors to look around the observatory and access our large telescope in the dome, all with-in the allotted two-hour slot.

Feeling confident after my talk, I presented the same forty-minute talk about the formation of West Yorkshire Astronomical Society and building of the observatory once again, this time to a group of elderly gentlemen, and with the original author in the audience.

Thankfully, I received an assured thumbs up, and he also took part in the questions and answers throughout the presentation, especially when needing first-hand knowledge and confirmation about a few points and topics.

All in all, everyone enjoyed a good night, fully rounded off when a few of these elderly gentlemen actually climbed the rather steep steps into the dome, for a look at the clear night sky through our telescope.

I have a prepared PowerPoint presentation of my own, arranged and shown via Zoom to the observatories committee members, when most of us, including a large percentage of workers, confined to their homes during the first period of covid lock-down.

The use of Zoom, to link various people from locations far and wide via "live" video, originally created in 2011, in San Jose in California.

This function bringing working from home, a commonplace initiative, now used worldwide for meetings, family gatherings and TV, amongst a variety of other convenient uses.

My PowerPoint presentation "An Unexpected Journey," bringing together space and music, inspired by a talk and meeting, carried out at Wakefield's "Museum of the Moon" in August 2019.

A two-week extravaganza of space, dance, and music celebrating the fiftieth anniversary of the moon landing on July 16th-24th, 1969.

These performances covering a variety of singing, dancing, and concerts, held at the former market Hall in central Wakefield, where my verbal presentation, a talk about the formation of West Yorkshire Astronomical Society,(WYAS) and the building and running of our Pontefract observatory will take place.

Including chatting about many outreach activities carried out by the observatory volunteers, to an audience of around one-hundred and twenty ticket holders.

On stage with me, a chap I did not know of until asked to present my talk by our chairperson of WYAS, when he contacted me while on my holidays in Benalmadena, Spain.

The initial enquiry told of a short talk about the observatory, then to obtain five or six questions about the 2003 Mars lander, Beagle 2, from our WYAS members.

Once an introduction has taken place, a special guest will join me on stage to answer these prepared questions.

All sounding good in theory, but having to wait until returning home from my mainland Spain holiday to make these arrangements.

Or so I thought.

Told during the telephone conversation to expect a further telephone call from my special guest, and visitor to Wakefield, a David Rowntree.

A chap having lots of knowledge and experience, and could talk until the cows came home about the subject matter of the Mars lander, Beagle 2, so told I need not worry.

Quickly looking on my phones search engine for "David Rowntree," and to my surprise, none other than the drummer of nineties pop group, Blur, an English rock band formed in London in 1988.

The observatories former chairperson did say the two of us has lots in common, a drummer myself, I now know what he meant, although soon to learn, not exactly lots in common.

David Rowntree, the multi award winning drummer of Blur, with over thirty-five chart topping single records, thirty chart topping LP records, and thirty-seven music videos, and counting, to his name, furthermore, millions upon millions of YouTube views of live concert performances.

A wealthy musician, local councillor, astronomer, astrophysicist, film producer, animator, pilot, and the list goes on and on.

Lots in common, I don't think so...

Feeling more than nervous about taking his call, so much so, vacating the somewhat lively outdoor sunny pool area of our hotel, and making a dash to our seventh-floor room.

Dressed in my almost dry swimming shorts with a towel around my shoulders, making the sprint just in time, although a little precarious running on glossy tiled floors with flip-flops on my feet, not a simple undertaking.

Slumping on my bed, slightly out of breath, and just in time, as not recognising the eleven-digit number displayed on my now vibrating phone, hesitantly answering.

"Hello..." not polite by any means.

"Hello, is that Terry, this is David Rowntree...

Almost asking him if a wind up, but keeping my composure, taking a deep breath, and speaking in what I assumed a confident clear voice.

"Hello David, so lovely to hear from you."

Our relaxed chat lasting quite a while, David commenting he had just returned from a holiday in Spain, also the subject of our shared music interest, raising quite a few laughs, and then my role with-in our observatory, before delving into the reason why he needed to speak with me.

Talking about his invitation to Wakefield's museum of the moon, and what will become our Mars Beagle 2 mission, questions, and answers presentation.

David rounding off our chat by saying, "take care Terry, and see you in Wakefield."

My early arrival at the former Market Hall certainly made my jaw drop, as there, suspended from the ceiling, a huge 1:500,000 perfect scale model of our celestial partner, the moon.

Designed by artist Luke Jerram, and what an amazing sight, using high-resolution imagery of the luna surface supplied by NASA, and no doubt a complicated job to put it all expertly together.

Walking all around this authentic looking sphere numerous times, taking in all the craters and moon landing sites, and killing a bit of time until notified David Rowntree and entourage, now on their way.

David flying a light aircraft from London South East airport, landing at Doncaster airport, and chauffeur driven in a council limousine to Wakefield.

Our meeting in the former market hall did not disappoint, such a lovely gentleman, a pre-chat taking place in our dressing room dispelling any nerves, as I took to the stage.

Almost dumfounded when I asked if anyone in the audience knew of our thirty-six-year-old observatory, located just a few miles away from Wakefield.

Only five people from over one hundred and twenty spectators, showing their hands as a response.

Nevertheless, completing my twenty-minute talk with-out further ado, and then to present the star of our little get together.

Giving a short, but informative prologue of my guest, before introducing David to the stage to thunderous applause.

Almost two hours of chatting, not a dull, awkward, or embarrassing moment, David a natural when talking and delivering answers about Beagle 2, and raising lots of laughter during our laidback tete-a-tete.

At one point discussing a bands equipment set up on the stage behind us, for a later in the night music show.

Both commenting on the nicely polished red drum kit, and saying, "almost feeling like home sat on here," to an amused audience…

Also, David joining the audience for photographs, including me, a day I will not forget in a hurry.

I do digress…

Following a committee meeting, agreeing to give my presentation "An Unexpected Journey," to this year's heritage night at the observatory.

Bringing together my former band Black Lace, and nineties band Blur, with a few slides showing photographs, and giving details and statistics of how David Rowntree and myself met, and delivered the story of Beagle 2 to an optimistically captivated audience.

That said, still plenty more to arrange with our last Friday of the month's Young Astronomers Evening, and subject of "Moons of the Solar System," requiring a twenty-minute talk, and a number of arts and craft activities yet to plan.

To think, I thought of retirement as a time in life when possible to take things easy, to relax and take each day as it comes for the remaining years of my life.

Not wanting to sound presumptuous, but perhaps if not involved in various projects that I genuinely enjoy doing, I doubt for one minute I could in fact relax for any meaningful length of time.

Of course, I still have the use of my mobile phone or laptop available, making my "down time" a little more of an enjoyable experience.

Making me wonder, what did the population do with their time during those childhood years, before this particular "invention" of communication and play came to most people on the planet.

Bringing back an old joke, but recently "aired" on a social platform:-

I wonder what my parents did to fight off boredom prior to the internet becoming the norm.

Asking my seventeen brothers and sisters, and they didn't seem to know either.

Anyway...

I think from my point of view, I need to thank mum and dad for the initial conception, and bringing about my birth at just about the right time.

My 1952 beginning, allowing me to not only witness these astounding innovative technological achievements of our journey into space, and after my trip to the USA, actually seeing for myself some of this progress, past, present, and future with my own eyes.

Enabling me to personally use at least some of the marvellous available apparatus, my fingers and thumbs working overtime, tapping away like no tomorrow.

An enlightening revealing experience, with the full and last version of 2010 Encyclopaedia Brittania, 32,640 pages worth of information, and so much, much more obtainable, and all available in a millisecond on a device that fits in the palm of my hand, and snuggly in my jeans back, or coat pocket.

My subsequent viewing of many documentaries on the subject, made aware that the Apollo 11, had a guidance computer with over one million times less memory power than contained in a modern iPhone, and still managed to land astronauts on the moon in 1969.

Unbelievable...

For me, definitely the right time, and right place.

CHAPTER THIRTY

Trouble at the Mill

Throughout my life I have attended meetings, or confabs with working colleagues, band mates, girlfriends, wives, children, and neighbours when things do not go, or progress exactly as planned or intended.

These meetings, sometimes arranged as a matter of some urgency, definitely a good proposal to clear the air.

An opportunity to discuss the subject matter causing concern, and optimistically arrive at a compromise, but all efforts made to avoid shouting, banging on a table or desk, or fighting to get a point understood.

This action a polite way to resolve issues, instead of careless talk behind a friend or colleagues back.

I remember lots of occasions when these so-called airing grievances during meetings, resulted in raised voices, the dispensing of unnecessary sarcastic comments, also walking out of meetings, and at times almost coming to blows, thankfully as yet, none have.

An unruly atmosphere of this nature to avoid at all costs, if possible, although sometimes easier said than done, as feelings can run high when issues left to rumble on for some time.

Confrontation between adversaries over a particular subject, or perhaps more than one issue that has come to the surface, as one person, family, group, business, or country feels aggrieved at another, for either things said or done, or worse.

Nothing new with that statement, as arguments within all societies, and at all levels, filling this description have flourished over millennium, resulting in sackings, resignations, demotions, fines, protests, murder, prison sentences, amongst other unpleasant antagonistic occurrences, or all-out war.

In my lifetime of seventy-two years, I have witnessed all of the above at one time or another.

Not exactly face to face, but on TV news channels, radio, or lately on social media platforms, where photographs or videos of a particular incident "shared" on various devices for everyone browsing to become judge and jury, with minimal evidence of the so-called event.

The unquestionable "verdict," at times achieving the role of a vigilante or kangaroo court, taking matters into their own hands, from the comforts of their own homes or surroundings, their fingers damaging many lives.

With working careers and livelihoods, slammed into oblivion, as it appears that every picture or video tells a believable but at times biased story.

The person or organisation complaining of an alleged "wrongdoing," requires evidence to prove that an "offence" has taken place.

For instance, take a typical speeding offence reported on a digital motorway speed camera.

Evidence should include photographs of the car, the registration number, the driver, the alleged speed, speed limit of the area, and not forgetting a date and time.

The absolute minimum requirement for an offence of this type, and usually appears via a postal delivery direct to your home address.

Sometimes knowingly, as the driver mindful of exceeding the speed limit, and expecting to receive information, while for others, an envelope comes as a surprise, and total shock, as not aware an offence has taken place.

At this stage a right of appeal exists, especially if you can prove the car on the image provided, not your car, or not the driver at the date and time the offence committed, and can provide evidence to support an appeal of the alleged offence.

Otherwise, a fine due with-in a set time limit, the surrender of your driving licence, and penalty points added as a consequence for exceeding the speed limit on the road in question.

Simple...

However, what if just one person making an accusation to another, a one-to-one scenario, what next.

If a verbal communication, no doubt "you said, he said, I did not say, you did say," a never-ending merry-go-round of finger pointing and verbal diarrhea, with little chance of a compromise.

Unless of course, one or the other agrees to disagree, and perhaps a sympathetic apology, with an accompanying handshake or hug, a solution of sorts reached.

Simple...

However, when both parties confident of their own actions believing them honest, true, and correct, a total impasse may emerge where neither party refuse to back down.

What then you may ask.

I have known lifelong friends, and family siblings that fall into this category, even going to their deathbed without ever rekindling their former friendship or family reunion.

Maybe a so-called accusation a petty one, with a possible solution easily obtained, if only either one could or would meet to discuss.

Perhaps a close friend that does not have an allegiance to either faction, a go-between or third-party arbitrator engaged, if both individuals wish to accept this to bring about an attainable resolution to the argument.

However, what if the scenario so involved, solicitors required as that third party, then a financial implication for both parties, resulting in a possible court case to bring about a solution.

Conceivably a triumph over one, and defeat for the other, and possibly the defeated person footing a huge bill, to finally settle the argument once and for all.

Not the ideal solution, but when one or the other so confident, truthful, and precise with their argument, this the only way to bring about a definitive clarification of the matter.

All of the above brings to mind an incident at my home a few years ago, and the first indication received in the post, that someone had an issue with my rear boundary fence.

Opening a rather large A4 envelope from a solicitor based in Leeds, to find a copy of not only my official property register of title deeds, but also those of my next-door neighbour and title deeds of those making the complaint.

Looking through a plethora of information supplied from a solicitor, including a number of photographs taken from every conceivable angle, and copies of an H.M Registry Ordnance Survey Plan Reference.

Also, a two-page letter indicating that my fence erected approximately one-metre to the wrong side of the official boundary.

Apparently, my next-door neighbour, and myself accused of encroaching onto land belonging to the complainant.

You can imagine my surprise, as my fence, although renewed some years earlier on the exact fence line as before.

Although, this accusation bringing to mind a conversation with the previous owner of the property, now belonging to the complainant.

However, before I explain that, I did visit who I now know as the new owner of the property bringing to light my alleged encroachment, when on my return from holiday astounded to see that the conifers to the rear of my fence totally removed.

My privacy totally ruined, as the former hedge a full metre higher than my fence, giving me ultimate privacy from the properties at the rear of my home.

I can now see into the gardens of the properties to the rear of my home, as the land slopes upwards, and more to the point, they can also look down over my fence, directly into my property and rear garden.

Totally dismayed at the action of my rear neighbour, although my visit initially to seek permission to enter his garden to inspect the rear of my fence, took on a new objective.

In the first instance, to receive an explanation as to why the new owner felt the need to destroy both our privacy, and that of all the gardens around us when removing a well-established conifer hedge, with-out consultation.

As an explanation, told that the conifer hedge out of control and unmanaged for years, had grown far too large, both in width and height, reducing the size of their garden.

I explained my side of the hedge always maintained to a good standard, trimmed flush with the fence and above, and had he visited me and looked in my rear garden before taking the hedge down, he could have seen for this for himself.

My somewhat angry rendition falling on deaf ears, as he had every intention of removing the hedge regardless of my comments, and whether at home or not, as the hedge firmly with-in his own boundary to do what he likes.

Upon inspection, my fence undisturbed and as good as the day I put it all up, so at this time, nothing further I could complain about.

Bringing me back to the accusation letter received from the solicitor, and a previous memory.

In 2004 just before the purchase of our home, Liams mum, Tricia, asked if I would have a look around the property, an inspection of sorts, to see if the valuation, and property conditions suitable for our future home.

Tricia explained, that when first visiting the property, the owner confirming amongst other things, that a new fence ordered, and contractors already confirmed a date to erect the new fence.

Clearly taken place, as Tricia commented to the owner, "the garden looks smaller than the last time I visited."

"Yes I agree," came the immediate reply, also adding, "more than likely, as this new fence now over six-feet high, while the other older dilapidated one, only three-feet high."

I confirmed more of an optical illusion, rather than the garden actually smaller.

However, when completing the property purchase and all moved in, the previous owner of the complainants property, came around to welcome us to our new home, with a card and bottle of wine.

Saying that the previous owners of our properties children, constantly around to pick up a football, or other flying objects that had appeared in her garden.

Liam only just three-years old, and while enjoying kicking a ball, doubt he would ever clear the rather high conifer rear hedge between both our homes, into her garden.

That said, when the rear neighbour returned home, I raised up, with little problems, one of the new fence panels, fitted between channels of two concrete posts, to look at what lies behind at root level of the conifer boundary.

Yet another surprise, the new fence erected almost one metre from the original fence, and pointing it out to Tricia, confirming that indeed our garden much smaller, over a metre shorter.

Obviously not acceptable, and pointing it out to our new rear neighbour, thankfully she confirmed that indeed the older fence hers, and also the official boundary when she moved in when the property built in 1976, even saying she would go halves on the cost to move, and reinstate to the original boundary.

With lots of other work on the cards, moving the fence back to the original line a low priority, but confirmed that it will take place at some point, and at no cost to our friendly and obviously concerned rear neighbour.

Looking at the new side fence, and counting the posts and panels, clearly the contractor or the then owner of our home did not want a half panel, instead reducing the length of the garden to suit an easier and possibly cheaper objective.

Sadly, Tricia would never see the garden returned to its former and correct size, as she passed away just eighteen months into our home ownership.

A year after Tricia's untimely death, me and Liam took on a derelict bungalow, bringing it back to life, leaving our family home, to move lock stock and barrel into our Abri, our oasis.

Living there just about five years, before moving back to our family home, but not with-out its challengers.

Deciding on some renovations, structural alterations, and decorations to our family home beforehand, and fitting a new kitchen, although the later waiting until fully moved in.

Transporting anything that could burn, back to our bungalow, where a number of evening fires lit to destroy old and rotten decking, unwanted damaged furniture, from our family home and anything left in the bungalow before finally handing in the keys.

The rear garden not an uppermost priority, but the fencing erected before our purchase had seen better days, with panels rotting or broken.

Deciding on building a conservatory as number one priority, as our Abri bungalow home having much larger rooms, a big "footprint," compared to our family home, as a comparison feels a little claustrophobic.

All the rooms in our bungalow much larger and higher ceilings, requiring more furniture to fill the space, although now greatly reduced, in moving back to our family home, our excess furniture and items either given away or sold.

A conservatory will help with opening up the through kitchen, dining room and new conservatory into a much larger family entertaining space, with lots of light, and all overlooking our yet to start rear garden.

Manually digging out the foundations and barrowing all the soil and debris into skips, two extra large ones required, taking all of three full days to complete, and all before concrete poured.

Warren helping me when he could to build the brick lower section and a UPVC manufacturer completing the top section of a fully glass conservatory.

Moving on to the rear garden next, in the first instance making the gently sloping garden level, that required removing the rear fence, including posts, some of which now rotting, and not re-useable.

Almost ten years after first recognising our garden over a metre shorter than the original boundary line.

Our neighbour joining in a conversation through the hedge, and welcoming us back to our home once again, saying "finally getting around to sorting out your fence then."

Taking a little time to explain what would happen during the next few weeks, and my adjoining neighbour in full agreement.

Our garden completely levelled off, new fencing erected to the either side and original rear boundary, decking constructed, astro-turf laid for easy low maintenance, and the summer house brought from the bungalow, now in place on the decking.

I had either sold or disposed of all my gardening equipment, including a petrol lawn mower, hedge cutters, and strimmer's, all a necessity when dealing with the huge gardens at the bungalow, nothing required here.

My garden a peaceful place, tranquil AND private, so much so purchasing a hot tub, named Hector, where I spent lots of evenings in bubbly hot water gaping into the heavens.

Following the removal of the conifer hedge, my new neighbour then proceeded to erect a fence to the rear of mine, although not the slightest bit interested, the mutilation of the hedge and my privacy now ruined.

Not offering a reply when he shouted, "all ok over here, my fence finished and not touched your fence."

I could not say "thank you" to save my life, instead just putting up my hand, and walking towards the house, and not sure I would waste any more of my time talking to my new rear neighbours.

Not many months later when the accusation of encroachment, a violation of my new neighbours garden, arrived.

Considering arbitration to resolve this impasse not an option on my part, as I see no need or reason to ever talk to my rear neighbours ever again, as no love gained or lost at this juncture.

My correspondence and that of my adjoining neighbour directed to the solicitor acting on behalf of my rear neighbour, so never the two should ever meet.

Now fully understanding the complaint, my rear neighbour believes I have taken approximately one metre from his garden, where my fence erected in 2004 once stood.

I explained to the solicitor, with a full report, original boundary photographs before the conifer hedge removed, clearly showing my fence erected to my side of the conifer trees remaining stumps, as much as one foot in places.

Clearly constructed either on, or at my side of the boundary, and matching the H.M. Land Registry plan, also including photographs taken from a drone footage, a friend from our observatory providing these.

What could go wrong...

Everything...

My new rear neighbour persistent to say the least, the solicitor forwarding three signed statement of so-called facts from his neighbours saying they had witnessed me building my fence, and taking land that belonged to his client.

Fuming...

How they could see me working behind these huge conifers beyond me, never mind, sticking to my guns, persisting with further letters disputing these so-called facts, and ignoring their request to employ a solicitor of my own.

My adjoining neighbour also taking the same stance, and also continuing to supply evidence to the contrary disputing these claims of encroachment.

No further responses received for months due to the covid epidemic, and almost believing both adjoining neighbours had succeeded in convincing the solicitor our facts correct, and not those of his client.

However, sadly not the case, a full two years later, and out of the blue, a suggestion to resolve the matter, arbitration, the solicitor arranging it, and a date agreed when me and my next-door neighbour available.

Finally, me and my adjoining neighbour can put our points forward to a third party, with no influence from any other source.

To our surprise the solicitor acting on behalf of our accuser arrived, with a colleague solely to act as arbitration between both parties.

What nonsense, how is this allowed to happen, however, listening to his proposals, then giving us the opportunity to respond.

The solicitor, along with his colleague, and a tape measure entering my garden and that of my adjoining neighbour, double checking all measurements I had given, also my neighbours measurements too.

Finally agreeing that indeed correct, with one small anomaly, my neighbour had erected his fence at ninety-degrees to my fence which is not correct, and as per the H.M. Land Registry plan.

The solicitor acting as the go-between to all parties, back and forth between all three properties, before coming to a definitive suggestion.

My boundary can remain untouched, whereas my adjoining neighbour should alter his rear boundary fence, only a few centimetres, then and only then will his client drop all accusations at no cost to either of us.

A sigh of relief from me, but at a cost to my neighbour, as he has to alter his fence, but reluctantly agreeing to bring this despicable, and totally unnecessary accusation to an abrupt end.

Nothing much really gained at all, as the true line of each of our boundaries virtually the same, but confident our accuser will pick up a substantial solicitors bill for the work they have put in.

The moral of this particular story is to prepare good precise evidence to support your claim, covering as many aspects as possible to ensure that your accuser in no doubt you are to challenge their accusation.

Disregard the initial accusation made against you, and in circumspect, provide an honest, accurate account as possible of all events.

Thankfully, on this particular occasion, common sense prevailed, and at no cost, or minimal expense for my adjoining neighbour.

Trouble at the Mill avoided on this occasion; however, you never know what might appear on your email account...

Or drop through your letter box.

CHAPTER THIRTY-ONE

What a Fight

(For Life)

I have never liked visiting the doctors, dentists, opticians, or hospitals for as long as I can remember.

However, as of today, I have tolerated all of the above over the last few years, either due to a misadventure, or perhaps due to age, and for one reason or another, certain parts of my anatomy have now started to fail.

My teeth for starters, taking after mum for failing gums and loose teeth, not helping when having one knocked-out while washing my silver VW Passat CC, DSG,GT, car over fourteen-years ago.

At this time, my chosen model of car did not have a doorframe fully surrounding the door window, with just glass protruding above door handle height.

The window cleverly dropping down a few centimetres to allow the door to detach from its seal when opening, and doing the exact same in reverse when closing, German engineering at its best.

Having had all door windows up and down a few times while cleaning, I thought all in the lowered position, now I know, sadly, not the case.

Inadvertently stooping over rather quickly to remove a cleaning cloth from the near side doors lower pocket, knocking out one tooth, and loosening three more on the door window.

The upper acute corner of the window had also penetrated my lower lip and bottom gum, blood everywhere, and the pain indescribable.

Telephoning the dentist, although not sure how my voice sounded with a missing tooth and three loose ones, but obviously understandable as the receptionist said to make my way there as soon as possible.

Quickly cleaning myself up, having to wash and change, especially my t-shirt, now covered in blood.

Driving rather quickly in my impeccably clean car to Ossett, to see my dentist for an emergency appointment.

The receptionist at my dentists welcoming me at the door, and with a hand gesture, requesting that I make my way to the stairs, to an upper floor room.

After a full inspection, making an impression for one lower central tooth, and temporarily saving three loose teeth, the dentist applying a sort of glue and brace to my teeth and lower gum, so that I can once again offer a smile.

The loose teeth now secure, and remained in good shape for over eight years, however, these extracted after becoming loose, and replaced with a denture.

After a year, my denture developed a wobble, and even when using denture adhesive, not offering much of a secure bond.

A bit of an embarrassment, more so when eating in company, and more to the point, in serious danger of swallowing it, just like an upper single tooth denture mentioned in an earlier chapter.

This single tooth now a permanent fixture, adhered to teeth at either side, so not in danger of dropping out, although required refixing after only one-month.

Following a further impression at my dentist, I have a new much improved fitting lower denture.

All good, so far, with no other dental issues to report, nevertheless, a different story when it comes to my vision.

Having had an eye test through a scheme at work over twenty years ago, this examination identified the need to wear glasses for reading, and while working at my computer.

Purchasing two pairs of glasses subsidised through work, and I have used these for years, however, noticing that my vision had deteriorated shortly after retirement.

Making an on-line appointment for a further eye test, which identified a well-established cataract on my left eye, suggesting imminent laser surgery to have this removed.

An operation quickly arranged with a local NHS clinic, and following a hastily arranged pre-op visit, the procedure to remove the cataract, only taking ten-minutes.

No pain at all, or discomfort to call of, and I can report a significant improvement to my overall vision.

The optometrist arranging a prescription for new glasses, but with so many different frames to choose from, my decision taking much longer than the operation.

Finally, choosing frames for two pairs of glasses, and when wearing them, along with the cataract removal, has improved my close-up vision for reading and computer work no-end.

All of this taking place over three-years ago, and told at the time, that my right eye will require surgery in the near future, but told not to worry, my long-range vision particularly good, so not required to wear glasses for driving.

Further regular tests following my surgery, revealed no further deterioration, although believing my right eyes condition had changed, especially when looking through telescope eye pieces or binoculars.

Frequently having to alter the focus to bring a target clearly into view, and considerably more than previous times when our weather permitted observing a clear night sky.

Requesting a further eye test, which confirmed my prescription had indeed changed, and not for the better.

Referred to the same clinic as three years ago, and following a pre-op test, the optometrist confirmed a right eye cataract, which needs removal.

Agreeing laser surgery should take place sooner than later, a date booked, although becoming a bit of a compromise to fit in with other duties already in my diary.

The disappointing bit, told not to drive under any circumstances for at least twenty-four hours, or lifting heavy weights, or stooping for around seven days after the operation.

Debilitating to say the least, however, good vision a more important alternative.

A personal need during my seventy-two years to attend hospital, remain few and far between, thankfully, although visiting patients in hospital, have developed into a full-time, and costly occupation.

The car journeys to either Pontefract, Dewsbury, Leeds, or local

Pinderfields hospitals not only time consuming with continual traffic congestion, but also finding and paying for car parking, and of course the rising cost of fuel.

Considering public transportation not an option, as this form of transport hopping from one bus to another, likely to take best part of the day.

Not for one minute do I object to visiting family and friends in hospital, on the contrary, with the number of visits recently taken to all of the above hospitals over the last few years, I would not want it any other way.

As long as I am the one visiting, and not actually the patient...

However, I must emphasise a lack of available spaces, and expensive parking charges, particular at Pinderfields hospital, mums apparent second home.

One day when visiting mum, I along with others, driving around for over 30 minutes to find a space, noticing other drivers had parked their cars on double yellow lines, grass verges, and raised tarmac borders throughout the vast carpark area.

Car horns blaring out, as frustration amongst some drivers reaching boiling point.

Noticing one space, although not an actual marked out bay for a car.

Other drivers had parked on a zebra crossing area that runs from top to bottom, and central to the car park, and the only remaining "space" available, so immediately reversing into this spot.

Walking just a few feet away, when a hospital car park traffic attendant confronted me, frantically waving his arms, and saying I should not park there.

Pointing out hundreds of other vehicles already "illegally" parked on the various crossings, and in other parts of the carpark to the attendant.

Explaining my urgent visit to see my ninety-three-year-old mum, and my annoyance of driving around for over thirty-minutes looking for a marked-out parking bay.

Obviously not his fault at all, as I imagine also frustrated too, at the acute parking issues progressively unfolding on the hospital car park.

The attendant saying not to worry about it, a reprieve for all of two seconds, then saying it is his job to point out unlawfully parked cars, and if left there, leaving him no choice but to give me a parking ticket.

My turn to raise my arms, but keeping frustrations to myself, I carried on walking towards the hospitals main entrance.

What a dilemma, and no different to my other repeated visits to see mum, parking always the problem, never mind the charges, as in no doubt upon my return, having to acknowledge a "ticket," also having to pay an exorbitant charge to leave the carpark.

Some good news though, mum so much improved than the day before, and day before that, a limited but positive recovery from what I can only describe as a life-threatening illness.

I will explain…

A further addition and anecdote to my chapter "Queenie" our mum.

Would you believe after spending just one full night, and one part night in mums new home, Stella House, mum would fall ill during the night.

Clearly not her usual self at all, night staff requesting an ambulance to give mum a check over.

The care home manager contacting me at 03.00hr, saying paramedics have carried out a thorough examination, and mum now on her way to her second home, Pinderfields Hospital.

I arrived at the hospitals A&E department around 03.45, coming across a female paramedic that had examined and transported mum to the hospital.

Explaining her reasoning along with another female paramedic, why it became necessary to admit mum, and at the same time enquiring about my paramedic son Warren.

News travels fast, as mum evidently able to communicate long enough with the paramedics while in the ambulance, to expect her eldest son at the hospital, and if they knew of her paramedic grandson, Warren.

Both paramedics accompanying me with a short walk through the reception area to A&E, confronted with mum in a distressed terrible state.

Unmistakeably agitated, constantly speaking, but inaudible, all the time fighting for breath, not a welcoming sight at all.

At this point thinking her emphysema, and chronic obstructive pulmonary disease (COPD,) finally about to take its toll on mums frail ninety-three-year-old body.

Doctors and nurses busily working on mum, placing an oxygen

mask over mums mouth and nose, mum pulling it off, saying she cannot breathe,(mum hates anything on her face,)the nurse persevering while explaining without oxygen you will die.

An eye opener for sure, as to what goes on in this emergency department, as a nurse embarked on trying to extract a blood sample from the dorsal side, or back of mums right hand.

While another nurse fitting a canula to mums antecubital fossa, or inner elbow at the same time.

Getting some fluids into mum seems the highest priority, also giving oral medication and an injection to her tummy, no time to lose looking at mums present condition.

Distressing to say the least, not only mum, but me too, as I had never witnessed a human being, namely my mum, clearly fighting for her life, trauma at its worst.

The doctor explaining that her blood pressure absolutely rock bottom, while her heart racing at double quick time, all clearly adding to mum panicking, and her irregular respiratory problems.

Feeling every bit in the way, as this commotion continued, specialists relentlessly and busily working on mum, taking a good few hours to bring her around to a stable and relaxed condition.

Mum exhausted, now calm and appearing fast asleep, her breathing even and controlled, the facial emitting oxygen mask helping immensely.

Almost 11.00hr, a full seven hours since my arrival at A&E, with mum awake and appearing settled, but with no beds available, still receiving attention in cubical 5.

Feeling a little sleepy, but hiding my yawning from everyone, how could I feel tired when doctors and nurses from the previous shift, and now other staff attentive, making sure mum comfortable.

Aware that patients in cubicles at either side of mum, also going through lots of pain and suffering, with constant shouts of "help me," "I need somebody," "nurse, nurse," and loud shrilling screams and deathly groans.

I don't know about feeling safe and secure in a hospital, but my presence seems more like an extra in a horror movie.

However, with mum looking so much better, clearly not her healthy self, but a vast improvement from just a few hours ago, deciding to agree with mums suggestion, and go home.

My brother Brian, a porter at the hospital had called to see us a few times during breaks of his daily duties, said he would keep everyone informed of progress, and when mum transferred to a ward.

Walking through a busy, and what appears chaotic A&E, with patients on beds throughout the corridors, in fact any available space taken up with beds.

Patients, along with relatives, all persevering with a similar dilemma to mum, waiting for a bed on an appropriate ward.

Thinking at the same time, could take hours, depending on priority, or illness, as I reckon, mum much later in A&E than others waiting, fingers crossed a bed may come available for our mum soon...

At 15.43hr, Brian adding a comment to our family WhatsApp group, "Moving mum to Gate 41, bed become available," just about the time I awoke from having a catch-up nap.

Good news, yet over twelve hours from mums arrival, at least mum now on a ward, a high dependency one at that, and away from all the hustle and bustle of A&E, where I am sure in the coming hours, mum will receive the absolute best attention Pinderfields staff can offer.

All of the above taking place four days ago, mum transferred from the high dependency ward to Gate 43, after showing good signs of improvement.

Mum still not 100%, nevertheless appearing "at home," with constant fault-finding about this, that, and the other.

Our mum almost back to her old self, showing significant signs of recovery.

Diagnosed with a severe chest infection, causing indescribable trauma, a definite near-death experience as far as my limited knowledge can describe.

Thankfully that unpleasant experience behind the both of us, as sitting at mums bedside she can offer lots of smiles, and joking about other patients and herself, all while receiving fluids via intravenous drip, and constant attention from the ward nurses.

Making my way down three floors of steps, all the time thinking

Liam proud of me not using the lift on any occasion since he pointed out I needed to keep fit, some two-years ago.

Using the hospital foyer ticket machine, generating an extortionate fee of £9.20, and then dispensing my ticket, required to lift the barrier, allowing me to exit the car park.

Quickly walking to the carpark, not sure what to expect following my earlier altercation with the carpark attendant.

Heading towards my car, and spotting other cars unmistakeably parked "illegally," all having tickets attached to each of the cars windscreens, my car no different.

Sharply pulling the self-adhesive clear envelope from my windscreen and tossing it on the front passenger seat.

Feeling a little cross and deflated after days upon days of driving around looking for spaces, paying whatever fee appears on the ticket machine to allow my exit from the carpark, and now faced with a fine.

Yes, "illegally" parked, as lots of others, some who may have travelled much further than me to get to see their loved ones, a frustrating dilemma, as I had considered walking a few times, the steps alone an advantage helping with my fitness.

The just over two-mile drive takes around seven-minutes each way, subject to traffic and parking, while walking could take around forty-minutes each way, and depending on what fine I receive, an option to consider from now on.

Our weather hasn't been exactly walker friendly, with lots of rain, and more rain, including high winds for the last week, so driving appears the best option for now.

Driving home with all these thoughts of the day's events, and what I should write on our WhatsApp group to inform family of my visit and conclusions obtained.

Reversing the car on my drive, taking note of the constant beeping, informing me I am nearing my stopping point, locking up, with Alexa and my phone informing me someone at the front door...

Yes, me, I'm home, with parking ticket in hand to read once I have made a drink of tea.

Imagine my surprise when opening the envelope, just a plain piece of folded paper inside, no writing on it whatsoever.

The envelope has blue writing on it, informing me that I have received a fine, but clearly on this occasion, appear to have a full reprieve.

I would like to think my brief nonetheless emotional explanation to the carpark attendant, perhaps hitting a moral chord.

Who knows, but I am smiling, and almost burning my mouth, with my freshly made hot cuppa.

Speculating, if all the other cars parked illegally have received the same surprise as me, I would like to think so, as it seems so unfair when all the "illegally" parked cars, have still to pay a fee to leave the car park, never mind paying a fine, all netting huge profits for the hospital trust.

Oh well...

Today has come to an end, and on reflection, with the exception of mum, an exceptionally good day all around, for all sorts of reasons.

CHAPTER THIRTY-TWO

— ⋙ ◦ ⋘ —

Work in Progress

How many times have I started a DIY project, only to come to a grinding halt because of one reason or another.

Usually running out of the correct size screws, nails, or glue, or just recently, sandpaper.

Deciding to resolve this issue once and for all, in future, checking I have everything required and on hand, before starting.

This particular blunder giving me the impetus to sort out a variety of drawers and two huge, larger than a bucket, plastic tubs, all in the shed.

The drawers and tubs currently full of anything and everything, in particular items purchased over and above needed, or the wrong size, or thought it or they would come in handy at some point.

While purchasing sandpaper, I also bought a purpose made polypropylene interlocking drawer organiser, with twenty compartments.

My new case has interchangeable or removeable sections to alter the size, larger or smaller compartments, ideal for storing screws, nails and other bits and pieces.

Where to start, firstly empty everything from two drawers onto the shed carpet, and sort items of different sizes and shapes into their respective trade.

Joinery, electrical, plumbing, decorating for starters, quickly beginning to fill up various compartments in my new drawer organiser, more screws than originally thought I had for sure, and many different sizes.

Clearly, all purchased for other completed jobs, thinking I did not have any of the size or length of screws required.

The two empty shed drawers also starting to fill up, lots of plumbing stuff, copper fittings in particular, in fact, hundreds of bends, "T" joints of various diameters, number ones, (straight couplings) of fifteen and eighteen-millimetre diameter, also PTFE tape, metal alloy solder wire, steel wool, almost filling one drawer.

A third drawer emptied onto the carpet, even more screws of different lengths, and nails, panel pins, self-taping screws, a multitude of different objects, door handles, hinges, latches, and locks, enough to open up a shop.

Four drawers all sorted, a joinery drawer, electrical, plumbing, and decorating drawers, and anything other than those, remaining on the carpet.

The heaviest of these, the plumbing drawer, now placed at the bottom, to offer the whole cabinet some stability.

The lightest at the top, holding decorators stuff, not much in here, just a few brushes, scissors, roller, and sandpaper.

My new drawer organisers twenty compartments almost all full too, with a complete range of screws, nails, panel pins, grub, and self-tapping screws, that will hopefully bring about vast savings on my next project.

Emptying one of two tubs, also full to the brim, the carpet awash with items of every trade, more drawers needed if to fit in everything in front of me.

Did I say everything on hand, BEFORE starting.

Nipping down to Wickes for a reasonably priced four drawer plastic cabinet, that will certainly hold the remainder of "stuff" held in the two tubs, and previous items on the carpet, but only just.

Taking over four hours all told, to finish what I had thought only a couple of hours job.

At least I know I have lots of everything, from screws and nails for starters.

While on holiday in Florida, USA, my sister Marcia, and husband Dave, dwelt at my home for three of seven nights, to babysit Lottie and Ted, our two aging mum and son, Lhasa Apso dogs.

On my return from holiday, Marcia and Dave dropping quite a few hints on my kitchen rejuvenation project.

Mentioning this a few weeks earlier, saying that I wished to replace my stainless-steel sink top, gas hob and extractor unit, but finding it difficult to locate the same sizes, regardless of how many internet sites I viewed.

Even visiting our local Wickes builders merchants, they carried out my kitchen renewal some ten years ago, informing me that they had standardised all of their appliances, so doubtful they could help.

Thinking no alternative, as well as my new appliances, also having to replace the worktops, because of the existing appliance cut-outs being too large.

Marcia, saying they found a company that carried out worktop replacements in Morley, a town close to Leeds, and at a reasonable cost, as they had used them to supply and fit a rather long quartz worktop in their utility room.

Visiting my son Warrens home, I did like their sink and electric induction cooker hob, both in black, and looking so neat, and modern.

If deciding to replace my existing chipboard laminated worktops, I would like to have quartz ones fitted, especially if purchasing new appliances too.

Picking a five-ring induction hob, one and a half bowl sink top, and cooker hood, all in black, and rapidly delivered to my door in just three days.

Also sending an on-line set of measurements of my present worktops, to the same Morley company Marcia used, to obtain an estimated price for supplying, and fitting new quartz worktops.

All in all, the start of my kitchen transformation now in progress, and currently estimated to cost around two thousand five hundred pounds, with further quotations required for a plumber and electrician to fit the new appliances.

I can see my little modernisation program could turn out a rather expensive job, although, looking forward to the worktop company attending to measure up more accurately.

No tape measures, or wooden pocket rulers, this company use a top of the range tripod mounted laser, to measure worktops.

What a piece of kit, amazing, fully mapping out my worktop design, including where the "cut out" for the new sink and electric induction hob located.

Setting up the tripod about a metre from, and ruffly central, to my row of floor and wall units, the operative began to set up the laser, all moving automatically, gathering as much data needed for the quartz worktops to fit snuggly into place.

Once manufactured, alterations almost impossible, as shaving using a plane, or cutting to fit, with a hand or power saw, not an option, as what arrives should, in principle, fit precisely.

The operative asking for the cut-out size leaflets for both the induction hob, and sink top, so that he can feed these details onto his computer.

The "mapping" out of my new quartz worktops taking around an hour, with all angles and wall deformities taken into consideration during the lengthy, apparently accurate process.

Seeing the laser and tripod standing in my kitchen, reminding me of the arrival of my latest telescope, recently purchased to "keep up" with several members of our observatory, that have also acquired this latest electronic innovation.

Unpacking and setting it up in almost the same spot, just to look at this stage, and to make sure all as purchased.

My See Star telescope, once set up proper, and linked to my mobile phone, almost one-hundred percent automated, making searching for deep sky objects a lot less complicated, and of course time saving, gathering selected images, and processed for viewing, all with-in the telescope.

Amazing.

Although, more dark clear skies needed to fully get to grips with my latest technological wonder.

Back to my kitchen and worktops.

Also, asking the operative, over a coffee and KitKat, (a bit of bribery,) could he accommodate a few of my requests prior to manufacturing.

Firstly, to manufacture precise circular corners on all outside edges where the quartz worktops come to an end.

Secondly, asking to extend my breakfast bar a further one-hundred millimetres past the "island" unit, as my existing laminate worktop a tad shorter than preferred, and in my opinion, not looking professional at all.

Furthermore, to fit two-hundred-millimetre-high matching "splash backs," around all the new worktops, as the seventy-millimetre ones I removed, looked rubbish, a pea on a drum comes to mind.

Scheduling a visit to the Morley showroom, as the company require a colour and design choice so that the manufacturing process can begin.

I had gazed at some length at a variety of brochures, but without success, and looking at them in the "flesh" made no easier, as picking a suitable colour and design for my quartz worktops, easier said than done, becoming a job in its self.

Walking around various kitchen set ups, deep in thought, do I pick black as my previous chipboard laminated worktops, or perhaps choose the exact opposite.

As usual, more than enough designs and colours to select from, my decision making made all that more difficult.

Thinking, a partner for a second opinion could help immensely, someone to fire off ideas, to give and receive constructive suggestions, and arrive at a compromise, or negotiate an agreement.

Oh well…

A showroom assistant coming to my aid, offering some good sound advice, and pointing out the latest preferred popular designs.

After almost an hour of pacing up and down the showroom, looking and touching the surfaces on each section, time after time, various fitted worktops, and smaller wall mounted sections, just so many.

Eliminating, what seems like hundreds, my thoughts focused between just two colours and designs.

Both almost similar, and at the point of making my decision. should I toss a coin to choose, a heads, or tails scenario.

Making my choice, and confident my preferred option of worktop, and the design and colour, will make a massive difference.

Bringing my kitchen, and dining room, along with my new one and a half bowl sink, and new appliances, up to date.

The Al-Murad Morley company such a pleasure to work with, and my choice of 30mm thick, Super White Quartz worktop design, has arrived via email for my perusal, along with a new quotation that considers my additional "extras."

A date now received for fitting, just seven-days' away, giving me an adequate few days to prepare.

Prior to the operative arriving to "map" out my new ones, I removed all the chipboard laminated worktops and matching upstands, taking them to our local tip, save for a short piece, a surface for making cups of tea, and making sandwiches on.

Deciding to fit the new cooker hood, ahead of the worktop fitters, a necessity, as not wanting to drop anything on the highly polished quartz worktop surfaces.

Just a few holes to drill using the provided template, and putting together the glass canopy and extractor motor, easy, and only two wires to connect, and a bit of filler here and there required.

Upon examination, looking slightly smaller than the recently removed stainless steel one, the glass and black cover design appearing good to me, although once again, no one here just yet to offer a second opinion.

Also considering a change of cooker splash back, as the previous one, only a plain dull black, not exciting at all, removed at the same time as the wooden worktops.

Talking of black objects, remembering those Black Lace days when taking part in the Eurovision Song Contest, (I know, you have heard about this often,) the Premier drum company, gifting a drum kit to me absolutely "free" of any charge, to use when performing at all our TV and live appearances.

I suggested black as the shell finish, however, the chap dealing with my order announced, black is black, (a Rolling Stones classic,) and will always look black, no matter how many different colour stage lighting beams, shine on your drum kit.

Proposing that I choose a different colour, perhaps silver, as this shell covering, along with all the new high-hat and chrome cymbal stands, sure to look much more appealing to the audience under stage lights.

Taking him at his word, and following my drive south on the M1 to Nottingham, to pick them up, absolutely delighted with the look of my new drumkit, and confident that he had made the right choice for me.

Using my drumkit for many years, and pleased with "his" choice of colour from then on.

I do digress, back to my kitchen.

Peering at lots of web pages for a suitable design of cooker splash back, yet again a plethora of choices, a do I, don't I, occasion yet again.

However, showing a few of my picked designs to friends, not forgetting Marcia, and also sending a few images to Liam, patiently waiting for a response.

Favouring two totally different designs myself, images produced on highly polished heat-resistant glass, yet another heads, or tails moment, although when receiving comments, all liking both.

My decision then… oh heck.

Choosing a white background, with high-definition images of two angled wine glasses, one with white wine, and the other red, and both looking as though falling from a tray, as a splash of wine spilling from both glasses.

However, and beforehand, choosing the same company to produce a much smaller splashback of a different design, to fit at the back of our downstairs toilet washbasin.

Choosing a close up of a drummer playing on a red kit, sending off the measurements, paying for my order, and waiting patiently for its arrival.

Receiving a text message to say my purchase now on its way, and to expect delivery the following day.

Alexa, and ring doorbell informing me that my delivery had indeed arrived, rushing to the front door in anticipation.

Instant disappointment, the cardboard carton looking way too small to contain my eagerly awaited splash back.

Carefully removing the packaging, and gazing at my chosen image on glass, looking amazing, but clearly not wide enough.

Producing my tape measure to check if a fault of mine, or the manufacturer process had made the mistake.

Over the years, my ruler, or tape measure an absolute must in making anything, and fortunately all without incident, rarely measuring wrong.

Told by peers in my apprentice years to measure two or three times, and double check, cut once, until now, how could I miss-measure, and a full two-hundred millimetres at that.

Investigating my original order information, definitely my error, and not the company, the height perfect, but how I misprinted a 3 instead of 5 on the width measurement, anyone's guess.

Perhaps I should wear my glasses more often.

However, so pleased with the production process, value for money, delivery procedure, packaging, and the overall look of what I have received, had I measured correctly, deciding to use the same company for my cooker splash back.

Warren visiting to ask how things coming along with my kitchen, and having a look at my new induction hob, and sink top, and suggesting that I also purchase a "Quooker" style tap.

I had used Warrens Quooker tap, and liked the as much as you like boiling hot water facility, incorporated within the hot and cold tap.

Instantaneous hot water at that, set at ninety-eight degrees, using an electrically controlled boiler located in the unit directly beneath the sink top.

Warren saying if I do want one, he will order, as he had fitted not only his own, but future mum in-laws too, and would also fit mine.

Receiving a text message to say the worktop fitters on their way, anticipating their imminent arrival, putting the kettle on, and checking enough biscuits to go around.

Good that I have Alexa, AND my Ring doorbell, yet another suggestion from my son Warren, as I spend most of the daylight hours in the conservatory, at the rear of my home.

After ten-years, my Lhasa Apso dogs have never barked to let me know someone either knocking or ringing the doorbell, not necessarily ferocious guard dogs by any means.

More than likely wag their tails and lick you sort of dogs, expecting a treat, rather than bark or bite.

The fitters certainly not hanging around, taking just twenty-minutes to install my brand new, amazing looking quartz worktops, and no time to ask if they would like a cuppa.

Not that much conversation at all, as the team of three, proceeded to carry in, and fit the worktops and splashbacks into place.

All fitting perfectly, the operative and accompanying laser, certainly making a marked difference to the installation process, as they quickly packed up their minimalist tools, and left.

So pleased all my "extras" taken care of, as I began to methodically examine the finished job.

Perfect, ten out of ten, both in quality and workmanship, pleased, an understatement, such an improvement, the first phase of my kitchen refurbishment almost complete.

Giving the worktops a further wipe down, and when tapping with my knuckles, sounding like a solid and hard surface, unlike the former wood laminate finish, hollow, and a sort of bargain-basement product, although in place for almost ten years.

This fantastic looking worktop merchandise almost infectious, as taking my time to fully appreciate and clean all the quartz outward facing exterior.

Quartz, a man-made stone product, consisting of between ninety, and ninety-three percent pulverised natural quartz, and seven to ten-percent resin, giving a durable glass like, smooth as ice finish.

The extremely glossy smooth surface reminding me of touching ice.

Although, feeling or falling on ice, a memory I still hallucinate about.

Liam and I, joining Amanda and daughter Holly at a garden centre ice rink just before last Christmas.

I had some experience on roller skates while performing at Butlins holiday camp in 1977, but only once since then, had I put anything on my feet that potentially could injure me.

Taking to the ice, for just the second time in around ten-years, the first at Doncaster Dome ice-rink with family, that did not turn out too bad.

This time, enjoying over an hour skating, or should I say wobbling in an anticlockwise jerking movement, umpteen times around the rink.

The one thing I am proud of, although falling onto the ice numerous times, I did not break any bones, or gather any bruises, and raising lots of laughs in the process.

The cooker hob splashback next, taking extreme care to measure the space between the wall cupboards, cooker hood, my just fitted quartz worktops, and quartz splashbacks, what could go wrong.

Measuring not once, but three times, checking and double checking, a former joinery term, as once cut, the item wasted if the wrong size.

Placing my order, and paying via PayPal, confident that enough care taken to ensure my measurements correct.

A full seven days before receiving confirmation that my wine glass cooker splashback out for delivery and on its way, everything in this jigsaw puzzle of a job, falling into place.

Warren and I fitting the new one and a half bowl sink top, waste piping, and of course my new Quooker instant hot water tap, that also has a traditional hot and cold supply.

A fully qualified electrician friend of Warren carried out the induction hob installation, and double checking my cooker hood connections at the same time.

All good, and patiently waiting for my wine-glass cooker splashback to arrive.

At the very least, the cardboard wrapping, covered in "fragile glass" stickers, looking about the same size as my measurements, as carefully taking the package from the delivery drivers hands.

Cautiously carrying the package through to the dining room, and removing all the tape with a sharp knife, revealing my splashback in all its glory.

Wow, looking good, but, and a big but, will it fit.

Cautiously offering the splashback up to the vacant space, placing the bottom onto the worktop, at about forty-five degrees, and with both hands at the top, slowly pushing the splashback forwards, and away from me.

Faultless, fitting perfectly between the wall cupboards, cooker hood, and quartz splash backs, my measurements millimetre perfect, and picture-perfect too.

Gently easing the splashback from the wall and placing it flat on my carpeted dining room floor, applying clear adhesive around all edges and a zig-zag pattern throughout the rest.

Once again offering it up as before, and gently but firmly pushing the splashback to the wall, finishing off by sealing the joint between both the worktop and splashback, and around all the edges.

Job done.

Already used to making a cupper with my instant hot water Quooker tap, sipping away while admiring my wine glass image, and workmanship.

No need for a kettle, and most things that cluttered my previous worktop, toaster, blender, tea, coffee, sugar canisters, and kettle, now placed either in the top cupboard, or beneath worktop drawers.

Already looking neat and tidy, with just a different colour emulsion required to fully finish off the worktop area of the kitchen.

Choosing a slate grey emulsion to compliment the worktops, applying two coats, and with only a few square metres to put on, not taking too long.

At last, following five weeks of planning, my kitchen area now complete.

Phase two, another story, and as yet no plan in progress.

But never say never...

CHAPTER THIRTY-THREE

Meeting Julia

(Part One)

Approaching people in a friendly smiling manner, always my intention, and rarely does this fail, until shaking hands, and can often result in progressing our introduction conversation much further.

Usually offering a comment of "blimey you have large strong hands, and a firm grip."

Always repeating, I would think it's both my joinery and drumming days that have helped improve my robust grip.

Possibly while tightly grasping a number of joinery hand tools, working in workshops, on a building site, or while at home involved in many of my DIY projects.

Otherwise, clutching 2B drum sticks while playing my drum kit for years on end, and all the required activities that entailed.

More often than not, occasionally pushing, wheeling, and carrying tons of musical equipment from our van or truck, into working mens clubs and pubs, required for our performances for almost fifty-seven years.

That task could involve climbing many steps indoors, or external fire escapes, and all while carrying equipment, and the same in reverse, or along lengthy corridors, or both, just to get all our paraphernalia to a stage.

A workout of sorts keeping me, and all our bands members fighting fit, thankfully the fighting bit, certainly not required, throughout these years.

Perhaps my many years of DIY work, including the building of house extensions, handling everything from timber to bricks, roof tiles and a plethora of other weighty materials.

Who Knows, but one thing for sure, a different approach of sorts when introduced to a lady, that could also involve the shaking of hands, certainly a more relaxed approach, a firm grip not essential, or perhaps a hug and kiss on the cheek more appropriate.

Sometimes a little hesitant in knowing which gesticulation to act on first, a handshake, kiss on the cheek, or hug, or perhaps all of them, and in any order, depending on the occurrence.

Remembering one such occasion when invited to Amanda's home for an early evening meal, and officially meeting Julia, who had driven from her home in Heckmondwike.

Amanda and husband Dave, friends of mine for over ten years and counting, and both Amanda and Dave becoming friends with Julia, when moving from their Middleton home near Leeds, to their new home on Lindale Grove Wrenthorpe, and at the same time a change from their local Christadelphian ecclesia, to Heckmondwike.

While regularly attending Bible class and Sunday school activities at the Heckmondwike ecclesia, Julia becoming a close friend to the family, including children, Holly, and Rosie, for over twenty years.

My introduction to Julia coming about due to my interest in visiting Israel once again, a bucket list item for over forty years, and now a reality.

First visiting this amazing location in 1979 when our band Black Lace, represented the UK in the twenty-fourth Eurovision Song Contest, stories mentioned in all my previous publications.

Amanda saying that I had met Julia at many a school concert when I attended to help behind the counter.

Serving tea, coffee and freshly baked buns and cakes, then watching my youngest son Liam perform, along with Holly and Rosie, many times in the schools orchestra.

I could not place Julia, even when looking at photographs on Amanda's phone, however, in just a few short minutes I will formally meet her, along with friends Amanda and Dave, while tucking into delicious home cooked food, and sure, many captivating conversations will follow.

Julia organising trips to Israel at eighteen-month intervals for around thirty-years, and while in conversation with Amanda, I spoke about my fixation to visit Israel once again.

Amanda saying that she would speak to Julia at their next ecclesia meeting, to ask if an unfilled place available, or added to the growing list of interested travellers on the next sight-seeing trip.

A full two years later, and taking account of the Covid epidemic, Amanda arranging the evenings get together tea, to bring about cementing friendships before our planned exciting trip takes place in just a months' time.

Yes, finally after all these years, I am actually going to Israel once again, and Amanda to thank for asking Julia in the first place.

My personal details and fees already disbursed to Travelink tour company, including an additional cost to Julia for pre-arranged tips that she gives out at over forty planned destinations once our party of twenty-seven tour of Israel commences.

My laissez-faire meeting with Julia, our first and last, before meeting at Dewsbury bus station for our National Coach trip to Luton, and the beginning of our ten-day sight-seeing trip to Israel.

Informed that red wine will accompany our meal, deciding to leave the car, and walk just over a mile distance to Amanda and Dave's home, although fully aware of a long steep ascending section of road ahead of me, and drizzling rain, the sort that appears to soak you through to the skin.

So, if not dripping wet due to the rain, perhaps a little perspiration on the cards too.

No matter, dressing for the occasion, and setting off in earnest, not forgetting an additional bottle of wine, just in case more required.

Locking the front door, and walking at a fare pace, making it to Amanda's home in around fifteen minutes.

A slight short cut following the up-hill bit, giving me chance to recuperate, in the now clearer weather, the light rain baiting just as I reached level ground, and my route deviation, partly taking me across muddy grass to a tarmac footpath, not helping.

Noticing a silver Ford car parked at the front of Amanda and Daves home, a tell-tell sign of a visitor, maybe Julia had already arrived.

Just a little on tenterhooks, as my pace faulted when walking to the side kitchen door, taking a deep breath, and apprehensively knocking.

Amanda answering, "hello, come in."

A hug for Amanda, hand shake for Dave, both in the kitchen, Julia in the dining room, but heading my way.

Taking the initiative, "Hello Julia, lovely to meet you," a gentle squeeze of her hand, hug, and kiss on the cheek, all three, and all four adults now smiling, clearly the start of what I am sure a lovely evening to come.

Firstly, removing my shoes, cleaner than I thought, no mud evident, leaving them at the side door, and removing my jacket, feeling a little damp to the touch, but just on the exterior.

Amanda taking my coat and disappearing into the room, with a comment, "tea almost ready."

A delightful aroma of cooked beef entering my nostrils, uppermost on other pleasant odours, making my mouth water, and realising not hungry at all, but starving.

A full six hours since a morsel of food past my lips, two coddled eggs on toast, around 11.45, and so looking forward to tucking into tonight's roast beef tea, and of course, meeting and chatting with lovely company.

Julia directed to a chair with her back to the dining room wall, a vacant seat for me, sitting next to her, Dave sitting across from Julia, and a chair for Amanda directly opposite me, once sorted in the kitchen.

Amanda backwards and forwards to the kitchen, tea towel in hand, a little protection from the hot crockery.

Piping hot serving dishes, all full of a variety of mixed vegetables, roast and mash potatoes, a plate loaded with pre-cut slices of tasty looking beef, and a gravy boat full to the brim, all neatly laid out on the large refectory table.

A "help yourself" meal, and viewing this appetising spread, so looking forward to tucking in, picking up a serving spoon, as Dave announced he will give thanks.

Ooooops, my first mortifying moment, although amongst friends, but an apology from me after Dave concluded his "with thanks" before meal prayer, a "no apology" required answer.

The open bottle of red, stood to "breathe" for quite a while, as Dave began to pour out our wine, not actually saying stop, but more than enough in my glass, for starters.

Julia drinking water, as driving the return six-mile journey home to Crawley Lane, just off Heckmondwike High Street, when our evening ends.

Now I can tuck in, Amanda offering vegetables, and placing them on my plate, plenty more where those came from, as I removed two rather thick slices of beef, fitting snugly on my plate, and helping myself to roast and mash potatoes.

My plate looking full, and awash with gravy, a little salt and pepper to taste, and all making a start, although looking at Julia's almost empty plate, and thinking, not enough there to keep me going for a breakfast, never mind tea.

Julia apologetic, saying not a big eater at the best of times, and so careful what she consumes, a diet problem she has to address daily because of a past serious illness.

I had already thought at the age of eighty, (Amanda told me her age) Julia the organiser of umpteen trips, I would think involving the taking hundreds of Christadelphian Brothers and Sisters to Israel already, this lady of slight build, looking extremely good for her age.

Thoroughly enjoying my main course, savouring every fork full, and dipping in for a few select "seconds," in particular the roast potatoes, delicious.

Of course, I enjoyed the tasty beef, my favourite of red meats, although, I do delight in eating chicken, in whatever format, with pasta, caesar salad, plain roasted, and I don't mind a KFC boneless meal, and whatever else too.

Any food, I enjoy, not only my own cooking, and Liams vegan dishes too, and also eating out at one or more of my favourite restaurants.

Lots of talking taking place, and one conversation I prepared for, Julia asking where I visited during my 1979 visit to Israel, and how they compare with the current itinerary Julia has produced, before my up-and-coming Israel trip.

Spending a lot of time reading through my booklet, a first-class professional production, itemising each daily location, with lots of historical and biblical references throughout.

I would think, a mammoth task for Julia in creating thirty brochures for our sight-seeing trip, never mind all the other associated preparation stuff, and doing the same for over thirty years, mind boggling.

With lots of "cutting and pasting," attaching location photographs, typing up individual place references, and printing hundreds of pages.

Finally, putting each expertly presented multi page by page catalogue together, and eventually writing out all the addresses on large A4 size envelopes, and posting to everyone.

A few photographs and places bringing a huge grin, The Dead Sea for one, looking forward to "floating" once again in the rich salty waters, also a kibbutz stay mentioned too.

Not sure if the same kibbutz Alan and I visited while with the BBC entourage, but looking forward to spending three nights there.

Also, the location where the Dead Sea Scrolls found, and Masada, a mountain top Roman fort, that our 1979 short tour should have visited, but due to time constraints, sadly, did not take place.

Of course, looking forward to visiting all locations mentioned on the demanding itinerary in Julia's brochure, some of which have a caveat attached, depending on the at times instability in Israel, some locations may change at short notice, however, all that aside, not long to wait.

Our first course finished, and all dinner plates looking pristine, not a crumb in sight, fully clear of delicious tasting cooked produce.

The table expertly cleared away, and clean pudding dishes and spoons set out, and all while our chatting continued throughout.

Apple pudding for afters, a further "help yourself" large flattish dish brought to the table, straight from the oven, and piping hot.

Placed on two table mats, with a large spoon neatly tucked beneath the surface, Amanda putting a huge helping in my pudding dish, Julia requesting just a tiny bit in hers.

Our conversations covering many subjects while eating our meal, in particular, the time-consuming sorting out each of the Brothers and Sisters personal details.

Travel arrangements, finance for the Israel trip, and room sharing allocations, all carried out over many months, involving hundreds of emails, texts, and phone calls.

Our meal now finished, and the table all cleared away, Julia introducing me to her Bible.

Amanda also presenting me with a King James Bible, and a Christadelphian hymn book, her grandma gifted both of these when just a child.

Feeling a little emotional, in receiving these significant keepsakes, and two publications I will take great care of.

Both required for my Israel trip, as informed meetings take place each evening shortly after our meal with "Christadelphian Brothers and Sisters," in a large, designated hotel room, although Julia saying not to worry, as no need to take part, if not wanting to.

Definitely a moreish taste, my pudding soon devoured, and reluctantly not asking for seconds, as politely asked to vacate the table, and retire to the living room.

Amanda taking orders for drinks, tea, coffee, or other refreshments.

Thinking about the amount of crockery and cutlery that requires washing up, electing to get my marigold free hands wet, and do the honours.

Not taking too long with Amanda drying, keeping the worktops clear, offering everything into their respective cupboards and drawers.

A drink of tea or coffee time, and no doubt more enlightening conversations taking place.

One such revelation coming to light of two long-ago coincidences, and both involving our band Black Lace.

Just after our Eurovision Song Contest appearance, our band became aware of a recording studio, at a reasonable price per hour, situated in Heckmondwike.

The property owner, a sound engineer, and musician, a former member of clubland bands and groups himself, who also enjoys recording good quality demo tracks with artists, and all types of music.

Our recording session booked, and making the short journey, parking up at the rear of the studio.

The recording studio constructed in what appeared a former best room, or front lounge, and large enough to accommodate a drum kit, backline guitar amplifiers, and a singing booth, more than adequate for our needs.

On this particular day, looking to put together a re-work of The Tremolos 1967 hit, Silence is Golden.

American band, The Four Seasons, released this single in 1964, Bob Crewe, and Bob Gaudio the composes, a "B" side tune to the hit song, Rag Doll, the same writers also composed this famous song too.

Our Black Lace version, more up tempo, and a rejuvenated dance type tune in the genre of Ellie Hope, and Liquid Gold, and the 1979 hit tune, "Dance yourself Dizzy," that may at some point become a single, or album addition.

I do digress...

Would you believe this very building and recording studio home, all part of the Christadelphian hall structure, possibly built at the same time, and unbeknown to me, our van parked to the rear of the ecclesia hall.

All the Brothers and Sisters mindful of the studio and its regular musical visitors, as sometimes pleasant-sounding melodic reverberations escape from the attached stone-built recording studio, while a service in progress.

The recording part of the building long gone, possibly returned to its former living room once again, as new owners now live there, and not of a musical background, unless of course you include the number of hens, and a constantly crowing cockerel, cock-a-doodle-do.

Julia also explaining in more detail where she resides, and again, coincidentally, I have driven past her Crawley Lane Heckmondwike home numerous times, from around 1994 to 1995, when Alan giving me directions to his home.

Not only driving past, but facing her bungalow home many times, when pulling up at a "T" junction following visits to Alan Bartons home on Churchill Grove before his sad untimely death in March 1995.

Another coincidence, or fate.

Sending a bit of a shiver down my spine, when realising these chance instances, and of course meeting Amanda some ten years earlier, bringing my arranged trip to Israel into realisation, and now an evening's meeting with Julia, too.

Sadly, our enjoyable and entertaining evening would draw to a close, and not necessarily because all had run out of things to talk about, on the contrary, lots and lots of subjects covered.

In the majority, faith, God, Jesus, Christadelphian history, previous trips to Israel, our children, and their musical careers, of course Black Lace, and all that entailed, and also the night closing in, as Julia prefers when possible, not to drive in the dark.

Julia offering to take me home, as it had started to rain once again, and the only one of four that had not had an alcoholic drink, my home just a few minutes out of her way to her home in Heckmondwike.

Meeting Julia as planned at Dewsbury bus station, a 07.15 arrival on May 3rd 2022, and a cold Tuesday morning at that.

My youngest brother John, dropping me off in his taxi after a 06.50hr pick-up from my home.

During my holiday to Israel, and subsequent holiday to the same location, exactly one-year afterwards, becoming Julias bag, and suitcase handler, and of course a close friend.

My role, to ensure that Julias baggage reach the appropriate destination, when either at the airports, on our arrival, or when leaving the hotels in the UK, and Israel.

Most of which you will have read in my previous chapters, Israel 2022, and Israel 2023.

Shortly following our return in May 2023, I have begun to attend Sunday afternoon Bible study meetings.

Rather than arrive for the meetings start, attending early, for a light lunch, and informal chat, before the meeting commences.

Starting at one-fifteen with an introduction, a voluntary, the singing of a hymn, prayers, and scriptures themed talk, concluding with an announcement of the following weeks meeting, a further hymn and prayer, then closing the afternoons meeting with a further voluntary.

An informative and enjoyable three hours, that have given me a positive perception of the Christadelphian faith, whilst meeting other Brothers and Sisters, including Amanda and husband Dave, and on occasions, daughters Holly and Rosie too.

Not forgetting Julia.

Since the completion of sale of the Christadelphian Heckmondwike Hall in August 2023, that involved the total clearance of the hall and its many adjoining ground and first floor rooms, including the attic.

Some rather old unwanted items taken to the tip, but not before Julia fully vetted each item, wanting to keep almost everything.

Filling up my car with some items that Julia wished to save, taking them to Julias home for safe keeping, until required.

That short journey from the hall bringing back so many memories of when I visited Alan Bartons home, and just as described earlier, Julia's bungalow directly opposite the right hand turning into Churchill Grove.

The meeting hall totally empty, and convinced lots of items purposely escaping Julias thorough inspection process, disappearing into the abyss forever.

Relocating into a new hall situated within Batley community centre, much smaller, but adequate for the number of attending Brothers and Sisters.

Following the Sunday morning meeting, attending on Sunday afternoons, joining Brothers and Sisters for lunch, prior to the meeting start.

Setting out collapsable tables in an end-to-end row, three today, as lots in attendance, beverage made in the adjoining kitchen in a huge aluminium teapot, and pushed through to our meeting room on a two tier trolly, along with milk, and enough white porcelain beakers for those present.

Amanda saying not to bring any food, as she will organise, bringing sufficient for the three of us.

Feeling a little uncomfortable, and me being me, wanting to join in, also bringing along a few savouries purchased with my weekly shop too.

Although, an abundance of tasty looking food Amanda has prepared, sandwiches, lots of mixed vegetables, sweet peas, peppers, radish, cut carrots to name a few.

Adding to this, grapes, melon, and other assorted fruits, also homemade buns, and cake, making my meagre input look a little insufficient to say the least.

Julia bringing along her own prepared lunch, but also taking three chive and onion twist sticks, and only three, never more, to eat later, from a pack that I bring along each week.

Julia had previously read the package label in some detail, and informed a common practice before preparation, to ensure the salt content, and other ingredients of all her food, below her recommended intake, and ok to eat.

I fully enjoy this delightful lunch, and also conversation that the whole table become involved in, ahead of the afternoons forthcoming meeting.

My visits and delicious lunch repeated week after week, unless Dave speaking at another meeting, as Amanda will also join husband Dave for the journey.

I then fend for myself, making a few sandwiches, usually made up of corned beef slices, smothered in brown sauce, a few savouries, and a chocolate biscuit.

Not the buffet lunch Amanda kindly provides, however, other Brothers and Sisters spoiling me, with continual offers of supporting food, usually slices of porkpie or cake.

Feeling a sense of belonging at these meetings, even though only a few hours each week, none more than with Amanda, Dave, and Julia.

Julia always asking if ok, and happy with the content of the afternoons talk, that Brothers give each week, sometimes travelling from as far away as Lancashire or further south to present their oration.

Following the afternoons meeting, all saying our goodbyes, giving Amanda a hug and a big thank you for providing lunch, and not forgetting my role while in Israel, carrying Julias heavy bag to her car.

When stood at Julias car, our chatting usually extends way past the meetings end while in the carpark, regardless of weather, at the Batley community centre.

Time and time again, Sunday after Sunday, the same procedure, also questions, and answers both ways, before Julia realising she has to go to another meeting, in this case, when arriving home, a further Bible study meeting, held on zoom.

At times, our Batley meeting room not accessible for various reasons, either decorations, maintenance required, or too few Brothers and Sisters available to make the meeting worthwhile.

As an alternative, most attending the Cleckheaton Christadelphian ecclesia for the Sunday service, and afternoon talk.

Wanting to continue attending meetings, also making the journey via the M62, westbound to exit at junction 32, and just a short drive to the meeting room.

This healthily attended meeting starts a little later, a one-pm arrival, instead of 12.15 at Batley ecclesia.

All attending brethren supplied a varied mixture of food, served in a first-floor kitchen/dining room, that includes cooked produce too, although once again bringing along some savouries to add to the more than enough tasty looking provisions.

The hall located quite some distance from a parking area, taking Julias heavy bag, to walk the few hundred yards to our parked cars.

Once again, our chatting continuing, sometimes a full thirty-minutes after the meeting concluded, and possibly everyone else home having a cuppa, or late afternoon nap...

Also, Kathryn, attends this ecclesia, involved in the 2023 Israel sight-seeing tour, and regularly joined our little group in the bar, following the days travels, tea, and evening meetings, so good to catch up.

Over the last year or so, visiting this meeting location quite a lot, the most recent just a few weeks ago.

The conversation over lunch discussing the recent Christadelphian Monday to Friday conference.

On one of those days while attending the conference, Julia becoming unwell, only for a few minutes, but having worked in the medical profession for most of her life, instantly realising the possible consequences.

Explaining this to me, and other Brothers and Sisters while eating lunch, and saying she has an appointment to visit her family doctor on Monday, the following day.

Julia said that she knew she had a NSTEMI, or mild heart attack, her doctor confirming this, giving her a prescription for medication, and told that she must take it easy, and unfortunately for the foreseeable future, not allowed to drive.

This announcement hitting Julia for six, but taken in what I now know as the usual Julia spirit, other Brothers and Sisters helping out, bringing Julia to our Batley meeting, and also taking her to the supermarket.

The following weeks meeting, yet another held at the Cleckheaton ecclesia, Julia attending and looking exceptionally good, considering, joining her and other Brothers and Sisters at a table from the Heckmondwike ecclesia, ready for lunch.

I had brought sandwiches today, as Dave and Amanda not present, Dave speaking in Grimsby, but customary at the Cleckheaton ecclesia, visitors told to help themselves first at the food table.

Joining the queue, and putting a few hot crispy looking golden-brown chips, and some salad on a plate, thinking these will go nicely with my smothered in brown sauce corned beef sandwiches.

Julia already eating her pre-packed lunch, as I offered her some of my usual chive and onion twists, taking just three, and placing them in her plastic container to eat later.

At the meetings close, Julia chatting to lots of Cleckheaton Brothers and Sisters, and today of all days I had planned to visit mum in Dewsbury Hospital, so made the lengthy walk to my car alone.

Spotting Julia coming out of the hall along with other attendees, slowing my car almost to a stop, pipping my horn and waving, before accelerating away.

Noticing a Christadelphian Brother holding her bag, Julia waving back, heading to where the cars parked, and a lift to her Heckmondwike home.

Receiving a WhatsApp message the following Saturday from Amanda at 21.42, "I have some bad news."

Almost instantly a further message, "Julia has passed away today, her neighbour found Julia, who called the Police, they think she had a stroke."

Totally speechless, my fingers doing the talking, saying how deeply sorry to hear such devastating news, placing lots of sad emoji's in my reply to Amanda.

A feeling of helplessness coming over me, such a sad and untimely ending for this lovely lady...

A comment often said by Julia, I am not eighty-one years OLD, but I am, eighty-one years YOUNG.

Always thinking positively, and saying she hasn't the time to feel old, no doubt thinking the same until her last breath...

CHAPTER THIRTY-FOUR

Meeting Julia

(Part Two)

The shock news of Julia's passing spreading quickly, first amongst the Heckmondwike brethren, all close friends and family, and a post put on our last year's 2023 WhatsApp trip to Israel participants.

Thinking about the last time meeting Julia, just six days ago, and disappointingly, not our usual talking session, but waving with a smile on her face, a lasting memory of this lovely lady.

To say everyone so upset, an understatement, Julia known throughout the UK Christadelphian community, and in countries around the world, most of which have travelled to Israel on many sight-seeing tours, the responses heartbreaking.

Two executors Julia had aspired to act on her behalf should the unexpected arise, dealing with all Julia's affairs, in particular, the arrangement of Julias funeral, and succeeding collective wake.

Also, the sorting out, and clearance of all belongings from Julia's bungalow home, clothes, furniture, and lots of sundry items, some dating back over many decades, including an abundance of possessions, also accumulated over many years, stored in the huge loft area.

Wednesday, October 23rd, 2024, a date now in everyone's diary, 11.15 at Dewsbury Crematorium, with a celebration of Julias life held afterwards at the Lakeside Restaurant, both venues local to Julia's Heckmondwike home.

Leaving home around 10.20 for the lone sombre seven-mile journey to the crematorium, not the best of days, as still in recoil at such a sad end of life.

So sudden, and certainly not foreseeable as far as close friends and relatives would believe, such abrupt and an unexpected end of life.

As a comparison, when recently passing the open doors of mums care home neighbours, perhaps, and although terribly sad for everyone, sudden, a more "fitting" way to go.

Obviously I understand a statement of this magnitude can potentially "open" up so many differing conversations, and perhaps one or more for another day.

Reflecting on the past two years of knowing Julia, most proceeding throughout my fragmented night's sleep, and not helped, or improving, as a lone fox yapping from 03.30hr until after 04.00hr.

My TV alarm waking me at 07.15hr, and looking at my watch app over breakfast, it appears I had an "alright" night's sleep, 87 points, my references "normal," clearly my watch and app, unaware of my thoughts and crazy dreams.

Collecting a performers music stand, purposely left behind the garden gate of Amanda and Dave's home, required at the afternoons gathering in celebration of Julias life.

A chilly almost free from cloud day, and thinking I should have put my suit jacket on, instead of leaving it in the car.

Arriving at Dewsbury Crematorium a good fifteen minutes before the service due to start, and meeting up with Brothers and Sisters from Heckmondwike ecclesia, and others that have made the further afield journey.

Lots of frivolity with memories of Sister Julia, the main topic of conversation, as the funeral director, walking at the head of the black hearse and car, slowly making its way to a stop beneath the covered entrance to the chapel.

Gradually following on behind the casket, and into the chapel, taking our seats, some directed left, and others right from a central walkway, Julias casket placed on an ornate pedestal directly to the front of us.

Joining a couple from the Heckmondwike ecclesia, along with two others that had travelled from down south, and part of last year's Isreal trip to the righthand side, about the fifth row, four rows and either side now full of mourners, with lots more taking seats behind.

Dave giving the order of service, expertly conducted throughout, presenting a narration of Julias active life, amidst a chosen selection of appropriate hymns and prayers, certainly a tear jerker, and with fits of laughter too.

The Order of Service.

- ❖ Entrance Music.
  Largo – by Handel.
- ❖ Welcome and opening prayer.
  Darren Peach.
- ❖ Spring.
- ❖ Julia's story.
- ❖ Hymn.
  In the buds of early Springtime.
- ❖ Summer and Autumn.
- ❖ Reading.
  Psalm 86.
- ❖ Hymn.
  Teach me thy way, O Lord.
- ❖ Winter.
- ❖ Closing Prayer.
- ❖ Exit music.
  Pray for the peace of Jerusalem – Meditation from Massenet's Thais.

Following the service, lots congregating outside the crematorium chapel, as clearly most have not seen each other for ages, a catch up needed, but also to reminisce about the life of their Christadelphian Sister.

Feeling such a sincere privileged sensation amid so many friends of Julia.

Other mourners starting to arrive for the funeral succeeding Julias, giving an indication that parking spaces required in an already overflowing carpark.

Making our way from the chapel, and heading out to reconvene at the Lakeside Celebration Venue, just a few miles away.

I know I have visited this location before, bringing our much younger children many years ago, however, the Ponderosa Zoo and surrounding buildings, looking completely different.

Most likely an age thing, even the long winding road, making its way through a huge well-established acreage, could not bring anything at all to mind.

Finding space between two other cars on a large unmade gravel carpark, others in front of me already parked, walking back towards the venue entrance.

Other cars following, all searching for that illusive space without having to step out from the car into nearby puddles of water.

Instantly recognising a couple arriving in a red mini, not at the Chapel service, heading directly over for a quick cuddle.

Names, I could not remember, and always embarrassing when both remember your name, but knowing they had travelled all the way from Glasgow, as toured Israel in May of both 2022, and 2023, in Julia's group of Christadelphian sightseers.

A welcoming drink of tea and coffee or soft drinks on our arrival, recognising and meeting other Christadelphian Brothers and Sisters, and even more mourners from both our 2022, and 2023 Israel trips too.

Placing the music/conductors stand on the stage, and adjusting the height, before making my way for a much-needed cuppa.

Appreciating an image of me and Julia on the TV screens and overhead projector, one image as part of a number of images sent to Amanda, and passed on to Darren.

Darren from the Heckmondwike ecclesia prepared a slide show presentation using these images, to include and play while everyone attending, helping themselves to a cuppa, before taking to their seats in preparation for the afternoon service.

Unfortunately, the slide presentation appeared to have stuck on just two slides, me and Julia on one, and an image of our 2022 group gathered in the garden of Gethsemane, beyond the walls of Jerusalem singing hymns, in particular Pray for the peace of Jerusalem.

Feeling a little embarrassed, continually gazing at my image, on screens around the large room, as I had expected around forty other images continually rolling from beginning to end, and then repeating.

Such a lot of exposure, an image of just Julia preferred, but now around thirty-minutes, and beginning to wonder if speculation rife.

Circulating amongst Brothers and Sisters in the room, speculating as to who this man accompanying Julia on the image, in particular those that had not met me...

Let me explain.

This particular photograph of Julia and me, taken at Amanda and Dave's home prior to an evening meal, and my first trip to Israel with Julia over two years ago.

Also, to remember when Amanda presented me with a King James Bible, and Christadelphian hymn book, and recognising my trip to Israel with Julia in May 2022.

Our meeting, the first between Julia and me, cementing a relationship lasting almost three years, with my name already added for a further trip in May 2024.

Due to current circumstances in Israel and surrounding lands, postponed until November 2024, and further deferred until May 2025, until Julia's sudden passing, bringing our proposed trip to an immediate cessation.

Also, considering the extended troubles from October 7th 2023, the May 2025 trip unlikely to take place anyway, or further ones for the foreseeable future.

Taking an aisle seat, with Amanda, Rosie, Holly, and Dave on the same row, about a third of the way from the stage, my now empty cup and saucer placed on the floor between my legs.

An accident waiting to happen, especially when all quiet and within lines of a speech, knowing my luck, gently pushing them out of the way beneath the seat in front.

Other Israel sightseers from the 2022 and 2023 Israel visits coming over for a quick chat, and catch up, including the couple from Glasgow, sat in seats directly behind.

Conversation now including Amanda, at this point introducing Amanda as the lady that had initiated my meeting with Julia, and because of our introduction, my trips to Israel taking place.

Embarrassingly, I had to ask the names of the couple from Glasgow, Kathy, and Lyndsay, came the instant response from Kathy.

My excuse, calling everyone love, so not remembering their names, and to think of the time spent together in Israel, and also part of a small group that met in the bar for a nightcap, and discussion of the day's events too.

Kathy also the keyboard player at all the after-tea evening meetings while staying in various hotels, and the Kibbutz on our sightseeing trip around Israel.

Paul, and wife sitting to the front of me, turning around and quietly asking for my autograph, even though I see him every week at our Batley meeting, clearly saying a popular chap.

One o'clock sharp, the Service of Remembrance began, and the image of Julia and me, still on the TV's and overhead projector screen around the room.

Many Christadelphians watching Julias service via a YouTube live stream in countries far and wide, and in particular Israel.

Da'vid, our guide during the tours of 2022 and 2023, and many more years before, also a close friend of Julia, joining everyone on the pre-arranged live stream, along with wife and children.

Also, Travelink representatives from the long-established tour company, responsible for arranging these Isreal tours on behalf, and in partnership with Julia.

Julia Mary Fentiman

Service of Remembrance – Order of Service

- ❖ Opening Music.
  God so loved the World.
- ❖ Welcome and opening Prayer.
  Darren Peach.
- ❖ Hymn
  Now thank we all our God
- ❖ Reading
  Ecclesiastes 12
- ❖ Reflections on Julias youth.
  Early Days - Nigel Patterson.
- ❖ The Teenage Years
  Chris Brook

- ❖ Hymn
  Life is the time to serve the Lord.
- ❖ Reflections of Julias visits to Israel
  Darren Guy.
- ❖ Hymn.
  Pray for the peace of Jerusalem.
- ❖ Personal reflections on the life of Julia.
  Andrew Wilson.
- ❖ Hymn
  Come thou long expected Jesus.
- ❖ Prayer
- ❖ Closing Music
  God be in my head.

The service leaving me breathless, and shedding many a tear throughout, both in sadness, and laughter at the many depictions of Julias personality.

So pleased that I wasn't asked to speak to anyone sat in close proximity, as not wanting to turn around, or to my righthand side, as my eyes awash with fluid…

Close friends and Brothers bringing personal and emotional reflections of Julias life to the lectern, raising extensive amounts of laughter, and noticeable sadness too, but huge amounts of love and affection shown towards Julia.

Brother Darren Guy adding lots of laughter too, as reminisced about the ten days while on our Isreal tour, speaking of Julia with love and utmost respect, commenting time after time about her commitment and overall unadulterated faith.

Also, commenting on the image of me and Julia, still present on all the screens, stating that everyone knows Julia, and will now know who I am.

Darren announcing the both of us have two things in common.

Declaring the two of us have actually represented the United Kingdom, and just six-years apart.

Darren saying, I represented the UK in 1979, taking part in the Eurovision Song Contest, held in Israel, and finishing 7th, while Darren representing the UK in 1985, in a dancing competition in Europe, finishing last.

A little magic intervening, as the slide changing from Julia and me to an image of the garden of Gethsemane, Darren instantly remarking that he also enjoyed gathering together, and singing at this location last year.

Just as Darren finished this comment, the slide once again returned to the image of Julia and me.

Meeting Darren Guy for the first time while at Dewsbury bus station, along with Julia and Kathrine, while waiting for our National coach to Luton, prior to our 2023 Isreal trip.

Getting on famously, and thoroughly enjoying his company and wit throughout our holiday come sightseeing tour.

Becoming so emotional during the hymn, pray for the peace of Jerusalem, further eyewatering moments, and finding that I could not utter the words.

Bringing back a memory of listening to the hymn while visiting a chapel on the edge of the sea of Galilee on our 2023 visit to Israel, once again an emotional occasion.

So pleased that the service did not end directly after this hymn, as taking quite a while to compose myself.

Thinking about Christadelphian beliefs and faith, Julia sleeping, awaiting the second coming and resurrection of Jesus, bringing about a sense of joy, rather than sadness.

As the service drew to a close, total silence for a few minutes, as everyone gathered their own individual thoughts of a lovely lady.

The Lakeside restaurant staff quickly getting to work, producing large circular tables from a storeroom, and re-arranging the chairs and added tables for after-service refreshments.

More conversation, in between toilet breaks, and a trip to the bar, as tables and chairs just about ready, as too the food.

A served cold buffet, with plates upon plates of assorted sandwiches, cakes, and lots of scones, complete with help yourself jam and cream.

Joining the lengthy queue, and feeling rather peckish, taking quite a plate full back to our table, and taking an order for a round of drinks, shandy for me, and likewise for Dave and Rosie, with Amanda and Holly drinking Lime and Lemon.

Making a further trip to the food counter, a few extra sandwiches, piece of cake, and a scone with ample cream, and large dollop of jam.

Highly satisfied with the quality and taste of all the prepared food, thoroughly enjoying the banter around the table too.

As others started to leave, some on our table deciding to have a walk around the lake, and as also a zoo, take a look at some of the animals.

It had rained earlier, but now almost dry, and reasonably warm, not needing anything over my suit jacket, as Amanda, Holly, and Rosie, including Holly's friend, up front pushing baby in a pushchair heading outdoors onto the gravel footpath.

Lots of interesting animals, Deer, Tortoises, Alpacas, Otters, monkeys, some so tiny, Porcupines to name but a few, and sure many more to see, although almost closing time, making our way back to the restaurant.

Only a few guests remaining, and saying I would say goodbye to Kathy and Lindsay before I or they left.

Hurriedly making my way to the carpark, Kathy, and Lindsay on their way to meet me, hugs, and handshakes, keeping in touch a must on our WhatsApp group.

Kathy and Lindsay staying over in Bradford tonight, as a planned sleep over at Darren Guys home not possible, as he left shortly after the service conclusion not feeling good at all, suffering flulike symptoms since his return from an earlier meeting.

Waving them off and returning to the restaurant, to work out how to get Amanda, Dave, Holly, and Rosie, to the Morley home of Julias cousin and husband.

Dave's car parked there, using my car, with four spaces, and Darren Peach's car, however, Darrens wife, and Sister Helen already passengers.

Holly and Rosie travelling with Darren, with everyone else tightly squeezing into mine.

Enough seat belts for everyone, although setting off before Amanda had located the female end of hers, neatly tucked away in the seat fabric.

Had Amanda taken the driver's seat, the car would not have moved until everyone firmly belted up.

Both cars arriving safely in the now rush hour busy areas of Heckmondwike and Morley, as the sliding gate slowing opening up into a private courtyard area.

Saying our goodbyes, and all three cars leaving with just a few minutes between each for the not too long, but busy drive home.

For me, further time to reflect on the day's events, and wondering if Liam having a good time in Manchester with Alice and their friends.

Liam on leave, and Alice concluding her university course, both home from London until Saturday, and spending two days in Manchester, due back in Wrenthorpe the following day.

Parking the car, and at home now, getting changed into shorts and t-shirt, and then making a cuppa, settling in to again reminisce of knowing Julia, and the times spent chatting before, during and after our Sunday afternoon meetings.

I have to say as funeral services go, this service giving both tears of laughter, joy and sadness, and a big thumbs up for Dave, Darren Guy, and other Christadelphian Brothers mentioned, who carried out todays service, and so much more, with the utmost precision, love, and respect.

In my personal opinion, all appeared to run exactly to plan, sort of, the slides needing some minor attention.

Darren Peach assuring everyone that all the individual images amassed for the slide presentation had worked perfectly at his home.

Possibly a fault with the equipment used on the day, although raising quite a few laughs for those in attendance, and the many at home watching on YouTube.

Rest in peace Julia XX

CHAPTER THIRTY-FIVE

A Trip to the Seaside

(With a Difference)

What is the attraction with wanting to paddle or swim in the sea.

More to the point, at some of our coastline towns, the sea almost difficult to actually see, especially when the tide elsewhere, and not on the beach.

The dark brown looking North Sea not exactly appealing, and appearing miles away, almost taking a twenty-minute walk to even reach water.

On the other hand, what about pollution, combined with fast tidal waves, although recent testing giving the Yorkshire coast a good rating for cleanliness.

Our Yorkshire coast spanning close to one hundred miles, from Redcar to Spurn Point at the tip of the Humber estuary.

To travel by car from Wakefield to any of these amazing resorts, either for a day trip, or to devote longer periods at the seaside, definitely a must.

Bridlington, Scarborough, Filey, Hornsea, Robin Hoods Bay, and my favourite, Whitby, and surrounding area, all taking between one and two hours to make the journey, depending on traffic and the time of year.

As a child, a day out always something to look forward to, our families once a year "holiday," arranged by the committee of Balne Lane working mens club.

Mum and Dad members of this institute union (CIU) club, for many years, at one time, mum even doing a bit of cleaning at the club.

Only in the job three-days, when following an altercation with an irate committee man, handing in her notice.

Apparently, mum not allowed to stand or kneel on the rather expensive snooker tables plush green baize surface, even in stocking feet, when attempting to clean years of accumulated dust from the over-head lighting and red velvet cover.

Remembering Scarbrough and Bridlington, and the steep hills leading up from the beach, and at the time, my favourite, Cleethorpes, although not actually a Yorkshire coast attraction.

The railway station of this North East Lincolnshire resort, directly across the road from the sea front, although twice a day, this coastal towns sea, as far as the eye can observe from the promenade.

Leaving an embankment of soft sand for digging holes, and deckchairs, and a vast flat sand surface, ideal for playing many games without fear.

Possibly why the club prefers this resort too, as visiting the location quite a few times during my early childhood.

On one such occasion I remember purchasing a Chinese Junk sailing boat, a sort of airfix equivalent plastic kit model, using most of my saved-up pocket money.

Mum not at all pleased, taking me, no, marching me along with my purchase, back to the shop for a refund, as felt far too expensive, and leaving me with no money left to buy an ice-cream.

Oh well...

Our steam train ride from Westgate station, always exciting, bringing to life my attention, and attraction to our local railway line, evidently, according to my parents, unaware of the dangers that can result.

As you can imagine the train full of kids, and for some, an opportunity to run up and down the many carriages, mayhem, unquestionably causing a nuisance for everyone.

Not a problem if the carriages have compartments, with a corridor, much better for families, no such luck on our trains, as in most cases a table between two sets of bench type seating, great for eating our "free" food boxes

Our family totally under control, mum, and dad quite strict, at least a window view, and not allowed to budge one inch from our seats, unless wanting to visit the toilet.

I must have had a weak bladder at the time, as a steady unaided walk to the toilet, the only chance to put my head through an open railway carriage window.

The smell and taste of the billowing steam giving the impression our train really travelling fast, when in actual fact, perhaps only reaching sixty miles an hour, unlike the electric and maglev trains from around the world, attaining incredible speeds.

Dad did not own a car during my early years of childhood, reliant on a day trip to get all the family away to the seaside, for at least one day a year.

Over the years since these memorable day trips, I have continued to visit the eastern coastline, traveling by car, or van to not only Yorkshire, also to Lincolnshire, Skegness, and Great Yarmouth to name a few.

Not enjoying the drive or resorts on the western coast, Blackpool, or Morecambe, preferring to travel a little further south to the Wales coastal regions, in particular, Llandudno, Port Maddock, Pwllheli, Abersoch and Aberdaron.

Visiting these regions for almost thirty years, a reunion of friends dating back to 1996, when meeting on the same Turkish Gullet cruise around areas of the Mediterranean Sea.

Friends from this time, often visiting these north Wales locations each August bank holiday, and the first weekend in December, and frequently mentioned in my other publications.

A suggestion from my stargazing friend Amanda, while on our way to Friday night's observatory open night, would eventually take me to Bridlington for a threesome day out.

I will explain.

For around ten years Amanda has carried out volunteer work, one such undertaking, taking a dog called Hugo for walks each Thursday afternoon, a pet, belonging to a lady called Doreen.

Over a number of years, Hugo developed blindness, and also severe hind leg problems, creating a difficult scenario for Hugo to using two steps when needing the outdoors from Doreen's bungalow.

Amanda asking, if at all possible, could I make a removeable made to measure ramp, to allow Hugo to exit, and enter the bungalow easily.

Doreen providing a drawing of the side door area where this temporary wooden incline will fit.

It just so happens I had a few lengths of timber decking, left over from one of my DIY home projects, perfect for the job in hand.

Making the ramp to measurements provided, and also giving the surface a makeover, fitting astroturf, an ideal surplus piece making Hugo's none-slip doggie-ramp, look like a professional purpose-made job.

Receiving a thank-you from Doreen, and saying Hugo has taken to the ramp, instantly using my just made incline to visit the garden, and when Amanda calls to take him for a walk around the estate.

Moving on almost three years, sadly Hugo becoming seriously ill, the vet suggesting he has no quality of life, and with permission, putting him to sleep.

Euthanasia for pets always a tough decision to make, and one I am accustomed to, with our family having to make this self and same sad, upsetting, and difficult choice on numerous occasions.

Amanda continuing to visit Doreen each Thursday afternoon, as they had become close friends, and on one such occasion suggesting a possible day out, perhaps a trip to the seaside.

Other days out had taken place with Amanda and daughters Holly and Rosie, along with Hugo, but during the last few years, Doreen's health had deteriorated, spending time in hospital, and requiring frequent visits by nurses to apply dressings to leg lacerations.

Doreen now requires a zimmer frame to aid with her walking around the house, and the use of a wheelchair when outdoors.

Amanda just about handling the wheelchair, and able to squeeze it into her cars boot, managing this function for a few arranged outdoor visits to appointments, or just out and about to give Doreen some fresh air, but not without hurting her back.

The wheelchair quite heavy, and awkward to squeeze into Amanda's car boot, bringing about yet another angle to our many deliberations while traveling to the Pontefract observatory.

Amanda asking if a day out to the seaside would interest me, the caveat, also taking Doreen along too.

My usual comment "not a problem," when, and where to, and setting off at what time.

Various locations discussed between Amanda and Doreen, finally settling on a reasonably level location with long promenade walks, Bridlington.

There you have it, a date in my diary, Thursday August 10th, a 09.30hr start, picking up Amanda, and then to Gawthorpe for my second passenger.

Dressing accordingly for a seaside visit, t-shirt, shorts, and trainers, and a just in case coat for the car boot.

I can now understand why Amanda hurt her back, this particular brand of wheelchair quite heavy, unlike mums, relatively light by comparison.

Once collapsed, Doreen's chair satisfactorily fitting in my car boot, along with a refreshment bag of eat on the way goodies, these removed and put on the rear seat.

Apparently, Doreen not a good backseat car traveller, preferring to sit next to the driver, on this occasion, Amanda sitting in the rear, directly behind Doreen.

Not that I minded one bit, and fully understanding Doreen's needs and requirements, however, driving over an hour and a half with a total stranger sat beside me, an enjoyable first.

Arriving in Bridlington with no traffic issues at all, the conversation riveting, mainly one-sided, and learning such a lot about Doreen's past eighty years, most of which Amanda had listened to before, many times.

Also gathering that Doreen digresses quite a lot, covering many years of her life, and at times not sure some discussions actually arrived at a conclusion, to rectify this, maybe more of the same when on our way home.

Looking busy around this locale of Bridlington, the Palace carpark almost full, certainly no extra wide car spaces with additional hatched areas available.

After a few minutes driving around, finding a single not over wide solitary space, a tight fit, and up driving directly to the gable end of a house gable wall.

Parking my driver's door as close to the next car, leaving me just enough room to get out, and to give a little more space to fit Doreen's wheelchair between my car, and the next car, parked in the adjacent bay.

Pay and display parking fees these days costing a fortune, particularly when in coastal resorts, and most not allowing the use of free of charge disabled parking permits.

Feeding pound coins into a greedy ticket machine like no tomorrow, but giving us a full day to meander around the many streets, shops, arcades, and promenade.

Doreen able to exit my car, although steadily, sitting in the wheelchair with inches either side, handbag, shopping bag, walking stick, and my duffle bag in tow.

Gradually reversing Doreen's four-wheel aid from between cars, and onto the pavement.

Amanda giving instructions of how to tilt the wheelchair, placing my foot at the rear of the chair frame, pressing down on a purpose made bar, the front lifting high enough to clear the average height kerb.

Making our way to the sea front, steering this contraption with reasonable ease on the downhill stretches.

All agreeing a fish and chips dinner, and uppermost on everyone's mind, with the refreshing sea air breeze welcome on an increasingly getting hotter sunny day.

Not often in the UK's hourly fluctuating climate can you plan a day at the seaside, a date far in advance, and arrive in glorious sunshine, but today, one of those days.

Luckily locating a just vacated bench overlooking the harbour, and a fish and chip shop just over the road, and after our long almost all downhill walk, about ready for a tasty lunch.

Manoeuvring the wheel chair and putting on the breaks, giving Doreen a sea view from the North Pier.

Placing bags on our bench, the fish shop queue not looking too long, Doreen more than happy to guard these seats with a view, until our return.

Receiving a pink numbered ticket and receipt from the cashier, in anticipation of our freshly prepared lunch, only half a dozen in front of us, so hopefully not taking too long.

Lots of holiday makers walking past, and some joining our queue, as both constantly checking on Doreen, just about visible amongst airborne seagulls and a glut of other full seats.

From information available about this seaside town, the current population around 35000, but on a warm sunny day like today, now thinking this number quite a few thousand more.

Chatting with Amanda in the queue, saying how hard everyone working behind the counter, and deciding where to take a walk after eating lunch.

Number after number called, finally our turn at last.

Gathering our wrapped-up order, and walking the few metres back to Doreen, guardian, and solitary minder of our bench.

Doreen said lots of people asking if these seats taken, and disappointed when told her two carer's just collecting our lunch.

Told many times you cannot beat quality fish and chips from the seaside, and once again, I fully agree, tasty indeed, but keeping alert, and our eyes wide open for these swooping thieves from the sky, lots of seagulls around our location.

I wonder why.

Without any doubt, a constant stream of people eating quality cooked food, and the gulls readily available to either steal, or pick up dropped or thrown morsels.

Walking over to a café for hot drinks, and asked "are you leaving" more than once, by other seat hungry holiday makers.

With today's forecast saying it will remain hot, and reasonably cloud free for the remainder of the day, and wanting to make the most of it.

Finally, and to the delight of those holiday visitors hanging around, clearing up our belongings, leaving our sort after bench and heading towards the north bay along the promenade.

Taking hold of the handlebars, beginning a steady walk, not taking too much energy to push at all, and commenting how lucky to make the decision to travel to the coast on a day like today.

The tide on its way out, with little or no swell, ideal for a customary seaside paddle, Doreen happy to stay put on the promenade, and look out at two adults behaving like kids.

Removing my trainers and socks, but not the first into ice-cold North Sea water, Amanda beating me down the steps, just wearing slip-ons with no socks, so much quicker.

Doreen above us, a good ten-feet higher, both brakes on her wheelchair, and tight up to the rails facing out to sea, camera in hand, taking lots of images.

I did have a smile on my face, and for all the wrong reasons, why I should think about Lou Todd and Andy Pipkin, fictional characters from the BBC's Little Britain, anyone's guess.

Played by actors David Walliams and Matt Lucas, looking back at Doreen using a wheelchair when outdoors, and thinking, one-minute hands free, and the next eating an ice-cream, dashing off to purchase a Cadbury 99 while our backs turned.

I'm sure Doreen and Amanda would see the funny side if mentioned, but on this occasion, keeping the thought to myself.

A bit of a walk to reach the sea for Amanda and me, and as I thought, freezing water, but others enjoying a swim and splash around, particularly children, loving a hot sunny day in the North Sea.

Making our way back to Doreen, drying off our feet, and putting on our footwear, walking much further on this rather busy walkway.

Getting the hang of pushing Doreen's wheelchair on a reasonably flat and level walkway, and so far an easy downhill push towards the beach, so an uphill walk/push still to complete when eventually making our way back to the car.

Sharing the pushing, covering the full walkable length of the promenade and back, and maybe in places, a joint effort when finally deciding to leave the bustle of the seafront.

Doreen thoroughly enjoying her time by the sea, as too Amanda and me, delighting in tasty ice-creams, an afternoon coffee, and also a tasty tea, before heading back to the car.

Thankfully a larger gap between cars, a good job too, after such a long day sat down, Doreen's legs now rather stiff, as she tried to slowly stand up, and then sit down once again into the passenger seat.

A wonderful sunset while driving home, Doreen making the most of the views, taking lots of photographs.

Arriving at Doreen's home just after ten o'clock, a full twelve hours, but such an entertaining day out.

Thoroughly enjoying the day, relishing a long paddle, tasty food, lovely company, and getting a bit of a tan in the process too.

Also, giving me firsthand experience, and an insight into just how difficult a job pushing a person sat in a wheelchair on our streets, especially when crossing roads, mounting kerbs, or just encountering uneven block paving or irregular tarmac footpaths and carriageways.

Able-bodied people take so much for granted, daily managing all of the above, and with relative ease, until faced with requiring others to help with getting you about, and thankfully, in my case not one aching bone in my body, just yet.

This particular full day occurrence, a first for me, and not put off at all, or Doreen, as just three months later, Amanda once again asking if a further threesome trip could take place.

Not another coastal day out though, instead Christmas shopping, at a local garden centre.

The recently opened, Tingley Garden Centre, certainly Christmassy, lots of ornate and decorative items, hundreds of artificial Christmas trees, of all heights and designs, in particular most with LED lighting already attached, and of course an excellent quality café, what a surprise.

Lots of wide isle space, ideal for pushing a wheelchair, made so easy to manoeuvre Doreen around this huge garden centre.

I should admit I have visited garden centres numerous times, usually a café the attraction, where good quality food, and limitless amounts of tea, and coffee available.

A breakfast time visit always appealing, a full English preferred, and then a walk around, just looking, and not sure what at, but occasionally buying something.

In my case, anything but plants, in particular, garden furniture, ornaments, mirrors and even furniture for the home, in particular a pine TV stand, a matching nest of three tables, and countless other items that I am not sure actually needed, but seemed a good idea to purchase at the time.

However, other than visiting pound type stalls with-in garden centres for our Young Astronomers events, and a visit to by some potting plants, quite a while since my last trip to a garden centre, and non the more exciting than a pre-Christmas shopping expedition.

Doreen trying on and purchasing shoes, also lots of family Christmas presents, Amanda joining in too, obtaining festive gifts for family, whilst on this occasion, I didn't buy anything, thinking more of looking forward to lunch time in the café.

The menu has lots of tasty looking food available, and not long before all tucking into a delightful lunch, including a scrumptious pudding.

A last slow look around, just to see if any buying opportunities missed, then heading back to the car, and Doreen's bungalow home.

Admiring Amandas wheelchair skills, and to a point emulating them, as I seem to have managed quite well so far.

Not only pushing and manoeuvring, combined with guiding in and out of tight corners, and without catching Doreen's feet, and finally folding to put into the car boot.

A further seven-months later, and yet another trip to the seaside.

Wednesday July 31st, 2024, and on our way to the East coast yet again, and seaside towns of Withernsea and Hornsea, including a visit to Hornsea garden centre.

All former places Doreen has visited in her past, and a bucket list item now completed.

The journey involved even more life stories from Doreen, this time some of them actually concluding, especially those when visiting these areas, although once again, four or five different deviations before finally getting to a finale.

During conversation while on our journey, Radio two playing in the background, perhaps a tad louder in the rear seats, arriving in Withernsea in no time at all, Amanda commenting, almost finishing her knitting during the journey.

Once again, our arrival coinciding with lunch time, and a not over busy carpark, and available extra wide bays giving more room between vehicles for Doreen to safely exit the car, and onto her wheelchair.

While at the seaside, fish, and chips a must for lunch.

Two fish butties, a portion of chips for sharing, plus two cans of Dandelion and Burdock for Amanda and me, a fish and bottled water for Doreen.

No harbour view this time around, instead picking a reasonably quiet spot in the Valley Gardens Park, on the perimeter of an open-air auditorium.

Sadly, no entertainment booked to appear on the covered stage today, however plenty of posters advertising shows, so still in use during the summer months.

Delicious fish, and tasty chips, much needed energy to begin our walk, pushing wheelchair and Doreen along the sea front.

Bringing back memories of visiting this seaside town many years ago, a regular Black Lace venue our band performed at during the late seventies/ early eighties, just a few hundred yards away.

From memory, a timber constructed building overlooking the sea, a bingo hall during the day, and a night club from 21.00hr, until 02.00hr.

Sadly, just a vacant site, with foundations just about visible when the tidal swell allows, the main building and infrastructure long gone, and many years ago looking at what remains.

Not sure if a huge storm destroyed the building or not, but after all these years, looking like no apparent plans to rebuild.

Once again taking in the sunshine, another hot a day, although a little breezy, welcomed as a few more hills to tackle, although not demanding from a pushing Doreen point of view.

Sun glasses required when walking on the front, and of course a customary paddle taking place, Doreen happy to look after our footwear.

Remembering sun cream too, as I did get a little sunburnt on our last coastal adventure.

Having a look around in a few wheelchair friendly stores, even buying a few bits and pieces.

Doreen purchasing a silver chain to add a gift from her daughter to put around her neck, and I actually bought something, two memento fridge magnets.

Not that I have a fridge door to put them on, as my fridge-freezer with-in a unit, but sure I will find somewhere or something metal to put them on.

Back to the car, and a seventeen-mile coastal road journey to Hornsea, and yet more memories disclosed by Doreen while on the way.

Passing Hornsea Mere, and the former Wakefield seaside school, now long gone, with new high specification properties built on the land.

Bringing back my two weeks school holiday at the camp, an amazing experience, as I am sure others throughout the years enjoyed it as much as I did.

Parking up the car, quite a few spaces available in Eastgate car park, and plenty of room for Doreen to safely access her wheelchair.

Further walks along the sea front, not forgetting another paddle, and more browsing around shops, before heading out to the Hornsea Garden Centre.

Although a few miles from the town centre, through a quaint village called Seaton, and just past a turning for Sigglesthorne.

These days, most garden centres follow a similar pattern, from all the usual garden plants, and concessionary stores, all having a restaurant style café area, and some much larger than others, as the case at this garden centre.

Only just in time for tea, last orders given out ten minutes after arrival, picking pie chips and peas, and a chocolate brownie from the menu.

Amanda and Doreen buying small hanging garden knick-knack type ornaments, then a final browse before heading back into Hornsea for a last look at the sea, and on our way home.

More verbal stories, a catalogue of intrigue and mystery, Doreen has certainly enjoyed her eighty years life, and counting.

Further short journeys to local garden centres around Wakefield taking place, and a few appointments later, planning yet another trip in the not-too-distant future.

I am looking forward to whatever journey Doreen and Amanda come up with next.

CHAPTER THIRTY-SIX

"The Rocket"

(And not into Space)

Each year the bangs get louder, and the colours and sparkles more vivid.

The so-called 5th November bonfire night firework display commences around the start of October, a bursting charge of colourful crackles, and loud explosions giving this away.

Each night a continuous sum of these premeditated discharges begins to increase, until the chosen night of the bonfire, depending on what day of the week November 5th lands on, and still many days afterwards.

Organised bonfire nights, with admission charges, that also include a "supper" of hotdogs, burgers, hot drinks, and the like, and a prepared fireworks display, now a preferred option for most families.

In most cases bringing the local community together, with health and safety uppermost on the controlling body investing their time, and money, putting on the night.

Amazing pyrotechnics giving a phenomenal display, previously only witnessed during the bringing in of New Year celebrations.

However, remembering our excited kids looking forward to one of these council arranged bonfire nights, however, receiving news the night of fire and fireworks, cancelled due to high winds, safety concerns the reason.

Disappointment beyond belief, but not putting off individual estate fires and displays, instead watching these through a cosy lounge window.

Bonfire night merriments taking place on various nights closest to a weekend, and on all three nights too, or more, if fires lit on the actual midweek day.

The skies full of glittering delights, and loud bangs and booms heard around our properties at all hours, through a period of up to three weeks, regardless of the weather.

Over the years the premature letting off fireworks has caused lots of controversy, from all sorts of protesting groups, mainly the owners of pets, or anti-social behavioural consortiums, and of course the Police.

Technology bringing about some amazing displays, and virtually noise free, an innovation of these manufactured tiny flying wonders.

Huge shapes and simulations instantly formed over towns and city landmarks, using expertly pre-programed controlled drones.

Some drone shows actually release a product looking like flames, perhaps actual effects as in rockets, to give the display even more authenticity, the results looking amazing to the viewing public.

I would imagine the preparation for such an event involves a few operatives, the brains behind countless hours of computer programming, as too the expense of hundreds of drones required for these incredible looking displays.

Some drone companies advertise over six -hundred drones used for a single night's 3D performance.

Perhaps in the not-too-distant future, a combination of pyrotechnics, laser, music, with the drones taking centre stage for these displays, and no need for bonfires at all.

The Grange in Pontefract organise a bonfire and fireworks display each year, and this year no different.

Noticing lots of wood and tree cuttings starting to appear at the end of the carpark.

Our observatory also in these grounds, and the members and visitors carpark utilised for the crowds that attend, with an organised bonfire as far as possible away from any buildings.

However, some self-set trees in the locality, and each year they seem oblivious to the heat immitted from these fires, scorched a little, but recovering in just a few months.

These self-set trees have grown far too high from our observatory members point of view, taking out some of the South West horizon sky, so much so, our committee approaching the Grange management committee to have them reduced in height.

Some arboriculture work did take place, and told at a considerable expense, however, only thinned out, and not reduced enough in height, if at all, certainly not making any significant difference for our stargazing members and visitors.

This year's bonfire might just get a little hotter, burn a little longer, and perhaps a fire extinguisher or the emergency services not available.

I mustn't speculate on such an occurrence, but it does make you wonder with so much heat dispersed from the bonfire, and perhaps hundreds of potentially dangerous fireworks, a catastrophe hasn't already happened.

To think most average rockets, contain the following explosive elements, and appearing to have no control of where they go from launching, hypothetically, who knows what could happen.

> **Black Powder:**
> Gunpowder, made from potassium nitrate, charcoal, and sulphur.
> **Stars:**
> Contain metal salts for colour, oxidizer, and charcoal.
> **Fuse:**
> Carries Heat to activate the black powder.
> **Lift Charge:**
> Black powder, located at the bottom of the shell, launches the rocket skyward.

Thankfully, I am not aware of any local occurrences of major fires as a direct result of a firework display or bonfire.

Although, just recently on the local news, a huge amount of fireworks and rockets discovered in a local domestic garage.

The owners attempting to sell over one-hundred and seventy-five KG of fireworks rather cheaply on various social media platforms.

These T4 classified illegal fireworks immediately confiscated as confirmed dangerous, as deployed only at large scale professional run events.

Specially trained officers removing all the fireworks, and I imagine raising lots of questions, such as where from, and how they had obtained them.

The news bulletin pointing out that had a spark set them off, nothing much left of the garage or the council estate.

Of course, these nights involving fires, and fireworks, not taking place at all if not for Guy Fawkes, also known as Guido Fawkes, born on April 13th, 1570.

Born and educated in York, Guy became a member of a group of provincial English Catholics involved in the failed gunpowder plot of 1605.

His motive, to assassinate King James VI, and members of the houses of parliament.

Apprehended on November 5th, 1605, and convicted of high treason.

Fawkes had the responsibility of safeguarding the gunpowder, and following receipt of an anonymous letter to the authorities, the basement of the houses of parliament searched, and Guy Fawkes found while guarding the powder.

Seemingly, due to the amount of gunpowder discovered, had he succeeded in lighting the fuse, most of the houses of parliament, and a huge region of London raised to the ground.

Following days of torture Fawkes confessed, and as a result, suffering an indescribable death of hanging, drawn, and quartered, on January 31st, 1606.

Guy Fawkes night commemorated since November 5th, 1605, with his effigy traditionally burned on a fire.

Bringing to mind, and on the very same estate as where the fireworks found, an explosion that occurred some years ago.

My mum raising the alarm when hearing a loud boom while in her first-floor kitchen, and noticing a huge plume of black smoke billowing skyward.

Telephoning me to say there's a house on fire on our estate.

As a housing surveyor for the local council, immediately getting into my car, heading from my Wrenthorpe home and in the direction of mums.

Only just home from work, leaving my tea, and almost immediately seeing the huge cloud of black smoke, intermingled with flames high above properties in front of me.

Arriving just behind two fire tenders, a police car, and hundreds of astonished and inquisitive on-lookers.

Access cordoned off until the fire put out, thankfully not the house, but yet again, a garage, situated in the garden of a corner semi-detached council house, although so close to other houses, and commercial properties.

Hundreds of windows blown out, chimney pots and roof tiles off, and in all directions, clearly a huge explosion, and following a call to the councils emergency services, joiners and glaziers motivated to make these homes secure for the night.

A number of trades started to appear in vans loaded with glass and plywood sheets, making an immediate start.

To make matters worse, the fire brigade had removed two remaining large acetylene bottles used for welding, from the remnants of a now isolated and smouldering garage.

Immersing them in a large pre-prepared eight-foot diameter paddling pool, a fireman constantly dowsing them with cold water.

A fire officer commenting had these exploded too, they could have gone up like rockets, and causing untold damage throughout a large region.

Returning home, and finishing my left-over tea as a late supper, leaving workmen working through the night, and thereafter.

Taking almost three-weeks to replace glass, chimney pots and roof tiles, and surveying all the effected properties.

Thankfully all coming to a good conclusion, from a no injuries point of view, but a costly experience for the local authority, and tenants continuing to live with damaged items in properties.

Most not having insurance, the council footing the bills for damaged items with-in the homes.

To avoid any further huge explosions and potential airborne missiles, notices served to properties containing garages in gardens.

Issuing a warning not to store these cylinders, to help in preventing a catastrophe of this magnitude ever happening again.

I do digress,

A much safer, easy rocket to make and launch, with products containing no inflammable fuel, a rocket made from soft plastic drink bottles, using water as a propellant.

I will explain.

As part of the observatories outreach program of activities, a solar Saturday, (former solar SUNday) takes place.

During the day, attending children involved in sticking fins, a cone and various self-adhesive stars, planets, and even glitter to two or three litre size bottles, and joining a queue for me to launch them.

Pouring water to about a third full in each bottle, and connecting a screw finned fitting to allow the bottle to stand upright.

Using a large battery, and my electric tyre pump, generating air to pressurise the void remaining in the bottles.

The rubber grommet fitting contained in the screw on fitting, only allows a certain amount of pressure to build up.

Each decorated rocket looking impressive, with lots of bubbles produced in the contained water, before whoosh, the air hose discharged, and the rockets zoom into the sky.

Try and better try to gauge the release with a countdown, numerous attempts commencing at ten, nine, eight, down to zero.

Sometimes the countdown only reaching five, and the rocket shoots into the sky, while other times starting at ten down to zero, and then commencing once again.

Only a few times have children, including me, succeeded in getting the countdown exactly right.

In some cases, the rockets no more than a bottle with a crooked shaped cone stuck to the top with cellotape, and still launched to the delight of the child that made it.

On one such day, launching upwards of fifty rockets, and some more than once, an exhilarating five hours of fun and laughter.

I may get a little wet from expelling water as each rocket soars into the sky, other than that, all parents, and children in no danger at all.

Some masterpieces excelling, launching vertically, straight upwards, no deviation whatsoever, making a good fifty feet in height, whilst others traveling a similar distance, but horizontal, no two bottle rockets appear to perform the same.

A few years ago, the time before covid, a fellow stargazer contacted a committee member asking if he could bring along his telescope to the observatory, and obtain some help with setting it up from our knowledgeable members.

Travelling south from Redcar on a cold evening in cloudy skies, this duly taking place, and requiring a few hours to fully sort, all to the delight of Mick, the owner of the scope.

Mick making numerous attempts to pay our member for his services, all to no avail, however, Mick saying that a friend of his called George, has built a model Saturn five rocket, and although reluctant to part with it, wanting to donate the rocket to our observatory.

Following lots of correspondence, our secretary, Amanda, born in Marske just a few miles south of Redcar, offering to pick up the rocket when visiting her parents during half-term school holidays.

However, once given the overall measurements, a pickup not possible due to the size of the rocket, complete with gantry, and servicing arms, as it would not fit in Amandas car, especially with two further passengers, Amanda's daughters Holly and Rosie.

A bit of a stalemate, but one easily sorted, making the offer of driving to Redcar to collect it.

Amanda sending the email correspondence to me, complete with contact details of Mick and George, and the address of where to collect the complete rocket.

Immediately telephoning George to make the arrangements to pick up the rocket, leaving a message, explaining who, and what my call all about.

George returning my call, however, not anticipating this George, not the correct George that owns the rocket.

Explaining in a strong north east accent, he knows nothing of our observatory, or a rocket, and I must have the wrong number.

A little shocked, but laughing under my breath, asking if he knows of Mick, "Oh yes, I know Mick very well, in fact, both regularly go shooting together."

Quickly deducing that Mick had inadvertently given me the number for the wrong George, but not before George (number one) giving his hobbies of pigeons, and breeding love birds, and at eighty-three years old, a really good conversationalist.

Listening to George and his north eastern accent bringing back so many memories of our band playing music in clubs all around this region, over many, many years.

Deciding the best option to ring Mick, and let him contact the correct George.

Upon contacting Mick, realising his error, saying that George who owns the rocket, currently on holiday in Krakow, and due back to the UK, early Tuesday morning.

However, saying he would send him a text, indicating arrangements may follow shortly.

Ironically, George saying to pick up the rocket on Tuesday November 5th, bonfire night, and to arrive around lunchtime at his Redcar home.

Sorted, finally, and laughably could not wait to meet both Mick, and the correct George.

Leaving home just after breakfast, around nine, a little early, but as usual always giving myself plenty of time, no rush at all, and once on the M1, setting my cars cruise control to 65mph.

A regular route in our band days, M1, A1, A19, A174, no real need for a sat nav, but setting the navigation system anyway, putting in the post code to take me direct to George's home.

Bringing along a hot drink of coffee, a packet of Red Leicester cheesy cheddars (I'm sure Lottie and ted will not mind,) and a Cadbury Twirl, for some in car refreshments, while driving the eighty or so miles to the northeastern coastal town of Redcar.

My sat nav saying I will arrive at ten-thirty-five, way too early, so deciding to drive into Marske, and park up.

Strange to pass a school with the Outwood name and logo, the very same school as in Outwood Wakefield, and senior school that Liam attended.

This Marske school, clearly part of the same school trust as our local Outwood Academy, Sir Micheal Wilkins, principle of the trusts namesake, founding the Outwood Grange Academy, and board of trustees in 2009.

While at the coast a traditional paddle a must, but failing to bring a towel to dry off my feet, not a problem if only my feet get wet, the cars heater will soon dry them off.

A first, a parking meter where you put in your car details, no fee to pay, and issuing a ticket to display on your dash, just a limit of four-hours, with a no return policy in the same day.

Spotting a steep unmade sand path winding its way to the beach below, with the sea a good hundred yards in the distance.

Almost a sprint, as when I started downhill, I couldn't stop, getting

432

faster and faster, accelerating all the time, my long legs having all on to keep up with the momentum of my body.

Thankfully not falling, but taking a few meters to come to a halt, and looking back up towards the car, far steeper gazing up, than it appeared looking down.

Walking across a band of water beaten rocks, stretching the length of the beach, before taking off my trainers and socks, and paddling through a shallow sort of lagoon area, long before reaching the sea.

Surprisingly the sea not feeling too cold, although without a towel, or shorts, a swim totally out of the question.

Not many people on this vast expanse of flat beach, a few dog walkers, and me, paddling in a few inches of the North Sea, with little swell, and no fear of getting soaked.

Looking around for fossils, nothing catching my eye, except one, washing off the sand, and putting it in my coat pocket.

Laughing at my attempt at balancing on each leg to put on my socks and trainers, made all the more difficult when stood in soft sand, rolling down my jeans, no such luck at keeping my socks or trainers dry, before making my way back to the car.

I have no idea what it takes to become a mountaineer, as judging my steep and exhilarating climb, not sure a profession I will take up.

Thankfully reaching the top of the almost vertical, (it did feel like it,) incline with no slips or falls, but requiring an input of oxygen, out of breath an understatement.

Contacting Mick to say I am a few miles away in Marske, and can arrive at the home of George in just a few minutes.

Mick confirming George at home, although not answering his mobile, and to meet there in twenty-minutes.

Terraced properties at both sides of Fitzwilliam Street, with cars parked at either side too, not leaving much central width of road available.

Driving slowly towards I presume a waving Mick, directing me to a reserved space directly outside George's home.

A while since I reversed into such a tight spot, with cars only a few inches away, thankfully lots of beeps from my back and front parking sensors, a significant help with my limited manoeuvring abilities.

A good firm handshake with Mick, before meeting George, yet

another firm handshake, and immediately feeling I have met both of these characters before, so friendly and welcoming, obviously pleased to meet me too.

Immediately coming across a huge gantry arrangement in the front living room, definitely a wow experience, as George connected it to a mains supply, flooding the whole gantry in tiny LED lights.

George also pointing out the rocket, in three parts, and protected in bubble wrap, laid on a table.

Discussions about the observatory, stargazing, and of course the amazing model rocket, and illuminated gantry assembly taking place.

One thing for sure, when displayed at the observatory, the whole model requires a glass lockable surrounding, to not only keep the model safe from tiny inquisitive hands, but also dust.

George leading the way through the lounge, dining room and kitchen, to a rear attached shed and working space, pointing out a variety of model aircraft hung from the ceiling and placed on shelves.

Clearly, George a keen model maker, and telling me he flies them all, including a blackbird spy plane, currently dismantled for travel and storage, and over five-feet long, and with-out wings.

Bringing back a memory of just a few months ago, when visiting the Imperial War Museum (IWM,) and due to my rushing to meet family at the destination on time, totally missed seeing a larger than life, now retired actual Lockheed SR-71 Blackbird spy plane.

Although, this model in the shed looking amazing, George explaining its flying capabilities, and how quickly it uses up fuel if at full throttle.

Other models include double winged world war one type planes, some fully assembled, while others because of their size, requiring building before flying.

Putting down the rear and front passenger seats, as George carefully lifting and placing the whole gantry assembly into my car, and only just fitting.

I cautiously carried out the larger S- IC first stage rocket booster assembly, with Mick following, bringing out the S-11 second and IVB third stages, and the capsule complete with the launch escape system (LES) fitted.

Just a few months ago, me and Warren actually at the Kennedy Space

Centre, viewing the original launch site of the amazing Saturn 5 rocket launch tower, feeling delighted to have a scale model of one of these, including rocket, in my car.

The original tower on launch pad 39A, standing over one-hundred and sixteen meters high, with base measurements of eighteen meters deep, and thirty-four meters wide, tapering to just twelve meters square at the top.

Inviting Mick and George to our observatory anytime they wished, preferably on a Tuesday evening, as this particular night unlikely to clash with any outreach events or family open nights.

Both duly accepting, and with any luck not taking too long to visit, but long enough to locate and exhibit this amazing model rocket.

My drive home taking just over one and a half hours, a little busier than my earlier drive, and just making the toilet.

George offered drinks at his home, but having just returned from Krakow, he didn't have any fresh milk.

A good job too, had I downed a cuppa, a definite on the way home stop required.

The gantry and rocket unloaded, and temporarily set up in my hallway, with no fear of touchy-feely kids, while I attempt to locate a glass display case at a reasonable cost, as most I have looked at so far, in the thousands of pounds range.

I am sure when placed at the observatory, the rocket display certainly a centre piece attraction, and absolutely positive everyone visiting, will enjoy looking at the complete rocket assembly, and admiring the amazing skills of Redcar George.

CHAPTER THIRTY-SEVEN

"360"

Following the purchase of my second telescope, a Dobsonian ten-inch diameter manual reflector scope, a non-expensive deep-sky visual aid, that replaced my Celestron Nexstar 5SE computerised more expensive telescope.

Finding my second-hand Nexstar telescope frustrating to set up, and for me, difficult to star align.

Once star aligned, the scope worked fine, just a long frustrating process for my limited brain cells to comprehend, and additional poor weather conditions, that at times added to an annoying waste of time in preparing the scope for viewing.

Just as everything set, after numerous attempts, of seeing the message "star alignment failed," the clouds come rolling in, bringing a sense of why bother with this hobby.

Clouds and bad weather 10.

Satisfaction 0.

However, when using Amandas six-inch Dobsonian model during a visit to the rear garden at her home, instantly preferring my recently purchased no-nonsense instant viewing version of scope to the Nexstar.

Immediately delighted with my second-hand acquisition, purchased with money left over following the sale of my Nexstar to a delighted stargazing member of our observatory, and after my selling and purchasing, still a little money left over.

The Nexstar telescope now third hand, as I too purchasing it from an observatory member who bought it from new, and this latest exchange keeping it with-in the observatory family, so to speak.

My Dobsonian telescope manually operated, a full three-hundred-and-sixty-degree continual rotation, and from horizontal to vertical or azimuth, and any angle with ease.

No actual setting up required, as the scope can remain in an assembled position, provided you are reasonably strong to lift and move it around.

Although, when wanting to take the telescope to the observatory or other location, Amanda's scope travelling on the rear seat of my car, made much easier by removing the actual telescope from the base.

Two rather long handle type bolts quickly removed, and placing the base in the boot, and wrapping the telescope cylinder in a blanket, using the rear seatbelts to secure, taking all of five-minutes to prepare for travelling.

Nevertheless, not fully content with the scope base, and following an idea from an observatory member, deciding to design and make a further adjustable platform for the telescope base to securely fit on.

Why you may ask, when the Skywatcher Dobsonian telescope arrives fully working, and almost instantly usable, subject to a clear night sky.

The additional base made fifty-millimetre diameter larger than the existing telescope base.

Fitting three seventy-millimetre-high legs, all adjustable to allow levelling, using two attached small spirit levels for accuracy.

Next stop, the printers, to prepare and print on card, a six-hundred-and-fifty-millimetre diameter three-hundred-and-sixty-degree circle.

The circle divided into 36 individual markings, like the hours on a clock face, then sub-divided further into 360, similarly like the seconds on a clock, giving a fully marked out circumference to facilitate the scopes azimuth alignment.

For example, ninety degrees, corresponds to East, one-hundred and eighty degrees, South, two-hundred and seventy degrees, West, and three-hundred and sixty degrees, North, or zero.

Simple...

Placing the telescope onto the new base, ensuring that zero at 90 degrees from the scopes tube, and adding a magnetic fitting "wixi" to the telescope tube, close to the eyepiece, allows a full and precise zenith orientation of the visible night sky.

The battery operated "wixi," once set, enables the accurate horizontal to vertical angle from any fundamental direction.

Little did I know at the time, until researching the type and styles available for the printing of a 360-degree circle, I came across some additional surprising information.

Evidently, during the reign of Nebuchadnezzar (605-562 BC) in the Chaldean dynasty in Babylon, divided the circle into 360 degrees.

The Babylonians continuously observing the sun, moon, and planets against a pollution free backdrop view of millions of stars, that all lie on the ecliptic.

The Babylonians calculated that the sun appeared to advance around one degree each day, using the information to accurately divide a circle into 360 equal parts.

Making it much easier when using factors of 2, 3, 4, 5, and 6, with 6 equilateral triangles fitting together to span a circle, helping to solve many mathematical problems thousands of years ago, and making 360 degrees a natural tested foundation for today's geometry.

However, in the Gregorian calendar used today, a normal year consists of 365 days, a sidereal year, or year that the Earth revolves once around the sun, or even more accurately 365.2425 days, a leap year of 366 days used every four years, to disregard the three shorter years.

All that information aside, making two bases, one for Amandas telescope too, then adding a "lazy Susan," an aluminium ball race, sandwiched between the existing telescope friction base, to aid a much smoother transition when turning a full 360 degrees.

Impressed with how it all works, and could not wait to try out both our scopes to see if accurate readings for a particular deep sky object location, equate to setting up, and locating through an eye piece.

The first outing of both our scopes a complete success, accurate to with-in a whisker, making our manual go-to scopes equally as good for viewing to an electronic version of telescope.

However, not practical to use our type of scopes for astrophotography, but if wanting a lasting memory of what objects, such as planets, nebulas, or other deep sky targets viewed, a product available to assist with this function.

A reasonably priced Celestron NexYZ-3 Axis adapter, a contraption that fits to the telescope eyepiece, and once fully attached and adjusted, a mobile phone then fitted.

Using your phone screen as an eyepiece, much easier to view the selected subjects, and also giving the opportunity to take as many images as possible to edit and enjoy.

A bit fiddly, and a reasonable DIY version of what a dedicated astrophotographer can produce, but once set up and used, the adapter easily removed for storage in its set position, allowing a quick fit to take even more images, and a keepsake of what targets viewed during a nights viewing.

I prefer to look for objects using my amended traditional method of the new 360-degree base, and eyepiece viewing, even more so now that I have had a further cataract sorted.

Using this method of viewing bringing my attention to the deterioration of my right eye, and as indicated in a previous chapter, an appointment made at the opticians.

Surgery sorted with the optometrist, and my eyesight as good as new.

However, technology moves on, and at an incredible pace, so much so, a new affordable telescope hitting the market, capturing the imagination of astronomers wanting to take up astrophotography.

A rather compact unassuming device, not much larger than a football, and comes with instructions, carry case, small tripod, sun filter, and aptly called, Seestar.

This electronic device capable of automatically finding and taking images of excellent quality, getting rave reviews throughout the astronomy world.

One member after another at our observatory acquiring one of these impressive telescopes, and once witnessing them in use, and looking at the quality images on mobile phones, or tablets, feeling a little left out, also deciding to make a purchase.

Placing my order directly with Rother Valley Optics, for an all-encompassing price of £539.00, receiving a confirmation email informing me I will receive my ZWO SeeStar S50 all in one Smart APO Telescope, in just two days' time.

Deciding my purchase of this telescope a pre-to-self, birthday present, a little early, but my anticipation far out-weighing my fast-depleting patience.

Feeling like a child at Christmas, opening my cardboard parcel, frustratingly almost like a Russian nesting doll, or "Matryoshka," layer after layer of brown cardboard and wrapping paper, certainly protected during delivery.

Surprised at the actual size of the black carry case containing my telescope, tiny by comparison to my 10" Dobsonian, but often told I shouldn't judge something by its size, as "good things come in small packages."

Having seen these telescopes in action and the images they produce, I have no concerns at all, and looking forward to trying it out once I have read, and fully understand the instructions.

Our members using these telescopes seem to make it look easy to operate, all via a downloaded mobile phone or tablet app.

What can I say, other than if I can do it, anyone can, not the best when it comes to sorting out electronic technology, both Warren and Liam usually helping me with sorting out any issues.

Impressed with my abilities, my telescope fully charged and functional, using the downloaded app.

Although daylight, and of course cloudy, no chance of imaging anything at present, nevertheless, directing the scope to a partly visible Sun, just to see if my scope performing as instructed.

With a product name of, ZWO SeeStar S50, all in one Smart APO, a shorter memorable name required.

Never getting to grips with all these complicated stock and product names.

Often hearing our members discussing particular types of camera, lens, tripod, telescope, or software and hardware, using exceptionally long words, letters, and numerals, to describe, far too complicated for my brain to take in, however, still impressed with their capabilities.

Keeping names of my own purchased products relatively simple, my Dobsonian, appropriately named Big T, and a name to identify my SeeStar, Marvin, picked by Amandas daughters Holly and Rosie.

I am impressed with the name Marvin; but other identification required if all our members owning one of these turn up at the observatory at the same time to set up and view.

Fitting a pair of self-adhesive wobbly eyes to the outward facing side of my tiny piece of fascinating technology, apt under the circumstances, as it appears to have no trouble finding anything in our super immense universe.

Not a problem at all for this telescope, billions of stars, galaxies, nebulas, and other fascinating objects, tracking and imaging whatever requested, and all at my fingertips, using my SeeStar mobile phone app.

I am so looking forward to discussing progress, and sharing these amazing images with fellow SeeStar users at our observatory.

While tucking into a delicious Sunday lunch of chicken, roast potatoes, and a selection of vegetables at Warrens home, announcing my recent purchase, and explaining the potential of my new telescope, when he revealed a surprise acquisition of his own.

I do remember Warren mentioning this device while at The Kennedy Space Centre in April, discussing its use with an operative at a themed ride.

Our ride, a fully immersive 3D experience, bringing together visuals, and a sensation of speeding skyward.

So realistic, as though I would know, still, enjoying everything while wearing the headset device, and could not wait to try Warrens VR headset out.

Our pudding first, a delicious helping of apple crumble and custard.

Of course, Warrens headset visual and sound only, unless he has a floor, or chair that can give full body vibrations, tilt backwards, forwards, and to either side.

The Meta Quest 3 Virtual Reality headset certainly looking the business, as Warren carefully removed it, along with two handsets from the packaging.

Placing the goggles on my head to adjust and snuggly fit, and giving me a few instructions as to where to place my fingers on the handsets, which buttons, or trigger does what, bringing the selected visuals to life.

To life, an understatement, Warrens chosen first 360-degree film of me becoming an astronaut actually floating in Space.

The International Space Station finger tips away, and ultra massive to the front of me, and the Earth directly below, almost losing my balance when coming to terms with my imaginary, but ever so realistic precarious position.

Blown away with the quality of this device, technology transporting me directly into space, and I mean space.

Viewing billions of miles in all directions, and not surprised at all when looking at an abundance of cloud directly over the British Isles, no change there.

Turning around on the spot, looking up and down, in every direction, a FULL immersive experience, oh wow, amazing, believe me when I say, I feel as though I am here.

Who needs a rocket, with view such as this.

Admiring our huge Earth, the thin blue line of our atmosphere around its circumference, the intricate construction and detail of the ISS, along with millions of visible stars, our Sun, and planets.

Hooked already, and a profound, "I have got to get me one of these" moments.

A full forty-minutes later, and other than floating in space, I have visited numerous locations around the world.

Stood at the Jaffa gate in Jerusalem, where I visited in May 2023, and other memorable sites in the city, fully immersive viewing.

Warren did say I could take the headset home with me, but reluctantly declined, however, while driving home, thinking I should have agreed with him, a little more evening viewing before bedtime.

Aware that Warren about to travel to Abu – Dhabi, Capital of the United Arab Emirates, in the next few days for two whole weeks, so perhaps he may offer to drop off his headset before then.

During my realistic viewing experience looking at Earth from space, I did wonder what the first-time in space astronauts must feel when having an actual view of our planet.

Astronauts having a view of our Earth from portholes/windows of the International Space Station every day, in between work-related experiments, or when on rest breaks, I know I certainly would, and as often as possible.

To think an uninterrupted view of this calibre, witnessed only with working astronauts to date, unbelievable, nevertheless, all no doubt soon to change, when the private sector space vehicles fully up and running.

Trips into space as common as traveling on an aeroplane coming our way soon, provided that as a fee-paying passenger, your bank account can support such an immense expenditure.

I remember thinking on one of my first visits to the observatory, and looking through the telescope at a deep sky object thousands of light-years away, and wondering if anyone out there looking back at our Earth.

Also, imagining I am just one person, out of seven-billion people on one planet, out of eight planets, orbiting one star, out of three-hundred billion stars in one galaxy, out of two-hundred billion to two trillion galaxies, mindboggling, and makes your head hurt.

Warren sending me a text message to say on his way to my home prior to his holiday, also saying, rather than travel separately, me in my car, Warren, and Sommer in theirs, and happy to drive to Pontefract for us to see mum at Stella House in Pontefract,

Making lots of sense to me, suggesting afterwards, to call in at The Cobblers public house for a delicious carvery tea.

I can say delicious, because on a previous occasion when visiting mum, Liam, and Alice on leave and up from London, my brother John and wife Gill, all called to sample the delights of this popular eatery.

A proposal already making my mouth water, but instantly discounted, as two further surprises coming my way.

Warrens partner Sommer, let slip that following our visit to see mum, arrangements already made to call at her mums for tea, AND bringing along the Meta Quest 3 headset for me to use while Warren away, ecstatic.

A slight detour on the way from seeing mum, calling back to Warrens home to pick up Sommers daughter, Imogen, then on to Val's home,(Sommers mum.)

Our prepared Indian food not quite ready, Val busy in the kitchen/ dining room, with us all sat around the table patiently waiting.

Well not exactly, out comes a games board, scrabble, and some discussion with Warren and Sommer as to who had won the last game.

Joining in, for the first time playing scrabble in years, and in my opinion doing quite good, finishing second of three, not too bad, with not particularly a high scoring round, Warren licking his wounds coming in third position.

Tea delicious, so tasty and not overpoweringly hot, my taste buds tingling, helped to sooth with a yogurt dip, and finishing off with a pudding of apple crumble and ice-cream.

Now a little tight for time, Warren wanting to finish off packing, added with the urgency for us all to watch the nine pm start of the Royal Albert Hall commemoration of Armistice day on TV.

Armistice, Latin, to stand (still) arms, marked with two-minutes silence throughout the UK.

As a musician in the Band of the Irish Guards, Liam taking part, playing cymbals and Xylophone along with other musicians and choir, on stage at this prestigious building.

Dropped off at home a good fifteen minutes before the TV program start, giving Warren a hug, and saying to take care while in Abu-Dhabi.

Sommer joining Warren in a weeks' time, both enjoying a week together before returning home to the UK.

That said, they arrive home on different days, Warren making a mistake when booking the flights home, but actually convenient.

Warren, leaving Abu-Dhabi now a few days later than planned, possibly Thursday, Sommer due home on Saturday, quite a few days before Warren, all laughing at his simple blunder, considering he had booked and organised our trip to Florida without incident.

Oh well.

TV turned on, and with a freshly made cuppa, instantly picking out Liam, feeling so proud throughout the show, not only of my youngest son, but how the BBC represented the loss of millions of soldiers and civilians.

The events, and selected memories portrayed of those that survived the horrors of World War One, including recent, and ongoing wars.

I have Warren's headset in my possession for at least two weeks, but what next, and what to view first.

Acknowledging my patience, as tempted to turn it on following the Armistice shows end, instead pouring a glass of red wine, and reflecting on what I had just watched.

Liam sending a text, to say on his way home to Hounslow after the shows end, although it had started at 19.00hr in London, the recorded, and possibly edited version shown on TV, starting at 21.00hr.

Feeling so pleased with today, especially from around 16.00hr.

Mum in good spirits considering the events over the last year, our scrabble game and tea an absolute delight, and the BBC's commemoration show, and finally time to hit the sack.

Sunday, up at my usual time of 07.15, letting out Lottie and Ted to the rear garden, a glass of orange, a banana, shower and dressed, carry out a few household chores, and then, to give my borrowed Meta headset from Warren a try.

What should I watch on the headset this morning, but mindful of the "live" TV coverage of the WW1 cenotaph presentation, starting at ten-fifteen.

Liam playing cymbals, joining fellow musicians taking part in the eleven am memorial of wreath laying, the marching past the cenotaph in London off thousands of retired, and those surviving military and voluntary personnel coverage.

Scrolling through hundreds of potential films and short videos, finally selecting a documentary.

My immersive viewing this time around, a visit to the Caribbean Sea, in particular just off the Yucatan Peninsula, to swim alongside Tiger and Hammerhead Sharks.

Absolutely fascinating, enthralled at my 360-degree view, almost losing my balance, as turning around and around on the spot, almost dizzy, but managing to capture as many of these sea creatures as possible.

Whatever you may think, I am actually there, beneath the sea, thousands of miles away in a flash, with sharks and divers, experiencing what others have paid thousands of pounds to see.

An amazing tool, making me wonder what other useful applications this equipment, or the technology capable of, and absolutely sure already in use.

Early evening, and following the day's events, my on-loan headset now fully charged, and ready for yet another around the world visit.

Choosing a further documentary, Helen Sharman narrating, a British chemist, and cosmonaut, becoming the first British woman, the first western European woman, and the first privately funded woman in space.

An enthralling full spherical panoramic short film, and getting late, I should go to bed, but after scrolling through yet more selections, now settling down to view a full two-hour long film.

My first full length movie using the Virtual Reality apparatus, Oblivion, with Tom Cruise and Morgan Freeman.

Staying awake for a further two-hours may become a problem at this already late hour.

An amazing viewing, and surround sound experience, a film released in 2013, with lots of CGI, but certainly worth staying up for, and fully convinced I should also own one of these VR devices.

The following day, with my VR headset on, and riding a rollercoaster for starters, a position preferred considering my last actual ride while in Florida.

However, today all the noise and excitement of many twists and turns, up and over, inverted or reversed, a treat, and sure my body compensating, even though sat on the sofa in the comfortable surroundings of my home.

To visit anywhere in the world, whenever I have the time, to view thousands upon thousands of documentaries and films, of all genres, utterly amazing.

However, only at day two of fourteen, maybe an option to stretch to sixteen days, when Warren can reclaim his headset, and return it to his own household.

In the meantime,

Where should I go next...

CHAPTER THIRTY-EIGHT

The Final Chapter

(Possibly)

Not thinking for one minute I would, or could write enough words for a chapter, never mind a book, and not sure how they relate to other self-penned biographical autobiographies, nevertheless, a fun experience, and enjoyable to do.

This manuscript taking almost eighteen-months to complete, yet another volume speeding towards the finish line, making a grand total of five published books.

My personal memories of many people, past, present family, and friends, that I have come to know, reflecting on many incidents or occurrences that have taken place during my life, now in words, along with selected photographs for posterity.

My somewhat embellished weekly diary accounts, recording most things involving close family, acquaintances, and of course me, that have transpired throughout many years.

An all-embracing number of recitals, telling of many events, that although at times causing untold trauma, with many upsetting manifestations, as well as happy ecstatic times, bringing me all the way through to where I am today.

Albeit, quite a few stitches, many bruises, and many sticking plasters here and there, along with mental and physical wounds requiring imperative attention.

Healing fine, until making a further bad decision, or choice, taking me beyond the lowest of low, before directly bouncing back to a form of established normality.

All of these occurrences fully behind me, and now looking forward to my remaining years in a reasonably fit, and healthy condition for my years.

The original idea of putting pen to paper, so to speak, coming from the mum of my youngest son, when leaving a get-together celebration, at the Mirfield home of the ex-wife of Alan Barton, Elaine Schofield, formally Barton, or maiden name of Killey.

A night full of laughter, made all the more jovial with a little added alcohol, or should I say lots for some, involving former band mates of Black Lace, members of Bradford band Smokie, including manager, wives, partners, and close friends.

Elaine arranging the gathering, along with sons Dean, Lee and Joel, and many friends, to remember the ever so sad and untimely passing of our dear friend, and band mate, Alan Barton.

A help your-self delicious buffet supper, and an assortment of drinks on hand to indulge as required, creating a wonderful memorable atmosphere.

My partner Tricia, thoroughly enjoying the evening, and meeting everyone, some for the first time.

An evening purposely orchestrated around lots of reminiscing, many stories coming into conversation about our early years, our musical career's when starting out on the path to stardom, from our early teens, up to around mid-2005.

While on our way home, Tricia commenting on the lovely evening with my friends and band mates, and thoroughly enjoying listening to the many stories, some of which not fit to repeat, or print.

I know, as quite a few times embarrassingly finding myself centre of attention, even wondering if our relationship strong enough to withstand the mickey-taking, and my constant ridiculous red face, and not as a result of sun burn.

Not on my own, all suffering at the hands of seasoned jokers, consequences of those early years, and absolutely sure some stories made up just to shock.

Furthermore, Tricia enjoying herself so much, saying that I should, and with-out delay, put all the evenings banter, and many recollected stories I could remember onto paper.

Not to hold back, throwing in as many profound printable revelations as possible, a book in the making, and all prior to me reaching the age of retirement, or perhaps before I begin to lose my marbles.

Grasping Tricia's initial comments with both hands, and making a start, my brain working overtime.

However, after labouring with just a few paragraphs, putting things on a semi-permanent hold until finishing a remote, part fast track twelve-month degree course, at Huddersfield University.

Sadly, and totally unexpectedly, Tricia departing from our lives during the early hours of July 17th, 2006, the consequence of an acute asthma attack, never to see the results of her constant bantering.

More often than not, a "well then," or "have you made a start yet," "how are you doing," all fun-loving remarks or pokes, made with a smile, relating to the commencement of a biographical account of my memoirs.

Certainly, an enjoyable time-consuming obsession of sorts, as not adjourning since that fateful day, jotting notes on bits of paper, or remarks on my PC, reminding me of an incident or occurrence, documenting anything and everything to write about at a later date.

The first results of these many anecdotes, "And then came Agadoo," reaching the shelves, and on- line stores on November 16th, 2009, becoming the catalyst for three further books, with "Alive and Kicking," my fifth publication.

The ever so sad and untimely death of Tricia, bringing together a bond that would see father and son, a duo of unbreakable unity, resourcefulness, and love, that assisted in producing my second book, "Abri – My Oasis."

The translation of the French word Abri, a refuge, shelter, protection, a compromise of sorts, telling a story recalling the rejuvenation of a onetime family home.

Taking possession in the summer of 1957, constructed for the McCauley family, and empty since 2006, three children, now adults, moving far and wide, and the elderly couple leaving Wrenthorpe for good.

The single storey property becoming repeatedly and unremorsefully vandalised, almost to the point of no return.

A seven-year-old Liam, joining me in bringing the former distinctive almost derelict McCauley home, back from total obscurity.

Set in almost three acres of land overlooking the village of Wrenthorpe, our new bungalow home, once again fully occupied, although sadly, only with my family a further five years.

A large construction company taking charge of the whole area, bulldozing our Abri, our shelter and protection once and for all, construction of eighty-eight properties on the land taking place.

Now almost ten years ago, nothing remaining of our temporary, but valued Abri, always knowing during the time of all our hard work, the final and absolute demise on the horizon for the former McCauley, and Dobson family home.

Warren has now taken over my mantle of home renovation.

Our former family home in Ossett has undergone various "improvements" over the years.

Way back in 1988, the first of these taking place, building a rear extension to obtain further living space, Warren at this time not even born.

A second extension to the property side gaining an extra bedroom, and internal alterations to complement the additional rooms.

A new fitted kitchen, open staircase, new bathroom, fitted wardrobes, you name it, I either built or manufactured whatever required.

Thirty years later, and from the time when Warren purchased the property from his mum, work once again beginning in earnest to replace all what I had accomplished.

Warren removing even further walls, making an open plan kitchen dining room, removing all fitted wardrobes, fitting a new kitchen, bathroom, and new flooring throughout.

Also, turning a former attached shed come utility room, into a ground floor toilet, most of the above I had some involvement in helping Warren to accomplish a modern family home once again.

Totally rejuvenated, the property, Warrens home, unrecognisable from its original build date of 1980.

A strange experience for me, permanently departing from our former family home, way back in 1992, following the divorce of Warrens mum, and now assisting my eldest son to revitalise his home, in most cases seeing all my work of the late eighties, entirely remodelled.

Commenting numerous times, home DIY and alterations a passion for the both of us, remembering, Warren at three years old, helping me, always my tools in hand, trowel, bucket, level, hammer, brush, and ironically training to become a bricklayer when joining the army in 2006.

For me, a pleasant way of helping Warren, and listening to his many ideas, "many hands making light work" comes to mind during my so-called retirement, and just the other week, helping to fit a remote garage door to the front of the house.

When will it all end.

Taking all of the above into consideration, and the saying "time waits for no one," or "You can't turn the clock back, BUT you can wind it up again," and with that in mind, so pleased to hear of a knew duo taking up the mantle of becoming Black Lace.

Performing at summer festivals throughout the UK, bringing those fun time Black Lace party-party songs of yesteryear into the current year, and beyond.

Agadoo, always a crowd favourite, forty-years after the tunes release, when first played on many radio stations throughout the UK and Europe, not forgetting Superman, Do the Conga, and Musicman, to name a few of many.

Nonetheless, a small number of concerned family members and friends saying its cheating, those two young men using the name Black Lace, when they have had nothing to do with recording and performing the tunes, and now earning money singing them.

In my opinion, I think it's an amazing compliment, two chaps actually enjoy performing those fun Black Lace tunes, and seeing the crowd reaction, popularity once again, and after all these years, merriment not dwindling one bit.

Even when those enjoying the song and dance routine, not yet born when first performed, or aired on national radio, and positive, an equally as good a feeling as when Alan and Colin performed the songs for the first time, around many countries all those years ago.

Testament to lots of hard work during the early to mid-eighties, Alan and Colin putting in many hours of musical and dance creation, required in the first instance.

Recording the songs, never ending promotion gigs, radio and TV interviews, and appearances throughout the UK, and Europe, and absolutely sure, the both of them willing them on.

Colin continuing throughout the remainder of his musical career, performing those tunes for over twenty-years in Tenerife, until retiring, and sadly just two weeks later, passing away.

The new Black Lace duo, not exactly a covers band per say, as the name remains the same, unchanged management, identical or new agencies, and even dressing in similar colourful bright, pineapple adorned, stage attire.

Just a band name to some, but to us, and all involved, a name presented to four lads from Wakefield, via a well-established Doncaster entertainment agency, way back in 1974.

From that date on, Black Lace synonymous with the 1979 Eurovision Song Contest, and party type dance tunes intended for all ages, to enjoy for ever and a day.

Personally thinking, not much different to a football team, as throughout the years, players, managers, trainers, and back-room staff, continually come and go, but the team name, colours, and team support remaining, conceivably attracting new fans season after season.

Some of which, far too young to remember the players, failures, or successes of yesteryear, through to their current status.

Just the other week, listening to a Sunday lunch time Paddy McGuinness Radio two show, playing Agadoo after announcing Black Lace will join him on stage at the 2023 Radio Two in the park, held in Preston Lancashire.

Furthermore, Paddy talking "live" to manager John Wagstaff the following week, once again playing Agadoo, and chatting to guests about their memories of the1984 summer hit.

The week after, talking live to Black Lace on his show, and also during Paddy's amazing Ultra Endurance Cycle Challenge.

Black Lace, meeting up with Paddy and Sir Chris Hoy in the car park of Cairn Lodge services in Westmorland, singing Agadoo with everyone present joining in, even a knackered Paddy and Sir Chris, at the end of a tough day's cycling.

Paddy riding a slightly revamped 1970's children's chopper bike, called patch, and painted in the colours of Pudsey Bear, cycling from Wrexham to Glasgow.

Covering three-hundred pedalling miles, over five gruelling days, raising over ten-million pounds of around thirty-nine-million pounds in total, for the BBC's Children in Need program.

Also, four consecutive weeks of "free" spontaneous promotion, with Radio Two, and TV air time, mentioning Black Lace, and playing Agadoo, a tune once again on everyone's lips.

The Black Lace duo are now, Phil Temple, and Craig Harper, a vocalist and comedian, previously appearing on Britain's Got Talant, Michael Barrymore's TV show, and Jane McDonalds Star for a Night.

What's there not to like, amazing, and in my opinion keep on rocking, and above all, giving my blessing to not only keep the name Black Lace going, but also the memorable tunes too.

My final point about the new Black Lace taking to the concert stage once again, reminding me of a Fools and Horses episode, when chatting in the pub about the life span of a well-maintained sweeping brush belonging to Trigger.

Trigger happily reports that his old, but very much in use brush, has had seventeen new brush heads, and fourteen new handles in its time.

Sid laughingly responding, saying, "how the hell can it be the same bloody broom then," to which trigger shows them a photo of the said brush, commenting, "there's the picture, what more proof do you need."

Long live, Agadoo, Superman and the like, and whoever enjoys singing them in front of a welcoming participating audience.

New for old comes to mind, to change the old for new, not a bad thing at all, to rejuvenate, or perhaps regenerate, like our city centres.

Instead of busy roads, consider open plan walking, cars banished to perimeter carparks, making a much safer environment to enjoy city centre shopping.

Innovative ideas to improve our lives, taking a fresh look at what the population has always done, to making logical and wise decisions, bringing about changes for the better.

Just the other week when visiting a local working mens club, to see my friend and founder member of Black Lace, Ian Howarth, perform his music on stage.

This particular club bringing back lots of memories of when our five-piece band first took to the stage, playing our music in clubland, and possibly fifty years since I last walked through these doors.

The region in question known to artists and agents as the Heavy Woollen District, and at the time, seemed hundreds of clubs to perform in, every day or night of the week.

Sadly, most now gone, except this one, just one of the few I know of remaining in this area.

Ian already set up on stage, plugging in the final few cables, and remarking so pleased his equipment light in weight, and only a few items to carry up the steep steps to the first-floor concert room.

About right for his age, and stamina, and so pleased our band not performing here tonight, as certain once our equipment carried up the stairs, and once set up, possibly too knackered to play or sing a single note.

Looking busy, most tables and chairs set in an elevated area, already full, eagerly awaiting the musical entertainment on stage, or perhaps many games of bingo.

Lots of people around my age, not necessarily a good sign, as expecting to see a younger audience, or at the very least, more youthful than Ian or me.

Asking Ian if he would like a drink from the bar, declining, pointing to a can of something, saying he brings his own.

Shock and panic setting in, as noticing a sign above the bar till, CASH ONLY.

Did I have any cash on me, pulling out my wallet to find a solitary ten-pound note.

Ordering a pint of Guinness, and not enough change given to purchase another pint, maybe a half will suffice, although rarely having more than one drink throughout the night when driving.

A chap at the bar commenting that they do not get many visitors to the club, what you see here are members that return week on week to watch the entertainment, and play bingo.

Getting me thinking that in not too many years, perhaps another club that will bite the dust, and not exist.

Especially if no visitors start to attend, and become new members, doubtful if operating a cash only till, with youngsters, including me, using their phone or card to pay.

Whilst I appreciate cash verses card payments a contentious issue, in particular with small businesses putting a minimum spend on using card or phone payments, my personal finances have certainly benefitted using this method.

Utilising this manner of payment a few years ago, mainly due to constant bickering from my children, so much easier, and perhaps one of the reasons this particular working mens club, not attractive to younger visitors.

A sad time indeed, however, on a brighter note, Ian's guitar playing and singing, going down a treat, everyone enjoying his choice of songs, especially me.

Sunny Afternoon, The Kinks, a favourite of mine, also guitar tunes of the Shadows, Apache in particular, Ian commenting to an attentive audience, "playing this tune much better as a twelve-year-old, than now."

Listening to two of three spots, and leaving just before his last set, not before Ian playing the Black Lace Eurovision song, Mary Ann, with a short but profound story of its existence, our band, and bringing me into the conversation.

Thoroughly, enjoying the evening, not joining in with bingo, although a few times our talking receiving a shush from keen hard of hearing bingo stalwarts on nearby tables.

All in all, a good night, and home for around ten-thirty, a far cry from arriving home at two-thirty in the morning during our many years of performing up and down the country.

Pouring a glass of red wine from an already opened bottle, and thinking of Ian's introductory tune, "Take it Easy," a song originally prepared and rehearsed for last year's heavenly birthday concert held at St Georges Hall Bradford, now a chosen song for Ian's repertoire.

Bringing to mind a saying picked up on social media some years ago, for some, a useful thought when undertaking anything and everything.

Happiness keeps you sweet, while trials keep you strong, sorrows keep you human, whereas failures keep you humble, success keeps you glowing, but only family and friends keep you going.

A treat tonight, and great to catch up, who knows the two of us will meet up once again, perhaps in a club or pub, reminiscing about our time together in those early bustling clubland days.

Who knows what will become of those remaining clubs, and venues employing entertainment, one thing is for sure, they need to move with the times.

YOU CAN'T TURN BACK THE CLOCK, BUT YOU CAN WIND IT UP AGAIN...

CHAPTER THIRTY-NINE

Post Script

"Mick"

I received some terrible news today, information about a band mate, a close friend, mentioned quite a few times in my publications.

A friend for as long as I can remember, from the early stages of putting our little band of musicians together.

Micheal Linskey, Mick or Mike, known to many for his phenomenal musicianship, besides his ability at playing anything he could lay his hands on.

From traditional four, six or twelve string guitars, or for that matter, any stringed instrument, to penny whistles, mouth organ, joinery panel saws, you name it, and absolutely sure, Mick will get an audible tune from it.

The only item of his body I have not seen him use, no pun intended, are his toes, but positively sure if he could, he would.

From my first memory of meeting Mick, always a positive, "I can do" sort of person, regardless of whatever problem may raise its head.

Known as fireman Bill to some friends, due to the many years of involvement in the miniature railway at Thornes Park.

Volunteers from the Wakefield Society of Model and Experimental Engineers, building the track, in a sort of huge figure of eight, to run the steam engines around the full perimeter numerous times, weather permitting.

Taking my kids there for a ride on the seven-inch passenger gauge track, on many a Sunday afternoon, with a selection of miniature steam trains pulling hundreds of passengers.

From memory, an Amtrack train, and an old western film imitation, and I'm sure lots of others, the engineers either using their own, or club steam engines, driving them throughout the day.

Mike always looking the part in faded blue uniform, including hat, red scarf, not forgetting his whistle, and loose change shoulder bag.

The train ride fares, as I understand, all, or most given to support the Wakefield Mayors fund.

Twice around the circuit, waving at the many on lookers, either waiting in the station, main road, or carparking area, fun times for children, and adults alike.

I have performed in bands, duo's, and trios with Mick, as a temporary replacement drummer on numerous occasions, also recording backing tracks to aid his many years performing in local clubs and pubs.

My absolute best memories of our early days with Mick, and girlfriend Angela, when becoming our driver come roadie at the conception of our band in 1970.

At this time, no individuals old enough to drive, when local agents began to book our five-piece band into clubs and pubs, Alan Holberry, and his side kick, the Milky Bar Kid, in particular.

Our earlier band name of "Penny Arcade" and then "Love or Confusion," when Mick, and Angela, taking all of us, and our equipment, to many a venue to perform our music.

Mentioning this before, but always a scramble as to who would sit in the front passenger seat of Micks J2 van.

I will explain.

The J2 commercial van, has two front seats as standard, the driver and passenger seat, however, a soft cushion placed on the raised central engine cover, between both seats, making a sort of full width bench, for a further front seat traveller.

No seatbelt laws in those days, Angela sitting on this centrally placed springy, and ever so warm vibrating pad.

Angela wearing, if you can call it that, a rather short mini skirt on most of these engagements, and all thinking that's all her wardrobe contained.

Adorning a selection of mini-skirts and tops, and with five virile young men joining Mick and Angela, making travel arrangements on our nights playing in clubland, an absolute delight.

Alan the smallest in build, better to sit as front seat passenger, giving everyone a little more space in the front cab area.

Although, Mick at the time no lightweight, and the J2 van not an excessively wide-bodied van, so much so, all three front seat passengers looking a little squashed.

Not exactly a fight to sit there, but always a bit of fun poked Alan's way, as favoured to sit on this privileged van seat.

The rest of us mere mortals sat in the vans rear, our bottoms on equipment strategically placed to form seats of sorts, made all the more cosy, if Steves girlfriend coming along too.

As mentioned earlier, no seat belts, often ending up on top of each other when braking or taking corners a little too fast.

The J2 van not exactly the most stabilised or perfect vehicle for our use, especially when loaded with musical equipment, and a minimum of seven young bodies.

A little frightening to say the least when thinking about our travel engagements in this day and age, compared to the carefree let's do it approach, way back then.

Lots of weekend bookings filling our diary, enabling our band to save enough cash to purchase a van, with Alan's sister's boyfriend Ronny, taking over driving duties.

Mick and Angela (Angie) getting married, and two daughters later, becoming a close happy family.

A cousin of Mick, also doing a bit of driving for us, until totally self-sufficient, when old enough to learn to drive, and passing my driving test on the first attempt.

That said, on a few occasions prior to taking my test, I had taken the wheel to drive our van, a bit of driver instruction going on, and usually after midnight when on our way home from a gig.

Not ideal, but with no other vehicles, or few on the road at this time, much safer for a wet behind the ear novice motorist like me.

Attending many a birthday of Micks, fortieth, fifty, sixty, seventy, and seventy-fifth birthday do's.

Most held in working mens clubs, the last three in Alverthorpe working mens club, but a memorable fiftieth birthday celebration held in Thornes Working Mens Club.

Receiving an invitation to attend this February 1995 birthday get-together, a young band booked to appear on stage, "Kiss This," Alan Bartons eldest son Dean, taking centre stage, singing, and playing guitar.

An excellent performance, and the band more than capable of playing their respective instruments, the drummer in particular, great rhythm, and beat throughout their forty-minute first set.

The night made all the more special when Alan joining them on stage, including birthday boy Mick, to sing and play "Living next door to Alice."

A great sing along, but omitting those immortal words, that everyone now enjoys to blurt out when arriving at the chorus.

The later version with Alan on lead vocals originally performed as a fun gimmicky record, aimed for a 1995 summer release, Roy Chubby Brown involved with "Alice who the F*** is Alice."

Alan able to fit in an appearance as just returned home from a busy schedule of European gigs as lead singer with Bradford band "Smokie."

Planning a visit to his home the following weekend in Heckmondwike, spending many hours over numerous cups of tea and coffee, chatting about anything and everything, and sadly the last time I would see him.

Alan died as a result of injuries received while on tour in Germany with "Smokie," March 23rd, 1995.

Our band, including other musician friends of Alan, including Mick, and Angela, attending his service at Wakefield Cathedral, and funeral wake afterwards.

The rude version of Living next door to Alice, including the narration from the infamous Roy Chubby Brown, released shortly after Alans death, as a fun record in remembrance of Alan, the "F" word beeped out when appearing on Top of the Pops.

Micks seventieth birthday held at Alverthorpe club, and the last time seeing Angela, as shortly after this event, Angela passing away following a cancer related illness.

Just last year, rehearsals for Alan Bartons heavenly 70th birthday memorial charity concert, held at Micks home, Mick joining us in a put-together Black Lace band performing live on stage at St Georges Hall Bradford.

Mick the exemplary host, providing not only his front room come rehearsal studio, and equipment, but tea and coffee in abundance too.

Many weeks putting a set list together, with lots of fun, and constant reminiscing, along with Ian Howarth, Steve Scholey, Neil Hardcastle, Stuart Duffy, and Richard Black, even my son Liam joining us when home on leave.

Mick involved in music throughout his life, and the last time playing together at this September 2023 memorial gig at St George's Hall.

However, over the years Mick has many more interests too, in particular the engineering and building of model steam trains, also reconstruction work of full-size steam engines in Sheffield, as well as writing clubland articles in the Wakefield Express, and many other regular publications.

All of these many memories and so many more came flooding back in an instant when receiving a text from Micks partner.

Judy, informing me that Mick admitted to Pinderfields Hospital, complaining of severe pain in his abdomen.

Only a few weeks earlier returning from a trip to South Africa, with band mate Richard, thinking he may have picked up something while there on holiday.

Undergoing many tests, Mick remaining positive throughout, until receiving further upsetting news, a prognosis not what everyone wanting to hear.

Ian Howarth, and many of our friends visiting Mick in hospital, all reporting Mick in good spirits, but clearly, extremely poorly.

I have mentioned numerous times in my publications, visiting patients in hospital not a favourite activity of mine.

Nevertheless, over the last three years, mum in and out of Pinderfields, Pontefract, and Dewsbury hospitals, including convalescence homes for physiotherapy sessions so many times, difficult in keeping track.

Mum becoming a fixture in these hospitals for weeks on end, giving me a wealth of experience, and a respected acceptance, to visit almost every day during those distressing times.

Travelling many miles throughout our district, offering encouragement in keeping positive, when at times, easier said than done.

Receiving a further text from Judy, Mick getting transferred to Wakefield Hospice, as soon as a bed becoming available.

Terrible news, shocked an understatement, replying almost immediately, saying I will visit in a few hours' time.

Ironically, just the other night while at Jim's (Mr-fix-it Trueman's) home, having a much-needed knock about in his recording studio, our many conversations between songs, all about Mick, his deteriorating condition, and what about to happen next.

Jim saying, he will visit Mick on his way home from work the following day.

I must admit visiting mum one thing, but a little more courage required when going into the unknown.

Lots of what if's coming to mind, no imagination required, all acutely obvious when receiving the earlier shocking news.

Bumping into a former work colleague in the carpark, more spaces available today, at the time just before lunch arrival.

Steve talking about his forthcoming retirement, and wife Tracy who should have accompanied him, but for spraining her ankle.

Parting company in the Hospital foyer, Steve disappearing to the floor below ground level to visit his ninety-one-year-old father, while I sort of scurried up the stairs to the third floor.

Gate thirty-three, in room twenty-four of four patients, bed four, and Mick fast asleep when I arrived at his bedside, and not looking much different from just a few weeks ago, although a tad jaundice.

Taking a seat at the end of his bed, Mick stirring when a patient in the next bed started a bout of coughing.

"Hello Terry" instantly recognising me, and asking what time I arrived.

"Just a few minutes ago Mick," only awake a few seconds before drifting into a deep sleep once again.

Eyes open once again, repeating he needed the loo, and quickly.

Over the next twenty minutes, a few unsteady attempts to get to his feet, before nurses successfully getting Mick to the toilet.

Moving his bed, and cabinet, including accessories, such as phone, tablet, and chargers from pod four to pod one, next to the toilet, so much easier for nurses to get him quickly sorted.

Judy arriving just as completed, Mick still in the loo, giving time for some explanation of events over the last few minutes, and earlier days.

Sadly, no positive comments at all, bleak to say the least, upsetting news, you bet, as Mick wheeled out from the toilet, looking pleased to see Judy.

However, after a further forty-minutes of general chatting between the three of us, saying my goodbyes, to a once again sleeping Mick, and attentive Judy.

Taking the stairs down to the hospital foyer, paying for my carparking in one of two pre-payment machines, with thoughts about the last hour heavily on my mind.

In particular one comment coming from Judy.

Only last week, Mick looking forward to planning his forthcoming February 2025 eightieth birthday celebrations, instead, now preparing plans for a destined funeral.

How things can change in just two days, receiving the following text reply from Judy, when making enquiries about Micks wellbeing.

"Sorry Terry, but he's in the hospice, out of it, probably tonight or tomorrow they're saying."

Totally devastated when receiving this terrible update, the inevitable closer than all of Micks family, and friends thought possible after a diagnosis of just a few short weeks.

So, so incredibly sad, an insurmountable feeling of grief coming over me, and cannot imagine how Judy, Micks daughters, and families feel when receiving this information.

Wakefield Hospice, or any Hospice for that matter, definitely a preferred residence when needing expert end-of-life care, providing physical, emotional, and spiritual support for the patient, and close family.

To give the patient some much needed pain free comfort during their time there, and slip away with dignity.

Sadly, Mick peacefully passing away at 22.00 on 9.12.24.

Shock beyond belief, and so rapidly from initial diagnosis.

I can only imagine everyone in his immediate family, and huge friendship circle, completely numb when hearing this devastating news.

Could things get any worse as 2024 almost ending, Ian ringing me with information that our close friend and bandmate of almost fifty-five years, admitted to York hospital with severe abdominal pains, just a few hours after his return from a Fuerteventura holiday.

Steve Scholey our Black Lace bandmate, undergoing tests for suspected prostate cancer.

More terrible news, difficult to comprehend, and put into some form of perspective as to what the resulting prognosis will ensue.

Taking to the M1, and A64 to visit Steve in York, Ian driving, thankful for that offer after my around trip drive to Keithley and back, a route I am so pleased I do not have to drive on a regular basis.

Only some twenty-six miles, one way, but when driving over the tops via Queensbury, and Denholme, totally missing out Bradford, in dark foggy conditions, not an ideal car journey at all.

Our drive to York, much quicker, the M1 and A64 relatively clear at this evening time, made all the more pleasant in Ian's super charged white Tesla.

Parking directly outside the front door, in spaces reserved for drivers with Blue Badge permits.

Quite a long walk to a lift, second floor, ward eight, Steves beaming smile has not lost its significance, certainly looking pleased to see us.

A four-bed ward, however, the three of us remained standing throughout our visit, and surprised to exceed the visiting end time of 20.00, by a full twenty-five minutes, and not told to leave.

Steve explaining his prognosis, following an earlier operation to fit two drainage bags, waist height at either side of his body, these depleted by a nurse while me and Ian looked on.

Hard to believe that Steve remained in great spirits all the time both with him, even raising a few laughs about his catheter, and mega-size testicles, regardless of pain he appeared to tolerate, until requiring further treatment relief.

The return journey home full of conversation about our visit, and possible scenarios that Steve had discussed with us, and looking to make the journey once again with-in the next week.

Conceivably, a fingers, toes, and everything else crossed, for a much-improved available prognosis.

Unlikely so close to Christmas that Micks funeral arrangements will take place before the festive period, making the inevitable upset for family, and friends, continuing throughout until a confirmed date announced.

Meanwhile, family, and many friends have to prepare for a Christmas without Mick, with an understanding his children have to lay him to rest soon afterwards.

Difficult to comprehend, what manner of Christmas and letting in the New Year will take place, as I am sure had Mick survived his illness, local clubs, and pubs his preferred location, along with Richard, performing their entertaining music.

Confirmation of Micks funeral arrangements now received, taking place at Wakefield Crematorium on January 7th, 2025, at 11.20, with a wake at Horbury Working Mens Club, absolutely typical, no surprise at all, as most of Micks, and many musician friends nights, over a myriad of years, spent playing live music in these establishments.

Steve now out of York hospital, staying with his partner Cheryl, over the Christmas and New Year festive period.

Who knows what 2025 will deliver, bringing to mind the following.

You can't change the past, and you certainly can't predict the future, but you can annihilate the present by worrying about both…

EVERYTHING HAS ITS TIME

To everything there is a season.
A time for every purpose under heaven:
A time to be born, and a time to die.
A time to plant and a time to pluck what is planted.
A time to kill, and a time to heal.
A time to break down, and a time to build up.
A time to weep, and a time to laugh.
A time to mourn, and a time to dance.
A time to cast away stones, and a time to gather stones.
A time to embrace, and a time to refrain.
A time to gain, and a time to lose.
A time to keep, and a time to throw away.
A time to tear, and a time to sew.
A time to keep silence, and a time to speak.
A time to love and a time to hate.
A time of war and a time of peace.

The Holy Bible – Ecclesiastes – 3

West Yorkshire Astronomical Society
The Rosse Observatory
Carlton Road
Carlton
Pontefract
WF8 3RJ

The Sky at Night
BBC Four
Broadcasting House
LONDON
W1A 1AA

Dear Sir/Madam

My name is Terry Dobson, Chairman of The West Yorkshire Astronomical Society (WYAS), and next year our observatory celebrates its 50th year.

If it is at all possible, and absolutely fantastic if the observatory could have signed photographs of Dr Maggie Aderin-Pocock, Professor Chris Lintott, Pete Lawrence, and Dr Lucie Green in celebration of this.

Sir Dr Patrick Moore OBE, former creator, and presenter of Sky at Night officially opened the observatory on September 25th, 1983, following ten long years of hard graft by our then members, friends and family raising funds to build it.

This amazing accomplishment was realised by holding a variety of regular events, and receiving donations from well-wishers to allow members to build and fit out the structure, the opening event televised and supported by the whole community.

We now have a fantastic observatory, a knowledgeable supportive membership, and great up to date equipment, for use by its members and visiting public at large, including scouts, cubs, and school, and private visits, and we subscribe to the Sky at Night magazine too.

We feel it is important to involve children in astronomy, and achieve this by running what we consider is an amazing Young Astronomers Evening on the last Friday of every month.

This YA evening regularly attracts over 40 children aged between 4 and 12, and along with their parents, grandparents, aunties, uncles, and anyone else who likes to stargaze.

Everyone enjoys looking at the night sky, stars, planets, deep sky objects, astrophotography, videos and prearranged arts and crafts, at this two-hour family orientated occurrence, regardless of our unpredictable weather.

A number of events are planned throughout next year in celebration of our upcoming 50 years, and a signed photographs of Maggie, Chris, Pete, and Lucie would add to our pleasure in showing them, along with photographs of Patrick Moor, at these up-and-coming events.

Thank you so much in anticipation.

Kind Regards

Terry Dobson.

Chair, West Yorkshire Astronomical Society.

West Yorkshire Astronomical Society
The Rosse Observatory
Carlton Lane
Carlton
Pontefract
WF8 3RJ

Hello Clara

My name is Terry Dobson, former drummer with the Wakefield pop band, "Black Lace," and I had the delight of a fleeting chat when meeting Brian some 43 years ago at a London E.M.I party/get-together.

As fans of "Queen," and their music, it was such an amazing pleasure.

"No Dice" performing on stage on the night, in mid-March 1979, when our band "Black Lace", also at that time, signed to E.M.I., had just won the BBC's Song for Europe competition, (8th March) to represent the UK in the 24th Eurovision Song Contest, to be held on 31st March 1979, in Jerusalem, Israel, Brian hearing of this, congratulating us, and wishing our band lots of luck.

Black Lace, came a respectable 7th with a song called Mary Ann.

I am now the Chairman of The West Yorkshire Astronomical Society (WYAS), and already have a signed photograph of Brian, with his now legendary guitar in hand "stance," (attached) sent to us quite a number of years ago, which takes pride of place on our wall of fame at the observatory.

If it is at all possible, it would be absolutely fantastic if our observatory could have another signed photograph of Brian, in celebration of our 50th year.

Following ten long years of our members raising funds, holding a variety of events, and receiving donations from well-wishers, to allow members to raise enough money to build and fit out the structure.

Dr Patrick Moore, Brian's astronomy, and music lover friend officially opened the observatory on September 25th, 1983.

The whole community supported the live opening event, also televised and shown on local TV channels.

We have a fantastic observatory, a good knowledgeable supportive membership, great equipment that members can use, and visiting public including scouts, cubs, and school visits.

Our observatory feel it is important to involve children in astronomy, which I have read close to Brian's heart, running what is described by others as an amazing Young Astronomers Evening on the last Friday of every month.

This YA evening regularly attracts over 40 children aged between 4 and 12, all joined with their parents, grandparents, aunties, uncles, and anyone else who likes to stargaze.

They all enjoy looking at the night sky, stars, planets, deep sky objects, learning about astrophotography, watching videos, and getting creative with prearranged arts and crafts, during this two-hour, family orientated event, regardless of our unpredictable weather.

Our members are carrying out a number of planned events throughout next year in celebration of our up and coming 50 years, and an up-to-date signed photograph of Brian, would add to our pleasure in showing him, along with photographs of Patrick Moor, at these events.

Thank you so much in anticipation.

Terry Dobson
Chair West Yorkshire Astronomical Society

CRICKET IS QUITE SIMPLE

Poem

"You have two sides, one out in the field, and one in.

Each man that's in the side that goes out, and when he's out, he comes in, and the next man goes in, until he is out.

When they are all out, the side that is out comes in, and the side that has been in, then goes out, and tries to get those coming in, out.

Sometimes you get men still in, and not out.

When a man goes out to go in, the men who are out, try to get him out, and when he is out, he goes in, and the next man in, goes out, and goes in.

There are two men called umpires who stay out all the time, and they decide when the men who are in are out.

When both sides have been in, and all the men have been out, and both sides have been out, and both sides have been out twice after all the men have been in, including those who are not out.

That is the end of the game."

Author unknown

An important job needs to be done, and everybody was sure that somebody at some point would do it...

ANYBODY would have done it, but NOBODY did it.

SOMEBODY got angry about that because it was EVERYBODYS job.

EVERYBODY thought that ANYBODY could do it, but NOBODY realised that EVERBODY wouldn't do it.

It ended up that EVERYBODY blamed SOMEBODY, when NOBODY did what ANYBODY could have done.

Charles R Swindoll

"Change is the law of life"
"And those who look only to the past and present are almost certain to miss the FUTURE."

JOHN F KENNEDY

A remarkable family man!

"My final message to you is whatever your personal
battle, be brave and face it.
Every single day is precious.
Don't waste a moment.
In a world full of adversity, we must STILL dare to
dream.
ROB BURROW - Over and Out"

ABOUT THE AUTHOR

Born in March 1952 to parents Jean and James living on a large newly built council estate in Wakefield.

Terry attended Flanshaw infants, Alverthorpe Junior, and Ings Road schools.

Attending Huddersfield University in his later years to obtain a degree in management.

From 15 years of age Terry worked as a joiner for Horners Building Contractors in Ossett while attending Wakefield building college on day release and night school.

As a founder member of the pop band Black Lace along with school friend Ian Howarth in 1969, Terry toured with the band all over the UK in pubs, social and working men's clubs and night clubs.

Turning professional in 1976 to perform at Bottons Fun Park in Skegness, and further summer season work at Butlins Skegness in 1977.

Black Lace represented the United Kingdom in 1979 in the 24th Eurovision Song Contest held in Jerusalem Israel, finishing the competition in a respectable seventh place.

Also, in 1979 performing in the InterVision Song Contest held in the amphitheater Lesna Opera, Sopot, Poland, Czestaw Niemen overall winner of the competition.

This appearance over four days giving the band a huge leg up to perform in and around Europe including the former Iron Curtain countries of East and Western Germany.

The author ended his professional career in music early 1983, when returning to full-time work in joinery for Wakefield Council until 2005, and Wakefield and District Housing until retirement in December 2018.

A full 35 years, taking on many roles and responsibilities during this time, finally bringing about retirement when working as a Survey Manager.

The author continued to play drums with his former professional Black Lace band mates, Alan Barton, Colin Gibb, and Ian Howarth, and various sessions with other artists in recording studios, and playing live music with Stormer, Aircrew, and finally Mister Twister.

Performing our music, and those likeable tunes of preferred artists in the clubs and pubs throughout the UK.

However, Terry now finds lots more time to continue with his hobby of stargazing at the Pontefract Observatory, West Yorkshire Astronomical Society, (WYAS,) and voluntary work with Supporting Music for All, (SM4LL.)

Other social activities include performing and playing his drums in working men's clubs around Yorkshire, with local band Mister Twister, until their demise in the summer of 2023.

Printed in the United States
by Baker & Taylor Publisher Services